Sisterhood and Solidarity

Workers' Education for Women, 1914–1984

I would like to write a poem,
But I have no words;
My grammar was ladies' waists,
And my schooling, skirts.

A student in a 1934 class for women workers, from *Concerning Workers' Education*, No. 3 (Washington, D.C.: Federal Emergency Relief Administration, 1934).

Sisterhood and Solidarity

Workers' Education for Women, 1914–1984

Edited by Joyce L. Kornbluh and
Mary Frederickson

Temple University Press   Philadelphia

Temple University Press, Philadelphia 19122

© 1984 by Temple University. All rights reserved

Published 1984

Printed in the United States of America

Library of Congress Cataloging in Publication Data
Main entry under title:

Sisterhood and Solidarity.

  Bibliography: p.
  Includes index.
  1. Working class women—United States—History—20th century—Addresses, essays, lectures.
  2. Working class women—Education—United States—History—20th century—Addresses, essays, lectures.
  3. Women in trade-unions—United States—History—20th century—Addresses, essays, lectures.
I. Kornbluh, Joyce L.
II. Frederickson, Mary.
HD6068.2.U6S57 1984   305.4′890623   84-8734
ISBN 0-87722-328-9

*What dreams may grow, as young vines
planted in the spring,
Their roots thrust down in deepest soil of truth;
Till workers all the fruits of understanding bring,
Borne from our borders in the hands of youth.*

Hilda Worthington Smith

*To Hilda Worthington Smith (1890–1984) and
Barbara Mayer Wertheimer (1926–1983)
with our love, respect, and appreciation.*

Contents

Contributors *xiii*
Preface *xv*
Acknowledgments *xix*

CHAPTER 1

Robin Miller Jacoby
The Women's Trade Union League Training School for Women Organizers, 1914–1926 *3*
  Girls' Stories *21*
  How I Escaped from the Factory *22*
  At the League's Training School *26*
  Notes *30*

CHAPTER 2

Susan Stone Wong
From Soul to Strawberries: The International Ladies' Garment Workers' Union and Workers' Education, 1914–1950 *37*
  The Unity Movement—The Soul of a Union *57*
  We Shall Be Free *62*
  Why I Joined My Union, and What It Has Done for Me *63*
  Notes *69*

CHAPTER 3

Mary Frederickson
Citizens for Democracy: The Industrial Programs of the YWCA *75*
  The Social Ideals of Club Suppers *97*
  What I Want from Workers' Education *98*
  Workers and Students *99*
  Thoughts *102*
  Color Equality *102*
  Notes *103*

CHAPTER 4

Rita Heller
Blue Collars and Bluestockings: The Bryn Mawr Summer School for Women Workers, 1921–1938 *107*
  The Song of the Factory Worker *129*
  The Machine *130*
  Thoughts in Patterns *131*
  My First Job *132*
  My First Strike *133*
  Excerpts from the Lantern Ceremony *135*
  Notes *137*

CHAPTER 5

Mary Frederickson
Recognizing Regional Differences: The Southern Summer School for Women Workers *147*
- The Marion Manufacturing Company *171*
- A Strike against the Stretch-Out *172*
- My Struggle to Escape the Cotton Mill *173*
- I Was in the Gastonia Strike *175*
- Mother Jones' Tin Pan Army: The Women Mop Up Coal-Dale *177*
- Notes *182*

CHAPTER 6

Marion W. Roydhouse
Partners in Progress: The Affiliated Schools for Women Workers, 1928–1939 *187*
- Your face, beautiful with belief *205*
- Corky Row *207*
- Workers' Education, 1939 *208*
- Notes *217*

CHAPTER 7

Alice Kessler-Harris
Education in Working-Class Solidarity: The Summer School for Office Workers *223*
- We Went to the Summer School *242*
- We Take Our Stand *244*
- Notes *248*

CHAPTER 8

Joyce L. Kornbluh
The She-She-She Camps: An Experiment in Living and Learning, 1934–1937 *253*
- For Sale *274*
- Excerpts from papers written by participants in the New Deal camps for women workers *276*
- Notes *279*

CHAPTER 9

Barbara Mayer Wertheimer
To Rekindle the Spirit: Current Education Programs for Women Workers *285*
- Interview with Barbara Kohn, United Auto Workers *309*
- We Came Here Stripped *316*
- Better Than B-12 *316*
- Valedictory Speech *317*
- Factory Worker *319*
- On the Wings of a Dove *319*
- Sisterhood *320*
- Hope *321*
- Conviction *321*
- Notes *322*

CHAPTER 10

Lyn Goldfarb
Memories of a Movement:
A Conversation *325*

Photographs *343*

Selected Bibliography *357*

Index *363*

Contributors

Mary Frederickson is currently an assistant professor of history at the University of Alabama in Birmingham where she teaches women's history. She spent a post-doctoral year at the Wellesley College Center for Research on Women in 1981–1982, and is now writing a book on the Southern Summer School for Women Workers.

Lyn Goldfarb has been the Assistant Education Director of the Service Employees International Union, AFL-CIO, and currently heads an independent media firm in Washington, D.C. Co-author of the article "Labor Education and Women Workers: An Historical Perspective," in *Labor Education for Women Workers*, she is co-producer of the film *Babies and Banners: The Story of the Women's Emergency Brigade*.

Rita Heller is completing her doctoral work at Rutgers University where a Bevier Fellowship has supported her research on the Bryn Mawr Summer School. She is the recipient of a National Endowment for the Humanities grant to produce a film, entitled "Women of Summer," about the Bryn Mawr Summer School.

Robin M. Jacoby is a Lecturer in History and Assistant to the Vice President for Academic Affairs and Provost at the University of Michigan. She teaches courses in history and women's studies, and her scholarly work, including numerous published articles, has focused on class and gender issues in women's labor history and the history of feminism in the early twentieth century.

Alice Kessler-Harris is professor of history and co-director of the Center for the Study of Work and Leisure at Hofstra University. She is the author of *Out to Work, Women Have Always Worked*, and numerous articles on wage-earning women and women in labor history.

Joyce L. Kornbluh founded and directs the Program on Women and Work at the Labor Studies Center of the University of Michigan. A workers' educator since 1947, she teaches credit and noncredit classes on women and work. She edited *Rebel Voices: An IWW Anthology,* and co-edited *Poverty in America* and *Negroes and Jobs.* She is currently working on a study of workers' education during the New Deal.

Marion W. Roydhouse is a visiting professor at St. Joseph's University in Philadelphia. She taught for the previous two years at the University of Delaware. Her research has been on the political participation and labor reform efforts of southern women in the early twentieth century.

Barbara M. Wertheimer was the founder and director of the Institute for Education and Research on Women and Work at the New York State School of Industrial and Labor Relations, Cornell University. Involved in labor education from 1946–1983, she wrote *We Were There: The Story of Working Women in America* and edited *Labor Education for Women Workers.*

Susan Stone Wong is a graduate student at Columbia University completing a dissertation on the workers' education movement from 1921–1951. She has worked as an historical consultant for television and has published an essay on Fannia Cohn in *Notable American Women: The Modern Period.*

Preface

The essays in this collection survey a number of innovative workers' education programs for women that span the years between 1914, when the National Women's Trade Union League initiated its Training School for Women Organizers, and the present. Our aim is to document and to analyze the contributions these programs made to labor history, women's history, and social history. The historians and labor educators writing here explore the relationship of female workers' education to changing patterns of women's work, to the trade union movement, to the meaning of feminism in the context of workers' education, to class conflicts within these programs, and to the changing nature of workers' education in the labor movement today. We also include some of the rich documentary material—essays, poems, plays, oral histories, and photographs—that was produced as part of these programs.

The reader will find in this volume new interpretations of the Bryn Mawr Summer School for Women Workers, the Southern Summer School, and the Affiliated Schools for Workers—organizations designed specifically as female workers' education programs; analyses of groups like the National Women's Trade Union League, the Young Women's Christian Association, and the New Deal-sponsored educational camps for jobless women that turned to workers' education to achieve their goals; and discussions of workers' education programs that were carried out within unions. Finally, we point to the important connections between the pre-World War II programs for women workers and the contemporary programs initiated by unions and universities.

By creating this anthology, we have in many ways given structure to a movement that had very little cohesion. The education programs for women workers documented in this collection had a multiplicity of specific goals. However, each program sought to provide experiences that would give women workers needed information, personal and organizational skills, and support for their participation in the labor force and in workplace organizations.

The cross-class coalitions of women who organized and staffed these programs envisioned the expanded participation of women in the labor movement as a means of democratizing organized labor and strengthening the role of trade unions within American society. Early education programs for women workers built on the activism of middle-class women in social reform organizations, in the suffrage movement, and in campaigns to extend opportunities for women in institutions of higher education. Although the women differed in identifying themselves as feminists, the programs reflected the collaboration of women educators, social reformers, feminists, YWCA and settlement house staff along with representatives of unions and the worker-students themselves.

The founders of the early programs helped shape the workers' education philosophy that classroom learning must lead to social action. They developed new educational methods that linked the learning setting to the community context, and aimed to increase the participation and power of women in the public sphere. They experimented with teaching techniques—new for that time and accepted in ours—of involving adult women students in an informal, nonhierarchical learning process that afforded a critique of traditional teaching methods.

These early education programs for women workers were testing grounds for relating group work to education and involving participants in defining their own educational levels, developing their own curricula, and sharing in the governance of the projects. The founders of the programs drew on the work of progressive educators such as John Dewey, Eduard Lindeman, William Kilpatrick and James Harvey Robinson as they helped students learn from their experiences, relate "schooling" to the "real world," and integrate their learning in a process leading to social change.

By focusing on individual growth as well as systematic change—the synchronization of personal and political transformation—many of these education programs offered a wholistic approach to social reconstruction. As women attempted to transcend the dichotomies of their private and public lives, the workers' education programs helped them to use their individual experiences to develop a political analysis. This concept and process were later used by women's consciousness raising groups in the 1960s that dealt with women's family relationships and affirmed for a new generation that "the personal is the political."

Workers' education for women flourished in twentieth-century America because it offered a way of mitigating conflicts between class and gender. For middle-class women it provided one way to become involved with the labor movement. For working-class women, the programs offered opportunities to interact with women of a different race, ethnic group, or region on common personal, workplace, union, and community issues.

Initially developed in a period when relatively few working-class women finished high school and when there were few unions that organized unskilled or semi-skilled women workers, the early programs combined economics, labor history, and public speaking with classes on literature, art, music, and women's health issues. Later programs, developed for women workers with more formal schooling and in the context of a stronger labor movement, included more functional courses designed to empower women within their unions and communities.

From the earliest years to the present period, workers' education programs for women have advocated an increased response by government to the needs of women workers. Efforts to overcome economic barriers through legislation began with support for protective legislation and a minimum wage that would benefit women workers at the bottom of the pay scale. After World War II, the focus shifted to support for an Equal Pay Act, affirmative action, an Equal Rights Amendment, and legislation that would outlaw such practices as sexual harassment and protect the health and safety of women workers as well as men.

Women have had to overcome discrimination and institutional barriers in unions as well as in workplaces. The early programs were developed at a time when conservative leaders of the AFL openly excluded women from union membership on the grounds that their unskilled labor would deflate the wage scales of males. Union hiring practices also reflected this discrimination. In 1924, only eight national unions hired women organizers, and even the garment and clothing workers' unions with huge female memberships counted few women on organizing staffs or in elected positions.

Fifty years later, in 1974, when the Coalition of Labor Union Women (CLUW) was founded, there were still no women on the AFL-CIO Executive Council, and only two international unions were headed by women presidents. Today, when only seven million women belong to unions or to labor associations out of twenty-three million organized workers, organized women hold only 12 percent of all elected positions in unions, and only 7 percent of the elected and appointed positions in union offices on a national level. Current programs aim to give women union members the information, skills and support to become more active in workplace organizations and to run for office at all levels of their unions.

Contemporary programs continue to bring working-class and middle-class women together around common concerns. Black and Hispanic women are attending in greater numbers, coordinating workshops, and running for leadership positions in their unions and communities. The need to organize more women workers remains constant, and female workers' education continues to respond to these issues through programs sponsored by individual unions, by the Coalition of Labor Union Women (CLUW), and by university labor extension programs.

Today, the female workers' education movement serves as a bridge to the contemporary women's movement. Throughout the schools and educational programs, issues are discussed that affect women's personal as well as public lives. Child care, sexual harassment on the job, health and safety, reproductive rights, birth control, domestic violence, rape, substance abuse, assertiveness training, goal setting, the relationship of racism to sexism, and alternative family structures are discussed along with workplace issues of job discrimination, affirmative action, the opening of nontraditional jobs for women, comparable worth, on-the-job training and laws guaranteeing equal rights.

Over the past seventy years, education programs for women workers have played a unique role in developing working women's collective potential and individual concerns. As Sylvia Maniloff wrote to her union newspaper almost forty years ago, her program "taught me how much there is to learn and that I am going to make not an end but a beginning." At the end of the 1982 Southern Summer School for Women Workers, cosponsored by the University and Colleges Labor Education Association (UCLEA) and the national AFL-CIO Education Department, postal worker Betty Tsang touched on a continuing theme: "If I learned nothing more this week except that I am not alone, that there is a bunch out there making waves, causing changes, being heard, and at the same time being themselves—sincere, people-oriented and union-minded women, I'd still be proud."

Acknowledgments

We are indebted to a number of people and institutions in the preparation of this book. We appreciate the resources, support and cooperation of the Labor Studies Center of the University of Michigan's Institute of Labor and Industrial Relations, the Department of History of the University of Alabama in Birmingham, and the Wellesley College Center for Research on Women. We especially want to thank Hy Kornbluh, Tennant McWilliams, Laura Lein, and Margaret McIntosh for their support and cooperation.

We are deeply grateful to the many archivists and librarians who helped make the time we spent in their libraries productive and pleasant: Debra Bernhardt and Jon Bloom of the Robert Wagner Archives and the Tamiment Library at New York University; William Emerson of the Franklin D. Roosevelt Library; Kenneth Fones-Wolf and Frederic Miller of the Urban Archives, Temple University; Patricia King of the Schlesinger Library, Radcliffe College; Eleanor Lewis of the Sophia Smith Collections, Smith College; Dione Miles and Marjorie Long of the Archives of Urban and Labor Affairs, Wayne State University; Elizabeth Norris of the National Board, YWCA; Richard Strassberg of the Archives of Industrial and Labor Relations, Cornell University; Robert Spink of the New York City Public Library; Robert Warner of the National Archives and Records Service; Edward Webber of the Labadie Collection, University of Michigan; Gloria Weinrich of the New York State Department of Labor Archives, and Lucy West of the Archives, Bryn Mawr College.

We appreciate the permissions from the following archives to use the graphics illustrating chapter title pages: the Library of Congress for the National Women's Trade Union League graphics used in Chapters 1 and 5; the Urban Archives at Temple University for the illustrations from the archives of the Kensington (Philadelphia) YWCA used in Chapters 2 and 8; the Schlesinger Library for the illustration used in Chapter 3; the Bryn Mawr College Archives for the drawing used for Chapter 4; the U.S. Department of Labor Women's Bureau for the illustrations used in Chapters 6 and 7; Helen Elkiss, faciliator of the 1983 UCLEA Midwest School for Women Workers, for the drawing used in Chapter 9; and Lyn Goldfarb,

Anatoli Ilyashov, and Charles Harrington for the photographs used in Chapter 10.

The lines by Hilda W. Smith on page v, are from her poem "Song for the Hudson Shore School for Women Workers" in the *Collected Poems of Hilda Worthington Smith*, Bryn Mawr College Archives. The stanza "I should like to write a poem" on page i was originally published in *Concerning Workers' Education* Vol. 1, No. 3 (Washington, D.C.: Federal Emergency Relief Administration, March 1934). We appreciate Edith Berkowitz Parker's permission to use her song "We Are Free" on page 62.

In editing this collection of original essays and documentary materials, we had the cooperation and enthusiasm of the chapters' authors. We are especially appreciative of the help given by Lyn Goldfarb in the initial planning of the volume.

A number of other colleagues and friends have been especially helpful at different stages of this book: Brigid O'Farrell of the Harvard University Trade Union Program; Judi Catlett of the Center for Labor Education and Research, University of Alabama at Birmingham; Patricia Cahill of Wellesley College are colleagues who responded to different sections of the manuscript. Betty Eisler, Gay Gullickson, and Jane Sherwin provided hospitality during our visits to archives in their communities. Jeanne Holloway and Andree Naylor expertly typed many of the sections of the book.

Our families—Clint and Megan Joiner; Hy, Peter, Eliana, Jane, and Kathe Kornbluh—have helped us in so many ways for which we are always grateful.

Michael Ames and Zachary Simpson, at the Temple University Press, facilitated the production of this book with imagination and professional expertise. We are grateful also to Joan Vandergrift and Lisa Waciega for their editorial assistance, and to Susan Holbert for her careful preparation of the index.

Our two dear friends and colleagues, Barbara Mayer Wertheimer and Hilda Worthington Smith, died before this book was published. We dedicate *Sisterhood and Solidarity* to them both for their vision, inspiration, and lifelong commitment to developing workers' education programs for women, and for the vital roles they played in our lives.

Sisterhood and Solidarity

Workers' Education for Women, 1914–1984

Chapter 1

The Women's Trade Union League
Training School for Women Organizers,
1914–1926

Robin Miller Jacoby

The history of educational programs for women workers in the United States effectively begins with the efforts of the National Women's Trade Union League (NWTUL generally known as the WTUL) in the early twentieth century.[1] The pioneering ventures of the WTUL, of which its Training School for Women Organizers was the most influential, reflected a combined commitment to principles of feminism and trade unionism as well as a profound belief in the efficacy of educational solutions to social problems. Moreover, the WTUL's educational activities and especially its training school embodied many of the goals, tensions, limitations, and achievements that characterized subsequent programs developed to offer women workers specific skills and general enrichment.

When the WTUL was founded in 1903, women workers were characteristically young and single and tended to think of themselves and to be regarded by others as only temporary members of the work force. As both a cause and an effect of this pattern, women workers were overwhelmingly clustered in the least skilled and lowest paying jobs and were almost totally ignored by the labor movement.[2] The WTUL, whose membership consisted of leisure-class and working-class women brought together by a shared concern for the plight of women workers, responded to the situation of women in the industrial labor force through three different but chronologically and conceptually overlapping sets of activities. It sought to organize women workers into trade unions; it lobbied for legislation that would regulate the hours, wages, and working conditions of women; and it developed educational programs aimed at women workers, trade union men, and nonworking women on the special problems of women workers and the value of organization and legislation on their behalf.

Within this tripartite program of unionization, legislation, and education, for reasons both external and internal to the WTUL, education emerged by 1913 as the WTUL's dominant focus. From its inception and throughout its existence, the WTUL sought to identify and respond to the educational needs of women workers, and it was in this arena that the league had its most prominent successes and its greatest impact. Its programs for women workers were designed to imbue working women with the motivation to unionize and to provide them with the skills necessary to function effectively in the labor movement. To this end, local leagues offered instruction in parliamentary procedure, public speaking, and the writing of business letters; several leagues developed libraries of works on industrial questions; and most local leagues sponsored periodic lecture series on trade union practices. One of the WTUL's earliest and most innovative educational ventures was the formation of free English classes for immigrant women, accompanied by the creation of a special primer so that the women could learn the value of trade unionism along with English.[3]

Most local leagues also sponsored various social, recreational, and cultural activities, and these were seen as part of the WTUL's educational program of enriching the lives of women workers while winning them to the cause of trade unionism. Local league meetings usually included refreshments and entertainment, such as music, dancing, travel slides, and literary recitations. Leagues often sponsored annual balls, and in the summer months most of them organized picnics and excursions. The Chicago WTUL even ran a small summer camp for its trade union members. Various leagues offered music, drama, art, and creative writing classes, and the Chicago WTUL's chorus, which performed at Hull House functions and at WTUL national conventions, was reported to be one of that league's most successful activities. Despite some instances of class and political tensions that developed, these activities were vital and important aspects of WTUL programs. They met real needs of women workers, they humanized the labor movement for many women, and they reflected the WTUL's commitment to a world of "bread *and* roses" for women workers.

Within this context of perceived needs and attempted responses, the WTUL's most ambitious and historically significant educational program was the Training School for Women Organizers it began in 1914.[4] The league had few models for any of its activities, but in this case it was truly a pioneer, for the school was the first residential workers' education program established in the United States. Even after other similar programs were begun in the early 1920s, the WTUL school remained unique because its curriculum included fieldwork as well as academic classes.[5] The school did not have a very long history; financial programs and the disruption caused by World War I led to its temporary suspension in 1915 and again in 1918, and it was permanently closed in 1926. Nevertheless, despite its limited existence and achievements, the WTUL's training school occupies an important place in the history of workers' education, for its goals and residential format provided an influential model for subsequent programs.

The impetus for the school was the need for more female labor organizers. WTUL leaders, especially the league's leisure-class president, Margaret Dreier Robins, had come to see the creation of a larger pool of women organizers as an essential prerequisite for increasing the number of unionized women workers. The fact that the WTUL national office received requests for women organizers from groups in nineteen states between 1911 and 1913 made the WTUL leadership feel there was not only a need for women organizers, but a greatly increased demand for them as well. Ten years of organizing work had also shown WTUL members that the scarcity of female organizers contributed to the tendency of gains won by women workers through strikes to disappear, because solid unions were not sustained in the aftermath of the crises that produced the strikes.

With these perceptions in mind, Robins introduced a proposal at the WTUL's 1913 convention to create a training school for women organizers. In her presidential address she stressed her conviction that "the best women organizers without question are the trade union girls."[6] The problem was that "many a girl capable of leadership and service is held within the ranks because neither she as an individual nor her organization has money enough to set her free for service."[7] Grandly characterizing the WTUL as "representing . . . the hope and aspirations of the great women's working group of America, organized and unorganized," Robins urged that "if we are to serve our time as we ought to serve it," the league should undertake to provide the funds and training necessary to enable more women with leadership potential to become organizers and labor leaders.[8]

The proposal met with an enthusiastic reaction, and Robins immediately appointed a committee to formulate plans for instituting a training program for women organizers. To head the committee, Robins appointed Mary Anderson, a member of the Boot and Shoe Workers' Union who had left her factory job in 1910 for a full-time position with the Chicago WTUL as an organizer (and who eventually became the first director of the Women's Bureau when it was created as part of the Department of Labor in 1920). The full planning committee consisted of three other trade unionists and three "allies," as leisure-class members of the WTUL were called.[9]

Once the committee had worked out a preliminary plan, the WTUL wrote to trade unions and labor federations throughout the United States, soliciting their reactions to the proposed school, whose students would be selected by the WTUL national executive board on the basis of recommendations from unions and local leagues. The responses were uniformly enthusiastic, and the training program advocated by the planning committee became the basis of the school's curriculum throughout its history.

The training was to consist of a year's residence in Chicago, where the students would be instructed in labor history, industrial relations, labor legislation, the theory and practice of trade agreements, English, public speaking, and parliamentary procedure. Fieldwork was to be divided between organizing and administrative activities. Under the supervision of the WTUL and union officers, the students were to gain experience in the planning, conducting, and publicizing of union meetings, the recruitment of unorganized workers, the handling of employee grievances and negotiations with employers, and the writing of reports, articles for the press, and business letters. The students would spend time in the offices of the WTUL and the Chicago Federation of Labor, where they would be exposed to basic bookkeeping procedures and general office practices. This aspect of their fieldwork was to give them insight into the bureaucratic functioning of labor organizations.

It was understood from the beginning that the program would be one of full-time study and fieldwork. Financially, this meant that all students would have to be on full scholarship, for the WTUL realized that the wage levels of women workers made it inconceivable that applicants would have savings to cover a year of unemployment. Since operating the school would involve overhead costs as well as the student scholarships, the decision to institute the training school signified the willingness of the WTUL to make it a major financial priority in the league's budget. This decision was yet another demonstration of the WTUL's optimistic belief in the connection between education and unionization.

The school actually began in the winter of 1914 with the arrival of the first three students: Louisa Mittelstadt, a brewery worker from Kansas City; Myrtle Whitehead, president of a 400-member, all-female local of the Crown, Cork and Seal Operatives' Union in Baltimore; and Fannia Cohn, a garment worker from New York, who was president of her ILGWU local (Local 41 of the Kimona, Wrappers, and Housedress Workers' Union).

Louisa Mittelstadt, who was secretary of the Kansas City league and a member of the WTUL national executive board, was a very capable but extremely diffident young woman.[10] Upon hearing of her selection as one of the first students in the program, she wrote a short letter conveying her "appreciation and thanks for giving me this honor" and earnestly promised to make "every effort to realize your hopes."[11] The Kansas City Industrial Council, a local federation of trade unions, subsidized the first four months of Mittelstadt's year in Chicago, and the WTUL was quite pleased by this indication of support for its school from an American Federation of Labor body.

Myrtle Whitehead, who had been working in a bottling plant since she was eleven years old, was partially sponsored by the Baltimore WTUL. She was eighteen or nineteen when she arrived at the school and was characterized by Stella Franklin, the national WTUL secretary-treasurer, as "a splendid girl with plenty of go and good humor and common sense."[12] Margaret Dreier Robins shared Franklin's positive response to Whitehead, but she revealed her deeply paternalistic attitudes toward young women workers when she described Whitehead to an important WTUL benefactor as "one of the dearest children, spontaneous, and full of spirit and an ardent little Methodist."[13]

It may be because she was a Socialist, but it is nonetheless surprising to find virtually no mention of Fannia Cohn in WTUL documents concerning the school at its inception or assessing it in retrospect, for of all the students who attended it throughout the years, she was the one who achieved the greatest prominence in the labor movement.[14] She has been described as "a sensitive, slightly irritable woman," and compared to the other students, her personality and her politics may have made her more aloof and independent, not as openly grateful to the WTUL for the opportunity it was offering her, and less accepting of the WTUL values and attitudes she encountered at the school.[15]

An indication of the atmosphere in which Cohn found herself and the only comment about her in WTUL records during the period she was at the school comes from the minutes of a staff meeting held shortly after she arrived in Chicago. Presumably in response to a request from her, the staff delegated Alice Henry, the editor of *Life and Labor*, to put Cohn in touch with leading Socialists in Chicago. This prompted Margaret Dreier Robins to make a series of remarks that "dwelt upon the necessity of getting our revolutionary spirits to do constructive work."[16] Robins, who had a very proprietary attitude toward the WTUL in general and the school in particular, was willing to have Socialists in "her" organization, but she was skeptical of their revolutionary theories and accepted them as colleagues only when they proved their willingness to do what she considered to be constructive work. By 1918, Cohn had apparently met Robins's criteria, for in a fundraising letter she praised Cohn as "among the finest of our women leaders . . . a woman who is able to move to the best possibilities in them the rank and file of our poorest workers."[17]

WTUL allies provided much of the instruction during this first year, with supplementary sessions on trade agreements and judicial decisions affecting labor conducted by Chicago area (male) labor leaders. A University of Chicago professor taught a class on public speaking one evening a week, and this class and the sessions on trade agreements and labor legislation were open to other women workers as part of the educational program of the Chicago WTUL. The public speaking class was especially popular, attracting more students than could be accommodated. A sense of the way this particular class offered relaxing camaraderie along with serious skill building comes from the following account:

Mr. Nelson is a modern, up-to-date man with no professional taint. . . . He makes the girls really get on their feet and say something clearly and to the point. He is death on digressions and long-windedness and altogether the class is a splendid thing. . . . Not only are the new speakers developed but the practiced ones are corrected. Miss Henry has been rebuked for lack of clearness, Mrs. Robins for being too tense and Agnes Nestor for being too talky. You can imagine how this is enjoyed by the lesser mortals and how it encourages them.[18]

As part of their fieldwork, Mittelstadt, Whitehead, and Cohn attended shop stewards' meetings, distributed leaflets for a union organizational drive, and participated in a meeting at Hull House called by "the women of Chicago" to protest police treatment of picketing waitresses on strike at

Henrici's, a well-known Chicago restaurant. WTUL leaders felt this Hull House meeting was an especially valuable experience for the students, for it "gave the girls a particularly fine opportunity of seeing the League getting that publicity and cooperation with citizens which is one of the distinctive features of our work in labor troubles."[19]

Even though the WTUL had been able to accept only three students for the first year, there was a general sense that the school had gotten off to an encouraging start. All three young women completed the course and went on to become full-time organizers. Fannia Cohn initially remained in Chicago, working as a general organizer for the ILGWU, and she was instrumental in unionizing striking workers at the Herzog Garment Factory into Local 59. She subsequently returned to New York, serving as a member of the ILGWU national staff until her death in 1962.

The other two had much shorter careers as labor activists; by 1918 both had given up their organizing work for marriage and motherhood. Myrtle Whitehead spent 1915 as an apprentice organizer in New York under the supervision of Melinda Scott, who was then president of the New York WTUL and had had considerable organizing experience with garment workers in New York and New Jersey. Whitehead then spent most of the following year as an organizer for the Philadelphia and New York leagues. She also, however, became engaged that year and resigned her position with the WTUL in November 1916, just prior to her marriage.[20] Louisa Mittelstadt returned to Kansas City, where she worked as an organizer for the Kansas City Industrial Council and the Brewery Workers' Union until her marriage in 1917 or 1918. By 1922 she was the mother of three children and was very pleased to be living in a home on the outskirts of Kansas City where her children "could grow up in the open air."[21] Because of the demanding nature of labor organizing, it is not coincidental that over the years the women most active in the WTUL and in the labor movement were almost invariably single, either by choice or by happenstance.

The school staff consistently attempted to devise programs of study and fieldwork that took into account each student's previous academic background and her experience in the labor movement. In 1916 the school's year-long program was divided into four months of academic work and eight months of fieldwork. This plan was followed until 1922, when financial problems caused the WTUL to reduce the training program to a six-month course—three months of classes and three months of fieldwork. A few students who did not need the fieldwork component of the program came only for a period of academic study. One such student was Julia O'Connor, who was president of the Boston WTUL and of the Telephone Operators' Union of Boston when she came to the school for four months of academic work in the fall of 1916. A few others did the reverse and participated only in the fieldwork program; one of these was Irene Goins (who Margaret Dreier Robins, in another unconsciously patronizing comment, characterized as "an extremely fine colored woman"), who in 1917 worked under Mary Anderson's direction organizing black women workers in the Chicago stockyards.[22]

In response to a suggestion in 1920 from Julia O'Connor and Rose Sullivan, another telephone operator who attended the school in 1919, the school staff decided to add a "short course" to the school's program. Five students came for an intense three-week session in January 1921; shortly after returning to her job, one of them wrote the director of the school that what she had learned in the three weeks had enabled her to settle "an organizational dispute" that she would not have been able to handle previously. Explaining the effect of being at the school for even this short time, she wrote, "It put pep and some very vital facts into my head at a time when I sure needed it."[23]

After the experience with the first group of students in 1914, it was decided that the school's academic goals would be best served by having the students take classes at local educational institutions whenever possible. The WTUL broached this idea to administrators at schools ranging from the University of Chicago to Crane Junior College and generally met with a favorable response. Most of the schools were willing to allow WTUL students to attend as auditors, but the University of Chicago stipulated that they would have to enroll as special students, which meant taking courses for credit. Not knowing whether their students could handle the pressures of examinations and grades, WTUL officials were annoyed at the University of Chicago's insistence on this policy.[24] However, since of all the schools in the area, only the University of Chicago offered a course on "Trade Unionism and Labor Problems," which the school staff felt would be useful to the WTUL students, it was decided to try placing selected students in the course.

Dora Lipschitz, a garment worker from Philadelphia, and Julia O'Connor, the telephone operator from Boston, enrolled in the course for the fall quarter of 1916, and there was great rejoicing at the league when they passed their first exam with grades of C+ and B+, respectively. A WTUL staff member wrote the news to Margaret Dreier Robins, jubilantly pointing out that the college students had averaged a C on the same exam.[25]

The presence of WTUL students in classes at the University of Chicago provided an additional dimension for the regular students' study of labor problems. Professor Paul Douglas, the instructor of the "Trade Unionism and Labor Problems" course, reported in 1920 that not only were the WTUL students taking his course that year doing "distinctly creditable work thus far," but furthermore:

I am very glad that they have been in the class. They have brought a reality into the discussions which has enlivened the subject for the other students and had enabled the college students better to understand the point of view of the working woman. It is an excellent thing for our students to have two such intelligent women with first hand knowledge of the facts, associated with them.[26]

Another professor's report on the same two students (Bella Caspar, a feather worker from New York, and Kathleen Derry, a boot and shoe worker from Canada) indicated that while their work showed "the lack of an early education," they were both "good, earnest students, thoroughly intent upon their work"; in fact, he wished his regular University of Chicago students "were half as much in earnest as they are."[27]

After 1920, virtually all the WTUL students took some courses at the University of Chicago. However, since most of them had very limited educational backgrounds, their attendance in college classes was supplemented by intensive tutorials with WTUL staff members. Of the four students who attended the school in 1923, one had gone through the tenth grade, another had reached the seventh grade, and the other two had not finished elementary school.[28] Prior to each class the students would meet with the director of the school, and together they would go over the reading assignment paragraph by paragraph, discussing the meaning of individual words and summarizing the main points of the assignment. As a result of these sessions, the students were able to participate in classroom discussions "on about the same level as students who have had a great deal more schooling."[29]

The same intensive tutoring was given to help students prepare term papers and English compositions. The combination of these tutorials, the student's native intelligence, and a lot of hard work on their part enabled all four of the 1923 students to write term papers for the University of Chicago course on labor problems that received B's and to move from initial grades of D's to B's on themes written for an English class. Taking these college classes expanded the students' intellectual horizons, and discovering that they could do college level work gave them a new confidence in their own abilities.

The high point of academic achievement by a WTUL student was an independent study of Canadian minimum wage laws done by Kathleen Derry, the Canadian boot and shoe worker who attended the school in 1920–1921. The project was suggested to her by Professor Paul Douglas after she had taken his labor problems course in the fall. He supervised her research, and they produced a coauthored article that was published in the April 1922 issue of the *Journal of Political Economy*. The WTUL extended Derry's scholarship to allow her the time necessary to complete this work, and the league's pride in her accomplishment was echoed by Douglas, who remarked, "If anyone needed an argument for workers' education, it was at hand in this piece of work, done by a girl who left school early and had but scant advantages afterwards."[30]

Despite the WTUL's pride in the student's academic achievements, it always kept firmly in mind that the goal of the school was to train young women for leadership positions within the labor movement, not to make them into college students. The league encouraged the students to keep in touch with their own trade by attending meetings of Chicago locals of their unions. It also stressed the educational value of attending meetings of the Chicago WTUL, the Chicago Federation of Labor, and various public lectures and forums on topics relevant to the labor and women's movements. The WTUL considered these meetings and the sessions with WTUL personnel and male labor activities on industrial relations and union practices to be as important as the students' course work in more academic settings.

Despite valiant fund-raising efforts, inadequate finances hindered the school from its inception. In the ten and one-half years it was in operation, the league spent approximately $50,000 on the training program, virtually all of it donated by people outside the labor movement.[31] Most of these sympathetic individuals were women, and WTUL fundraising appeals stressed the notion of cross-class sisterhood in requesting contributions. In a typical fund-raising letter describing the school, Margaret Dreier Robins wrote:

I am very happy to be able to add that all the money which we have received for this work has come to us from women. It seems to me so significant of our time that women of all groups should get together, should learn to understand each other and should be of service one to another.[32]

Some of the fund-raising letters also mentioned the need to provide health care for the students. As Robins wrote to one WTUL benefactor, "No one who does not know intimately the terrible drain upon the physical strength and vitality of our young girls can have any conception of the universality of ill health among them."[33] The league did what it could to arrange for medical and dental care for the students, but serious health problems caused the premature departure of three students who began the training program.[34] Robins felt it would have been beneficial for all the students to have a month's rest before coming to the school and deeply regretted that such an arrangement was "of course quite out of the question."[35]

One of the ways the WTUL provided for the physical well-being of the students was to include recreational activities in the school's program. It was grateful to the YWCA for allowing WTUL students to take swimming and exercise classes free of charge, and in the summer months the school staff arranged excursions such as picnics in Chicago parks and boat rides on Lake Michigan. An indication of the league's continuing concern with the students' health and of the school's precarious financial status is that in 1922 an arrangement was made with a "first class" woman physician who would see WTUL students for the special rate of $3.00 for a full examination and $1.00 to $2.00 for ordinary office consultations; the school staff was pleased with this arrangement and hoped "that somehow we can meet these small bills."[36]

Given the limited financial resources of the school, the WTUL national executive board took very seriously the process of awarding the few scholarships it could offer. The board, guided by recommendations from members of local leagues and union officials, based its selections on its assessment of the applicants' intellectual abilities, union experience, leadership potential, and seriousness of purpose. The league's desire not to antagonize the AFL was a major factor in the board's decision not to award a scholarship to one of the 1923 applicants who was a member of the United Shoe Workers of America, a group that had seceded from the AFL-affiliated International Boot and Shoe Workers' Union.[37]

The board did, however, refuse to go along with racist tendencies in the AFL. One of the 1923 applicants it did accept was Marjorie Kemp, a black post office worker from Chicago; league officials recognized that racial prejudice might make finding fieldwork placements for her difficult, but they considered her a "splendid" young woman, one who had taken "exceptional interest" in the activities of her union and who, with the benefit of training, would be in a position to do "pioneering work among a group as yet scarcely touched by organization."[38]

Predictably, the students did not always fulfill expectations, despite the care that went into their selection. Two students were asked to leave the program in 1917: one partly because of health problems but largely because she did not "give evidence of possessing the qualities of leadership" considered essential;[39] the other because her prior experience in union activities proved too limited to give her the "background to profit by the course of training as outlined for the School."[40] The Boston WTUL, having highly recommended this student, protested the decision to remove her from the program after four months, but the school officials stood by their negative assessment.[41]

A compromise was offered to another student who told the school director that she had recently become engaged and was to be married the following month. Upon hearing this news, the WTUL executive board decided it could not justify continuing her scholarship after her marriage. The board acknowledged that "being a married women is not in itself any disqualification for either an organizer or student organizer," but it felt it must anticipate the reality that "very few young brides care to face the great amount of evening work that organizing involves, or the possibility of being sent away from home at short notice and for indefinite periods."[42] The student, Margaret Haray, an Hungarian immigrant garment worker from Chicago, was told that her scholarship would be continued for another month and that she could use the last two weeks of her grant for her honeymoon. She was invited to return to the training program after her marriage, but at that point it would have to be at her own expense, an option WTUL officials must have realized she was unlikely to be in a position to accept.[43]

On the basis of past experience, WTUL leaders were being realistic; but at the same time, this case illustrates their tendency to accept prevailing views about the incompatibility of careers and marriage for women. As single women, most of the WTUL's most active and committed members often had ambivalent feelings about women who gave up active roles in the WTUL and/or the labor movement for marriage. News of such "defections" tended to produce mixed feelings of pleasure and regret in WTUL leaders. When reporting that Alexia Smith, a student at the school in 1923–1924 and subsequently an organizer for the WTUL, was resigning her position with the league in order to marry, WTUL national secretary-treasurer Elisabeth Christman commented, "While I adore brides and weddings, I find myself wishing that Alexia could have remained with us a while longer!"[44]

Another problem that emerged was conflict over the orientation of the fieldwork program. Although the stated goal of the school was to train women to be union organizers, the fieldwork assignments in fact emphasized bureaucratic and administrative skills and did not provide the students with much supervised experience in day-to-day organizing work.

Dissatisfaction with the fieldwork program was first expressed by the six students at the school in the fall of 1916. The students, in a memo to the national executive board, affirmed their belief in the "purpose and the possibilities of the School," stated that they considered "the academic work valuable and entirely worthwhile," but asserted that they found "the opportunities for experience and practice in field work, the most important phase of the School's work . . . to be practically negligible."[45] As far as they were concerned:

Not a piece of work has been done by the students who are partly or entirely on field work that can be construed as experience in organizing work. We submit that office routine work is distinct from organizing work and that training in the former makes no contribution to the value of the latter.[46]

This astute and pointed criticism did not, however, lead to

lasting changes. The WTUL national executive board discussed the memo and decided to ask Mary Anderson, a WTUL organizer, to direct the student fieldwork.[47] She took charge of this aspect of the training program in 1917, adding the students to the group of women she was coordinating in an attempt to unionize the approximately 15,000 women workers in the Chicago stockyards.[48] Anderson, however, left Chicago the following year, and the changes she had effected in the fieldwork program apparently did not survive her departure.[49]

In 1925 Helen Hill, an ally who served as director of the school in 1924–1925, voiced reservations quite similar to those expressed by the 1916 students, claiming it was a "farce" to think the fieldwork was providing the students with experience in organizing. Her year as director had convinced her that "office and academic work we can do and have to some extent done; insofar as whatever we have taught is transferable, we may have increased the potentiality of whoever from our students may become an organizer, but we are not training organizers."[50]

Hill felt the WTUL would be justified in claiming it was training organizers only if the fieldwork actually required the students to attempt to unionize a group of unorganized workers. "Real training," from her point of view, would consist of picking a target group of workers and then having the students go through the following procedures: exploring legislation and union practices pertinent to the industry in question, making a preliminary survey to obtain names of workers in a given shop or shops, visiting them to discuss the advantages of unionizing, producing and distributing leaflets, and conducting a series of meetings. Such a program would provide the students with genuine organizing experience and, ideally, would produce a new, viable group of trade unionists.

As these perceptive assessments of the training program indicate, there was a serious gap between the WTUL's professed goals for the program and the kind of training it was actually providing. The league was not consciously betraying its commitment to organizing; the bureaucratic emphasis of the fieldwork program simply reflected the current orientation of the WTUL. By the time the school was established, the league, locally and nationally, had come to focus its time and money on educational programs and legislative activities it hoped would move women workers toward unionization, rather than on the actual unionization of women workers. Accordingly, the students at the school were being taught those skills which would be useful in these activities; the fieldwork program, reflecting the background and the experiences of the school's leaders, was producing women better trained to be labor union administrators than militant organizers of other working women.

A final problem worth noting was at least one instance of considerable student dissatisfaction with the attitudes of the school staff. The 1916 memo mentioned above, in addition to its criticism of the fieldwork program, indignantly complained about the staff's patronizing attitudes. Contending that "the School as it is being administered at present must fail of its avowed purpose—the training of trade union girls for leadership among their fellow workers," the students listed the following practices as reasons for their point of view:

1. *Because initiative and the qualities that make for leadership are neither permitted nor encouraged to develop.*

2. *Because past experience and knowledge of the movement are discounted and ignored; we resent being made over.*

3. *Because the treatment accorded us as students in the School has not been that of equals and co-workers in a great sense, but rather that of distrust and condescension.*

4. *Because on no matter, great or small, are we considered capable of making a decision for ourselves, although every one of us has for many years been not only permitted but forced by circumstances to meet her own problems and make her own decisions.*[51]

It is especially interesting to note that these complaints were directed at women who had once been in the position of these students, women whose leadership potential had been developed through their involvement with the WTUL. These complaints, then, were not an instance of class tension between middle-class allies and working-class unionists, for the WTUL personnel most closely involved in the administration of the school at the time were primarily trade unionists who now held staff positions with the league.[52] The charge of patronizing behavior, which the students had no reason to invent, undoubtedly reflects in part inevitable generational differences, but more important, it also reveals a tendency of league leaders, whatever their class backgrounds, to develop the self-righteous attitudes that characterize most social reformers.

The financial problems that beset the school from its inception in 1914 ultimately made it too great a drain on WTUL resources. The combination of a steadily decreasing budget and the development of other worker education programs in the 1920s led the 1926 WTUL convention to vote to discontinue the school. The league came to this decision reluctantly and expressed hope that some of the school's functions would be carried out less formally by the local leagues.

Financial constraints had allowed the WTUL to accept a total of only forty-four students into the training program. Of these forty-four, however, at least thirty-three went on "to serve the labor movement in some capacity."[53] Information about the specific career patterns of individual students is incomplete, but of the twenty-three about whom some information exists, sixteen worked as organizers for trade unions or for the WTUL for at least some period of time. The seven others may also have done some organizing work, but they are known to have been union staff members, government officials in labor-related agencies, and/or active in local leagues of the WTUL. While league leaders deeply regretted the limited number of scholarships they were able to offer, they were extremely proud of the school and considered it a significant aspect of the WTUL during the years it was in operation and in retrospect.

Overall, the school should be regarded as a qualified success. It served only a small number of students, and the fieldwork program was not designed to provide them with the best possible training in organizing skills and techniques. Nonetheless, as the first full-time, residential workers' education program, its establishment was an important event in the history of workers' education in the United States, and the WTUL school influenced the design of subsequent programs.[54]

In terms of the WTUL's history, the decision to establish the school and to devote to it the resources that it did signifies the WTUL's increasingly indirect approach to the unionization of women workers, an orientation that strengthened the league's identity as a social reform organization but weakened its links to the labor movement. However, the fact that 79 percent of the students who attended the school attained positions of greater responsibility and prestige within unions or related organizations is an indication that the school, albeit in a very limited way, did indeed serve to increase the pool of women labor leaders and thereby to improve the status of women in the labor movement.

Hundreds of young women needle workers on strike in East Coast and Midwest cities recounted their experiences to Women's Trade Union League members and supporters. In 1914, *Life and Labor*, the journal of the NWTUL, published these two reports of sexual harassment and the need for union organization under the heading "Girls' Stories."[55]

Girls' Stories

Rosie's Story

The boss from our shop was always fresh with the girls. He liked to see us blush, so we made a society, called "The Young Ladies' Educational Society," and we was not to stand the freshness of the boss. But we was afraid of him, and so we couldn't help each other. Once he touched me, very fresh like, and I cried, and he said, "Let's be good friends, Rosie, and to show you how good I means it, you take supper mit me in a swell hotel, with music and flowers, see?" And I says, "So! Supper mit you—swell hotel! Well, I ask my ma," and he said, "Don't you do it. You say you going to sleep at a friend's house," and I was scared and I said, "Oh! What you mean," and I was trembling so I couldn't nearly do my work, and when my ma sees me, she says, "What's the matter, Rosie?" and I says, "Nothing," because she's sad, my ma is, 'cause I have to work so hard and can't have no education, and she says, "Rosie, you got to tell your ma what's gone wrong," and we both cried together, and so the next day I went to another shop, and I told the *first lie I ever told in my life*. I told the boss I come from another city. I liked this new boss; he was not so fresh and I had a seat by a window, and my ma and me, we was so happy we laughed and I told her about the nice shop and fresh air, and then the next day the boss he come to me and he says, "I'm sorry, Rosie; we like your work, but your other boss telephoned he no discharged you and so we can't keep you here."

Becky's Experience

Well, we had troubles in our shop. The boss, he put a girl at a padding machine, which is awful hard work, the needles they break all the time, and, mind you, a $9.00 job it is, and he only gives her $6.50. Then there is another girl, a pale, quiet kind, and she doing a $6.00 job and gets only $4.00. And this quiet girl, I know just how she feels in her heart, as she sits there sewin'—it's so hopeless, it is—such poor pay, and a big family at home needin' money—and then when the boss comes around, he says to her, cross-like, "Thinkin' of the boys again? You girls can't work, thinkin' of the boys. Out late last night, was you?" And I know just how she feels when she hears that, and so I says to him, "Those two girls in this shop got to have more pay," and he says to me, "You mind your own business, making trouble here. You're satisfied with *your* pay, ain't you?" and I says, "Yes, I'm satisfied with my pay, but the other girls' pay is my business, too." He got mad, and he says to me, "Get out." And so I quit workin' and go home, and they told me after I was gone everybody in that shop quit workin', too, and says they won't do a stitch until I comes back. And so the boss he had to send for me, and we had a shop meetin' and a committee goes to the boss, and he raises the wages of the girls. Now we're organized fine, and everybody in our shop belongs to the union. But I know a shop where the girls don't belong to the union and my friend, she tells me the conditions is awful bad in her shop. So we are going to change places. She gets $8.50 and I get $10.00, but I don't care. I want to help organize these girls and see what's wrong in that shop. And besides, my boss, he hates me so. Gee! did you ever see a boss smile? He smiled at me today! Ain't it cute! Don't it just make you sick!

Submitted in 1914 to *Life and Labor* by a reader, this life history underscored the need for "the strong organization of the women and girl workers" supported by the WTUL. The editors also applauded the young writer's call for the vote.[56]

How I Escaped from the Factory

Grammar school had just closed for the usual summer ten weeks' vacation, and I entertained fond hopes of entering the high school at the close of the vacation, having passed my examinations successfully, but hopes of a high school education for me were soon to explode like bubbles.

My father, who had been employed as a machinist in a large factory had the misfortune of having several pieces of lead and steel enter his eyes, and the doctors were of the opinion that he would never be able to see again, and for weeks lay on a bed while my mother, sisters and brother took turns of supplying ice cold compresses to the almost sightless eyes.

My father recovered his eyesight, however, and because of the enormous expenses incurred, and loss of work, it was necessary for me to help finance the family.

I was about fourteen years of age and the oldest of five.

I shall never forget the day my father came to me and told me he had secured a job for me in the same factory in which he was employed, and expected me to be ready in the morning to go to work at 6:30 A.M.

I had been sitting on our front door step, quietly dreaming and planning my future career as a professional nurse with a high school diploma.

After my father proceeded to leave me, I got up too stunned to reply. It seemed as if an iron clamp had suddenly been pressed around my head. I said, "Alright, father," and walked and walked, not knowing or caring where the walk might lead.

Finally I arrived at the dark winding river which flowed near our large manufacturing concerns, and came very near wishing the river would swallow me up, so filled was I with disappointment, and so weary and tired trying to think this new thing out.

I managed to get back home about eight o'clock and, going straight to bed, gave vent to my disappointment by sobbing bitterly, until from sheer exhaustion I went to sleep.

The following morning mother came and woke me up at 5:30 A.M. I immediately arose, trying to conceal from mother and father just how badly I felt, but I couldn't deceive mother. She knew my ambitions and plans, I felt her ever watchful eyes on me all the time I ate breakfast. I had the feeling that she would question, but she very wisely said nothing. Just before leaving for work, however, she gave me a new sailor hat to make me feel brave I suppose. At another time I would have been delighted, but I was still too grieved and dazed, and the sailor hat brought no comfort.

Father and I walked to the factory together, and I was on the verge of tears all the way. I had hard work to keep from sobbing. I had never seen the interior of a factory, and upon entering, the machinery seemed so large, formidable and black, the floors so black, too, and the walls and ceilings so dirty and dusty that it satisfied my ideas of a prison.

I was assigned to a printing office, connected with the factory. The odor of poisonous inks and oils was unendurable.

I was immediately set to work running a Gordon press at slow speed for about a week, and learned to feed the machine so accurately and well that the very next week I was put on full speed, receiving the sum of three dollars a week.

The actual work was not hard; the hours were very long. Just as soon as an order had been printed, we would sit down in some uncomfortable corner and wait half an hour or an hour for another order to be printed.

After a few months the factory went into a trust, and we all felt the change before three weeks had gone.

We found, for instance, that we had departed from the old system into one of speed, speed, speed. We also had a timekeeper over us, which meant we were to have printed by 6:00 P.M. twelve thousand to fifteen thousand envelopes a day. This meant that we must repeat the one and same motion twelve or fifteen thousand times a day.

I used to be tired and weary about two in the afternoon, with energy and snap all gone. This was partially due to the poor ventilation we had.

There were about forty of us in all, men and women, boys and girls in this printing room breathing this bad air.

The only ventilation we had was open windows; but most people are aware that open windows give haphazard ventilation. We couldn't have even so much ventilation in winter. When one of the girls opened a window for a breath of fresh air, someone would surely call out, "Close that window. Do you want to freeze us to death?" So the windows generally remained closed. The air we breathed as a result was a mixture of carbonic gas and paper dust and floor dust. The floor was swept daily with a broom, never dampened, though we often begged the sweeper to "please dampen the broom."

Many of the men chewed tobacco, and would usually expectorate on the floor. If we admonished them they swore at us.

During my observation of them, two of these men, who were in the habit of thus expectorating on the floor or in the sink, were obliged to lay off on account of tuberculosis.

One day I plucked up courage enough to ask the boss for a "raise."

I was granted $3.60 a week. I thought I ought to have more, and upon saying so, "the boss" informed me that, since we were working for a trust, it was up to him to run his department as economically as he could.

That meant, I inferred, getting as much speed as he possibly could out of us—as reports and figures had to go to headquarters and be compared with reports and figures of the other five factories in the trust.

With the increase in speed, the dispositions of the girls changed. We became, as a whole, an irritable, unhappy company.

One day a paper came amongst us for our signatures. The paper agreed to give us Saturday afternoons for a holiday every week if we would agree to come back a quarter of an hour earlier each noon to work.

We all signed, for we all wanted Saturday afternoons off.

I never counted the cost of signing that paper then, but I did later.

Three quarters of an hour for a dinner hour. Think of it! It meant rushing home, swallowing your food whole and rushing back.

My home was a mile away from the factory, and I had to climb a hill to reach it, but a great many of the girls had farther than that to go.

I used to have severe attacks of indigestion; and the weariness and headaches began to tell. I grew thin, pale and lifeless and had all I could do to keep up with the speed.

When I could manage to work all day, I could hardly walk home at night. The hill climbing became almost an impossibility. Many times I prayed to die; I was too miserable to live.

I managed to plod along this way about three months when one day an accident occurred to one of the boys.

The young fellow was an apprentice, and had just "set up" a press for printing labels. Some of the labels, dropping on the floor, he stooped to pick them up, when the flesh of the upper part of his arm was drawn into the machinery and ground to pieces between two unprotected gears. I saw the accident, and went to his assistance with the result that a week from the day the young man was injured I entered a hospital, not as a nurse, but a general helper.

The interns of the hospital noticed my transparent, colorless appearance, and took a blood count and found I was on the verge of serious anaemia. Therefore my work was made lighter and a diet prescribed. I took walks in the open air, took the prescribed tonics and today I am a full-fledged state registered nurse, happy and well.

I never pass a factory without thinking and praying for those employed there. Women in industry are increasing faster than their birth rate, and girls are becoming unfit for motherhood because of the speed and grind of factory life.

The factory exists to produce dividends for the stockholder; that is all.

Give the working girls pure air to breathe, give them a living wage, and less hours of labor.

I often wonder whether we are always going to have laws in the interests of workers combatted by capitalists. So many courts are in the habit of declaring laws in the interests of workers unconstitutional.

There are eight million women today working for wages. They are not working for starvation wages because they want to; women are not working ten hours a day because they want to.

Speed the day when we shall have the minimum wage, eight-hour law, compensation and liability act, and the righting of an unjust industrial situation and the vote giving the working girl the chance to voice her own sentiments.

My experience as a factory girl has convinced me that women in industry need the vote for their protection.

—Unsigned, 1914.

Written by a student at one of the early sessions of the WTUL's Training School for Women Organizers, and published by *Life and Labor* in 1916, this essay reflects a rarely articulated concern for both women in industry and women "working in the homes of union men." Organized under labor's banner, the author argues that women could become a powerful political and economic force.[57]

At the League's Training School

"SCHOOL FOR WOMEN ORGANIZERS."

Up I sprang from the dining-room floor where I was engaged in putting down a carpet. I was all excitement, for here was something valuable—a golden opportunity, perhaps—and how near I had come missing it! For that copy of the "Mine Workers' Journal" which contained the article under the caption "School for Women Organizers" was about to be hidden away. Clearly opportunity had knocked more than once, for the paper was an old copy and this article had missed my eye before.

Hurriedly and excitedly I read this extract from an address made by Mrs. Raymond Robins:

"* * * If we are to serve our time as we ought to serve it, representing as we do the hope and aspirations of the great working women's group of America, organized and unorganized, we have to make possible an equipment to train and send forth organizers. * * * Will it be possible for the National Women's Trade Union League to establish a training school for women organizers, even though in the beginning it may be only a training class, offering every trade union girl a scholarship for a year? The course of study ought to include the philosophy of trade unionism, the history of trade unions in America, England and Europe, a study of all current labor legislation, current history of the woman movement and the need of full citizenship for women, lessons in parliamentary law, a study of the methods of trade union offices, including the office of the American Federation of Labor at Washington, and field practice in more than one city under the leadership of the trade union organizers of the Women's Trade Union League. Am I right in thinking that this is the great need of the hour in the industrial development of America? If I am right surely the delegates to this convention will find the means to establish a training school for women organizers so that we may be equipped to do our work. * * *"

At once I clipped the article and went on about my many Saturday duties, but all through the day the thought of that woman, of whom I had never heard before, was uppermost in my mind. Was it that through this bit of news, found by the merest accident, I was to gain the opportunity I had long desired? I, too, had felt the need, in a somewhat different way, of women trained for service in the industrial world; and here was a woman who had expressed this need excellently, and from her words surely this thing could be done.

But who was this Mrs. Raymond Robins and where could she be found? The writer evidently took it for granted that his readers knew all about the Women's Trade Union League. I agree that they should.

When my father came home from the mine that evening, I shared the news with him, saying, "If I only knew of such a school, I'd go there."

"Would you quit teaching?" he asked.

"I would go to that school," I declared, evading the question. "I would go as soon as school closes this spring for I can't help but feel that such a school would offer more of the vital things of life than we get at the Normal University."

But would it mean the end of my teaching profession? Would it mean giving up all that that had meant and might mean to me? I was not talking now, I was dreaming—dreaming of another school in which I might some day come to teach.

"Oh, I must learn more about it," I presently exclaimed.

It must seem strange indeed to you who have long been familiar with "Life and Labor," to know that it was a very difficult thing for me to get information about the Women's Trade Union League and to locate that woman, Mrs. Robins. But life in the coal camp and mining town, even in Illinois, affords little opportunity for one to come in touch with the big movements of the day. The "Mine Workers' Journal" was the only trade union publication with which I was familiar. My reading was largely confined to educational journals which give nothing, of course, of the activities of the big school of industrial democracy.

It was John Mitchell, a former leader of the mine workers, who put me on the track of the woman I was seeking. Without delay I began to bombard the National League headquarters with letters. We got acquainted.

The opportunity was given me, at the League's national convention in New York City last summer, to tell those present about the women I know. I was afraid I could not make the women of the League understand. The working women in the larger industrial centers had always claimed their thoughts and energies. Could I get them to see that the women in the isolated mining camp or small industrial communities were a large and important part in the development of an industrial democracy?

How happy I was to learn that another had been dreaming dreams akin to mine. Mrs. Robins could see the women of whom I spoke and she could see them in the future, intelligently active in labor affairs.

As I look back upon it now that wee, but valuable, bit of news I had read that Saturday was the key which unlocked to me a big new world, the world of women in industry, and led me on to that splendid New York convention which sent me back into my little world with a larger, a clearer and a richer vision. I saw my work before me and I must make ready for it. Would the word come, would I be given that opportunity?

October 1, 1915, it came. That scholarship, that wonderful opportunity, was mine.

And I am here in Chicago. And how happy and proud I am. I feel that there must be hundreds, yes, thousands, who if they knew, would envy me. I am here, for the present the lone student in this "School for Active Workers in the Labor Movement," as it has since been renamed, for we know that some of us will be organizers, some writers or lecturers, some will use their talents in other ways. This big work of women and labor needs many sorts of service.

We must gather into our movement the women working in small groups in the towns and the women, who, though they can hold no union card, are working in the homes of union men, and have a voice in political affairs; for all these women constitute a potential force both in the political and economic world, and organized, they will contribute much of strength and value to the cause of labor. We need them and they need us. Think what it would mean if when our representatives appear before the state legislature asking for such legislation as the eight-hour day and the minimum wage, we could have the voice of all these women heard in the legislative halls. The "doubting Thomases" would be convinced that women want these things and I feel sure that these women will be instrumental in the passage of such laws.

My field work in the fall came to a sudden close after I had been in Chicago only two weeks and it became necessary for me to go to a hospital for an operation. But with the beginning of the new year I began my studies at the University of Chicago. I am now getting the background, the setting, if you will, of present day labor activities and I am coming to have a more wholesome regard for history than ever before. And following this will come the study of labor problems. Besides this work at the university there is a wealth of material in the League's very valuable library. I cannot read these books fast enough. Then there are night classes for all the League girls in Chicago, one of these being a very interesting and important class in industrial history. And among the most interesting meetings I attend are the meetings of the Chicago Women's Trade Union League once a month, and the bi-monthly meetings of the Chicago Federation of Labor.

And now that I am here I cannot feel that I have lost any of the value of the teaching profession nor have I sacrificed any of its possibilities. Many there are to teach in that great institution, the public school, but to some of us it is given to teach in this equally great institution, the school of industrial democracy.

—Agnes Burns, 1916.

Notes

1. Modeled on a British organization with the same name, the American Women's Trade Union League was founded in 1903 by a coalition of social reformers and trade unionists. It remained in existence until 1950, but the steady decline in its membership and financial base that began in the mid-1920s makes the organization's first two decades the most interesting and important part of its forty-seven-year history. Its headquarters were in Chicago until 1930 and after that in Washington, D.C., and while the number of branches or local leagues fluctuated over the years, they were consistently concentrated in the East and Midwest. The New York, Chicago, and Boston leagues, the first ones to be established, were the strongest and most active locals throughout the WTUL's history.

For a fuller discussion of the WTUL, see Robin Miller Jacoby, "The British and American Women's Trade Union Leagues, 1890–1925: A Case Study of Feminism and Class" (Ph.D. diss., Harvard University, 1977); Nancy Schrom Dye, *As Equals and as Sisters: Feminism, Unionism, and the Women's Trade Union League of New York* (Columbia: University of Missouri Press, 1980); and Philip S. Foner, *Women and the American Labor Movement*, 2 vols. (New York: Free Press, 1979 and 1980).

2. For further discussion of this pattern and the position of women in the industrial labor force in the early twentieth century, see Alice Kessler-Harris, "Where Are the Organized Women Workers?" (*Feminist Studies* 3 [Fall 1975]: 92–110), and Leslie Woodcock Tentler, *Wage-Earning Women: Industrial Work and Family Life in the United States*, 1900–1930 (New York: Oxford University Press, 1979).

3. Rich and reasonably accessible primary sources describing these local and national programs are the WTUL-written "Women's Department" in the *Union Labor Advocate*, a monthly labor journal published in Chicago, and, from 1911 to 1921, *Life and Labor*, the WTUL's own monthly journal. A complete copy of the primer may be found in the WTUL papers at the Schlesinger Library of Radcliffe College; excerpts from it were published in the January to April 1912 issues of *Life and Labor*.

4. The name was changed in 1915 to the School for Active Workers in the Labor Movement. The school's goals did not change, but the new name more accurately reflected the

kind of training the school offered.

5. By the time the WTUL school closed in 1926, some of the resident worker education programs which had come into existence were: summer schools for women workers at Bryn Mawr, Barnard, and Sweet Briar; a summer program for women and men at the University of Wisconsin; and year-round sessions at Brookwood Labor College in Katonah, New York, and Commonwealth College in Mena, Arkansas. For brief surveys of these and other workers' education programs, see Spencer Miller, "Summer Schools for Workers" (*American Federationist* 32 [July 1925]: 569–71), and Mark Starr, *Workers' Education Today* (New York, 1941).

6. "The Fourth Biennial Convention," *Life and Labor* 3 (July 1913): 210.

7. Ibid.

8. Ibid.

9. They were Melinda Scott, who was national vice-president and a member of the New York WTUL and the United Hat Trimmers Union; Leonora O'Reilly, a working-class member of the New York WTUL; Stella Franklin, a Chicago league activist, who was national secretary-treasurer and a member of the Stenographers and Typists Union; Laura Eliot, a New York ally; Amy Walker, a Chicago ally; and Mrs. Henry D. Faxon, an ally who was president of the Kansas City WTUL.

10. Mittelstadt had been secretary of the Kansas City league since its inception in 1911 and was elected to the WTUL national executive board at both the 1911 and 1913 conventions. The characterization of her as diffident is based on letters written by her between 1911 and 1914; these are in the WTUL papers in the Library of Congress and the Schlesinger Library.

11. Mittelstadt to Stella Franklin, December 6, 1913, NWTUL Papers, Library of Congress, Washington, D.C.

12. Franklin to Executive Board members, February 27, 1914, Rose Schneiderman Papers, Tamiment Library, New York University, New York, N.Y.

13. Robins to Mrs. Willard Straight, February 15, 1916, NWTUL Papers, Schlesinger Library, Cambridge, Mass.

14. Cohn became a member of the ILGWU staff in 1919 and worked for the union until her death in 1962. She served as education director for most of that time, but was also the executive secretary and a vice-president in the course of her career. She gained a national reputation for her role in the development of workers' education programs, founding the Workers' Education Bureau of

America and helping to establish Brookwood Labor College.

15. See Alice Kessler-Harris, "Organizing the Unorganizable: Three Jewish Women and Their Union," *Labor History* 17 (Winter 1976): 14. (Kessler-Harris's discussion of Cohn does not include mention of her attending the WTUL school.)

16. "Staff Meeting Held March 12 [1914] to discuss work of National League and especially plans for the National Training School," Rose Schneiderman Papers.

17. Robins to Straight, February 22, 1918, NWTUL Papers, Schlesinger Library.

18. Franklin to Executive Board Members, February 22, 1918, NWTUL Papers, Schlesinger Library.

19. Ibid.

20. Whitehead's life had a tragic ending: her husband was killed in an accident a few months after their marriage, and she died very unexpectedly shortly after the birth of a child in May 1917. Her mother took the baby to raise, and WTUL members kept in periodic touch with the grandmother throughout the 1920s. At the time of Whitehead's death, the WTUL established a fund for the child's education, but, like so many of the league's undertakings, the fund proved to be one of those good intentions that was never very fully realized, for only about $200 was accumulated.

21. Alice Henry to the Alumnae of the Training School, June 29, 1922, Rose Schneiderman Papers.

22. Robins to Straight, February 22, 1918, NWTUL Papers, Schlesinger Library.

23. "Report from Secretary of Educational Department," February 11, 1921, NWTUL Papers, Library of Congress.

24. See "Report of Associate Director of the School for Active Workers in the Labor Movement" (pp. 3–5), June 1917, NWTUL Papers, Schlesinger Library.

25. Olive Sullivan to Robins, October 27, 1916, Margaret Dreier Robins Papers, University of Florida, Gainesville, Fla.

26. "Extracts from Reports of Professor Douglas and Professor Nelson," NWTUL Papers, Schlesinger Library.

27. Ibid.

28. See Elisabeth Christman and Penn Shelton Burke to Members of the Executive Board, November 30, 1923, NWTUL Papers, Library of Congress. This information on the educational backgrounds of these students in 1923–1924 was the only indication of the prior schooling of students who attended the WTUL school.

29. Ibid.

30. Quoted by Alice Henry, "Report of the Education De-

partment" (p. 3), June 5, 1922, NWTUL Papers, Schlesinger Library.

31. This estimate is based on reports indicating that the WTUL had spent slightly over $28,000 on the school by 1920 and over $35,000 by early 1923. These figures were found in untitled, undated documents in the NWTUL Papers at the Schlesinger Library. Since twelve more students attended the school between 1923 and 1926, another $8,900 was spent on scholarships ($750 per student). Taking into account overhead costs, as well as this sum expended on scholarships, $50,000 is probably a conservative estimate. While the WTUL never received much financial assistance from the AFL, its policy was to use AFL contributions only for WTUL organizing work.

32. Robins to Mrs. William Cochran, August 31, 1916, Margaret Dreier Robins Papers.

33. Robins to Straight, October 5, 1916, Margaret Dreier Robins Papers.

34. In one case the student was able to return to the school several months later, and there was a dramatic change in her after she had had the operation she needed and some time to rest. According to Robins, "It is almost impossible to realize that this healthy, quiet, and serene young woman is the same human being who was up in the heights and down in the depths, high strung and physically and nervously ill when she came to us!" (ibid.).

35. Ibid.

36. "Distribution of the Scholarship Fund," NWTUL Papers, Schlesinger Library.

37. See Christman to Maud Swartz, April 12, 1923, NWTUL Papers, Library of Congress.

38. Ibid. See also Christman to Members of the Executive Board, July 5, 1923, NWTUL Papers, Schlesinger Library.

39. Emma Steghagen to Members of the Executive Board, January 9, 1917, NWTUL Papers, Library of Congress.

40. Steghagen to Members of the Executive Board, January 11, 1917, NWTUL Papers, Library of Congress.

41. See ibid.; Mabel Gillespie to Steghagen, January 27, 1917; and Steghagen to Gillespie, n.d.; NWTUL Papers, Library of Congress. Florence Adesska, the student in question, returned to Boston, where she did very effective organizing work for the ILGWU, an indication that the school staff was not always correct in its judgments.

42. Christman to Members of the Executive Board, July 12, 1922, NWTUL Papers, Library of Congress.

43. The letter cited in n. 42, which is an explanation of the situation and of the action taken in regard to this case, was written while the student was on her honeymoon. It is the only document referring to the case, and the fact that it does not indicate that she was planning to return is probably a good indication that she did not complete the training program. There is unfortunately no evidence of her reaction to the executive board's decision.

44. Christman to Members of the Executive Board, May 23, 1927, Margaret Dreier Robins Papers.

45. Agnes Burns, Dora Lipschitz, Lilly Brzostek, Mary Thompson, Florence Adesska, and Julia O'Connor to the Executive Board of the National Women's Trade Union League, November 1916, WTUL Papers, Library of Congress.

46. Ibid.

47. The minutes of the executive board meeting simply state that a "full discussion" of the memo took place and that it was decided to appoint Mary Anderson as head of the fieldwork program ("Minutes of the Executive Board Meeting," November 4–5, 1916, NWTUL Papers, Library of Congress).

48. See Robins to Straight, February 22, 1918, NWTUL Papers, Schlesinger Library.

49. Anderson moved to Washington, D.C., in early 1918 to accept a government appointment to the Women's Division of the Ordnance Department, and she remained in Washington to become head of the Women's Bureau of the Department of Labor when it was created in 1920.

50. Helen D. Hill, "Report on Training School," n.d. (summer 1925, from internal evidence), NWTUL Papers, Schlesinger Library.

51. Burns et al. to Executive Board, November 1916, NWTUL Papers, Library of Congress. Despite their complaints, these students were not fundamentally alienated from the WTUL, for all six of them remained active in the organization in the years that followed.

52. The associate director, however, was an ally who had formerly served as head resident of a settlement house in Baltimore, and it may well be that she was the primary target of the students' criticisms, even though they do not explicitly say so in their memo.

53. National Women's Trade Union League, *Twenty-fifth Anniversary Program* (Chicago, 1929), p. 15. This summary indicates that, by 1928, three of the forty-four students who had attended the school had died and that thirty-two (or 78 percent) of the remaining forty-one had been active in the labor movement. Of the three de-

ceased students, I can identify only Myrtle Whitehead, but since it is known that she worked as an organizer for a period prior to her death, I am counting her in the total of activists. Discounting the other two who died, then, 79 percent (actually, 78.57 percent) of the students went on to serve the labor movement.

54. There were especially close ties between the WTUL and the Summer School for Women Workers established at Bryn Mawr College in 1921. The program was run by a joint administrative board consisting of an equal number of college and industrial women, and most of the latter were trade union members of the WTUL. The Bryn Mawr school, which ran for eight weeks and accepted about 100 students each summer, offered an academic program similar to that of the WTUL's school, but it did not include fieldwork and it was not nearly as trade union oriented as the league's school in Chicago. The Bryn Mawr Summer School remained in existence until 1938, when it moved to New York to become the Hudson Shore Labor School, a coeducational institution with year-round programs.

For further information, see Helen D. Hill, *The Effect of the Bryn Mawr Summer School as Measured in the Activities of its Students* (New York: American Association of Adult Education, 1929); Gladys L. Palmer, *The Industrial Experience of Women Workers at the Summer Schools, 1928–1930*, Bulletin no. 89 (Washington, D.C.: U.S. Department of Labor, Women's Bureau, 1931); and Hilda Worthington Smith, *Women Workers at the Bryn Mawr Summer School* (New York: Affiliated Schools for Women Workers in Industry, 1929).

55. Both from *Life and Labor* 4, no. 8 (August 1914), pp. 243–44.

56. From *Life and Labor* 4, no. 9 (September 1914), pp. 268–70.

57. From *Life and Labor* 6, no. 3 (March 1916), pp. 38–39.

Chapter 2

From Soul to Strawberries:
The International Ladies' Garment Workers' Union and Workers' Education, 1914–1950

Susan Stone Wong

The history of workers' education in the International Ladies' Garment Workers' Union (ILGWU) mirrored the history of the American workers' education movement. Born of the necessity to teach workers the rudiments of trade unionism, the ILGWU's educational programs flourished in the burst of idealism and hope that followed World War I. For a few short years, it appeared that the ILGWU's Educational Department and other workers' education enterprises would be the vanguard of a new movement dedicated to the creation of an economically and socially just society. As the 1920s progressed, however, idealism and hope gave way to conservatism and defeatism, and the workers' education movement floundered. Workers' education reemerged during the successful unionizing drives of the 1930s and 1940s, but it had changed to reflect the hard-nosed realism of the new labor movement. Workers' education had become labor education, and the link between education and social action was broken. Whereas workers' education had aimed to teach workers to build a new and better world, labor education endeavored to instruct them to manage in the world in which they lived. In the 1920s, workers' educators believed that workers' education would become the soul of the union movement. By the 1940s, labor education had become a union fringe benefit.

The workers' education movement and the ILGWU's Educational Department shared a similar concern for women workers. At the outset, the workers' education movement was composed of middle-class intellectuals, radicals, and reformers, many of whom were women. The architects of the ILGWU's Educational Department were two women from middle-class backgrounds. In designing workers' education programs, these educators paid particular attention to what they saw as women workers' special needs and desires. When workers' education became labor education, union leaders denounced this special concern as naive and sentimental.

The history of the ILGWU's Educational Department serves as a guide to the workers' education programs developed by other garment unions. In 1919, for example, the United Cloth Hat and Cap Makers, the Furriers' Union, and the Fancy Leather Goods Workers formed the United Labor Education Committee in New York City. For a few years the committee offered garment workers classes and lectures. In 1921, the committee sponsored the first workers' education conference in the United States, from which the

Workers' Education Bureau grew. In 1920, the Amalgamated Clothing Workers of America organized an educational department and launched a short-lived workers' education program. These unions, however, did not develop a continuing commitment to workers' education. During the next two decades individual locals sponsored occasional educational activities, but without the backing of the national unions these programs were little more than undersubscribed and underfinanced copies of the ILGWU's more successful ventures. Until the late 1940s, the ILGWU was more than the leader of the workers' education movement in the garment industry; it was the movement.[1]

The ILGWU initiated its program of workers' education because, as the Chicago Cloakmakers declared in 1910, the principles of unionism were like "a sealed book" to the majority of foreign-born needle workers. Most of these workers were women, and, although many had socialist sympathies, few had trade union experience. As early as 1905, Secretary-Treasurer John Dyche urged locals to teach their members the importance of the union label.[2]

The signing, in September 1910, of the first collective bargaining agreement in the industry added urgency to the need to inform members of the duties and benefits of unionism. Louis D. Brandeis, the Boston attorney and later justice of the Supreme Court who had negotiated what became known as the "Protocol of Peace," insisted that the ILGWU conduct an educational campaign to win workers away from the "radical" ideas they had acquired as a result of "a generation of miseducation." Thousands of workers learned about unions as participants in the 1909 "Uprising of Twenty Thousand" and the 1910 Cloakmakers General Strike. If the Protocol was to work, the workers had to be taught that arbitration and conciliation, rather than class struggle, were the basis of American unionism.[3]

The 1914 ILGWU convention, agreeing that the educational programs then available to workers were too sporadic and unsystematic to be useful, decreed that the time had come "to dwell particularly upon the more solid and preparatory work of education and not to devote much time to the mere superficial forms of agitation and propaganda which have been the main features of our educational work in the past." During the winter of 1914–1915, ILGWU president Benjamin Schlesinger initiated a joint program with the Rand

School to provide classes in trade union history, methods of organization, and English. The national leadership, however, did little else during the next two years to implement the convention's request.[4]

In the meantime, individual locals, especially New York Waist and Dress Makers' Union, Local 25, devised ambitious programs that laid the foundation for the International's future educational work. In 1915, Local 25 appointed Juliet Stuart Poyntz its educational director. Under her guidance, the first Unity House was established in Pine Hill, New York, to serve as a recreational retreat for union members and their families. Poyntz also organized Unity Centers at local public schools, where workers attended shop meetings, union lectures, and courses in English and physical training taught by Board of Education teachers.[5]

Prompted by the activity of its locals, the International created its own comprehensive educational program in 1916. In stating its objectives, the convention alluded to the past concerns of Brandeis, the Chicago Cloakmakers, and John Dyche. The aim of the program would be to enlighten "the great masses of our organization upon general labor questions" and "on the functions, aims, possibilities and limitations of a trade organization." The report continued,

They [ILGWU members] are to be taught about the contents of our existing agreements with employers, their rights as well as their obligations under the agreement. In short, this part of the educational system is to enlighten our members upon all matters concerning labor, and make of them a well disciplined and reliable body of men and women who cannot be misled and incited by anybody who desires to do so.[6]

The General Executive Board appointed a five-member Education Committee, appropriated $5,000 for its work, and designated Juliet Poyntz as its part-time director. Poyntz expanded the number of Unity Centers and Unity Houses and established a Workers' University at Washington Irving High School in New York City. There, workers could take advanced courses in labor problems, economics, American history and government, literature, and psychology. The 1918 convention demonstrated its approval of the work by increasing the Education Department's appropriation to $10,000. By late 1918, when Poyntz resigned and was replaced by Fannia Cohn, the basic direction of the ILGWU's program had been charted.[7]

Juliet Stuart Poyntz and Fannia Mary Cohn deserve joint credit for founding the union's educational program. Poyntz was the more original thinker, but her tenure at the ILGWU was short. From 1918 until a few months before her death in 1962, Cohn dedicated herself to explaining, expanding, and promoting workers' education. At first glance, two women could not appear more different than the attractive, college-educated midwesterner Poyntz and the short, stocky, Russian-Jewish immigrant Cohn. Yet both women were born into the comforts of the middle class, both chose to abandon their social position in order to champion the workers' cause, and both believed that workers' education was essential to the personal and political liberation of the working class.

Poyntz's background and education were typical of many women in the workers' education movement, but her commitment to revolutionary politics led her to leave the field early in her career. Born in 1886 to a middle-class family in Omaha, Nebraska, Poyntz came east to attend Barnard College. A brilliant student, she was awarded a fellowship by the General Federation of Women's Clubs to study at Oxford and the London School of Economics. She joined the Socialist Party in 1909, and besides teaching history at Barnard and working with the ILGWU, she headed the Rand School's Labor Research Department. In 1917, she left the Socialist Party to join the newly organized Workers' Party. The bitter disputes between the Communists and Socialists in the ILGWU forced her to resign her position in the union. In the early 1920s, she helped to organize the Communist Workers School in New York City, but she left shortly thereafter to become a top party official and candidate for public office.[8]

Cohn was born in 1885 in Kletzk, Minsk, Russia. Her prosperous family had Cohn privately educated in preparation for a professional career. Attracted to radical politics, Cohn joined the outlawed Socialist Revolutionary Party in 1901. Three years later she emigrated to New York City. For Cohn, socialism was a basic creed, an article of faith. Unlike Poyntz, however, she eschewed doctrine and formal party affiliations. As a result, she was able to work with both Socialists and Communists within the ILGWU.[9]

Cohn's American relatives offered her a chance to study pharmacology and eventually to join their drug supply company. However, in 1905, determined to dedicate her life to the labor movement, Cohn abandoned her studies and took a job in a garment factory as a sleevemaker. "I realized then that if I wanted to really understand the mind, the aspirations of the workers," she wrote years later, "I should experience the life of a worker in a shop." She began her life as a union official with her election in 1909 to the executive board of Local 41. In August 1915, she reached the high point of her organizing career when she headed the first successful strike of Chicago's dress and white good workers.[10]

Cohn gained a union-wide reputation because of her success as an organizer. She was elected the first woman vice-president of the ILGWU in 1916. A year later, she was appointed organizing secretary of the General Education Committee. Cohn and Poyntz did not work well together. Cohn lacked Poyntz's popularity and easy rapport with the immigrant women who Cohn considered her natural constituency. Despite these difficulties, from 1918 to her death in 1962, Cohn worked ceaselessly to promote the ideas Poyntz originated.[11]

The ILGWU's desire to school its members and leaders in the responsibilities and duties of unionism prompted the establishment of its educational program but, in itself, does not explain the strength of the union's commitment to workers' education. This commitment grew naturally out of the ILGWU's particular philosophy of trade unionism and from Poyntz's and Cohn's perceptions of the needs of women trade unionists. "Social unionism," as the ILGWU's philosophy was dubbed in the 1930s, moved beyond Samuel Gompers's formulation of "pure and simple" unionism by addressing not only the economic concerns of workers for higher wages and shorter hours but also the workers' need for recreation, education, health care, and housing.

Social unionism tied the building of a union to the creation of a new and better social order. In so doing, this philosophy reflected both the practical needs and the political ideals of its immigrant constituency and provided the theoretical underpinnings for workers' education in the ILGWU. In 1923, the ILGWU's educational committee summarized this credo as it applied to workers' education: "The International Ladies' Garment Workers' Union was practically the first labor organization in America to recognize the truth that in addition to providing for the economic needs of its members, a Labor Union has other functions; among the most important of these is that of providing for their spiritual needs."[12] As defined by Poyntz and Cohn, "spiritual needs" encompassed the workers' wishes for a general and wide-ranging education, for individual self-improvement, for social and intellectual respectability, and for recreation.

Most pressing of these "needs" was the immigrant workers' desire for an education. Cohn, in particular, believed that workers should not be deprived of the joys of a liberal education because of their age, their lack of formal schooling, or their class. Adult workers, as much as the sons and daughters of the upper classes, deserved exposure to art, literature, music, drama, philosophy, and history. On Saturday afternoons or Sunday mornings, union members could take classes in these subjects at the Workers' University; these were often taught by the same professors who lectured during the week to the children of the elite at such institutions as Columbia University. But "spiritual needs" could also be more mundane. Within the ILGWU there were hundreds of foreign-born men and women who required instruction in the basic skills of reading, writing, and arithmetic. Under a special arrangement with the New York City Board of Education, public school teachers came to local Unity Centers to teach the three R's in the evenings or on weekends.[13]

Poyntz and Cohn also recognized, especially among the young women garment workers, a longing for respectability. The very name "trade union" often conjured up in the minds of these women a picture of middle-aged men sitting in smoky taverns drinking and arguing interminably over the tactics of union organizing. Male unionists criticized their female counterparts for their reluctance to take part in union activities and for their unreliability as union members. But Poyntz and Cohn recognized that these women workers wanted their union to be more than a rallying point in the battle for economic justice; they wanted it to be a community in which they could learn, meet friends, and have fun. They also wanted it to be an institution of which they could be proud. Poyntz realized that through workers' education, the longings of these women could be met and, as a result, their loyalty to the union could be strengthened. Unity House, the vacation home in the Catskills, was described by Poyntz as a "center of spiritual inspiration," a place where:

The girls grew to realize that a trade union has a very powerful influence beyond the purely eco-

nomic field. Ties of friendship made then held. Devotion to the ideal of trade unionism acquired then strengthened many a Unity girl to continue her struggle as a chairman of her shop against an ignorant and deceiving employer. The union has found a soul.[14]

In 1917, Poyntz designed the first Unity Center, located in a public school building, with the same objectives in mind. In addition to attending their shop meetings, union members could join friends for a cup of coffee and a roll in the cafeteria, consult a nurse, listen to a concert, dance or exercise in the gym, take remedial courses, or attend a lecture in Yiddish on the history of the ILGWU. Poyntz realized what such centers could mean to young garment workers. She wrote:

The Unity Center seemed to the workers not a public school, but their own home, a home where they found cheer and familiar faces, a beautiful, clean, well ventilated home, well lighted and hung with beautiful pictures, a great change from the dirty, ill ventilated meeting rooms, often above a saloon, where trade unions most usually meet for want of a better place. The very entrance into the public school of a trade union raises it from the position of a social outlaw to that of a vital and recognized social group. . . . It provided a possibility of growth and development of the body and of the mind of the individual worker through his collective organization.[15]

An educational program designed so carefully to reflect and serve the needs and desires of individual workers posed a dangerous dilemma. How did one draw the line between individual and individualistic needs, between self-improvement and self-aggrandizement? Education is traditionally viewed as offering class mobility, but if one of the aims of the ILGWU education program was to facilitate entry into the middle class, the program risked betraying the very union that sponsored it. More, in seeking to cater to the immigrant worker's demand for a general education, the union risked accepting another bourgeois educational tenet—"Knowledge for Knowledge's sake." Why should a trade union sponsor a program that threatened to inculcate its working-class members with the skills that might enable them to leave their class and thus their union? These questions plagued the workers' education movement from the outset. The architects of the ILGWU's educational program were the first to address them.

For Cohn and Poyntz, the

answer to the dilemma lay in the motto chosen for the ILGWU's program—"Knowledge is Power." The difference between workers' education and what Cohn scornfully dismissed as "individual education" was its aim—the building of a stronger union. Cohn wrote in 1921:

The subject for study in workers' classes must be selected with the definite object of giving the students the mental and moral equipment which will best enable them to be useful to their class and which will inspire them to disinterested service to the labor movement. . . . To give such service, we must receive a specialized training which will strengthen and broaden character, develop discrimination, and create in us the ability to form sound judgments when we are confronted with serious problems. Labor is reaching out toward a new life, and educational training such as this is a necessary step toward its attainment.

The ILGWU developed a curriculum which reflected Cohn's goal. Courses that would enable workers to "form sound judgments" were emphasized. At the Workers' University in the early 1920s, classes in economics, political science, and trade union and industrial history outnumbered those in art, literature, music, and remedial subjects.[16]

The ultimate justification for workers' education was its ability to contribute to the creation of a new and better social order. The link between workers' education and progressive social change reflected the political consciousness of the ILGWU's educational planners and its membership. The socialist inclinations of a large number of garment workers and their leaders had led them to conclude that the aim of unionism was the rebuilding of society. Poyntz and Cohn believed that workers' education was indispensable to achieving this goal. Through workers' education, ILGWU members would become more aware of society's problems and possible solutions. By demonstrating the importance of unionism in society and in the personal lives of members, workers' education would create union loyalty, which in turn would contribute to a stronger union. The stronger the union, the more forcefully and successfully it could struggle to create a new order. Fannia Cohn put it simply:

It has always been our conviction that the Labor Movement stands, consciously or unconsciously, for the reconstruction of society. It dreams of a world where economic and social justice will prevail, where the wel-

fare of mankind will be the aim of all activity, where society will be organized as a cooperative commonwealth....[17]

Juliet Stuart Poyntz understood the relationship between workers' education and social change to be more subtle. For her, the creation of a better individual through workers' education and the achievement of a new and just social order were inexorably joined. "Body, mind, and will must be strengthened for the more effective participation in the great struggle.... The worker must become more truly and deeply than now a *person*, not only for the sake of his individual happiness and fulfillment but also for the sake of cooperative accomplishment."[18]

The ILGWU's workers' education program offered a vision: trade unions—whose members developed, through workers' education, social consciousness, understanding of economics and politics, and the determination to struggle collectively—would bring about the restructuring of American society. This vision inspired workers and educators alike, and it addressed the contradictions inherent in the very name "workers' education." By linking progressive, even radical, social change to workers' education, the ILGWU demonstrated that education need not be thought of merely as a means to escape the working class or as an inculcator of middle-class values and beliefs. Workers' education would make the worker a better individual. Only the best individuals, acting in concert, could create a new order.

The architects of the ILGWU's educational plan left the outlines of the new society tantalizingly vague and failed to provide a blueprint showing how workers' education would necessarily lead to it. In retrospect, their logic is less compelling than their vision. At the outset of the movement, these weaknesses mattered less than the ILGWU's accomplishments. The union had devised a theoretical framework for workers' education and had begun a program which would provide the movement with its first full-scale working model. Finally, it is significant that most of the credit for this achievement goes to two women who, in developing a workers' education philosophy and program, believed that they were reflecting the feelings and ideas and serving the needs of the union's women members.

Poyntz and Cohn built the ILGWU's educational program upon the desire to create a new and better world. For a brief time following the First World War, it appeared that this desire was about to become a reality. The Russian Revolution, the rise of the British Labour Party, the smaller revolts in Germany and Eastern Europe, and the wave of strikes which swept across America in 1919 seemed to presage a worldwide movement for social and economic justice. In the United States this yearning for social change was called "social reconstruction." The workers' education movement was a product of these heady and exhilarating times. Those who rallied to the banner of workers' education defined social reconstruction as the restructuring of society by the working class; the aim of workers' education was to educate the workers for this momentous task.[19]

The American workers' education movement burgeoned in 1921 with the launching of the Workers' Education Bureau, Brookwood Labor College, and the Bryn Mawr Summer School for Women Workers. The ILGWU's educational department assumed an important role in all of these enterprises. Cohn and the other Workers' Education bureau organizers hoped that the bureau would become the movement's centerpiece. The bureau was designed to encourage and coordinate programs and activities and to develop and disseminate a philosophy of workers' education. The ILGWU also provided Brookwood, the first residential labor college in the United States, with students, scholarships, and moral and political support.[20]

Cohn was less than enthusiastic about the summer schools for women workers. In 1914 she had attended the National Women's Trade Union League (NWTUL) school in Chicago. Later she wrote of her experience there:

I found the economics very orthodox and of the kind I had long ago almost forgotten. The professors themselves admitted that I did not need it. Their instruction in how to organize women was also of no use to me as I had had more actual experience from my activities in charge of strikes.

More than the conservatism of the curriculum and its seeming irrelevancy, Cohn resented the middle- and upper-class women who ran the NWTUL. She characterized them as "mere do-gooders" and told an interviewer in 1948 that her experience at the school had convinced her of the futility of working with such women. Cohn's attendance at the NWTUL's school reinforced her belief that workers' education would succeed only when provided by trade unionists for trade unionists. In the winter of 1921, Mary Anderson invited her to serve on the organizing committee for the Bryn Mawr Summer School for Women Workers, but Cohn declined. Throughout the 1920s and 1930s, however, despite Cohn's reservations, the ILGWU's educational department provided scholarships to send union members to both the Bryn Mawr and Barnard summer schools.[21]

The conflict between Cohn's feelings and actions toward the summer schools extended to her position on feminism. Late in her career Cohn was labeled by her detractors as "an old-fashioned feminist," and she was lumped together with the very summer school women she disdained. Yet Cohn considered herself a trade unionist rather than a feminist. Her deep concern with women workers arose from her commitment to the trade union rather than to the women's movement.[22]

Throughout the 1920s and the 1930s, Cohn wrote dozens of articles in which she expounded her belief that women needed trade unions and trade unions needed women. During the same period, she wrote to AFL president William Green to urge him to accelerate the federation's efforts to organize women workers. Her message was simple: in an industry where women dominated the labor force, unionism would fail without strongly committed and loyal women members. For this reason, Cohn worked carefully to design workers' education programs that would attract women. In paying attention to what she considered the special needs of women—be they a clean meeting room or a class in literature—Cohn's aim was to foster trade unionism. While she remained suspicious of the middle-class and feminist character of the summer schools, she sent workers there because she believed that the schools shared this basic goal.[23]

Even as the delegates to the first Workers' Education Bureau's convention assembled, the first students walked across Bryn Mawr's and Brookwood's idyllic campuses, and the ILGWU announced plans to expand its programs and create a new extension division, the spirit that had animated these enterprises began to wane. The strikes of 1919 had been lost, and the labor movement was in retreat. The "red scare" had driven many radicals underground, and increasing numbers of prewar progressives abandoned the arena of reform. In politics, Harding's normalcy replaced the tattered remnants of Wilson's idealism.[24]

Not surprisingly, the ILGWU Educational Department, as leader and guide for much of the workers' education movement, was among the first programs to feel the effects of this waning of spirit. By the mid-1920s, the program that had been so carefully designed by Poyntz and Cohn to reflect the needs and desires of the ILGWU membership seemed out of step with the realities of the decade. Fewer and fewer students enrolled in the Educational Department's programs. Classes in Marxism and public speaking could not compete with the allure of the burgeoning consumer culture—movies, radios, and Sunday auto trips. The idealism inherent in workers' education and the symbol of the worker as society's savior seemed hopelessly dated when compared to the cocktails, cynicism, and the Charleston that had become the cultural hallmarks of the age.[25]

The decade was particularly difficult for the ILGWU. Beneath the veneer of prosperity, garment workers were forced to cope with automation, seasonal unemployment, static real wages, and an absence of fringe benefits. They also found their union under attack. Emboldened by their successes in 1919 and buttressed by friendly courts and legislatures, employers devised a number of antiunion strategies ranging from the run-away shop to a nationwide antiunion campaign piously called the "American plan." Within the union, Communists and Socialists waged a bitter and sometimes violent battle for control.[26]

During the mid and late 1920s, Cohn alone kept workers' education alive in the ILGWU. Under such harsh conditions, however, it was inevitable that the program would change. The nearly bankrupt union often had no money for books, supplies, teachers, or even Cohn's meager salary. Cohn struggled on, compiling reading lists of books the union could not afford to buy, staging the occasional musical or play, arranging for concerts and lectures, and teaching the few classes the department offered.[27]

Cohn was horrified by the virulent battles between the Communist and the Socialist factions. She was determined to keep the Educational Department above the fray. As a result, both sides viewed her with suspicion, and in 1925 she lost her bid for a fifth term as an ILGWU vice-president. She continued as the department's executive secretary, but without the prestige and political clout her vice-presidency had conferred. Within the ILGWU, Cohn and workers' education were synonymous. As her importance within the union declined, so did that of the department she headed.[28]

Cohn's attempt to keep workers' education above politics had still other, more important, consequences. The link between workers' education and social action that had so vitalized the department during its early days was strained by the general conservatism of the 1920s. Cohn's efforts to remove politics from workers' education further weakened this connection. Given the highly charged political climate within the union, Cohn understandably preferred lectures on art appreciation to courses on political economy that might, at any moment, erupt into violent shouting matches between members of opposing factions. The belief that workers' education would train workers to create a new world became increasingly tenuous as classes in the social sciences were replaced with trips to museums and Broadway shows. Whereas Cohn had once designed programs to help unionists deal with the world in which they lived, she now increasingly offered entertainments to help them escape it. Ironically, despite Cohn's efforts to remove politics from workers' education, the department suffered from its past. When the Socialist faction emerged victorious in the political struggles of the late 1920s, the new leadership shied away from workers' education for fear that it embodied the political utopianism they had come to associate with their Communist rivals.[29]

Cohn's personal situation reflected that of the department she headed. She often complained of "extreme loneliness," of being misunderstood and neglected. The obsessive zeal and stubborn self-centeredness which enabled her to carry on alone during these years discouraged close friendships. With the exception of Theresa Wolfson, who lent a hand whenever her busy schedule allowed, Cohn had no sustained support from within her own union. Her few allies came from outside the ILGWU. The Brookwood staff—notably A. J. Muste, Helen Norton Starr, and David Saposs—provided teachers, educational material, and moral support whenever possible. There was never enough. Cohn, depressed and dispirited, wrote to Helen Norton, "To be a woman active in the labor movement is a very difficult task." But she realized that her lonely position was less attributable to her sex than to her union colleagues' low regard for workers' education.[30]

The decade which began so promisingly for the ILGWU and its educational department ended with both nearly destroyed. The union lost over half its membership, most of its treasury, and its preeminent position within the trade union movement. Its Educational Department abandoned most of the programs and philosophy that had once made it a leading force in workers' education.[31]

The 1920s was a bleak time for workers' education in the other garment unions as well. By the mid-1920s the educational activities in the Hat and Cap Makers, Furriers', and Fancy Leather Goods unions had petered out. Only the Amalgamated Clothing Workers of America (ACWA) created an educational department that, for a short time, rivaled the ILGWU's in the scope and depth of its programs. The men who ran the ACWA's educational program did not, however, share the ILGWU's commitment to workers' education. For men like J. B. S. Hardman, the ACWA's first educational director, the aim of workers' education was to equip workers, "individually and collectively, for a successful stand for what is theirs."[32] When workers' education failed to accomplish this goal, the men of the ACWA abandoned it.

In 1916, two years after its founding, the ACWA endorsed workers' education. Its General Executive Board made clear that it saw trade union education as a means to an end. The board declared that education, like union organizing, "is a means for a great purpose, the carrying out of the historic mission of the workers as a class."

Like their counterparts in the ILGWU, the ACWA's leaders believed that workers' education would lead to progressive social action by educating workers and by binding them more closely to their union. Education would make workers' "lives worth living" and would "tie them to their organization with those sacred bonds of love which though invisible are most powerful and cannot be sundered."[33]

Beginning in 1920 the ACWA's Educational Department launched a number of ambitious programs. J. B. S. Hardman, aided by Paul Blanshard and David Saposs, supervised the creation of Active Workers' Schools in New York City and Rochester, New York. In style and program, these schools resembled the ILGWU's Unity Centers. An ACWA member could attend formal academic classes in the social sciences and humanities, lectures by well-known radicals and reformers, remedial courses in the three R's, debates, concerts, dances, and plays. Within two years, similar programs flourished in a half-dozen cities. By 1924, all but a few of these ventures had closed their doors, and the ACWA's Educational Department had essentially ceased to function.[34]

The factors that had led the ILGWU to abandon workers'

education during the 1920s—the political climate, the state of the union movement, the decline of worker-student interest—played only a small part in the ACWA's action. The ACWA gave up on workers' education because workers' education failed to live up to the goals its leaders had envisioned for it. Countless lectures on "the Industrial Situation and Its Outlook," endless lessons on "Social Problems," and impressively staged May Day pageants had created neither class consciousness nor class action. As far as the ACWA was concerned, until workers' educators could translate study into action, workers' education was merely adult education. Fannia Cohn was willing to support this type of education, but J. B. S. Hardman and the ACWA were not. Workers' education did not reappear in the ACWA until the 1940s. It did so not because the philosophical problem of translating education into social action had been solved, but because by then the ACWA had forsaken its commitment to the radical restructuring of American society.[35]

With the coming of the New Deal, the ILGWU and its Educational Department revived. For both, this revival led to a transformation. David Dubinsky, the ILGWU's president, took advantage of the impetus provided by the National Industrial Recovery Act to launch an organizing drive in sixty cities. By the end of 1934, the ILGWU had quadrupled its membership. Unlike their elder sisters, these "NRA babies" were native born and unfamiliar with either radical political thought or the mechanics and philosophy of trade unionism. As had his predecessors, Dubinsky sought in his union's educational program an antidote to the membership's ignorance and a method to ensure its loyalty.[36]

Cohn sought to oblige Dubinsky, but she was rebuffed. In January 1935, the Educational Department was reorganized. Dubinsky appointed Mark Starr, an Englishman, as educational director. Starr was the son of a miner and was himself a hod carrier's helper in the mines of Somersetshire. He became a union activist and an ardent follower of the socialist Kier Hardie. Acquainted with workers' education first as a student and then as an employee of the National Council of Labour Colleges, Starr came to America to join the faculty of Brookwood Labor College in 1928. Julius Hochman, a Brookwood graduate, ILGWU vice-president, and, in 1935, chairman of the Educational Committee, recommended Starr to Dubinsky. Cohn retained the title of executive secretary, but she was increasingly relegated to marginal activities.[37]

Starr attributed his appointment to Dubinsky's desire to appeal to the "NRA babies." The ILGWU president believed that Cohn, with her heavily accented English and her immigrant background, could not do this as well. Cohn's personality undoubtedly played a role in her ouster. Dubinsky was heard to have said on numerous occasions that he would rather lead a general strike than deal with Cohn. However, the real significance of the 1935 reorganization, which Cohn failed to recognize or understand, lay in its repudiation of the workers' education philosophy that she and Poyntz had developed.[38]

Benjamin Stolberg reflected the views of the union's leadership when he criticized the original Educational Department. Cohn and Poyntz designed a program, he explained in his history of the ILGWU, that catered to the sentimental desires of women workers and centered on "the romantic concept of the Worker as the Redeemer of Society." This "old-fashioned feminist" approach to workers' education, Stolberg continued, appealed to middle-class female do-gooders but was irrelevant to the needs of a modern trade union. Thus the new ILGWU Educational Department discarded the special concern for women workers that Cohn and Poyntz had so carefully nurtured and dismissed "Miss Cohn" as "a missionary who must be judged by her good works among the heathen, not by the quality of her theology."[39]

The new workers' education—or, as it was increasingly called, "labor education,"—hearkened back to the dictums of Dyche and Brandeis. It aimed to create "a well disciplined and reliable body of men and women." "What is good for the union is good for the members" replaced Cohn's and Poyntz's intricate cataloging of unionists' intellectual and emotional needs. More important, the link between workers' education and progressive social action was broken. Labor education in the ILGWU was designed to serve the union, not the world. Occasional vague references to creating an informed and intelligent citizenry were all that remained of the fervor for social reconstruction of the 1920s. The new members were to be taught about unionism not so they could be forged into a fighting force for a new and better world, but so they would loyally follow their leaders. The public was to be educated about the union not to be introduced to a progressive blueprint for social change, but so that it would accept the union as part of the existing order.[40]

The work of the Educational Department after 1935 was roughly divided into three parts: recreational and cultural, traditional classwork, and the Officers' Qualification Course. The recreational and cultural division sponsored baseball, basketball, soccer, and bowling leagues, tennis and track and field teams, swimming and calisthenics lessons, choruses, orchestras, and dramatics. The offerings of the division combined what Cohn had called the members' need for "individual enrichment" with the public relations Dubinsky desired. An ILGWU mandolin ensemble presenting folk music on a local radio station, a fashion show staged jointly with the Metropolitan Museum of Art, a union all-star baseball team battling the Sing Sing prison team, and the long-running musical review "Pins and Needles" all contributed to the new image of American unionism that the ILGWU sought to project. No longer were garment workers foreigners spouting radical political doctrines in strange tongues. The young and attractive men and women who sang "Britannia Waives the Rules" at a White House command performance of "Pins and Needles" in 1938 symbolized the new ILGWU members. They were fun-loving, intelligent, all-American workers pursuing wholesome and self-improving activities.[41]

As the recreational and cultural activities expanded, systematic study classes, with two exceptions, dwindled. The New Members Course was designed to create union loyalty. Members were informed of their duties as unionists and introduced to a dramatized version of the ILGWU history. The Officers Qualification Course was created in 1937 when the ILGWU convention ruled that candidates for paid office who had not previously served must complete a prescribed course of study. Students attended fourteen to eighteen two-hour sessions where they were introduced to the bureaucratic structure of a modern union and to the intricacies of the garment industry. Subjects included how to keep union accounts, how to run a strike, and how to settle the price of neckwear.[42]

Critics complained that the courses ignored theoretical considerations. Where, they asked, were the classes in the humanities and social sciences that had once sought to stimulate workers to think about American society? Mark Starr answered with the department's new credo:

There is in workers' education the possibility of creating the perpetual student—the member who knows more and more but does less and less; the member who can argue about the fine points of disputed doctrines but does not know how to serve as the chairman of a meeting, [or] make a lively two-minute speech.... Then too workers' education has sometimes produced members who felt that they personally were so advanced in their views ... that they could sit down and wait for the rest of the world to catch up to them ... but who had little interest and no advice to offer concerning an immediate program of action.[43]

The workers' education movement of the late 1930s and 1940s followed a course similar to the ILGWU's. The ACWA revived its Educational Department in 1946. Its work, like that of the Textile Workers' Educational Department, closely resembled the activities developed by the ILGWU. By 1950, labor-management educational programs in state and private universities and union educational departments had replaced the Workers' Education Bureau, Brookwood, and most of the summer schools. The intellectuals, radicals, and feminists who had once flocked to the banner of workers' education had long since departed. Professional educators and trade union bureaucrats ran the movement, and its goal was in keeping with the character of the unions and universities that sponsored it: workers were taught to manage within the existing social order, not how to change it.[44]

Mollie Friedman, a delegate from the ILGWU to the 1918 American Federation of Labor's convention, closed her report on her union's educational activities by declaring,

In 1913 I came to New York City. I knew nothing about the trade union movement of America or any other trade unionism in the world. When I was asked to join the union I felt I had to join it, but now I feel that I would give my life for an organization that will educate its members.

Thirty years later, a *Reader's Digest* article described the ILGWU's Unity House as a resort hotel in the Poconos where members could swim, dance, canoe, play tennis and basketball, enjoy the latest movies, hear arias sung by Metropolitan opera stars, and watch shows put on by Danny Kaye. The article continued,

At mealtimes [a union member] could choose from many delica-

cies in the 1000-seat dining room. So splendid is the table that many a veteran dress operator will remember the early days in the sweatshops and get off the favorite Unity House gag:

"We used to say, come the revolution we'll eat strawberries and cream. This is the revolution. And I'm tired already of strawberries."

These two quotations epitomize the history of the ILGWU's educational program from 1914 to 1950.⁴⁵

Cohn and Poyntz believed that what made workers' education unique was that it reflected and made possible the workers' desire to create a more equitable and just social order. The pragmatists of the 1930s and 1940s contended that this was never the desire of the vast majority of garment workers, but rather the dream of two middle-class feminists. Dubinsky and Starr believed that Cohn and Poyntz had misread the workers and the time.

Worse still, they felt, was that these two women were imbued with a fallacious belief in the ability of education to lead to social change. The factional struggles of the 1920s convinced the ILGWU's leaders that a membership educated in the humanities and social sciences led to organizational chaos rather than to a bright new world.

The union's leadership did not find it ironic that what Poyntz had once described as the "soul" of the union was by the late 1940s a $4 million "vacationland." The new resort symbolized what the leaders saw as the goal of unionism—a larger slice of the pie achieved through negotiation and compromise. In their scheme, workers' education was to be a source of happiness, not the union's soul. Workers' education could never again hope to arouse the passionate commitment of a Mollie Friedman. She might have been willing to give her life to rebuild society, but not to watch Danny Kaye.

As education director of the Ladies' Waist and Dressmakers' Local 2587, ILGWU, Juliet Stuart Poyntz described her vision of the role education could play in transforming the lives of women union members and the mission of the union itself. In this article, published in *Life and Labor*, she traces the development of the earliest union education programs for women workers.⁴⁶

The Unity Movement—The Soul of a Union

We have heard tales from across the seas of wonderful institutions which have been developed in certain countries of Europe for the creation of a higher culture among the workers: the great Maison du Peuple in Brussels, which made every possible effort to bring the best modern inspiration to the labor movement and enrich it there. In France, the great cultural organization among the sewing girls, the Association of Mimi Pinson, as it was called, for whom the best in art was none too good.

We sometimes think these things cannot be done in our unimaginative America. And yet the so-called Unity Movement among the dressmakers of New York may, perhaps, humbly claim some distant relationship to its Parisian prototype. In the shops of that city are produced the dresses of a nation, as in Paris, the dresses of a continent, while an army of eager, thirsty young souls sits at the work table, here as there, dreaming, as they stitch, of all that life has in store. Through years of sacrifice these workers have built up for themselves a wonderful organization comprizing about 25,000 members and controlling the industry in New York City. But they dream not alone of better prices and shorter hours; they dream also of more joy in life, of more to learn, to see, to know. They are interested not only in higher wages, but in what those wages will buy. They are eager for the best in life and literature and art, and through their organization they are determined to gain these good things for themselves.

Girls Want Department of Education

It was as a result of a genuine and widespread demand among the girls working in the industry for more enlightening and educational activity in their organization that the Ladies' Waist and Dressmakers' Union established a special department of education a year ago. From this educational effort has grown up a unique movement in this and other organizations, which we may call for the want of a better name, "The Unity Movement."

It all began with Unity House. Last summer, the union leased a beautiful residence in the Catskills, formerly the property of a Wall Street broker, and organized there a summer center of recreation and education among its members. This new home was christened Unity House, because it was part of an attempt to draw together the membership of the union with ties of greater solidarity and unity.

House Becomes Inspirational Center

Unity House succeeded beyond all expectation. Under the able leadership of our comrade, Marie McDonald, it developed less as a mere vacation place than as a center of spiritual inspiration. The girls grew to realize that a trade union has a very powerful influence beyond the purely economic field. Ties of friendship made then held. Devotion to the ideal of trade unionism acquired then strengthened many a Unity girl to continue her struggle as chairman of her shop against an ignorant and deceiving employer. The union had found a soul.

Unity House seemed too good to the workers to leave behind them in the mountains, and they hoped fervently through the winter months that somehow, somewhere, it might be possible to find a Unity House in the city. This dream came true in January, when the union secured the use of an entire school building for every purpose of its organization. To the fine building on East Twentieth Street, which is christened the Unity Center, the union brought its entire life and activity, and began there a development of real educational work. Not only were regular shop meetings held there, often as many as twenty in an evening, but all sorts of other activities were developed. A cooperative cafeteria provided warm sustenance before the shop meeting, and prevented the impatience which had before spoiled the attempts of the workers to discuss their business in an organized manner. A nurse of the Joint Board of Sanitary Control gave physical and medical advice several evenings a week to workers in need of it. The two auditoriums provided space for general meetings and for concerts and lectures, the gymnasium for dancing and physical training.

In addition to these activities a beginning was made in labor education. Several classes were organized on such subjects as "Labor Problems," "History of the Labor Movement," "Literature," under the guidance of the ablest and most popular lecturers in Yiddish and English. The success of these classes and their popularity justifies a development on a larger scale during the coming season. A library on social and economic questions as well as for literary pursuits will complete the framework of this workers' university. Simplicity and clarity has been the chief aim of the classes. The most complicated subjects were taught in language simple enough for the average worker in the shop to understand and appreciate. The instruction given related to the facts and problems of his own industrial life and was in no sense an attempt to train him away from his own class.

Attendance Proves Center Popular

That the Unity Center filled a real need in this great organization is indicated by the fact that in six weeks 10,000 different individuals had attended 350 shop meetings there, and that at social affairs, concerts, etc.; during the same period, there had been an additional attendance of about 7,000. The Unity Center seemed to the workers not a public school, but their own home, a home where they found cheer and familiar faces, a beautiful, clean, well ventilated home, well lighted and hung with beautiful pictures, a great change from the dirty, ill ventilated meeting rooms, often above a saloon, where trade unions must usually meet for want of a better place. The very entrance into the public school of a trade union raises it from the position of a social outlaw to that of a vital and recognized social group. The school provides physical facilities and the space for the development of all the wonderful latent social, cultural and other possibilities of labor organizations. It makes upon society a claim for opportunity in the name of its most vitally important group. It provides a possibility of growth and development of the body and mind of the individual worker through his collective organization.

The same idea is being followed out in the development of the Unity House this year. An arrangement has been made with the Interstate Park Commission whereby a reservation of land will be granted to the union for the purpose of a summer house, and the Commission is even ready to build at its own expense a beautiful camp on the style of the Bear Mountain Inn, surrounded by smaller cabins for sleeping purposes. This camp will be situated on the shore of a beautiful three-mile lake, Cedar Palm, surrounded by fir clad mountains. The central headquarters, measuring about 50 × 100 feet, will contain a large dining room, seating over 200, and a great hall which can be used for lectures, concerts and gatherings of all descriptions. These will be open to the air and the mountain view on all sides and will have glass doors which can be closed in case of rain.

This new and greater Unity House will have accommodations for between 200 and 500 people. It will respond with great elasticity to the demands of this kind which are placed upon it. It will be within easy distance from New York, the round trip costing only $1.00. It will be a two or three hour trip up the Hudson by boat to Bear Mountain, and thence by bus for several miles up into the mountains. Until the new headquarters are completed, the state has provided for the use of the union at a moderate rental a large house in a beautiful location, which is now being completely remodeled for this purpose.

Park to Be Made Real Playground

The whole development of the State Park is one of especial interest, for here are being worked out on a large scale some remarkable projects of collectivism. This fine tract of land in the foothills of the Catskills, on the shore of the Hudson, is being developed by the Interstate Park Commission as a real playground of the people. In addition to the thousands of picnickers who every summer find recreation at Bear Mountain, provisions are being made all through the park for colonies of vacationists.

For all these camps, which together serve many thousands, a central economic organization is being perfected whereby transportation and food supply are guaranteed with cheapness and regularity. The state, through a special agent, buys food and camp furnishings on a huge scale and at a basis of lowest market cost for all the organizations participating in the advantages of the park. Buying as it sometimes does $75,000 worth of food in a single deal, it is able to bring to these organizations the advantages of real cooperation. Scattered through the park are various beautiful pavilions which contain thousands of tons of ice cut on its own lakes by the hired workers of the Commission and sold in the park at cost.

A special force of men is constantly at work hewing the trees and building them into charming woodland camps. While all the camps are attractive, it is being planned that that of the waistmakers shall be the finest in the park, as befitting an organization of such a size.

Such is the Unity Movement in all its diversity. The prospects are that very shortly this educational idea will extend rapidly beyond its present bounds, not only in New York but in other industrial centers of this country, for it meets a real need of the worker. It brings to his service all the vast social and educational resources of the community; it lifts him to his proper position as a citizen of the community entitled to share in these resources, and it brings to him a vision of labor with an idea, a hope and ideal.

—Juliet S. Poyntz, 1917.

Garment worker Edith Berkowitz, a member of the ILGWU, wrote this song in 1932 when she was a student at the Bryn Mawr Summer School for Women Workers. The song was sung frequently at ILGWU meetings and songfests for many years.[47]

"We Shall Be Free." Source: Edith Berkowitz Parker

The following three stories were the response of some trade union women to *Life and Labor*'s offer in 1920 of prizes for articles on the subject. The three stories included here were awarded prizes because "each answers the 'why' so definitely and so individually." They were written by members of the Philadelphia WTUL, the Office Employes' Association, and the Typographical Union.[48]

Why I Joined My Union, and What It Has Done for Me

Found It a Partnership

FIRST PRIZE

I was a lace worker in Philadelphia when I "joined my union." A business depression and lay off of two-thirds of our forces compelled me to seek a new job. I had grown so accustomed to spending the day at the old place that I felt wronged in some way by this order of ejectment, and it did upset my line of least resistance. Having learned only one line of work, to go to another meant much effort and low wages even if "paid while learning."

Naturally I turned to a place where I could follow the same trade. The only such place I knew was called a "closed shop." Just what that meant, I did not know, but it was said no one could work there without joining the union. I secured a price list from a person who had worked there, and used it to back up my arguments that our prices were about as good as theirs, and we wouldn't join any union. It was enough to have a forelady yelling at a person, I thought, without having anybody or everybody, just girls like ourselves, telling us what to do.

With my small knowledge of "unionism," of course I did not know that it was organization in other departments and in other shops that necessitated uniform prices in order to hold the workers.

It being the usual policy to secure a job first and later to learn the details concerning hours, amount per week, and rate per piece or dozen, when pay day came, I followed custom and awaited developments.

A week passed, and no one mentioned unions or gave orders, and the forelady did not yell, but everybody attended strictly to business. My first pay convinced me that a better system of giving out and completing work existed. It was more just and less exacting. The spirit of the girls was more independent and less slavish. This better system had enabled me to do better on what seemed cheaper work. I liked the place better than I had the other and asked for admission for a friend as soon as there should be room for her.

Another week passed, and I began to hope they would forget about the union. But no; just about quitting time a girl bent over me and in a cheery voice said, "I came to see if you wanted to join our union." I stopped my machine and studied her face. Only kindly comradeship was expressed there. "I did not come last week because we always wait till a girl gets a pay or two to give her a chance." I smiled at her frankness and after a few questions paid the dues and so became a member of a labor union because I had no further arguments against it. The Lace Finishers' Protective Association it was. Later, I think the Lace Finishers joined hands with the Menders' Union, and they with the Lace Weavers, and so finally became a part of the A. F. of L.

I soon learned that the union was a kind of partnership in which every advantage or injustice affected all concerned in exactly the same measure. We were a firm selling our time and labor under a contract of equal responsibility. Because of this fact, we took pride in turning out good work and refused to stand for a careless worker. But we stood firm when the worker was not at fault.

Finding that complaints kept coming concerning work from a certain part of the room, we insisted that the long neglected windows be cleaned to allow more light, and the complaints ceased. We demanded that the men's toilets be separated from those used by women, that proper repairs be made, and the vermin that had bred for years be destroyed. These and other improvements we could insist upon only as a union.

The improved system brought about by the union resulted in an increased efficiency in the workers that was of even greater value than the actual wage gain. This because it enabled many to reach out with courage in other ways, such as evening study courses, and so move on to other business and accomplish things long held in their hearts.

True, some sleep on and fail to get a vision of the possibilities or take advantage of opportunities. But after fourteen years as a union member I feel nothing else boosts one like this partnership in our business life. It not only increases our efficiency and courage, but it instills a spirit of comradeship that is greater than our love of gold. Witness the amazing struggles in times of strikes when to scab on the others would bring money to avoid starvation. Yet loyalty holds firm in all honest hearts.

—Leona Huntzinger, 1920.

Freedom in the Shop Appealed to Her

SECOND PRIZE

When I was about fourteen my father passed away. A year later conditions got so that I was compelled to go out and earn my own living.

At home I often heard my folks talk of shops. I could not imagine what they meant. I often wondered what kind of places they were or where such things could be located. Father had worked in a tailor shop and had talked much of how the people in the shop wanted to form a union because prices and conditions were not satisfactory. I was too small to understand this, though.

My first position was as errand girl in the basement of a department store. I studied every move they made. I was a stranger in that world, and when I was taken to my post, I worked as if it was an honor. As I became acquainted with the girls, I found that they were afraid of some one they called a boss. The girls would gather in groups and as soon as they saw a boss, away they flew. I remained and sometimes talked to the boss.

I said to the girls, "Are we not the same human beings as the bosses? You work more than girls of your age really can, which is a result of your weakness." I asked a boss why the girls were so afraid of him. He said, "Maybe their work is not done properly, or not done at all. Just do your work and all will be well." This interested me and made me think.

The days were hot and the girls did not like to work Saturday afternoons. They were the ordinary everyday type of girls who looked more dead than alive. They recalled to me what my father had once said of organization. I told the girls to get together and appeal to the firm for the half day. In a body a great deal can be done. I had the idea, but did not know what to do, or how. But I said, "I'll go to the firm." I went to the president's office and found all the heads of the firm there. I asked them if it was any more than fair to let the employees off Saturday afternoons, and whether they wanted sick and lazy workers instead of workers healthy and ready to do all work necessary. They listened, but did not answer. Later I was discharged and told that when they needed me they would send for me.

Then my friends asked me to join the Ypsls, (Young People's Socialist League.) Here I became interested in lectures and started to read a little, but I still kept the idea of getting together. I became more and more informed on what the working world is composed of. I got a job in another department store. Here I stayed longer, but kept on telling the girls to get together. I was laid off because of my affiliation with the Ypsls.

Later I learned what was meant by a union. I read on the subject and found it to be something worth while to all working people—especially young girls.

About 1918, I began to want to take an active part in the labor movement. I did what I could in the Ypsls. Young as I was, I spent a day at the polls during every election for three years. This gave me more food for thought as I saw the way the politicians went about their work.

In January of that year I was arrested by my brother and taken to the Juvenile Court. Here I saw only children, young girls and boys. I was told by the attorney and detectives that unless I made up my mind to keep away from the radicals, I would not be released for three years. At the court I became acquainted with the different social workers, who were doing all they could for the betterment of the children.

I spent one month in the Juvenile Home. The inmates were all working girls. Most of them worked in factories. Whether they were found guilty or not, they were convicted and sent to what they called an industrial training school, where they teach the girls to make good use of themselves. But I couldn't see that anything for the betterment of the girl was really accomplished. Working conditions, which really caused the downfall of the average girl, were never considered. A young girl is sent to work before her mind is mature enough to consider what confronts her in the working world, and the employers never thought of the value of the girl herself.

This made me think more and more of a union. I asked the officer, "Do you think the working conditions of these girls should be investigated before you let them go? Would it decrease your work?"

"Well," she said, "the girls are well taken care of here. They are sent to a training school. When they get out they are ready to make a decent living for themselves."

"It looks to me," I said, "as if they are worse."

We did not talk any longer. She called me a Red and that was the end.

A month later I was released and paroled for two months. I had some new ideas about labor. How wonderful it would be, I thought, to be able to have something to say regarding your own environment.

I got a job with a dental instrument firm. Here I carried bundles to the post office. They were quite heavy. Once the owner's wife was in the office when I had five heavy bundles to carry. She looked at them, but seemed not to care. I cried out, "If we had a union, I would only do the work in the office and not carry these bundles." I was fired.

Later the Boston Store strike occurred. I got a job there and went out to strike with the rest. It was interesting to see how the very ones who contributed, in a way, toward the welfare of the people would directly send sluggers to attack them. This showed me the great need for an organization of workers, if only to protest against that sort of thing. Also, I began to see that in order that any good for anyone may be accomplished, labor must be represented. It is the leading factor of society today, for practically the entire life of a person depends upon labor.

I am a member of the Office Employes' Union, and am working with the tailoring industry. The Amalgamated Clothing Workers had done a great deal for its members. When the slack time came in the clothing industry this year the employers were prevented from laying off their workers by the thousands because of the agreement the Amalgamated had made with companies. By this arrangement, every one gets his share of whatever work is going. It is due to the foresight of the union.

Freedom in the shop, and not to be under any obligation to a "boss," is worth much. The chance to develop leadership is open to all. Many have become great leaders only through the freedom which the union offers. All of which is, I am sure, of greater advantage than dollars, as well as a help in making them.

—Jennie La Zar, 1920.

Sanitary Conditions and a Real Pay Day

THIRD PRIZE

My reason for joining a union was the bright prospect of work in a union office with sanitary conditions, a real pay day, and real gentlemen and ladies as co-workers, contrasted with the dreadful conditions endured for three years in non-union offices.

At the age of fourteen, my sister Alice and I were taken to a dark, dirty shop to learn to set type. Windows opened on a court and light was poor at best. When too dark to see, gasoline torches were used. Poor light caused me to have granulated eyelids. The floor had a thick coating of tobacco spit. The towel was so black and thick it could stand alone. Often there was neither soap nor water to wash up with.

The first few weeks we received no pay, later we were to have $1.50 weekly, but that was not forthcoming on pay day and often was several weeks behind. One of the workers said her mother counted on the $1.50 she would bring home to buy something for Sunday. The money was not paid and she quit. Father came around and insisted we be paid. Sometimes part of it was collected. When too much was owing us we were laid off for a time. I went around to other offices and worked, but the first boss always came and tried to get me back.

Hours were 7 A.M. to 6 P.M., or later, until work in hand was finished. I was sent on errands, and down a business street with oil cans for oil. That hurt my pride. The proprietor and his wife both worked. The wife frequently had us race with her. I can understand now that it was to speed up production.

An occasional tourist was put to work. So little money came in that two of the tourists were taken home with the boss to board out salary. One tourist tired of that and had a telegram sent to himself saying his mother was dead and succeeded in getting out of town. The other frequently slept in a waste paper box and crawled out when we arrived at work. The office was frequently moved, to locations each worse than the former ones. They could not understand it was cheaper to pay rent than move a printing office. The proprietors kept moving their home until finally they took a single room and arranged to get meals at a hotel in exchange for printing. The office was moved to a hotel basement, but was only allowed to remain a week. The next move was to a building full of barrels of salt from fish. The odor was bad and the vibrations of the presses shook the building.

My sister quit and found work in a union office. That was the first I knew a union existed and that conditions were better there. Sister Clara started to learn and was put to feeding Gordon presses, furnishing the power with one foot while she stood on the other. This made her very sick.

At this stage such a gloom possessed me that it showed in my face. Father sued for my money, I being a minor, and then I lost out in that office for good. It was then that I had the chance to finish my apprenticeship in a union office. The thought of a real pay day and better working conditions brought smiles to chase away the gloom. I joined the union as an apprentice, not telling father until after I was initiated, because he would object to it. Union membership was not required at that time, but I wished to cast in my lot with successful people.

My early views of non-union conditions have not been altered by a quarter century's observation. Most non-union offices operate with beginners. One large office in Chicago conducts a school to teach printers, that it may have help. The help leave as soon as they know anything. Open shops are not friendly to women workers. I would have been crowded from a trade years ago had I not joined a union that believes "an injury to one is the concern of all."

A union card is a guaranty that one has graduated at the trade, while the open office stunt is to start one in at a small salary and raise when they think the worker is worth more, not wishing to give credit for time worked in other offices.

Proprietors have a strong organization; so should the workers. The Typographical Union has business headquarters on a par with the bosses themselves. Our best diplomats are sent to treat with the bosses, and they obtain raises in salary for us without any effort on our part, save our standing solidly behind the committee. Now, had each individual to treat separately for a raise, few would even be given a hearing.

The Typographical Union has a beautiful home at Colorado Springs for sick and aged members, an old age pension, a mortuary benefit, sick benefit society, rates in hospital for the sick, and lots in various cemeteries. It also conducts a school.

—Venus M. Heath, 1920.

Notes

1. J. M. Budish, "United Labor Education Committee," and J. B. Salutsky, "The Labor Education Program and Activities of the Amalgamated Clothing Workers of America," both in Workers' Education Bureau of America, *Workers' Education in the United States: Report of Proceedings, First National Conference on Workers' Education in the United States* (New York: Workers' Education Bureau, 1921) (hereafter cited as WEB, *Proceedings*), pp. 11–16 and 54–60.

2. Louis Levine, *The Women's Garment Workers* (New York: B. W. Huebsch, Inc., 1924), pp. 484–85.

3. Ibid.

4. International Ladies' Gar-

ment Workers' Union, *Convention Proceedings* (1914) (hereafter cited as ILGWU, *Proceedings*), p. 148; ibid. (1916), pp. 50–51.

5. ILGWU, *Proceedings* (1916), pp. 50–52; James Oneal, *A History of the Amalgamated Ladies' Garment Cutters Union* (New York: Ashland Press, 1927), pp. 265–66; Elise Glick, "The Educational Work of Local 25 of the International Ladies' Garment Workers' Union," in WEB, *Proceedings* (1921), pp. 49–51.

6. ILGWU, *Proceedings* (1916), pp. 197–201.

7. Ibid.; ibid. (1918), pp. 35–36, 236–38.

8. Poyntz disappeared from her New York City apartment in 1937 (see "Woman Communist Missing 7 Months," *New York Times* [December 18, 1937]). Her fate remains a mystery. My special thanks to Professor Alice Kessler-Harris for sharing with me biographical data she gathered on Poyntz and the FBI files she obtained through the Freedom of Information Act.

9. Ricki Carol Myers Cohen, "Fannia Cohn and the International Ladies' Garment Workers Union" (Ph.D. diss., University of Southern California, 1976); Susan Stone Wong, "Fannia Cohn," in *Notable American Women: The Modern Period*, ed. Barbara Sicherman and Carol Hurd Green (Cambridge, Mass.: Harvard University Press, 1980), pp. 154–55; Cohn to Evelyn Preston, May 22, 1924, Fannia Cohn Collection, Box 4, New York Public Library, New York, N.Y.

10. Cohn to Selig Perlman, December 26, 1951, Box 5; Cohn to Emma, May 8, 1958, Box 5; Cohn to David Dubinsky, October 12, 1932, Box 4 (all in Fannia Cohn Collection).

11. Interviews with Mark and Helen Starr, April 12, 1976, and July 27, 1978; Theresa Wolfson to Cohn, May 6, 1922; Cohn to Wolfson, May 15, 1922, Fannia Cohn Collection, Box 4.

12. ILGWU Educational Department, "Announcement of Courses Given in Workers' University" (1923–24), in David Saposs Collection, Box 3, Wisconsin State Historical Society, Madison, Wis.

13. Fannia Cohn, "What Workers' Education Really Is," *Life and Labor* 11 (October 1921): 228–34; Alexander Fichandler, "Workers' Education: Why and What?" *Socialist Review* 10 (April–May, 1921): 49–50; Fannia Cohn, "Our Workers' University," mimeographed (n.d.), Selma Borchardt Collection, Box 132, Archives of Labor History and Urban Affairs, Wayne State University, Detroit, Mich.; Louis Friedland, "The Workers' University of the International Ladies' Garment Workers' Union,"

School and Society 11 (March 20, 1920): 349–50; "Knowledge is Power" (1920 pamphlet), Selma Borchardt Collection, Box 145.

14. Juliet Stuart Poyntz, "The Unity Movement—the Soul of a Union, *Life and Labor* 7 (June 1917): 96; Fannia Cohn, "Unity House," *American Federationist* 32 (July 1925): 534–36.

15. Poyntz, "The Unity Movement—the Soul of a Union," p. 97.

16. Fannia Cohn, "What Workers' Education Really Is." The motto is from Francis Bacon's *Meditationes Sacre* (1597). Information on Cohn's selection of the motto is from an interview with Mark and Helen Starr, April 12, 1976. See also ILGWU Educational Department, "Announcement of Courses Given in Workers' University" (1923–24), David Saposs Collection, Box 3.

17. Fannia Cohn, "Educational Department of the International Ladies' Garment Workers Union," in WEB, *Proceedings* (1921), p. 47.

18. Juliet Stuart Poyntz, "The Workers' University," *Ship Builders News and Navy Yard Employee* 2 (September 1919): 13.

19. Burl Noggle, *Into the Twenties: The United States from Armistice to Normalcy* (Urbana: University of Illinois Press, 1974), p. 40; Lewis Mumford, "Reeducating the Worker," *Survey* 47 (January 7, 1922): 567; Eden and Cedar Paul, *Proletcult* (New York: Thomas Seltzer, 1921), p. 11.

20. "Report and Recommendations of Organizing Committee," April 2–3, 1921, Workers' Education Bureau Collection, Box 1, New York State School of Industrial and Labor Relations, Martin P. Catherwood Library, Cornell University; Ithaca, N.Y.; Charles Beard, "Workers' Education," *New Republic* 27 (November 9, 1921): 328; Jonathan D. Bloom, "Brookwood Labor College, 1921–1933" (M.A. diss., Rutgers University, 1978), pp. 34, 81.

21. Cohn to Florence Miller, April 16, 1928, Fannia Cohn Collection, Box 4; Robert J. Schaefer, "Educational Activities of the Garment Unions, 1890–1948" (Diss., Teachers College, 1951), pp. 44–45; Anderson to Cohn, February 23, 1921, Box 1; and Cohn to Anderson, March 14, 1921, Box 4 (both in Fannia Cohn Collection; Gladys L. Palmer, *The Industrial Experience of Women Workers at the Summer Schools, 1928–1930*, Bulletin no. 89 (Washington, D.C.: U.S. Department of Labor, Women's Bureau, 1931), p. 38.

22. Benjamin Stolberg, *Tailor's Progress* (Garden City, N.J.: Doubleday, 1944), p. 289.

23. For examples of Cohn's

writings see Fannia Cohn, "Workingwomen and the Written Word," *Labor Age* 16 (May 1927): 18–19; "Winning Workingwomen to Unionism," *Labor Age* 16 (April 1927): 18–19; "Can We Organize the Flapper?" *Labor Age* 16 (December 1927): 18–19; "Shaw Speaks to Women," *Labor Age* 17 (October 1928): 22–23; "Education Aids Workingwomen" *Labor Age* 17 (January 1928): 12–13. Cohn to William Green, March 6, 1925, and March 25, 1925, Fannia Cohn Collection, Box 4.

24. Cohn to Dr. Marion Philips, May 24, 1927, Fannia Cohn Collection, Box 4; "Workers' Education," *New Republic* 28 (October 12, 1921): 173–74; David Kennedy, *Over There: The First World War and American Society* (New York: Oxford University Press, 1980), pp. 88–92, 287–91.

25. WEB, *Proceedings* (1923), pp. 70–75; Schaefer, chap. 4.

26. Irving Bernstein, *The Lean Years* (Baltimore: Penguin Books, 1966), chaps. 1–4; Philip Foner, *Women and the American Labor Movement: From World War I to the Present*, vol. 2 (New York: Free Press, 1980), chaps. 7–8.

27. ILGWU Educational Department, "Report of the Educational Department to the Nineteenth Convention of the ILGWU," March 7, 1928, David Saposs Collection, Box 34.

28. Cohn to Evelyn Preston, November 5, 1923; Cohn to Preston, May 22, 1924; Cohn to Florence Thorne, June 24, 1926; Cohn to Sonia, August 28, 1928 (all in Fannia Cohn Collection, Box 4).

29. Cohn to Phillips, July 13, 1938, Fannia Cohn Collection, Box 4; Schaefer, p. 138.

30. A. J. Muste to Cohn, October 11, 1928; Wolfson to Cohn, May 6, 1922, and November 19, 1923 (all in Fannia Cohn Collection, Box 1); Cohn to Preston, November 5, 1923, May 22, 1924, and December 6, 1923; Cohn to Helen Norton, February 9, 1932 (all in Fannia Cohn Collection, Box 4).

31. Irving Bernstein, *The Turbulent Years* (Boston: Houghton Mifflin Co., 1971), p. 85.

32. Amalgamated Clothing Workers of America, *Documentary History* (1920–22) (hereafter cited as ACWA, *Doc. His.*) (New York: Allied Printing Trades Council), p. 246.

J. B. S. Hardman was born Jacob Benjamin Salutsky in Grodno, Russia, in 1892. He attended the University of St. Petersburg and became active in the social democratic and union movements. He came to America in 1909 and studied for two years at Columbia University before embarking on his lifelong career as editor, writer, and labor intellectual. In the early 1920s he changed his name from J. B. Salutsky to J. B. S. Hardman. Solon de Leon et al., ed., *American Labor Who's Who*, [New York: Hanford Press, 1925], p. 97; *Who's Who in Labor* [New York: Dryden Press, 1946], p. 150).

33. ACWA, *Doc. His.* (1914–16), p. 189–90.

34. ACWA, *Doc. His.* (1918–20), pp. 139–92; *Doc. His.* (1920–22), pp. 89–96, 245–67; Paul Blanshard, "The Rochester Labor College," in WEB, *Proceedings* (1921), pp. 17–20, and "Open Forums," WEB, *Proceedings* (1922), p. 158–62.

35. ACWA, *Doc. His.* (1928), pp. 241–44; J. B. Salutsky, "Journalism and Workers' Education," in WEB, *Proceedings* (1922), pp. 184–86.

36. In 1920, The ILGWU claimed 105,000 members. This figure steadily declined through the 1920s. In 1932, the union counted 63,000 members; in the early months of 1933, a mere 40,000 members. As a result of its organizing drive, the ILGWU had nearly 200,000 members at the end of 1934, making it the third largest union in the AFL (Bernstein, *The Turbulent Years*, pp. 84–89).

37. Interview with Mark and Helen Starr, April 12, 1976.

38. Cohn to Bertha, April 24, 1935, Fannia Cohn Collection, Box 5; interview with Mark and Helen Starr, July 27, 1978.

39. Stolberg, pp. 288–91.

40. ILGWU, *Proceedings* (1916), pp. 197–201; Mark Starr, "Education for Labor," *Forum* 55 (May 1946): 775–79.

41. ILGWU, *Proceedings* (1937), pp. 165–85; Ibid.(1940), pp. 132–45; ILGWU, "Report of the Educational Department," June 1, 1942, to May 31, 1944, and June 1, 1944, to December 31, 1946; Schaefer, p. 191.

42. ILGWU, "Report of the Educational Department," June 1, 1942, to May 31, 1944, and June 1, 1944, to December 31, 1946; Schaefer, pp. 180–86; "New Members Classes" (n.d.), Fannia Cohn Collection, Box 11.

43. ILGWU, Educational Department, *Training for Union Service* (New York: ILGWU, 1940), pp. 6–7.

44. ACWA, *Doc. His.* (1946–48), pp. 271–76; Per Gustaf Stensland, "Education and Action in an American Union" (Ph.D. diss., Teachers College, 1950); "A Memorandum on the TWUA Education Programs," June 28, 1950, Textile Workers Union of American Collection, Box 9; Wisconsin State Historical Society, Madison, Wis.; Starr, "Workers' Education Today"; Mark Starr, "Cap and Gown Meets Overalls," John Edelman Collection, Box 38, Wayne State University, Detroit, Mich.

45. American Federation of Labor, *Report of the Proceedings of Annual Convention*

(1918), (Washington, D.C.: The Law Reporter Printing Company, 1918), pp. 321–22; Victor Riesel, "Come the Revolution," *Reader's Digest* 53 (October 1948): 119–20.

46. From *Life and Labor* 7, no. 6 (June 1917), pp. 96–97.

47. From the collection of Edith Berkowitz Parker, Irvington, N.Y., used with permission.

48. All three from *Life and Labor* 10, no. 10 (December 1920), pp. 312–15.

Chapter 3

Citizens for Democracy:
The Industrial Programs of the YWCA

Mary Frederickson

The Young Women's Christian Association (YWCA) played a crucial role in the development of workers' education for women in the United States. At its peak, the YWCA's Industrial Department had an interracial membership of almost 60,000 women workers, brought together by the common experience of their industrial employment. The association's experiments in workers' education began during World War I and continued to develop through the 1930s. Through the YWCA women workers attended local classes and regional workers' education conferences planned by the industrial membership. The Industrial Department maintained close contacts with the developing independent women's summer schools, which recruited extensively from the association's vast membership. For many working "girls," YWCA Industrial Clubs provided a gateway to full participation in the labor movement. Workers' education programs within the association became important vehicles for a workers' growth into active union involvement. Likewise, for middle-class YWCA "secretaries," the YWCA Industrial Department focused enthusiasm for social reform and channeled it into a growing movement for women's workers' education.[1]

In the years between 1904 and World War I, the YWCA redirected its focus from providing minimal social services for poor women to scrutinizing the social consequences of industrial capitalism and demanding far-reaching economic and social reforms. The moving force behind this transformation was Florence Simms, a young midwesterner who had worked with industrial women in Michigan and who was appointed as the first YWCA National Industrial Secretary in 1904. In the early years of the YWCA's industrial work, Simms advocated the study of the social and industrial problems of working women and recommended teaching industrial women about the protective regulations being legislated in their behalf.[2]

After 1908, the industrial group gained autonomy within the national organization, and YWCA Industrial Clubs within factories, laundries, stores, and mills became self-governing units run by the local membership. As the newly organized Industrial Department began to address wage issues, industrial health standards, working conditions, and protective legislation, more and more working-class women began to participate. By 1914 there were 375 Industrial Clubs; by 1918, over 800 local clubs had an industrial membership of more than 30,000.[3] At the urging of the Industrial Department, the 1911 National YWCA Convention passed resolutions supporting a minimum wage and limited working hours for women.

During this period, an internecine competition developed between the Industrial Department and other factions within the YWCA. The national organization was closely tied to Protestant churches and required church membership as a prerequisite for association membership, and there were many local association members who continued to carry on traditional YWCA evangelism in factories, primarily through noontime Bible meetings, vocational training, and general adult education. Nevertheless, under Simms's leadership, the Industrial Department moved in new directions; it hired staff members trained in the social sciences, maintained independence from employers whenever possible, and assisted industrial women in raising questions about working conditions. As Simms wrote, "We began to change from the type of work in which we were doing *for* girls, thinking *for* them, to that in which we began to feel the solidarity of the whole human family."[4]

During World War I the Industrial Department extended its programs for women workers by establishing Industrial War Service Centers in newly developed industrial areas and in the industrial sections of large cities. Called "Blue Triangle Houses," over 300 YWCA-run hospitality centers provided rooms, food, recreation, and fellowship to women employed in defense industries, women visitors to military camps, and women waiting at wartime ports. The only admission requirement for women industrial workers was that they take a pledge stating: "It is my desire to serve to the best of my capacity in the ranks of the Women's Industrial Army. I pledge my loyalty by promoting in every way possible the spirit of service and good-will in my work and community."[5] Thus the YWCA initiated thousands of women into the work force by emphasizing the importance of labor unity and the critical significance of women's wartime participation in the industrial sector.

As the "women's industrial army" increased in size, the YWCA sought to sharpen public awareness of the need for industrial health and safety regulations for workers. At YWCA War Service Centers, newly hired women defense workers found a place to sleep and a hot meal in the company of sister workers; there they began to formulate concrete demands for the eight-hour day and the six-day week, equal pay for equal work, and collective bargaining rights. Under YWCA auspices, committees of women workers and War Service Center staff educated new workers about protective legislation and contacted individual employers to inform them of particular health and safety issues affecting women workers.

Middle-class women, concerned about the increasing numbers of women workers entering industrial employment because of the war, came to the Industrial War Service Centers to assist in programs for women workers. At the centers they heard about the employment policies of their capitalist friends (or even husbands). Disturbed by what they learned through the YWCA about wage levels and working conditions, these women demanded routine factory investigations and better conditions for industrial workers. Industrial Department staff members believed that during this period many women, both workers and middle-class sympathizers, discovered "the power of a woman in the world's work, the realization of her worth, and of the necessity of women's standing together."[6]

After World War I, the YWCA sought to carry over into peacetime the spirit of cooperation and fellowship among industrial workers and the sense of responsibility on the part of professional women and women of leisure. At the war's end, Simms argued for accelerating the YWCA's industrial efforts, saying that "we have a very great responsibility upon us because we have now the favor of the public and the ear of the public. I know of no other organization that is creating a program like this, and we seem to be the logical people to carry on." She believed that solving the industrial problems of the postwar world would result in the establishment of a new social order permeated with justice for women and workers.[7] In fact, the War Service Centers and the concept of cross-class cooperation among women formed the backbone of the YWCA's industrial work in the postwar period.

During World War I, in addition to expanding its industrial work and increasing the participation of middle-class women, the YWCA also substantially extended its work among black women workers. Although black women began to turn to the YWCA in greater numbers during the war, minority women had a long history of YWCA membership in segregated branches of the organization. Fourteen black student groups had affiliated with the YWCA in 1907, and southern student work in that year reached 2,300 young women (out of a total of 14,000 black women in secondary schools and colleges). The first city associations for black women began in 1907 in New York, Washington, Baltimore, and Brooklyn.[8]

Four years later, after the "mushroom growth of all colored Associations," work was being carried on in over twenty cities across the United States. Despite chronic short staffing and constant demands for more trained secretaries to meet the needs of women in the black community, two women carried the weight of coordinating all YWCA work among black women. They wrote in 1911 that "in nothing do we find greater satisfaction than in the knowledge that the crying need of colored women is finding some response," and they emphasized "the necessity of having definite provision in the budget for colored city work, which now appears as a provisional clause."[9]

In 1912, the first industrial survey of black women workers revealed "a picture full of deep shadows." In Winston-Salem, North Carolina, investigators reported "a story too dark, too depressing, too long, to be unfolded here." Later in the same year, black women workers from five states and the District of Columbia (women came from as far south as Alabama) traveled to New York City for the first conference of black city workers.[10]

During World War I, YWCA work among black women began to receive much-needed support from within the association. A field supervisor was named for the South Atlantic states, and thousands of black women took advantage of the services available at local YWCAs and at the Blue Triangle Houses established for the use of defense workers and women friends and relatives visiting military camps. By the end of the war, after working with "an undercurrent of race prejudice which is dangerous," YWCA fieldworkers had established dozens of new centers across the country, with 57 black Industrial Clubs comprising an industrial membership of over 2,000; more than 7,000 black industrial women attended the meetings of these clubs without officially joining the YWCA.[11]

As the YWCA Industrial Department broadened its focus to encompass new groups of women workers, Florence Simms, in her capacity as National Industrial Secretary, led a women's commission, with representatives from the National Consumer's League, the American Association for Labor Legislation, and the National Women's Trade Union League (NWTUL), to Europe to investigate conditions of women's work and to confer with European women who were also interested in bridging what Simms described as "the chasm between capital and labor."[12] As these women toured European industries, factories, unions, and shops, they were deeply shocked by the desperate conditions faced by women workers. The women of the commission pledged to continue to work together to improve the working lives of industrial women in both Europe and the United States.

As a group, members of the commission endorsed a set of minimum industrial standards, including the abolition of child labor, the eight-hour day, a minimum wage, equal pay for equal work, and the right to collective bargaining. The YWCA had endorsed most of these standards prior to the war, but the National Board had balked at collective bargaining, an issue that provoked considerable controversy among the more conservative board members of the association. Early in 1919, plans had been made to call a meeting of representatives of industrial women in the YWCA to formulate a statement about the conditions of women in industry. This pronouncement was to be presented at the first International Congress of Working Women convening in Washington, D.C., late in 1919.[13]

In Simms's absence, plans to hold a small meeting of a few industrial women had escalated, and in the fall of 1919, sixty-five delegates, representing 30,000 women workers in twenty-six states, traveled to Washington, D.C., to attend the YWCA's first National Conference of Industrial Women. This assembly of women workers included unionists and nonunionists, Protestants, Catholics, and Jews, the politically active and the nonpolitical. Many of these women represented new constituencies brought into the association through the Industrial Department. The statement these industrial representatives prepared included a blanket endorsement of collective bargaining and a recommendation that the YWCA work for passage of protective legislation for women workers.[14]

Impressed by the independent action of the industrial women and motivated by their endorsement of a formal set of resolutions, Simms began to lobby vigorously for the National Board's approval of collective bargaining as part of the YWCA's industrial platform.[15] In so doing, she encountered fierce opposition from many wealthy YWCA board women and touched off two years of heated debate. Reactions by members of the National Board ranged from enthusiasm to horror. One YWCA staff member recalled that many board women were shocked at the inhuman aspects of American industrialization, and "they felt guilty about their own privileges and determined to take some action." These women took a stand that was "in some cases a threat to their marriage and family life, but they stood firm because they were convinced it was right." Others, however, were more shocked by collective bargaining than by the working conditions of the industrial members. Some women opposed collective bargaining because of their own point of view, others because of their husbands' stance on the issue. When Simms visited in board members' homes, she was often challenged by their spouses. One staff member recounted the story of Simms and two of her colleagues being invited to the home of a board member whose husband was a railroad executive. After dinner, the host "harangued us about our 'socialist beliefs.'" Simms finally lost her temper and said, "Mr. ———, if we do have a revolution, it will be people like you that bring it on." That finished, she put on her hat and majestically led her party out of the house.[16]

At the YWCA's national convention in 1920, women on each side of the collective bargaining issue engaged in long and arduous debate. For two days over 2,000 women argued back and forth. Delegates representing women workers in the association addressed a YWCA convention for the first time and spoke for the adoption of the entire set of industrial standards, including collective bargaining. A Pennsylvania silk worker addressed the convention, pleading, "I beg of you to be the leaven among the girls in industry and help them rise to better conditions."[17] National Board members, clearly divided on the issue, argued on both sides. One wealthy board member suggested that the word "agreement" be substituted for "bargaining," a proposal soundly rejected by the industrial membership. Another board member protested that as YWCA members "we [are] losing our religion and [are] in danger of Communism," and a third resigned in the middle of the convention. Finally, a middle-class member of the board argued that "we are having a power put in our hands that we must use. Do not be afraid of it."[18]

Eventually sentiment turned in favor of the Industrial Department's position. The strength of Simms's negotiations with the National Board, the zeal of working-class and middle-class leaders within the Industrial Department, and finally the threatened withdrawal of the industrial membership from the association provided the necessary impetus for inclusion of a collective bargaining plank in the YWCA's set of standards for women in industry.

Mixed reactions met the YWCA's acceptance of a comprehensive set of standards for working women. The NWTUL, long suspicious of the domination of the YWCA by middle-class women, praised the women of the Industrial Department for winning a significant victory. On the other hand, wealthy women within the organization looked to the Industrial Department with increased suspicion. One member voiced her fear of "radical socialism," a trend she had found "even in certain departments of our Association that we love so much."[19] But the more than 30,000 working-class women within the association hailed the endorsement as a victory and as a measure of their growing power within the national YWCA.

In addition to recommending that the YWCA endorse collective bargaining, women workers at the YWCA National Industrial Conference in 1919 had proposed that the entire membership participate in educational programs designed to analyze social and industrial issues. Industrial women wanted these programs to be available to the association's board women, business clubs, and student groups in order to "prepare for citizenship and for our part as a Christian organization in helping solve the industrial problem."[20] This proposal resulted in increased cooperation between college students and industrial workers within the YWCA. As part of this movement, industrial women addressed college groups about the problems of women in industry, and after 1921 college students, under the direction of YWCA industrial secretaries, took industrial jobs for a six-week period to experience at first hand the working conditions in factories and mills. Finally, joint study groups of industrial and college women were formed in many cities where there had been little previous contact between women who worked in industry and middle-class students.[21]

From the beginning of the Industrial Department, Florence Simms had preferred "education" to "agitation" and had argued that "knowledge must precede reform." The Industrial Department's gradual efforts to educate middle-class women about industrial issues had proved generally successful, and YWCA leaders consistently emphasized the "solidarity of interest uniting the women of leisure and the wage earners" in solving social and economic problems. To conservative board members who supported the YWCA in local communities across the country, the implementation of educational programs for women workers appeared to be another logical step in the process of slowly implementing a new system of social justice.[22]

Within the Industrial Department itself, workers' education was viewed as a means of training leaders among industrial women and providing the necessary skills working women needed to push for industrial reforms and to build a new society. YWCA staff members and women workers had supported the development of a working women's educational movement as early as 1916, when the NWTUL proposed that women's colleges open their doors to working women during the summer months. Two years later, YWCA industrial secretary Ernestine Friedmann, later the assistant director of the Bryn Mawr Summer School, designed a program for Industrial Clubs that emphasized training the "natural leadership of the industrial group" and sought to supplement traditional YWCA educational courses in basketry, home economics, and nursing with classes on "Women and Industry," the "Industrial Revolution," the "New Place of Women in Labor," and "Politics and Economics."[23]

Experimentation with workers' education in local associations had ramifications throughout the Industrial Department. Women began to ask for courses that would help them understand the historical context of their lives and the particular economic realm in which they lived and worked. The demands of women workers resulted in the development of a series of courses for women workers in economics and history. Initially this new educational direction drew criticism for not being traditional YWCA "Bible study," but later a consensus was reached that "this kind of course was even more needed than the other."[24] In keeping with the collective goals of workers' education, YWCA secretaries felt strongly that YWCA classes in leadership, training, public speaking, parliamentary law, and writing should be designed to help a worker function better in workers' groups and cooperative enterprises, not to favor an "ambition for excellence in personal performance."[25]

Lucy Carner, who succeeded Florence Simms as National Industrial Secretary in 1923, argued that the YWCA's most continuous and widespread educational work among industrial women was done as young women learned to manage local clubs, departments, and regional and national organizations. Women who would not enroll in a "class" learned organizational skills as they elected officers and planned and executed programs. But she admitted that workers' education had redirected the focus of local programs and that "the few girls who had discovered the joy and responsibility of real study are making classes in economics and history and psychology the thing of which an industrial department has a right to boast and without which it feels a bit ashamed." In Carner's view, the finest thing was that the new educational interests of women workers were not being enjoyed simply for themselves, "but were being used as tools by increasing numbers of girls who in the process of education have caught the vision of a better social order."[26]

As workers' education programs spread through the YWCA, the Industrial Department transformed its summer conferences for industrial women, which had been held annually since 1912, from recreational camps into intensive educational sessions on industrial and social issues. After 1920, five conferences were held each year in the East, South, and Midwest. A total of 800 to 900 American women attended these programs annually. Women came to the conferences as representatives of their local Industrial Clubs and were instructed to return home ready to share what they learned and with proposals for new Industrial Club programs and activities. Industrial delegates administered their own conferences, invited economists and labor specialists to lecture, and led discussions on the specific labor problems they faced as women workers.[27]

Designed to meet the needs of the large number of women workers who could not leave their jobs or home communities for long periods, these ten-day, abbreviated summer schools for women workers were attended by a total of over 15,000 women workers in the years between 1920 and 1940. Union members, the unorganized, recent immigrants, native whites, and urban black women came together and worked to understand their common concerns as women and as workers.[28]

Former YWCA secretary Lois MacDonald saw the industrial conferences as providing a strategic educational opportunity to reach unorganized women workers, most of whom were "out of touch with any other agency which is interested in education and group development among industrial women."[29] Nationally planned but regionally executed, these summer educational programs for women workers provided women from industry, and eventually from domestic service, with the opportunity to enjoy "freedom from the ever-present rush" in a course of study focused on labor legislation, issues of women's work, industrialization, occupational health, and trade unionism. Through the YWCA conferences, women had the opportunity to analyze their own industrial experiences and to participate in working out their own educational programs.[30]

By the mid 1920s, as the women's workers' education movement expanded, a debate about the authenticity of workers' education programs within the YWCA began to surface. Lucy Carner took a circumscribed view of the work done in her department, writing in 1925 that: "It would not be honest to leave an impression that the Industrial Department of the YWCA is doing intensive or prolonged educational work. Few departments could be so described."[31]

But Lois MacDonald, writing in the *American Federationist* in 1927, the year she was involved in founding the Southern Summer School for Women Workers in Industry, argued that whether the YWCA Industrial Department provided "worker's education in the technical sense of the term, is too academic a question to be of much concern." She emphasized that both the industrial conferences and the YWCA's educational work in local Industrial Clubs were unique workers' programs, "made out and almost entirely executed by workers," and that the YWCA was in touch with more industrial women than any other organization. MacDonald was cautious about the incremental nature of the work. Few expected a ten-day summer course to transform a hosiery worker into a union organizer, but MacDonald concluded that the YWCA conferences, "real workers' education or not, were important experiment[s] in education for workers, education which looks toward a new day when all workers shall be united."[32]

Despite the fact that the YWCA never established its own school for women workers, such as the Training School for Women Organizers sponsored by the NWTUL, the association's experiments in workers' education reached more working women, and affected more women's lives, than did the educational efforts of any other contemporary organization. At peak membership, in 1930, the number of working women in local associations with Industrial Departments was 57,556. Out of this group, more than 15,000 women received specialized leadership training through summer conference programs.[33] By contrast, the NWTUL's Training School for Women Organizers admitted only three to five students a year, the Bryn Mawr Summer School reached 100 women each summer (for a total of about 1,500), the Southern Summer School had a total of only 350 students, and Brookwood Labor College and Vineyard Shores accepted under a dozen women each year. Workers' education programs within the unions reached thousands of women, but by the mid-1920s these offered women workers little except training in union administration.

Of all the workers' education programs established in the 1920s, only those carried out within the YWCA reached women at the grassroots level on a year-round basis. The YWCA Industrial Department brought women into an organization firmly established within a specific community. And for those industrial women who left their local organizations to attend a summer conference or a women's summer school, the YWCA provided a ready forum for discussion, support, and the dissemination of new ideas when they returned home.

What could, and often did, happen to women in the YWCA is eloquently illustrated in the life history of Jennie Spencer of Roanoke, Virginia. Born in 1917, Spencer became keenly aware of her family's working-class status when at age eleven she recognized that "my home wasn't as nice as the other children's and that while they had oranges everyday and money to spend, I didn't have these things." Spencer quit inviting her schoolmates home and "felt like an outsider." In her second year of high school, Spencer's father came out on a Norfolk and Western Railroad strike, and she had to drop out of school. She got a job with the American Viscose Corporation working as a reeler. Spencer had always wanted to go to the Roanoke YWCA, but "thought it was a place for the rich girl." Finally, some of her co-workers invited Spencer to attend their YWCA Industrial Club. Spencer joined the YWCA "and began to be happy again." She found that "the girls there were just like me; they had had to quit school to go to work to help their family out. They worked in the same mill as I did, we all made the same amount of money and their families weren't any better educated than mine."

Gradually, Spencer became a leader within the Industrial Club in Roanoke; after a year she was selected club secretary, and two years later her friends from American Viscose voted her their president. When still new to the YWCA, Spencer was named a delegate to an industrial conference held at Camp Merrie Wood. Each morning during the conference Tom Tippett, from Brookwood Labor

College, spent an hour discussing unions, but Spencer still "thought the YWCA was a social club, and . . . wasn't the slightest bit interested in anything that was said." From a union family, Spencer was not antagonistic toward the labor movement; she "just didn't think unions concerned me, and when I later began to think a little, I was afraid of strikes." Within the supportive atmosphere of the Industrial Club, Spencer continued to develop the self-confidence needed to examine her own attitudes about the labor movement and other difficult social issues. At their meetings, Roanoke's YWCA women followed the guidelines of the YWCA national convention, and as a result they frequently discussed "the race question." Spencer recorded that "it didn't take me long to lose my race prejudice because I was that timid easy going kind, and injustice to human beings to me was a terrible thing."

The YWCA's industrial program brought women like Spencer into contact with other young women of similar backgrounds. Working together, these women gained a sense of common purpose and the strength to develop their own programs, meet and recruit new members, elect local officers, and serve as delegates to regional and national meetings. Through the YWCA, thousands of young women were introduced to new ideas and different ways of viewing the world. With a strong national program, unassailable moral credentials, and firm footing in local communities, the YWCA could facilitate a woman's rejection of conventional racial mores and validate the role of women in the labor movement.

For Spencer, exposure to the labor movement through the YWCA occurred slowly, as she attended the Industrial Department's workers' education programs over a period of several years. In May 1936, the Roanoke unions sponsored a workers' education conference and Spencer attended. Tom Tippett was again on the program, and the following evening he addressed the local YWCA Industrial Club. "I don't know what he said," Spencer recalled,

but all at once I realized that it was my duty to myself and my fellow men to join the union and take part in the things so to make life more as I think it should be, regardless of what might develop, whether difficult or not. I knew I was a worker and I belonged on the workers' side.

Following the Roanoke workers' education conference,

Spencer became chairman of Pioneer Youth in Roanoke, and as an organizer of local youth clubs for union children she began attending the union meetings of the Viscose workers. Soon she joined the union. Pioneer Youth "expanded into clubs all over town," and Spencer and the women in the YWCA Industrial Department established a summer camp for thirty children outside of town. In the fall of 1936, Spencer ran for recording secretary of her local. During the election "one or two people objected to a woman having the office, as this was something new." But Spencer won by a large margin because she "had become well known to the membership by working with their children." As an officer, Spencer carefully followed events when her local transferred its affiliation from the American Federation of Labor (AFL) to the Congress of Industrial Organizations (CIO). As she put it "[O]ur contract expired and we just couldn't get Green [AFL president William Green] to negotiate for us. CIO's door laid the 'welcome' mat down and we walked in."

Under her local's new contract, Spencer sat in on grievance negotiations and once traveled to Pennsylvania with three other union members to meet with representatives from the other five locals covered by the same agreement with American Viscose Corporation. But Spencer "had many unpleasant experiences in the union," and during the period when her spirits "had been broken, all except a single thread," she almost left the labor movement. She wanted to return to the YWCA and "devote more time to the union" within the Industrial Department, where "a girl can be happy for her work is appreciated and encouraged." But a close YWCA friend repeatedly lectured her not to quit, and finally Spencer decided to continue her union work.

Although she became "much stronger as a result of staying on," Spencer found herself "usually in the minority on policies" and, as a result, unable to enjoy much of her local union work. But the union fulfilled Spencer's need for "the humanitarian work which is my religion." Eventually, she learned to "keep fighting and not let things break your spirit." After four years as an active union member, Spencer had negotiated grievances, recorded minutes, picketed local department stores selling Japanese rayon, marched down the main street of Roanoke in a strike parade with local furniture workers, and brought a carload of women to the picket line each day. Finally she saw her local begin to "accept the idea of girls being active," and Spencer saw herself as one who had chosen "to go through life fighting labor's battle."

Spencer recorded her history in 1940, in an essay she called "My Transition."[34] Her story embodied all that the YWCA Industrial Department sought to do for young women workers across the United States. Convention resolutions on equal pay, minimum wage, limited hours, and the hard-won plank for collective bargaining were directed toward making things easier for women like Jennie Spencer in communities like Roanoke, Virginia. The Industrial Department had designed workers' education conferences to expose the Jennie Spencers of the country to the ideas of labor educators like Tom Tippett and to give them the skills they needed to become local union officers.

Finally, the association's Industrial Department wanted to continue serving women after they became active trade unionists. Union women could, and did, return to the Industrial Department to obtain essential support and encouragement. Within the YWCA, appreciative friends could help mend broken spirits and then send women back to their unions with the strength to continue their fight for industrial justice.

As women in the YWCA began to integrate workers' education into their programs, they recognized the need for their more serious students to obtain training that went beyond what was available through the Industrial Department. Thus, the YWCA supported the institutionalization of women's workers' education in the growing number of summer schools for women workers. Many association staff members served on summer school boards; others taught in six- to eight-week summer courses or in the year-round programs sponsored by various summer schools in local communities. YWCA Industrial Departments helped select students to attend the summer schools and often provided the financial support necessary for women workers to leave home. The women's summer schools depended heavily on the cooperation of YWCA Industrial Departments across the country to put them in touch with those women workers who would most benefit from an intensive workers' education program.

In promoting women's workers' education, the YWCA joined with other groups that supported a broader cultural and nonvocational education for industrial women. In 1918 the YWCA had agreed to cooperate with Bryn Mawr College in writing courses for the training of women for industrial work. Bryn Mawr economics professor Susan Kingsbury reported on the proposed training course for industrial workers at a YWCA Conference in Kansas City in the spring of 1918. A year later, the National Industrial Department voted to "cooperate as far as practicable with working women, universities and churches in the development of a working woman's educational movement."[35]

This cooperation was tangible in the YWCA's participation in the opening of the Bryn Mawr Summer School in 1921. The National Industrial Department staff was involved in planning for the school, and the local YWCA Industrial Clubs raised money to send women from their ranks to Bryn Mawr. Over half of the eighty-two students in the first Bryn Mawr Summer School class in 1921 were recruited through YWCA Industrial Departments.

By the late 1920s, all of the workers' education schools looked to the YWCA as a "recruiting agency." The YWCA cooperated with six workers' education programs in different regions of the country: the Bryn Mawr Summer School, the Barnard School for Women Workers, the Southern Summer School, the Wisconsin Summer School, Brookwood Labor College, and Vineyard Shores. After almost a decade of cooperation, the association considered it "a very natural part of its program" to recruit for the summer schools and "to help prepare girls for more advanced education than we ourselves give."[36] As the recruiting agency for workers' schools eager to reach industrial women, the YWCA provided an invaluable service. Without this aspect of the Industrial Department's work, the summer schools for women workers could not have drawn women from local communities in all sections of the country to participate in their educational programs.

In addition to recruiting students for the women's summer schools, YWCA Industrial Departments across the United States coordinated workers' education fund-raising activities within local towns and cities. In select communities the summer schools themselves had local committees (of Bryn Mawr College alumnae, for example) that would choose industrial women to attend a summer school and provide scholarship support. But in the communities without summer school committees, women from the YWCA would contact a variety of local organizations and ask for contributions. In Duluth, Minnesota, in 1926, the Industrial Department organized a committee of seventeen women's organizations, including the Duluth Women's

Club and the Junior League. This group raised scholarship funds to send three women to the Wisconsin Summer School. The YWCA then successfully approached the Duluth Trades and Labor Assembly, asking them to provide the money for a local trade union member to attend.[37]

Once a local YWCA had selected one or more women workers to attend a summer school and raised the necessary scholarship funds, the Industrial Department usually provided some type of preliminary training in labor economics or trade union history aimed specifically at preparing women for their advanced workers' education experience. On returning to their communities, these women continued their study of industrial and economic problems within their local Industrial Clubs. Their enthusiasm and newly acquired expertise infused energy into ongoing YWCA Industrial Department programs. In many communities, groups of summer school alumnae assumed leadership positions within both the Industrial Clubs and local labor organizations.

Because of the YWCA's extensive network among industrial women, the association was directly responsible for the initial organization of several workers' education programs. These ranged from the Wisconsin Summer School for Woman Workers, to a small workers' school in Cleveland established under the aegis of that city's YWCA Industrial Department, to the Summer School for Women Workers in Industry, which was organized in 1927.

The Wisconsin Summer School began in 1924, when the Industrial Department of the Madison YWCA and the University of Wisconsin's Department of Economics started a summer institute for factory women. The university, then under pressure from the state's labor federations to provide specific programs for workers, requested the existing school for women workers to invite local unions to participate. For several years women workers recruited through YWCAs continued to dominate the school, but by the late 1920s more men than women attended the renamed Wisconsin School for Workers.[38]

In the 1920s the YWCA had more contacts with industrial women in the upper Midwest than any other organization, and this pattern also held true throughout the South. In 1925, a group of former Bryn Mawr Summer School students active in local YWCA Industrial Clubs worked with Louise Leonard, YWCA industrial secretary for the southern region, to plan a small summer school for southern women workers. The first session was held in Sweet Briar, Virginia, in 1927, and over half of the twenty-four women who made up the first class had come to the school through the YWCA. Southern Industrial Departments continued to recruit many of the school's students until the mid-1930s, when a majority of the women came as representatives of newly organized unions from across the region.[39]

Through the YWCA's intramural workers' education programs, its support for the industrial conferences, its large industrial membership, and the strong trade union advocacy of its leaders, the Industrial Department earned some measure of respect from organized labor. By the mid-1920s, the YWCA was widely recognized by many leaders in the labor movement "as a force making for more social thinking among young workers which they have such difficulty reaching." The national association regularly sent representatives to AFL conventions; during the early 1930s, the YWCA's fraternal delegate status was an acknowledgment of its representation of thousands of industrial workers. The Industrial Department considered this participation an important opportunity to keep abreast of developments in the labor movement and to promote the interests of women workers within the male-dominated AFL.[40]

As one of the few national groups firmly committed to the organization of women workers, the YWCA maintained an ongoing critique of the AFL's refusal to organize women. The YWCA fraternal delegate at the 1933 AFL convention raised issues of special concern to the YWCA, including the needs of women workers and the necessity of integrating black employees into the labor movement. YWCA members joined others at the convention in calling for new strategies to reach unorganized workers and in endorsing a shift to industrial rather than craft-based unions. The report of Helen Carr, the Industrial Department's delegate to the 1935 AFL convention, underscored the AFL's conservatism, which she considered to be exemplified in a stodgy group of older men "who had become so set in their ways that they will not even tolerate the thought of change."[41]

The AFL remained intransigent on the subject of industrial organizing and on addressing the needs of women workers. Only with the ascendency of the CIO in the mid-1930s did these issues finally receive some attention. In many ways, the industry-wide unions that proliferated under the CIO subsumed the role of the YWCA as a meeting place for industrial women. This was exemplified in Jennie Spencer's shifting her participation from the YWCA to her local union. Moreover, lack of funds during the Depression contributed to a gradual decline in the Industrial Department's influence within the labor movement.

As the YWCA Industrial Department worked through the labor movement to draw attention to the concerns of women workers, the department's staff members gained invaluable experience in both workers' education and the principles of labor organization. Most young women who went into the YWCA in the 1920s saw the association as a place where they could act on their own religious convictions to bring about Christian social reform. As Eleanor Coit, a Smith College graduate who became a YWCA secretary in 1920 in Bayonne, New Jersey, recalled, "I came from a very religious family . . . of course we could not have worked in the YWCA if we did not have some religious motivation."[42] Once in the YWCA, women like Coit witnessed at first hand the basic need for social reform and then recognized the trade unions as a vehicle for economic change. These women understood the importance of education as a prerequisite for the unionization of women workers, education carried on both within and outside of the YWCA.

YWCA secretaries who joined the Industrial Department in the years between 1915 and 1925 formed a cohesive group, a network of reform-minded women who had moved to New York City in the World War I decade. Many of these women came from elite Eastern women's colleges—Smith, Vassar, Radcliffe, Wellesley, Mount Holyoke, Barnard, and Bryn Mawr—and most attended graduate school at Columbia University, receiving social science training in the rapidly expanding fields of sociology, economics, and political science. At the YWCA's newly built National Headquarters Building on Lexington Avenue, Industrial Department staff members began to develop industrial reform programs and to experiment with women's workers' education in an urban atmosphere highly charged with social change.[43]

Each year National Industrial Department members were assigned to coordinate YWCA industrial work over six geographical areas. The National Industrial Secretaries traveled throughout their regions, meeting with local staff members and supervising the planning of regional industrial assemblies and workers' education conferences. Based in New

York, often living in the National Headquarters Building, these secretaries enjoyed socially compelling and intellectually challenging work which they executed collectively, within a supportive, female-dominated environment.⁴⁴

Scores of other YWCA industrial secretaries worked on the local level in both small towns and large cities, wherever women were employed in substantial numbers. Secretaries employed in far-flung community YWCAs faced the difficult task of transforming the Industrial Department's goals into reality. Many took YWCA jobs because they believed that the association would "prepare girls for getting into unions." Some risked their jobs in conservative communities by offering union organizers support and access to local contacts. Once involved at the grassroots level, YWCA industrial secretaries frequently found themselves in a "ticklish business" where workers often associated them with management and employers either viewed the YWCA as "harmless" or as unlawfully "preaching unionism."⁴⁵

Many women in the Industrial Department fought private battles over how to reconcile a growing ideological attraction to socialism with their YWCA work. Florence Simms encouraged politically committed women to stay in the Industrial Department, writing to one woman that "many of our people will feel and think as you do now. Just go right ahead being a Socialist . . . there is not the least difficulty in your combining your secretarial work and Socialism."⁴⁶ But often it proved impossible for staff members to continue working within the limitations of the YWCA where, as Louise Leonard McLaren put it, an industrial secretary had the difficult job of having to "cooperate . . . without compromising her ideals."⁴⁷ Despite major changes in the YWCA's program for working women and the substantial power gained by the industrial membership, the National Board of the YWCA remained in the control of middle- and upper-class women whose commitment to social change and industrial reform remained circumscribed.

Few YWCA Industrial Department secretaries, on either the national or the local level, made a lifelong career of association work. Of those who stayed active in the labor movement, a few became union organizers, while the majority left the YWCA to take a more active role in workers' education programs for women. In fact, most of the women who became leaders in workers' education began their careers as YWCA industrial secretaries: Ernestine Friedmann, a YWCA secretary in 1912, became assistant director of the Bryn Mawr Summer School, served on the staff of the Affiliated Schools, and was named director of the Barnard School; Eleanor Coit left the YWCA to become director of the Affiliated Schools and then head of the American Labor Education Service (ALES); Alice Hanson Cook taught in each of the summer schools and worked for ALES; Louise Leonard McLaren became director of the Southern Summer School; Grace Coyle originated the idea of a workers' education program for office workers. Alma Herbst worked with ALES on a Works Project Administration workers' education project; Alice Shoemaker became director of the Wisconsin Summer School; Ethlyn Christensen worked with the White Collar Workshop; Lois MacDonald taught at the Bryn Mawr Summer School and was instrumental in founding the Southern Summer School; and Brownie Lee Jones directed the Southern School for Workers.[48]

As these women changed their careers, they transferred the network of personal and professional relationships they had established in the YWCA into workers' education. This facilitated communication among the various workers' schools and was largely responsible for forging a diverse group of workers' education programs into a cohesive educational movement for women workers.

The YWCA's influence on workers' education for women was unparalleled. No other organization's membership even approached the vast numbers of working women involved in YWCA Industrial Clubs; and no other institution supplied the workers' education movement with as many leaders as did the Industrial Department of the YWCA. The workers' education movement for women could not have developed as it did without the pioneering efforts and the sustained cooperation of the women of the YWCA.

YWCA Industrial Departments in local communities across the nation brought young women who worked in a variety of factories within the same town or city together in lively meetings like the one humorously depicted in this cartoon. Concerned about child labor, working conditions, and wages and hours, YWCA Industrial Departments often brought labor and economic issues to the attention of manufacturers and community leaders in efforts to improve the working lives of their members.[49]

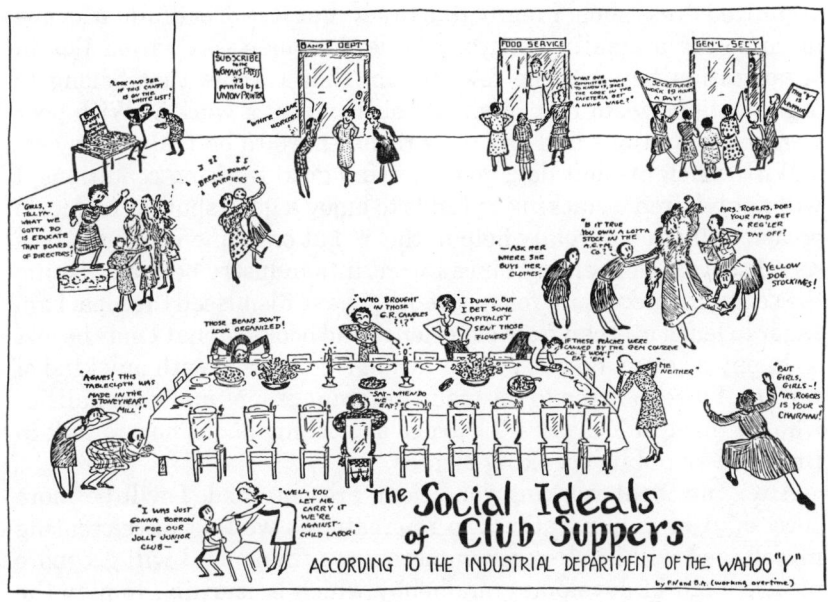

The essays and poems that follow were written by women workers who took part in YWCA Industrial Department programs. They were printed in YWCA newsletters and publications between 1928 and 1944. As a cross-class organization, the YWCA promoted interaction between industrial women and college students as a way to educate each group about the other and promote solidarity among women of different backgrounds. The organization also developed interracial programs for women and led integration efforts in hundreds of northern and southern communities.[50]

What I Want from Workers' Education

I enjoy working much more since my last three years of rich memories and experiences which I owe to the YWCA. As an underpaid worker, the ambitious girl has quite a struggle because to satisfy any ambition, particularly "forward," it takes money.

Since my study of economics at Chicago and Bryn Mawr [Summer School for Women Workers], I have been fired with enthusiasm for organization for women in all lines of industry. I am still in the ranks of the unorganized but I am waiting for my opportunity to work in an organized dress shop. I really like to sew but it is dreadfully irksome to do so for a small pittance. I believe women's salvation lies in organization because the few women that I know that belong to organizations seem rich in all the blessings of a worker. With poor working conditions and pay, it is rather hard to be truly happy.

With an eight-hour day, good pay and good working conditions, I will not be tired or lacking in funds to enjoy a good show or musicale occasionally and to really help in the Y. I at one time wanted to be a social service worker, but since I went into industry before finishing the schooling necessary for such work, I have dismissed the idea. I am eager to learn all I can from experience and books so that I may be just as happy as one who has passed through college as with any kind of worker. I love to listen to the many different groups and nationalities which I meet in Y classes. I learned something about how to talk in Bryn Mawr public speaking classes.

After my ideal working conditions are obtained, I will be more successful in helping others to re-create, as well as to re-creating myself, as I will be stronger in more ways than one. I will get more pleasure out of developing my hobby which is learning to play the piano. I have been trying to interest my co-workers in gym, as all needle workers really need it, and I will feel truly rewarded if I get a dozen girls to take part in such a class. I have just learned how to relax last summer. It is refreshing to be able to relax after an exciting but interesting day. My days are now very crowded with my work and classes of economics, drama, clubs and music.

Girls that couldn't be interested in economics would certainly be interested in gym or charm school. It will be wonderful to help girls show off their best in health-giving recreation or dramatization after hours. This program [at the Y] is very near social service, I believe. I will be compensated if I am able to make good money three fourths of the year and can also act as an open door, eye-opener, or beacon light to other girls or women in industry.

I love to sew but hate to be cheap labor. I love the contact gained in meetings or classes of industrial girls; and last but not least, the friends I have among my leaders in different phases of workers' education.

—Edna Monroe, 1928.

Workers and Students

I first became acquainted with the idea of the student-industrial movement in 1922 at a week-end party conducted by the Young Women's Christian Association. At that time I was not much impressed with its importance, and wished I would not be invited again; however, since then I have learned to appreciate the value of this movement.

When students actually go into industry, not for financial help only, but for the purpose of seeing for themselves what it means to work in a factory; and on the other hand when factory girls are actually given an opportunity to taste college life, the student-industrial movement becomes something more than good times and discussions; it is getting down to brass tacks, and stimulating thought and action which affects our whole industrial problem.

The best thing that happens to a student who has worked in a factory is that she has her illusions shattered on how to help the working class. She learns that it is not important to teach workers how to live properly, how to be good Americans or to be good producers. Nor is it important to teach them more religion or to inspire them to become millionaires or the President of the United States; but that it is important to awaken workers to the fact of the big role they play in industry and in helping to develop civilization, and to teach them that if they want respect and a square deal out of life they can not get [it] as individuals or with [an] "Everybody for himself" philosophy. Workers must learn that if one is hurt, all are hurt.

Some students do get that understanding out of their experience and decide to ally themselves with workers' movements and remain in industry. But few stick it out; the adjustment is too difficult. It often means the cutting off of all family and social contacts.

I would not discourage students who want to ally themselves with the workers' cause, but I would not encourage it. Instead I would advise them to go back to their professional and intellectual fields and do the job from there.

College students apparently do not realize their opportunities to influence workers' minds—what damage, what misleading and deadening work has been done by their group. If they are really interested in helping the working class, why don't they become teachers, and instead of glorifying kings, war lords and wars, emphasize the part workers play in developing civilization and tell what their heroes and martyrs have done in bettering working conditions.

When teaching economics, they should not glorify the wonderful opportunities our country offers for making profits. Instead, they should tell how our economic system can be run for service.

If they become social workers and wish sincerely to help the workers, they should not be satisfied with just patching up cases. They should question and trace back reasons. If they become lawyers they should see that the workers get a square deal in the courts, especially when involved in the industrial struggle. If they become journalists, they should not live off scandals and murders, but give the workers a little space when they are in a strike.

Some students hope to be active politically. In this field there are opportunities to help the workers "to clean up." If their ambitions spur them to become industrial engineers, why not give human beings at least as much consideration as machines and production? And ministers who tell workers that if they are denied things on this earth, they are made up in heaven are not the kind that will help the workers' cause. In fact, that kind of talk has a terribly deadening effect on the workers' mind. Students who become Y.W.C.A. secretaries should not be interested in teaching girls how to play; neither should they, when they realize the struggles and needs of the workers, find the Industrial Department too small and limited and go out into other fields. In that case, they are very often lost to the cause.

It is not going to be easy, this job of helping the working class from the professional fields. Those who try are going to have plenty of opportunities to experience that glorious feeling of martyrdom and suffering that always comes to those who stand for progressive ideals. They will get the same thrill that we workers get when we lose our jobs, go into strikes and get arrested. I know of three people of the professional class who in the past year have lost their jobs. It is much better to learn how to compromise, if it means getting a point a little later. But if they are put in a position where they almost sell their whole soul, then it would be better if they went out and sold vacuum cleaners instead.

What happens to my industrial sister when she gets a taste of the intellectual world? First a dizzy pain in the head. If she gets her taste at Bryn Mawr, Madison, Barnard, the Southern Summer School, or Brookwood, the dizziness is soon relieved with the help of teachers and tutors who understand the purpose of "workers' education." The second thing that happens is that the world begins to stretch out. They begin to see and hear things that have always been there, but to which they have been deaf, dumb, and blind.

For instance, at Bryn Mawr Summer School, the study of economics taught me that my employer was not the only one responsible for the struggle of workers. In fact, he too was a victim of forces such as inventions, discoveries, climatic changes, wars and new theories, all of which have resulted in separating our interests. Some understanding of the history of civilization gave me a feeling of importance as a factory worker. The study of English made speakers and writers out of us overnight. A taste of literature seems to flavor life and make a library look larger. We see books that have always been on the bookshelves but have meant nothing to us. The study of science opens our eyes to the skies and trees. A theoretical understanding of the trade union movement strengthens our faith in it, even when our fellow workers and leaders seem to fail us.

The biggest thing that the industrial girl gets out of a workers' school is the contact with the other working girl. She learns that though workers may be different in religion, nationality or color, they have one common problem as workers; that though they have many theories, philosophies, and tactics, the ultimate goal is the same.

I hope that the student-industrial movement will keep on growing. Students should be encouraged to go into industry and industrial girls should be encouraged to go to school. Students will find that any activity they engage in to help solve our industrial problems will enrich their lives more than any other activity can possibly do.

—Sadie Goodman, 1928.

Thoughts

(Passing through my mind as I sat in a conference called at Hollins College for working girls and college girls.)

I work, you play.
You have everything,
I have nothing.
Why should I sit here, afraid to take my coat off?
Is it because I smell so strong of acid?
Why don't I take my gloves off?
Is it because my hands are so rough and dirty looking?
Why do I keep my hat on?
Is it because my hair smells like a wet dog?
Acid again. Acid that smells like burning sulphur.
There are fumes of sulphur in hell.

You daughters of the rich,
You walk so easy and sure of yourselves,
You don't smell at all.
Your hands are well kept,
Your hair shines with cleanliness,
Your eyes are bright and eager looking.
But who makes your sweetness, your cleanliness, possible?
Is it not workers like me?
I work, you play.
You have everything;
I have nothing.

—Thelma Brown, 1937.

Color Equality

Will there be two heavens,
One for white, the other for color?
Or will there be two entrances?
For the superior and the lower?

Doesn't God stand for color equality,
Accept Christians of every kind,
And demand they serve in unity,
Put discrimination behind?

Can't we forget discrimination,
Since God is color-blind?
We are all of His creation,
And He's watching all the time.

There will only be one heaven,
And there'll only be one door.
There won't be any superior,
Nor will there be a lower.

We shall be our brother's equal,
When we enter the golden shore.
There will be no discrimination,
If we enter through heaven's door.

—Diamond Crouch, 1944.

Notes

1. For background on the YWCA, especially the Industrial Department, see Annabel M. Stewart, *The Industrial Work of the YWCA* (New York: Woman's Press, 1937); Mary S. Sims, *The YWCA: An Unfolding Purpose* (New York: Woman's Press, 1950); Grace L. Coyle, "A Historical Outline of the Work of the Industrial Department," November 1923, Sophia Smith Collection, YWCA Manuscripts, Smith College, Northampton, Mass (hereafter cited as SSC, YWCA); "The Work of the Industrial Committee" (pamphlet prepared by the Woman's Press [1924], SSC, YWCA, Box 16; "The Young Women's Christian Association and Industry" (pamphlet issued by the Industrial Department, National Board of the Young Women's Christian Association [1927/1928]), SSC, YWCA, Box 27, Folder 7.

2. For biographical material on Florence Simms and discussions of her influence on the YWCA, see Richard Roberts, *Florence Simms: A Biography* (New York: Woman's Press, 1926); Marion O. Robinson, *Eight Women of the YWCA* (New York: National Board of the YWCA, 1966), pp. 91–101; Edward T. James, ed., *Notable American Women: A Biographical Dictionary* (Cambridge, Mass.: Harvard University Press, 1971), 3:291–93.

3. Roberts, pp. 212 and 233.

4. Ibid., p. 193.

5. "The Young Women's Christian Association and Industry," p. 13–14. SSC, YWCA, Box 27, Folder 7.

6. Roberts, p. 217.

7. "Typed Report of the Industrial Conference, October 1–6, 1918," SSC, YWCA, Box 19, Folder: "Conferences, Industrial-National, 1918–20."

8. "History of Colored Work," compiled by Jane Olcott Walters, November–December, 1920, pp. 1–3, Archives of the National Board of the YWCA, New York, New York (hereafter cited as YWCA Archives, NB).

9. Ibid., p. 12.

10. Ibid., p. 16.

11. "Information from War Work Centers Indicating Industries in Which Colored Women Are Employed and Those in Which YWCA Club Membership Is Represented," YWCA Archives, NB.

12. Roberts, pp. 221–22.

13. Ibid., pp. 231–38.

14. The women of the Industrial Department also recommended that because the setting of industrial standards depends largely on legislation, the YWCA should work "for granting women the power to work for these laws through the ballot" (Roberts, p. 284).

15. Instead of working out an independent statement, the YWCA decided to endorse the "Social Ideals of the Churches," which had been prepared and adopted by the Federal Council of the Churches of Christ in America (see Sims, pp. 77–84).

16. Robinson, pp. 98–99.

17. Ibid., p. 100.

18. Ibid.

19. Ibid.

20. Ibid., p. 284.

21. Many delegates to the first industrial conferences compared their new position in the YWCA to that held by college women. One woman wrote: "For the first time in my life I feel that I have an equal chance with the college woman," putting into words her new sense of power and respect for herself ("The Young Women's Christian Association and Industry, p. 11, SSC, YWCA, Box 27, Folder 7).

22. Roberts, p. 57; "Our Second Line of Defense: Women's Industrial Army," June 4, 1918, p. 2, YWCA Archives, NB.

23. Ernestine Friedmann, "The Industrial Club and Its Program" (New York: National Board of the YWCA, 1918).

24. "Industrial Committee Minutes," October 17, 1922, YWCA Archives, NB.

25. Lois MacDonald, "Education by Conference," *American Federationist* 34 (February 1927): 188–90.

26. Lucy P. Carner, "Outline of Biennial Industrial Report, 1924–25," p. 7, YWCA Archives, NB.

27. "The Young Women's Christian Association and Industry," pp. 17, 26–34, SSC, YWCA, Box 27, Folder 7.

28. "Bulletin," Industrial Department, National Board YWCA, No. X, (November 1925), pp. 7–8, includes a description of the activities of black industrial women in a local association. In 1924–25, black and white delegates met together in industrial conferences, except in the South.

29. MacDonald, p. 188.

30. Ibid., p. 188.

31. Carner, p. 7.

32. MacDonald, p. 190.

33. Lucy P. Carner, "Biennial Report of Industrial Department, 1930–31, p. 7, YWCA Archives, NB.

34. Jennie Spencer, "My Transition," Operation Dixie, CIO Organizing Committee Papers, 1946–1953, Series III, Reel 32, Frames 72–74.

35. "Industrial Committee Minutes," 1919, p. 10, YWCA Archives, NB.

36. Roberts, p. 255.

37. "Bulletin," Industrial Department, National Board YWCA, No. XII, (July 1926), p. 11.

38. "The School for Workers" (pamphlet issued by the University of Wisconsin, University Extension Division, 1959).

39. See Chapter 5.

40. Carner, "Outline of Biennial Industrial Report, 1924–25," p. 11.

41. Helen Carr, "Report of the AFL Convention," November 1935, p. 12, YWCA, NB, Microfilm Reel 111.4, "Unions, 1919–1950."

42. Interview with Eleanor Coit, New York City, November 2, 1974.

43. Elizabeth Wilson, *Fifty Years of Association Work among Young Women* (New York: National Board of the YWCA, 1916), pp. 316–25; interviews with several former YWCA industrial secretaries are included in "The Twentieth Century Trade Union Woman: Vehicle for Social Change," Institute of Labor and Industrial Relations, University of Michigan—Wayne State University, Ann Arbor, Michigan.

44. "Tentative Set-Up of the National Industrial Staff for 1924–25," SSC, YWCA, Box 6, Folder: "Industrial-Inquiry Commission, 1924–27."

45. Louise Leonard McLaren Reports, Industrial Department, 1922–1926, YWCA Archives, NB.

46. Roberts, p. 56.

47. Louise Leonard McLaren Reports, Industrial Department, November 1925, YWCA Archives, NB.

48. "Tentative Set-Up," SSC, YWCA; Doris Cohen Brody, "American Labor Education Service, 1927–1962: An Organization in Workers' Education" (Ph.D. diss., Cornell University, 1973).

49. From the *Woman's Press* (1931), YWCA National Board Archives, New York, Record Files Collection in the Sophia Smith Collection, Smith College, Northampton, MA.

50. From the Industrial Department Papers, National Board, YWCA Archives, New York, N.Y.; "What I Want From Workers' Education," from Hilda W. Smith Papers, Schlesinger Library, Cambridge, MA., Box 13, folder 236; "Workers and Students" appeared in *Labor Age*, October 1928, p. 21; "Thoughts" appeared in the *YWCA Program Exchange*, January 1937, p. 15; "Color Equality" appeared in the *YWCA Program Exchange*, June 1944, p. 8, YWCA Archives, NB.

Chapter 4

Blue Collars and Bluestockings:
The Bryn Mawr Summer School for
Women Workers, 1921–1938

Rita Heller

During the winter of 1920–1921, Lena Richman, a twenty-six-year-old native of Skalet, Austria-Hungary, an ex-student of its gymnasium, was employed in New York City's millinery industry. She had immigrated to America ten years before. Richman belonged to the Young Peoples' Socialist League and to the United Cloth Cap and Hatmakers' Executive Board. That summer, 1921, the newly formed Workers' Education Bureau sent Richman to the first session of the Bryn Mawr Summer School for Women Workers.[1] There she joined eighty-one other students representing forty-nine trades and twenty-five nationalities.[2] Richman's summer school experiences entered family folklore, enabling her granddaughter to recount:

Among the faculty in 1921 were Estelle Frankfurter (sister of Felix) who taught English and thought the girls lacked proper manners and didn't study enough; Henry Wadsworth Longfellow Dana who also taught English and was the reigning radical; Laurance Saunders of Ruskin College, Oxford who used H. G. Wells' Outlines of History as a textbook; Paul Douglas, who taught economics and frequently upbraided the young women for not studying hard enough and only wanting to have a good time and Amy Hewes [economist from Mount Holyoke] . . . who despite her conservative bent was much liked and admired by the young women there. Guest lecturers included [socialist, pacifist and labor educator] A. J. Muste and British labor educator Henry Clay.[3]

Sixty years later, the granddaughter remembered hearing that the summer experience was punctuated by "ideological disagreements between right and left, high spirits and enthusiasm, and a belief in the possibility of creating a brave new world."[4]

Scholars now regard the Bryn Mawr Summer School for Women Workers, which continued from 1921 to 1938, as a social feminist institution.[5] As social feminists, the school's leaders gave priority to broadly based social reform. The school built on the accomplishments of organizations with similar goals. It emulated the National Women's Trade Union League (NWTUL), and the National Consumers League (NCL). Settlement houses provided another model, for they were mixed-class institutions engaged in evolutionary change. The Bryn Mawr Summer School for Women Workers and these kindred groups shared a belief in gradualism and voluntarism, and all wished to bridge economic and social classes.

During the three decades preceding the summer school's inception, women had been leading activists for social justice.[6] A number of historical forces had converged to produce this phenomenon. Beginning in the late Victorian age, leisure-class women seized opportunities to expand their public roles. A new human resource was also available to take leadership in social reform movements—the first graduates of pioneering women's colleges. Educated women sought a productive outlet beyond domesticity for their skills and energy. Between 1890 and 1920, more women joined groups seeking reform of civil service, municipal government, and conditions under which women and children labored. The reformers sought enactment of child labor, conservation, and pure food and drug laws. In particular, these women pursued careers in social service. The names Jane Addams, Florence Kelley, Lillian Wald, Julia Lathrop, Katherine Davis, Alice Hamilton, and Margaret Dreier Robins are writ large over the era and its accomplishments.

One scholar has shown that the newly won vote revitalized social feminism in the 1920s. His "new women citizens" heeded the message embodied in the suffrage. "These ... women citizens ... wanted to use their newly won citizenship to advance the reform effort. They created new organizations and established new contacts to promote progressivism in the 1920s." The vote was an imperative to action. It called women to further democratize, civilize, and humanize American life.[7] The Bryn Mawr Summer School for Women Workers can be seen as a prime example of a suffrage-inspired, social feminist institution.

At the Bryn Mawr Summer School for Women Workers, the women's social justice movement joined ranks with a fledgling labor education movement. The latter was a loose network of academicians, unionists, liberals, and socialists unified by a Jeffersonian vision of education and a commitment to organized labor. The pioneering effort at Bryn Mawr quickly gained recognition as a model. It set the pattern for subsequent programs conducted at the Brookwood Labor College, the Vineyard Shore School for Women Workers, the Barnard Summer School, the University of Wisconsin Summer School, the Southern Summer School, and the Summer School for Office Workers.

The appearance of a workers' summer school at an elite college resulted from the efforts of M. Carey Thomas and Hilda ("Jane") Worthington Smith.

One woman provided the vision, the other the stewardship. It was the autocratic educator and feminist, M. Carey Thomas, who introduced the idea of opening a workers' school at Bryn Mawr, the college she had dominated as dean and president for thirty-five years. And while innovative geniuses defy categorization, it is still fair to term Thomas's final enterprise, the workers' summer school, as surprising. How was it that this crusading feminist who had devoted a life's energies to the attainment of feminine academic elitism abruptly embraced the cause of downtrodden working women? A desire to uplift weavers and garment workers appears to be at odds with, if not alien, to Thomas's beliefs.

Evidence from the newly opened M. Carey Thomas Papers suggests that close relatives in the Whitall Pearsall Smith family influenced Thomas throughout her life.[8] Her mother's oldest sister, Hannah Whitall Pearsall Smith, was a formidable iconoclast,[9] an author and orator who embraced feminism, the temperance movement, and evangelical Quakerism. Hannah Smith emigrated to England in the 1880s, where she quickly joined the intellectual avant-garde. One of her daughters married art critic Bernard Berenson; another married philosopher Bertrand Russell. The latter daughter, Alys Russell, was a companion and correspondent of M. Carey Thomas.

Among the many interests of this group of British intellectuals was the Workers' Education Association (WEA), which was a thriving enterprise by the time of M. Carey Thomas's visit to London as part of a 1919–1920 world tour. The WEA, brainchild of Albert Mansbridge, a clerk and a product of the cooperative movement, had the support of a remarkable coalition of Anglican bishops, Oxford dons, and self-educated men. Activated by the Christian Socialist belief that the educationally deprived suffered primarily from spiritual malaise, the movement was suffused with a Christian Socialist spirit. Mansbridge's favorite phrase was "the glory of education."[10] The WEA curriculum was intended to prepare students for "life, not livelihood."[11] Although course material was grounded in the social sciences, classes provided no training in trade unionism and were strictly nonvocational. Instruction was carried on in tutorial sections of sixteen to thirty-two working men and women who met for two hours weekly for three successive winters. J. F. C. Harrison, historian of the British workers' education movement, has provided the following judgment:

The idea of an equal partnership between the university and the working class movement, the emphasis upon the scholarship of the tutor coupled with the necessity of teaching subjects from the angle of the students' needs and the conception of the social purpose behind all studies, gave a distinctive slant to the typical class.[12]

The workers' school, which rapidly assumed a reality at Bryn Mawr in 1921, drew heavily on the WEA as well as on other British models developed by the Fabians and the National Council of Labour Colleges. The Bryn Mawr experiment emulated the British in curriculum philosophy and tutorial approach and in deliberately fostering alliances among incompatible constituencies and institutions. The school brought privileged, educated women into a partnership with poor and uneducated women. The college establishment and its capitalist network were the main sources of financial support of a school created to benefit and nurture women workers and, indirectly, the labor movement.[13]

M. Carey Thomas later alluded to her visits to British workers' education programs when she described her inspiration for founding the school. Thomas was also moved by British enfranchisement of women and the impending passage of the Nineteenth Amendment in the United States:

One afternoon at sunset I was sitting on my golden hilltop in the Sahara rejoicing that British women had just been enfranchised and American women would soon be politically free. . . . I also saw as part of my vision that the coming of equal opportunity for the manual workers of the world might be hastened by utilizing before it had time to grow less, the deep sex sympathy that women now feel for one another. The peculiar kind of sympathy that binds women together seems to come only to those who have not been free. . . . Then with a glow of delight as radiant as the desert sunset I remembered the passionate interest of the Bryn Mawr College students in fairness and justice and their intense sympathy with girls less fortunate than themselves; and I realized that the first steps on the path to the sunrise might well be taken by college women who, themselves just emerging from the wilderness, know best of all women living under fortunate conditions what it means to be denied access to things of the intellect and spirit.[14]

The speech was vintage Thomas. It exemplified both her luxuriant rhetoric and her publicist's skill in behalf of what she had come to call THE CAUSE.[15] She now endorsed a broader feminist vision, one which included working-class women. Lacking direct evidence, one could presume noblesse oblige as Thomas's motivation. A closer look at her record suggests otherwise. In the preceding decade Thomas had shifted direction. After 1910, she began to retreat from scholarly isolation, turning instead to "social reconstruction and human betterment."[16] In 1913, she authorized the progressive Phoebe Anna Thorne model school. Even more audacious, and on a grander scale, was the Graduate Department of Social Economy and Social Research opened at Bryn Mawr College in 1916. It was the first graduate school of social work in the United States and the first to offer a Ph.D. The intrusion of socially relevant institutions at staid Bryn Mawr was not accomplished easily.[17] Disdain for the social work school and its director continued well into the 1920s, beyond Thomas's tenure as college president. The director was the pioneering sociologist, Susan M. Kingsbury,[18] known for her abrasive personality.

Against this background, the Bryn Mawr Summer School for Women Workers, if precipitously decreed, was neither an anomaly nor an exercise in noblesse oblige. Rather, it was a culmination of the shift that Thomas had begun in the previous decade. In the years from 1910 to 1921, Thomas added social reformer to her established identity as feminist, educator, and suffragist.

The evidence shows Thomas to have been an impassioned activist, particularly in her later years. Increasingly, she had embraced the experimental or practical—first in the progressive Phoebe Anna Thorne School, second in the Graduate Social Work school. The latter provided training for worldly careers. By 1921, Thomas was ready to invite the world onto her hallowed campus. The summer school would incorporate blue-collar women into the liberal humanist tradition. At the school they would be offered things of the intellect and spirit that had been monopolized by the privileged few. From all that can be known, Thomas appeared dedicated to her newest innovation. Sincerity cannot, however, be equated with depth of understanding. Thomas did not, in fact, appreciate the complex character of the enterprise she had endorsed. As Hilda Smith later reflected, "President Thomas didn't realize that a workers' school would plunge Bryn Mawr into the heart of the organized labor movement."[19]

The woman who offered this judgment was the second key personality, the one tapped by Thomas to transform her dream into a reality. She named as director of the Bryn Mawr Summer School for Women Workers Hilda ("Jane") Worthington Smith, who was dean of undergraduates and a trained social worker. Submerged by melancholia over her mother's death, yearning to break out of the confines of educating daughters of the middle class, Smith was electrified by the surprising assignment, for which she was well qualified. After college at Bryn Mawr she had attended the New York School of Philanthropy, and in 1916 she had become director of a new community center in the town of Bryn Mawr. Susan Kingsbury had devised the center to provide accessible fieldwork for her graduate students. In jointly developing the Bryn Mawr Community Center with Smith, Kingsbury became the latter's mentor, advisor, and friend. The center offered evening classes for adult workers in the community. Later, while serving as college dean, from 1919 to 1921, Smith followed the same interests. She organized an educational program for the college's gardeners, electricians, and cooks. In so doing, she displayed a bold originality and a capacity to surmount traditional class boundaries between administration and hired staff.[20] It was Smith, therefore, who took Thomas's nobly conceived but shallowly rooted idea and made it viable. She headed the summer school for thirteen years and became its revered symbol.

In addition to Smith, Thomas asked leading social feminists to design the summer school. Susan Kingsbury, since 1916 the director of the pioneering social work school, was Thomas's main link with women reformers. On March 19, 1921, in the exotic reception rooms of the College's deanery, Thomas convened a group that included Mary Anderson of the U.S. Women's Bureau, Fannia Cohn of the International Ladies Garment Workers Union (ILGWU), Mrs. Robert Speer of the YWCA, and labor economist David Saposs. In formulating plans for a women workers' summer school, they addressed an idea first advanced in 1916 when the NWTUL had urged women's colleges to make their campuses available to working women during the summer months.[21] Although no NWTUL representatives were present at the meeting, the organization became a loyal summer school supporter. It recruited students and participated in key advisory capacities.[22]

The Bryn Mawr Summer School for Women Workers was firmly rooted in the Jeffersonian belief that a vital democracy requires an educated electorate. Thomas's dynamic feminism caused her to extend this progressive vision to laboring women; she was convinced that they, too, could benefit from exposure to the liberal humanist heritage. At its outset, the school strove primarily to enhance individual capacity. However, what would become obvious over time was the necessity for collective action to change workplace conditions for women.

The school's purpose can be viewed either as idealistic, inclusive, and timeless or as ambiguous, utopian, and naive. According to the school's brochures and publicity releases, its purpose was "to offer young women in industry opportunities to study liberal subjects and train themselves in clear thinking." Instruction was to be conducted "in a spirit of impartial inquiry with freedom of discussion."

The School is not committed to any dogma or theory. The teaching is carried on by instructors who have an understanding of the students' practical experience in industry and of the labor movement. . . . It is expected that thus the students will gain a truer insight into the problems of industry, and feel a more vital responsibility for their solution.[23]

The school's founders aimed to create a community of industrial women, representing a cross-section of occupations, regions, religions, and races, with a balance maintained between union and nonunionized workers. The school welcomed as applicants women between the ages of eighteen and thirty-four who had an elementary school education and two years of industrial experience. The term "worker" referred to someone working with the tools of her trade, not in a supervisory capacity. Specifically excluded were teachers, clerical workers, and saleswomen. In selecting applicants, the school sought evidence of maturity, leadership, intellectual curiosity, and an awareness of economic problems. The Bryn Mawr College alumnae, the NWTUL, the YWCA, and unions all worked to recruit students. The college's established national alumnae club network became the primary recruiting body.

The predominantly white, Anglo-Saxon college alumnae groups were invited to work for the school and to recruit students among the heavily immigrant laboring classes. Beginning in 1926, blacks were welcomed as students. Within the student body were southern fundamentalists and Russian immigrant socialists, rural whites and urban blacks. Unionized city garment workers met provincial YWCA-affiliated factory operatives.

Margaret Fulton, a shoe factory employee of Syracuse, New York, was president of her branch of the Y, the Grey Shoe YWCA. Helen America of New York, an ILGWU member, worked in the Helene Dress Company. Both women applied to and were accepted by the Bryn Mawr Summer School for Women Workers in 1924. Ruby Haigwood, an R. J. Reynolds Tobacco Company worker of Winston-Salem, North Carolina, was president of the Sunshine Club of her Baptist church. Helen Maver from Tacoma, Washington, was an unemployed candy factory operative and a YWCA member. Haigwood and Maver were rejected in 1924. These four women were drawn from a sample of 197 applicants to the Bryn Mawr Summer School for Women Workers for the years 1924, 1929, and 1931.

These applications provide a rich body of data that permit a comparison between stated criteria and actual admissions policies.[24] The documents portray the student body as well as rejected applicants.[25] One can chart changes in the student profile between the years 1925 and 1931.

A demographic profile of the students attending the summer school in 1924, 1929, and 1931 emerges from the data. Almost one-half of the accepted students came from the Northeast, and almost all were from urban locations. A little over half were native born; approximately one-third were born in Russia or Poland. Almost two-thirds of the students were between the ages of twenty-two and twenty-nine. Approximately half voted, and the overwhelming majority were single. Very few of their mothers were employed. An eighth-grade education was most common, followed by entrance into the workforce between ages fourteen and fifteen. The YWCA was the primary recruiter, with unions and churches following behind.

The sample was representative of the American female industrial work force in the 1920s and 1930s with respect to age and marital status. However, there was an overrepresentation of unionized and garment workers. Students under the age of twenty-five accounted for 55 percent of the school population, the exact percentage in 1920 of urban working women.[26] In the sample, 93 percent were single; this corresponds to Tentler's description of the "typical" working-class daughter living in the parental home.[27]

Nearly half (46 percent) of the sample women were unionized. While the national figure for industrialized women in unions was 18 percent, this high percentage reflected the school's deliberate effort to recruit a student body from both union and nonunion industries. Eighty-three percent of its unionized students came from the needle trades (garment and hosiery industrial workers and seamstresses), double the national norm of 42 percent of unionized women (in the ILGWU, United Garment Workers, and Amalgamated Clothing workers).[28] Milliners, composing 12 percent of the sample, were also overrepresented, compared to the national figures of 4 percent in 1920 and 2 percent in 1930.[29] On the other hand, the percentage of textile workers was less than the national norms of 18 percent in 1920 and 20 percent in 1930.[30]

Compared with those accepted, rejected applicants tended to be younger. Fewer were of Russian or Polish origin. They were less likely to have voted or to be union members. They had worked fewer years, were less frequently in the needle trades, and were more likely to be unemployed. Their social affiliation tended to be a church and less frequently a Y or a union.

Over time, the student body changed. Most striking is the shift in origin of the sample. The native-born percentage fell by almost 50 percent between 1924 and 1931, while the percentage of recent immigrants (residents of less than ten years) increased. Between 1924 and 1931, there was also an increase in the number of students over age thirty and from the northeastern United States.

Analysis by occupation shows an increase over time in participation by the needle trades and the milliner group and a decrease among the other factory categories. Unemployment was unusual in the accepted group, reaching only 4 percent by 1931. There was an increase in union membership, so that by 1931 over one-half of the students belonged to unions. The YWCA remained a constant and major organization for student affiliation while union membership increased.

The foregoing data reveal a general congruence between declared criteria and admissions practice. However, over time, the sought-after balance shifted to favor immigrants from the Northeast who were union members. The reasons for this shift are conjectural, since direct explanations are lacking.

It may be that recruiters increasingly indulged their bias in favor of intellectuals. School participants, in both oral and written records, have focused particular attention on this fact. Eastern unionized immigrant working women displayed great sophistication and interest in economic questions. As students, they set the school's level of inquiry, dialogue, and tone. Hence, their presence was probably sought. Perhaps they were also seen as gaining most from the school.

At the school, course content and teaching method were continually evolving to meet changing student needs and interests. Three constants gave some stability to the instructional environment: a commitment to humanistic education; a faculty drawn almost exclusively from the eastern academic community and *not* from the labor movement (some instructors were YWCA Industrial Department staff members); and the presence of a policymaking arm, the Joint Administrative Committee, composed of equal numbers of Bryn Mawr representatives and industrial women.

Of incidental interest are the unlikely circumstances that surrounded M. Carey Thomas's decision to make labor an equal partner in the summer school. The story added to Thomas's reputation as unpredictable.

Hilda Smith recorded in her autobiography that the pivotal event occurred at a summer school board meeting in the fall of 1921. One of the school's leading students, a Baltimore buttonhole maker, acted as catalyst. It was Sadie Dressner who succeeded in winning over the formidable, legendary Miss Thomas. Dressner articulated her ideas on labor education to Miss Thomas. There and then, Thomas concluded that the students' objectives and hers were identical. "Convinced after that conversation that the workers desired a liberal course related to their own problems, rather than propaganda in favor of one viewpoint, Miss Thomas herself had proposed the motion that 50 percent of the members of the Board should be elected by the former students of the school." Since Smith had long realized that the school's future depended on labor's equal status, she greeted the decision with relief and delight.[31]

The curriculum underwent revision throughout the school's history. In the early years, students encountered an ambitious liberal arts program. The class of 1923, for example, had an eleven-hour per week course of study divided as follows: Modern Industrial Society (four hours), English (two hours), Hygiene (one hour), and an elective in either History, Art, Literature, or Science (four hours).³² Hilda Smith and her faculty discovered that so diverse a curriculum overwhelmed their average unschooled student. By 1928, the staff had redesigned the curriculum to focus on a core of practical English and economics, with science and the arts as secondary activities.³³ One economist and one English professor were responsible for creating an integrated learning experience for a twenty-member student unit.³⁴ From the school's inception, undergraduate tutors recruited from the Seven Sister Colleges supervised tutorial sections and provided one-on-one instruction.

In the course of overcoming educational hurdles—students' unschooled background and long absences from classrooms—the school created a learning environment that would bring it recognition as a model. Of necessity, it experimented with pedagogy inspired by John Dewey and progressive education.³⁵ The staff designed courses for the adult woman worker who had an elementary school education. They generally compensated for academic deficiencies by using students' work and life experiences as the basis for discussion of economic and social issues. Personal material was the departure point for most instruction. The women frequently wrote autobiographies and discussed current events in an effort to make their aptitudes and interests central to learning. Amy Hewes, a Mount Holyoke economist who through years of summer school service became one of its revered teachers, described the experimental learning process:

Classes in English composition often started with the writing of autobiographies. Hygiene might begin with the study of the physical motions required to perform an industrial operation. How could strains be avoided and energy conserved? In the case of a group of textile workers a study ended in the composition and performance of the "Dance of the Weavers," set to appropriate music.³⁶

In 1930 and 1931, the Depression was the unifying theme in economics classes. Students chronicled their unemployment experiences in Depression case histories: "The Effect of Unemployment on My Family and Me"; "My Experience of Being Unemployed"; "What Made Me Hold On."³⁷ In addition, each summer school class produced a yearbook—a literary magazine containing a variety of poetry and prose based on material drawn primarily from the students' work lives.

Besides the classes and writing projects, the students participated in a rich extracurricular program. This included field trips to historical sites, museums, and factories. Highlights of the 1924 session were a debate on the Equal Rights Amendment and the school's first international folk musical festival, which featured an ethnic cross-section—Scots, Russians, Czechs, blacks—of the student body. That summer there were discussions of the national political platforms and a weekend forum entitled "The Bargaining Unit of Labor." The cooperative store and the student paper, published twice during the term as in previous years, had their place in community life. And, as in other years, the lantern ceremony, held in the library cloisters, was the season's final event.[38]

In 1934, during a crisis at the school, critics alleged that the curriculum had become radicalized. The school's charter had mandated "impartial," "non-dogmatic" inquiry. Had it ever been possible to adhere to those principles? Economist Broadus Mitchell believed that "advancing the rights and influence of organized labor infused all instruction."[39] As early as 1922, in Amy Hewes's economics classes, for example, value-laden rather than value-neutral instruction prevailed. In her syllabus for "The Role of the Worker,"[40] Hewes argued that the economic power of the individual worker is less than that of the capitalist. An employer's assets are his superior knowledge of market conditions and his bargaining skill. He fights for profit, not life. In a competitive system, an employer must use his economic power against workers because the public demands that he lower prices.

Hewes's outline expressed union principles. Antagonism between employer and employee regarding output requires the formation of unions. The employer's chief goal is increased production and decreased cost. The union's goal is restricted output. The latter is seen as necessary for wage and job retention. To eliminate unfair bargains and job insecurity, workers must act as a unit.

In Amy Hewes's course there clearly was a prochange, pro-union bias. Twelve years later, a Communist party member was on the faculty, teaching from radical materials. The presence of this Communist, Emanuel Blum, showed the students' influence: they had lobbied for and won his hiring in 1933. The Emanuel Blum–Ellen Kennan teaching team used National Recovery Administration (NRA) Board member W. O. Thompson's statement. It read.

> *The trend of the National Recovery Administration has been and continues to be toward the development of monopoly capitalism in the United States.*
>
> *The NRA handed over the trade associations dominated by the largest corporations in the various industries, the formulation of codes of fair competition without representation of the consumers or workers. . . . As a result of these conditions, small business is being oppressed.*
>
> *The amount of goods that can be bought by workers with declining real earnings has dropped as a result of price advances created by monopolistic practice.*
>
> *The only solution involves a change in class relationships. Only a government by workers and farmers can plan production, produce goods for use and not for profit, eliminate poverty, and raise the standards of living of the entire population.[41]*

These cases indicate that ideology permeated some teaching during the school's first fourteen years. The school's reliance on experimental learning and current events made it particularly attuned to worldly politics. Classroom ideology ranged from Hewes's liberal prounionism to Blum's Marxism. Clearly, school participants enjoyed "a broad spirit of impartial inquiry and . . . academic freedom."[42] Academic freedom meant one thing in 1921 and quite another in 1934. In the latter year, alternative economic systems and "isms" increasingly engaged the entire school.[43] New Deal ferment brought too much reality to the Bryn Mawr Summer School and, with it, too much risk to the college.

By 1934, the Bryn Mawr Summer School for Women Workers had achieved success. It had educated 100 women workers annually. As indicated below, each summer many students left the school better equipped to take charge of their lives and to assume leadership positions in their communities and at work. But Depression-generated internal and external crises would wound its operation. The school had depended for its continuance on cooperation among incompatible forces: conservative and liberal college trustees and alumnae, union sponsors, industrial clubs of the YWCA, business and industrial leaders, and academicians. While it was possible for a tenuous equilibrium to be maintained in the quiescent 1920s, the charged political atmosphere of the 1930s proved its undoing.

Union representation at the 1934 session had increased to two-thirds of the student body.[44] More students with louder voices were interested in communism and socialism. By chance, the college's fiftieth anniversary $1 million endowment campaign coincided with the radical developments within the school. Conservative members of the college's Board of Trustees (Mrs. Learned Hand, for one, who had become increasingly uncomfortable with the college's "leftist" labor school) were eager to seize an excuse to evict the school. Their opposition was sharpened by the need to raise additional endowment funds for the college. The event that galvanized the opposing forces was the Seabrook Farms strike of 1934.

The particulars of the crisis are easily summarized. A longstanding agreement had barred the school's participation, as a school, in strikes. Individuals were free to express themselves in strike activities. What occurred during July 10–12, 1934, was the involvement, as individual observers, of economist Colston Warne and sociologist Mildred Fairchild in the strike called by the workers at the Seabrook Farms in Bridgeton, New Jersey. By going to the strike "to be damned nuisances, if possible,"[45] the two faculty members violated no agreement with the Bryn Mawr Board of Trustees and broke no rules. They observed a confrontation between police and teargassed strikers and gave a story to reporters. The next day, Bryn Mawr made the Philadelphia newspapers.[46] This, of course, was just the turn of events for which the conservatives, influenced by Frances Fincke Hand, were looking. They claimed that the school had violated the agreement not to participate in strikes. The controversy grew into a cause célèbre of hysterical proportions and resulted in the school's eviction for the summer of 1935. Although the summer school returned to Bryn Mawr from 1936 to 1938, much of its momentum was gone and its idealistic energies spent.

The school ended, but what happened to its women students? Until now, that paramount question has gone unanswered. How did eight weeks of English and economics affect factory women? To what did health education, astronomy, folk festivals, debates, outings, lantern ceremonies, and myriad human interactions add up? Did the school alter the lives it touched? My follow-up study of fifty-four student participants, a forty- to sixty-year retrospective, confirms the school's efficacy.[47]

The data thus uncovered point up the vitality and importance of the Bryn Mawr Summer School. They also portray the follow-up sample whose mean age was 72.7 years in 1982. Native-born, urban,

Protestant women respondents outnumbered Catholics and Jews. A majority came from the Northeast and had been recruited by the YWCA. Unions recruited the second largest group of students, who came primarily from the needle trades. Half of the women in the follow-up sample were union members.

There were some differences between the follow-up sample and the matriculant sample. The follow-up sample had fewer "other factory" workers, was somewhat better educated, and was more likely to be born in the United States and recruited by the YWCA and the NWTUL.

Most respondents credited the summer school with giving them an enhanced self-image, greater general knowledge, and changed personal lives. A comparable percentage viewed positively the interaction of diverse social and ethnic groups. Almost half the respondents noted improved social skills, while a majority believed the school had furthered their careers. One-fifth of respondents felt that the school had had no impact on their work.

Almost three-quarters of the respondents felt the school could not have been improved. One-third had no idea why it ended, while others thought its radical image and inadequate funding were the reasons.

The survey illuminates the school's impact on employment and careers. Worker-students clearly realized the founders' aspirations. Their subsequent lives followed widely divergent paths. Some experienced dramatic upward social mobility, perhaps a tribute to faculty role models. Others moved into trade union leadership. The canvass yielded the following: eight women continued in the same industrial work until retirement, twelve left paid employment for full-time homemaking, six left industry for either retail or white-collar work, and seven combined homemaking with community volunteerism. Five became middle-class professionals, while two gained college scholarships (to Barnard and the University of Wisconsin) through the direct intervention of summer school personnel. Fourteen provided no career data.

Twelve heeded the school's message to assume a greater responsibility for the solution of industrial problems. The ten who became shop chairladies and volunteer organizers for their unions are now chiefly remembered by co-workers, daughters, and granddaughters.[48] Carmen Lucia and Elizabeth Nord became vice-presidents of the United Hatters, Cap, and Millinery Workers International Union and the United Textile

Workers Union, respectively. Ultimately, Nord represented labor on the Rhode Island State Unemployment Compensation Board from 1956 to 1974.

Outside evidence has established the school's national contribution to union leadership training. Six of seventy-five subjects in the Twentieth Century Trade Union Women Oral History Project had been students at the Bryn Mawr Summer School.[49] They were Sara Barron (ACWA), Sara Fredgant (ACWA), Dolly Lowther Robinson (ACWA), Elizabeth Nord (UTW), Carmen Lucia (Hatters Union), and Bonnie Segal (ILGWU). Rose Pesotta, who predeceased this study, attended the school in 1922. She became a leading trade unionist in the 1930s and 1940s and the only female vice-president of the ILGWU's executive board.[50]

For many of the faculty, the school's impact was as powerful as it had been on the students. It was their first opportunity to help the disadvantaged, an experience that proved irresistible and pivotal. Teaching assistants and instructors Margaret Honour, Elizabeth Lyle Huberman, Anita Marburg Lerner, Oliver Loud, Millicent Carey McIntosh, Broadus Mitchell, Mark Starr, Susan Shepherd Sweezy, Caroline Ware, and Colston Warne said the school fueled their dreams for equal opportunity and social justice.[51] The faculty joined or returned to their home universities or social welfare and government agencies intimately acquainted with the problems of poor and exploited laboring women.

First at Wellesley and later at Vassar, Helen Drusilla Lockwood became well known for her activism. Lillian Herstein, a Chicago social studies teacher, moved into leadership in that city's American Federation of Teachers. Rosamund Tuve, a Connecticut College Renaissance scholar, said that teaching at the Bryn Mawr Summer School "left [her] left of center."[52] Brooklyn College's well-known Theresa Wolfson, a member of the 1928 and 1929 faculty, focused her reformer's energies on the workers' education movement.[53] Mount Holyoke's Amy Hewes, the University of Pennsylvania's Gladys Palmer, and the University of Chicago's Hazel Kyrk[54] made names for themselves through economic research. Margaret Berry and Marie Algor returned to their YWCAs with broadened perspectives. Alice Hanson Cook moved from the YWCA to a faculty position at Cornell's School of Industrial and Labor Relations.

The New Deal generated further opportunities. Hilda Worthington Smith herself was the first, in 1933, to join FDR's team. Harry Hopkins tapped her to train unemployed teachers as labor educators, first in the Federal Emergency Relief Administration (FERA) and later for the Works Progress Administration (WPA).[55] Those summer school faculty and staff members who joined federal agencies were for years part of a vital Washington, D.C., summer school network. These included Marguerite Gilmore (U.S. Women's Bureau), Katherine Pollak Ellickson (AFL-CIO), Jean Flexner Lewinson (U.S. Bureau of Labor Statistics), Constance Williams (U.S. Department of Labor), Esther Peterson (Amalgamated Clothing Workers of America), Ida Craven Merriam (Social Security Board), and Caroline Ware (Organization of American States). Other faculty staked out new territory. Colston Warne, for example, founded the Consumers' Union. Esther Peterson became a link to the contemporary women's movement when she was named as first chairperson of the President's Commission on the Status of Women in 1961.

While it appears that the quality of the educational program contributed to the school's effectiveness—well-trained academics and activists taught an innovative curriculum to carefully chosen students—its force derived in part because it fulfilled a need not met by other institutions. The school was in the vanguard of education programs for women workers, offering them scholarships, support, and awareness of their individual and group potential.

The Bryn Mawr Summer School was an experiment in residential living and learning that generated stimulating personal relationships. Many respondents wrote of acknowledging for the first time their collective identity as working women. In an age when working people seldom traveled, attending the school was a broadening experience. The school enabled its students to widen their acquaintance with other laboring women and to consider common problems. They valued opportunities to meet a cross-section of the American—and each year a few European women also joined the school—female work force.

The heterogeneity of the school's students often resulted in confrontations. A New York dressmaker wrote, "The School opened for me a lot of information about the status and backwardness . . . of women from all over the country who never heard about the class struggle."[56] An unemployed Lawrence, Massachusetts, textile worker remembered being labeled a "nigger lover" by her Winston-Salem, North Carolina, roommate after befriending a black girl. She was a Catholic for whom the summer meant first meetings with Protestants and Jews. She confessed to having feared them as "Satanic" and "Christ Killers."[57] A New York milliner remembered that some Christians experienced another sort of culture shock: "A few gentile girls from the Midwest were so disturbed when courses conflicted with their ideas about God and religion, that they left the School."[58]

Cross-class encounters were central to the entire experience. Academicians and collegiate tutors mixed with social classes known only from texts. Faculty women taught factory women. Some students focused on the summer's idyllic character, writing of the access to luxury and leisure. A Virginia textile worker wrote: "Bryn Mawr was a heaven on earth for me. I had a suite of rooms. The food was good. The nurse asked me if I wanted to put on some weight. I weighed 98—I gained 14 while there."[59] A New York clothing worker said: "In that day, just being on such a campus was very different in concept to what we from the factory were even aware of—only the rich knew that life. So it was a new world."[60] A neckwear finisher reminisced: "It was a terrific summer, especially for those girls who were really very poor and probably never lived in the environment we had there. To them, it was out of this world to have maid service and waitresses and meals."[61]

Elizabeth Nord was particularly moved by the faculty's capacity for empathy: "What really impressed me . . . was how well our professors, who had a different background from ours, knew so much about our problems, what affected us as workers. Lillian Herstein told us she had done laundry and ironing to go to College."[62]

Another student developed a deep six-year friendship with Vassar literature professor Laura Wylie. It began with an invitation to "Iolanthe."

That was only one invitation. Then one after another followed. I spent many weekends in her home and two weeks every summer. She gave me a list of books to read, encouraged me in everything I undertook. She wrote to me twice a week for all those six years that she lived (passed on in 1932), and insisted that I drop her a card once a week just to say I was O.K.[63]

After her summer at Bryn Mawr, the student left the dressmaker's shop. Passing the New York City teacher's exam opened for her a thirty-five-year career at the Manhattan

Trade School for Girls as a dressmaking teacher.

Faculty were more analytic about cross-class mixing. Many stressed what they had gained from the unique experience. Economist Jean Flexner Lewinson, Carter Goodrich's undergraduate assistant in 1925, remembered: "The students greatly enjoyed the companionship among themselves and with faculty and tutors and the beauty and quiet of the campus. Those with strong Marxist leanings could not be pried loose. We learned as much or more from the experience as they."[64]

Another teaching assistant recounted the class feeling aroused by a neighborhood party.

I remembered being delighted when many of the students were indignant at a supper party given by a would-be kindly neighbor. We had hot dogs and store rolls. But the girls had expected a good home meal, were hoping for it. They thought this was a condescending effort to give them what they were "used to." They would have loved something like steak or chicken.[65]

Susan Shepherd Sweezy, an undergraduate assistant and later a member of the English faculty for several summers, devoted most of her memoir to the students.

But the students were the big education for me. Girls my age who had often less than an eighth grade education, many had emigrated from Europe, many had fled pogroms, all had worked hard when they could get jobs. . . . They all had to be literate, but really had very little education. They were wonderful people, some full of flare and color, some repressed, rigid, many of them nursing strong grudges against the world. When I returned to Wellesley that Fall I changed my major from English to Economics.[66]

Elizabeth Lyle Huberman, another undergraduate assistant who taught English, credits the school with political conversion.

The students were wonderful. They were overflowing with knowledge of a world I didn't know but felt I should have because my grandfather was a fisherman and my grandmother was a factory worker. . . . The School turned my politics upside down. From being an unthinking Republican simply because I'd inherited my parents' view I became some kind of socialist. . . . My parents were shocked but persuaded and ended up voting for Roosevelt.[67]

Her transformation began in earnest when she went to work for John L. Lewis in Washington, D.C., upon her graduation from Bryn Mawr College.

The Bryn Mawr Summer School for Women Workers, 1921–1938, was rooted in M. Carey Thomas's idealism and social feminism. By unifying women through education, Thomas hoped to reduce social and economic inequities and to hasten "the coming of opportunity for the manual workers of the world."[68] Thomas provided the imprimatur for the ambitious experiment. She wisely tapped Hilda ("Jane") Worthington Smith as steward. Smith proved a transcendent figure capable of maneuvering among conflicting interest groups and ideologies. Into an institution that Mary Beard once described as "unnatural"[69] she infused a messianic dedication. Smith was the source of the Bryn Mawr Summer School's equilibrium, clear-eyed confidence, and continuity.

Two forceful personalities, Thomas and Smith, energized a small private college into committing its resources to laboring women's advancement.[70] Bryn Mawr College alumnae made the enterprise, which was costly and national in scope, possible. The college women brought a sense of mission to the lofty experiment. They annually collected $20,000 of the necessary funds and, in collaboration with the NWTUL, the YWCA, unions, and others, recruited applicants. The work brought reciprocal enrichment. While the summer school's existence required Bryn Mawr alumnae involvement, the work repaid them in challenge and sense of purpose.

The summer school was daringly original. It was the pioneering, and perhaps unequaled, school for women workers in the United States. Within its ivied walls it mixed ideologies, social classes, and races in unique and important ways. As a collective women's experience it was without peer. Communal living and studying, conducted in an atmosphere of mutual respect and admiration, deepen understanding as no textbook, rally, or lecture ever can.

The summer school was successful as well as original. Selected members of a generation of blue-collar and bluestocking women returned to homes, communities, factories, unions, universities, and YWCAs forever changed by the eight weeks. It enabled working women to "find their place on the side of right, justice, and humanity, to be in the mainstream of modern thought."[71] In its faculty, it sharpened a belief in education as a vehicle for nonrevolutionary change. Carmen Lucia and Elizabeth Nord assumed new roles as union organizers. Helen Schuldenfreid Selden went to Barnard College on scholarship. Sophie Schmidt Rodolfo eventually established a vocational school in the provincial Philippines. Elizabeth Lyle Huberman went to work for the United Mine Workers and later wrote about the Mexican labor movement. Esther Peterson remains vital and prominent in Washington, D.C.

The school carried forward liberal activism of the progressive era. In the politically quiet 1920s, it kept alive a commitment to social change, readying many of its students and teachers for the recharged world of FDR. It linked the world of Jane Addams to that of Hilda Worthington Smith to that of Esther Peterson. It linked Agnes Nestor to Rose Pesotta to Elizabeth Nord and Carmen Lucia. It enabled a generation of women to discover new inner and outer worlds. It groomed women for leadership.

Students at the Bryn Mawr Summer School for Women Workers wrote the following poems and essays between 1924 and 1933, which were printed in the school's paper, the *Bryn Mawr Daisy*. The final piece is from the annual "Lantern Ceremony," which was held in the cloisters at the end of the school session each summer.[72]

The Song of the Factory Worker

Red-brick building
With many windows,
You're like a vampire
For wherever I go,
You know
I'm coming back to you.
You have held many under your spell,
Many who have sewed their life away,
Within your walls.
You say to me,
O, you may leave
But you'll come back.

You'll miss
The whur, whur of the machinery
The click of the tacker,
The happy laughter of the girls,
Telling jokes.
You'll miss the songs,
They sing,
And the tired-eyed ones,
Watching the clock.
The pieceworkers,
Sewing fast
So fast till it makes you dizzy
To watch.
(They haven't time to look up.)
And under the skylight,
The red-haired girl
When the sun sets her head aflame,
You'll miss the noise and the bustle and the hurry.
And you'll come back
You'll see.
All this and more
You say to me,
Red-brick building
With many windows.

—Ruth Collins, 1924.

The Machine

Hello, you big monster.
I'm not afraid of you today.
Yesterday, you played me a dirty trick
By pulling in my hand,
And crushing it till I screamed.
You laughed and roared on and on.
Louder and louder, just like a wild lion
Full of joy that has just caught its prey.
I was helpless.
To fight you would be like fighting wild beasts.

You don't care what you do to me.
Cripple me for life or take it from me.

There is one who can compete with you
And that is Fate in all her glory.
If it wasn't for her,
I wonder where I would be?
When you took the notion, you fierce-looking thing,
That I no longer needed my hand,
Fate stepped in, and said to you,
"You have all the power in this world:
Your gears, your wheels, your huge rollers,
Why? The size of a human being compared to you
Is as great as a mouse compared to him.
This human body doesn't stand a chance with you;
You will go on living and roaring
Long after the human body is dead and buried.

So why should I let you take its life or disable it?"
You paid no heed to that, did you? Of course not.
Remember when you pulled that hand of mine
And how I screamed till I could scream no more?
Fate heard me and she stepped in,
Like lightning the power was shut off,
For what reason, no one knows but I.

Today, I am not afraid of you.
I don't hear your terrible noise,
I hear music, louder and louder.
Oh, how I wish to dance to you,
Your roaring wheels and your terrible curse.

—Mary Kosovicz, 1926

Thoughts in Patterns

Clatter, clatter, clatter,
As the shuttle flies in and out.
If we could only weave our thoughts in patterns,
What a history it would be.

Many songs of gladness,
And many tales of woe
Would be woven in the patterns.
As the shuttles go back and forth,
Ambitions and desires,
With a sense of humor too.
Discontent and admiration,
In the patterns would be woven.

—Sarah Burgess, 1930

My First Job

At the age of fifteen I took my first step in the industrial world, in the twisting department of the R. Mill, a branch of the American Woolen Company. The R. Mill is situated in the west of Providence on the banks of the Woonasquatucket River.

The first morning I reported to work, after I had taken off my hat and coat, I stood around talking to some of the girls I knew. All of a sudden out of the stillness of the room a loud shriek was heard which resounded throughout the mill and seemed to be right in the room, but to my surprise I soon discovered it was the whistle outside on top of one of the roofs.

After this loud shrieking had stopped, the girls I had been talking to all seemed to scatter in different parts of the room leaving me standing there alone in a quandary, not knowing what to do.

As the girls started their machines in operation the room became a mixture of different noises. The hum of machines and the shrieking of the belts on the pulleys which keep the shafts overhead in motion so the girls can run their machines, seemed to form a throbbing sensation through my head and vibrated throughout my whole body.

As I stood watching all the different wheels turning this way and that, looking like a jig-saw to me, the foreman, a short stocky Englishman, came walking up the room. He bid me, "Good morning," and introduced me to one of the girls and told her to teach me how to run a twisting machine.

As I walked into the alleys between the twisting machines, the din of the room seemed to become ever so much louder. The girl did her best trying to teach me how to run these machines but I was so frightened of them I didn't even want to touch them. The machines really frightened me so much that the girl who was teaching me told the foreman that I was too young to do this work and too small a child to be put on them. The girls working on these machines were all around the age of thirty.

The foreman then placed me on the Foster winding machines. This was a simple job and I soon learned to run these machines very efficiently. This work was on a piece-work basis and I averaged between $20 and $25 a week for full-time work. I hadn't been working on these machines very long when one of the yarn carriers for the twisting machines gave up her work to return to school and the foreman thought I would like this sort of work so I was moved again.

This was about the easiest work I ever did, and the most interesting to me because, while working on this job I could roam all over the plant talking to girls I knew who were working in different departments. Of course, this work did not pay as much as the Foster winding but I didn't have to work so hard. This job was a standard job and paid $17.50 a week.

—Madeline, 1933

My First Strike

When I first started to work in J & J, it was not a union shop. I didn't know what a union was. My boss was very friendly with me; she told me if I wanted her to be my friend I was not to make friends with anyone in the shop. The girls had told me to be very careful, because she was very fussy; she kept a girl a month then fired her and got someone else. I was afraid of losing my job and stuck by her and made no friends in the shop. Darn fool that I was, I was soon to know why.

A few weeks later there was a big argument in the shop. Mr. J. had gone over to the operators and told them he had to take five cents off every dress. The girls refused to take it. So he told them if they didn't like it, they could get the hell out. After much argument and discussion they all accepted the cut. More and more dresses were coming out each week. Girls were working twice as hard as before.

A few weeks later Mr. J. came around again and told them he had to take five cents more off as dresses were selling cheaper. There was no argument this time; no one said a word. A week later he came around again and told the girls he was going to give them a nickel more on the dresses as he had gotten customers who would buy dresses for their usual price. There was much discussion among the girls that week of which I could learn nothing.

Next morning when I went to work I found the workers from my shop in front of the building. As I came towards them, the men approached me and told me not to go up to work as they were striking. Everywhere you went you could heard the word, strike, strike, strike! By asking a few questions I found that the girls had not even been making enough to live on.

We had day in and day out of picketing in front of the shop without results. It seemed as though my boss got her work out just the same. So we kept a closer watch on the shop; this was very hard to do, because there were police everywhere; if you just stopped for a minute, you were told to move on and if you didn't do it, you were shoved right into the patrol wagon. On one part of the street the scabs in the shops above threw spools of thread at you and in addition to this the police would come prancing up to the sidewalk on horseback and try to scare you away. But it seemed the more the police threatened us the stronger our force grew. More and more people were joining us each day. People who knew nothing about our work used to come by and ask us how we were making out and wish us luck. We sure needed it.

One morning about 11 o'clock our shop was called to the union for a meeting. We were told that my boss had called up and told the organizer to tell the girls if they wanted to come back to come now, because after 3 o'clock he would take the five cent raise he had given them back. There was much laughter in the union, everybody took it as a joke. At noon we parted, the men went on the picket line and told us girls to go and have lunch, when we came back they would go, so we could have the shop covered all the time. Two days later my boss called the union again and told the girls if anyone wanted to come back they still had a chance. Everyone began to get uneasy; there seemed to be no results of our picketing and striking. It seemed as though the boss would not give in. The organizer told us to be patient; we would get what we wanted and more.

Next day the boss called up again and said he would give the operators five cents on every dress, but nothing to the finishers and pressers. This gave everybody courage. Girls said if he can give the operators five cents he could raise the finishers and pressers too. The organizer called back and told him we did not agree. This made him mad. That afternoon he called up again and said he would give five cents to the finishers and pressers but nothing more to the operators.

There was much rejoicing in the union; now we knew our strike was almost won; we knew we would not come back till he gave the operators five cents more and cut down our hours.

Well I joined the union and got two dollars a week increase; the operators got twelve and a half cents per dress; the finishers got seven and a half cents; the cutters were on piece work and they were put on week work at forty dollars a week. We went back to work the next morning. Now our boss cannot tell us, "If you don't like it, you can get the Hell out."

I am glad I joined the union because it gained so much, not only for me and my shop, but it helped to organize many other shops in Boston. Because when girls of other shops knew what we gained they were more than willing to join.

—Mary C., 1933

Excerpts from the Lantern Ceremony Held on the Steps of Denbigh Hall During the Closing Exercises of the Bryn Mawr Summer School

Jean: Now our all too short time has ended.—We came, each with the picture of our own lives, not knowing or seeing the same problems in the lives of others. But now we go, knowing that we are not alone—but that we are many—all working together in the same direction, though we will be far apart.

This is a strange kind of going out from school. Not to a world waiting eagerly for us—but to one where we must make our own places, quietly. It will be hard to open all the doors that are closed to us. Doors closed because of hatred; doors closed because of ignorance; doors closed, but waiting to be opened. Behind large doors that now may seem too secure to be opened, there are people wanting you, people waiting to ask, wanting to have things explained. They do not know how much they want and need you.

Girls: Who are the ones that want and need us?

Youth: We are the youth of America. Five million of us are unemployed. Where are our promised jobs? Jobs we need so that we can live decently. What are we to do with our high school and college education? Every year thousands of us pour from these schools. To what? ... We crowd into the machine of this modern world and, not knowing, become a part of its power ... become a cog in the huge wheel that is crushing us. Are we to keep it going—what have you to say to youth?

Student: You belong with us—in the labor movement. Here your power will be used, not to destroy you, but to build for you!

Woman: We are the wives of laborers. The mothers of their children. Our men are cruelly exploited in the mills of big business, big industry. They give their lives to these mills and have so little of themselves to give to us and our children. It is we who suffer, too! Always wanting, but not having. It is we who suffer when they strike—when we see our children hungry. It is we who keep them on the line—or send them back for a paltry sum because it means bread. Bread, yes—our fight, our mothers' fight, but is there not more? Can't we have for our coarse, tired hands roses too? What have you to say to us ... we women in the homes!

Girl: You, too, belong with us in the labor movement. Going side by side, we will fight for bread *and* roses!

Unorganized: We are the unorganized—we who are exploited in such ruthless ways because we do not have the knowledge of how we might work together in unity to protect our common interests. We are simply tools of the bosses—for so long we have seen only ourselves that now we are blind and full of hate and ignorance. This is our tragedy—we have no strength—we are afraid of ourselves and distrust each other. What have you to say to us, the unorganized?

Girl: Your place is with us, in the labor movement. There you will get fresh courage ... there you will see a way.

Unemployed: We are the unemployed—do you hear the steady tramping of millions of us? Can you see millions of feet marching from agency to agency asking for work and being refused? Can you see these weary feet resting in the public squares and watching the seeds of agitation being sown in the fertile soil of discouraged hearts and minds? What a ghastly farce, the army of unemployed, increasing a thousand-fold while manufacturers close up their factories, oil up their machines, and let life rot in back alleys because these owners decide there is no more profit in human life.

We are hungry, yet there are hundreds of idle factories. What is the answer, what have you to say to us, the unemployed?

Organized: We are the organized workers. We are in the labor movement; for years we have banded together to fight for our share of what we have created and in our fight we have fought each other, black against white, Jew against Gentile, union against union, leader against leader, worker against worker. We distrust ourselves; we do not know our power. Our leaders, those of our own people who have worked side by side with us, have gone from us, have forgotten the grind of the mill. Why are these things? What have you to say to us, the organized workers?

Student: We are coming to you in the labor movement, coming with eyes of youth, strength of youth strong in the knowledge that only together will we rise, but we must know. We come to you to learn with you, to rise with you (and not above you). We come to ask, to explain!

Jean: Ask and explain. Learn now the simple truth.

Notes

This research was funded by a dissertation grant from the National Council on Employment Policy, Contract No. DD 34-80-009.

1. The organizational files of the Bryn Mawr Summer School for Women Workers are located at the following repositories: American Labor Education Service Papers, School of Industrial and Labor Relations, Cornell University, Ithaca, N.Y. (hereafter cited as ALES Papers–Cornell); the Bryn Mawr Summer School for Women Workers Papers, Institute of Management and Labor Relations, Rutgers University, New Brunswick, N.J.; American Labor Education Service Papers, Wisconsin State Historical Society, Madison, Wis. (hereafter cited as ALES Papers–Wisconsin). Partial collections are located among the M. Carey Thomas Papers, Bryn Mawr College, Bryn Mawr, Pa. (hereafter cited as the MCT Papers); the Eleanor Coit Papers and Mary Van Kleeck Papers, Sophia Smith Collection, Smith College, Northhampton,

Mass.; and the Hilda Worthington Smith Papers, Schlesinger Library, Cambridge, Mass. (hereafter cited as HWS Papers). Within three years of the demise of the Bryn Mawr Summer School for Women Workers, Florence Hemley Schneider's *Patterns of Workers' Education: The Story of the Bryn Mawr Summer School* (Washington, D.C.: American Council on Public Affairs, 1941), appeared. Schneider's work, based on her doctoral dissertation from the Bryn Mawr Carola Woerishoffer Graduate Department of Social Economy and Social Research, is largely an institutional history. She worked primarily from published materials on workers' education. Her evaluative chapter drew on her analysis of the short-term level of communal involvement undertaken by returning Bryn Mawr Summer School students in three cities: Rochester, Niagara Falls, and Pittsburgh. Schneider's work did not address itself to the long-term impact of attendance at the Bryn Mawr Summer School for Women Workers.

2. Hilda Worthington Smith, *Women Workers at the Bryn Mawr Summer School* (New York: Affiliated Schools for Women Workers in Industry, 1929), Appendix D, pp. 281–82.

3. Lee Katcher to Rita Heller, September 6, 1981. Lena Richman's widower, Hyman Zieph, was the source of the reminiscence.

4. Ibid.

5. William L. O'Neill coined the term "social feminism" in *Everyone Was Brave: A History of Feminism in America* (New York: Quadrangle, 1971). Social feminists submerged their interests as women in a multitude of philanthropic efforts. They were distinct from "ultra" feminists, who focused exclusively on a women's rights agenda. The term "social feminist" is now commonly accepted and used in contemporary feminist scholarship. The Bryn Mawr Summer School, in its promotion of women workers' interests, neatly fits the label. Some Summer School faculty have recently reacted negatively to the designation. They deny any hint of feminist militancy. They wished to change a society that discriminated against the poor and powerless of both sexes. Social sex segregation made *women* workers more accessible (telephone interview with Caroline Ware, November 29, 1982; telephone interview with Susan Shepherd Sweezy, November 30, 1982; telephone interview with Alice Hanson Cook, November 29, 1982). The faculty's antipathy to the term "social feminist" is more clearly understood in the context of the 1920s and 1930s.

Then, "feminist" carried a pejorative meaning akin to that of "suffragette." Activists in the Bryn Mawr Summer School mold were critical of American feminists—e.g., Alice Paul and her Women's Party. They believed it to be narrow, extreme, and even ill conceived and harmful to most women. Susan Ware has shown in her study of women New Dealers that, although they were active women partisans, they were repelled by the term "feminist." "Today we would call the women in that network feminists because of their crusading efforts on behalf of women, but the women in the network consciously shied away from that label." As Ware has aptly observed, "Women activists in the 20s and 30s were not the first or last group of women to be confused and ambiguous about their priorities" (Susan Ware, *Beyond Suffrage: Women in the New Deal* [Cambridge, Mass.: Harvard University Press, 1981], p. 16).

6. The two comprehensive monographs that focus on the social justice movement of the 1890–1930 period, and on women's important contributions to it, are Allen F. Davis, *Spearheads of Reform, the Social Settlements and the Progressive Movement, 1890–1914* (New York: Oxford University Press, 1967), and Clarke A. Chambers, *Seedtime of Reform: American Social Service, 1918–1933* (Minneapolis: University of Minnesota Press, 1963).

7. J. Stanley Lemons discusses social feminist accomplishment in *The Women Citizen: Social Feminism in the 1920s* (Urbana: University of Illinois Press, 1973), p. ix. He argues that social feminists were chief bearers of the progressive impulse in the Harding-Coolidge era.

8. See correspondence between Thomas and Smith, MCT Papers.

9. Earl C. Kaylor, Jr., "Hannah Whitall Pearsall Smith," in *Notable American Women*, ed. Edward T. James (Cambridge, Mass.: Harvard University Press, 1971), 3: 313–16.

10. J. F. C. Harrison, *Learning and Living, 1870–1960: A Study in the History of the English Adult Education Movement* (London: Routledge & Kegan Paul, 1961), p. 263.

11. Albert Mansbridge, quoted in Margaret T. Hodgen, *Workers Education in England and the United States* (London: Kegan Paul, Trench, Trubner & Co., 1925), p. 140.

12. Harrison, p. 269.

13. The Bryn Mawr Summer School's financial records reveal that consistent donors, in the $1,000 and above category, included John D. Rockefeller, Jr., and the Carnegie Corporation,

among others. Other substantial regular donations came from individual Bryn Mawr alumnae, as well as from Alumnae Clubs throughout the country and Bryn Mawr undergraduates. The records are more intermittent and obscure regarding union support. Extant, however, are some letters acknowledging donations from the Amalgamated Clothing Workers of America (ACWA), the International Ladies' Garment Workers' Union (ILGWU), the Brotherhood of Sleeping Car Porters, and the Electrical Workers Industrial Union, to name the most prominent unions ("Bryn Mawr Summer School Finances," ALES Papers–Cornell, Boxes 1, 6, 10, 11, and 44).

14. M. Carey Thomas, "1922 Address to the Bryn Mawr Summer School," quoted in Smith, *Women Workers* p. 4. This speech is the only extended discussion Thomas ever provided about the summer school.

15. As the school's implementation proceeded, Thomas used her weekly chapel talks to keep the college community informed of developments (M. Carey Thomas, "Chapel Talks," February–March, 1921, M. Carey Thomas Papers).

16. M. Carey Thomas, "Notes for the Commencement Address June 7, 1907," quoted in Roberta Frankfort, *Collegiate Women* (New York: New York University Press, 1977), p. 37. Frankfort charts Thomas's initial absorption with and later movement away from the scholarly ideal in "Martha Carey Thomas: The Scholarly Ideal and the Bryn Mawr Women," (pp. 26–40).

17. M. Carey Thomas's niece, Barnard president emeritus Millicent Carey McIntosh, brings the clarity of an eyewitness to the issue of noblesse oblige. Mrs. McIntosh was at Bryn Mawr during the period under scrutiny. She was a member of the class of 1920, a summer school tutor in 1922, and an English faculty member in 1926. She rejects "noblesse oblige"—connoting a self-conscious do-goodism—as Miss Thomas's motivation. Instead, Mrs. McIntosh presents Miss Thomas as a committed reformer applying the values of her Quaker upbringing to social problems. She writes, "[Miss Thomas's] record in starting the Carola Woerishoffer [Social Work] Department, in sponsoring an ultra-progressive [the Phoebe Anna Thorne] School with attendant courses in Educational Theory, suggest that she took unpopular steps out of conviction that Bryn Mawr must make its contribution to social justice. Even when I returned to Bryn Mawr in 1926

... there was faculty resistance to social science and education courses as diluting Bryn Mawr's classical, liberal arts curriculum. If anything, the Summer School would (and probably did) get Miss Thomas into trouble with some of her more affluent alumnae" (McIntosh to Heller, October 23, 1982; telephone interview with Millicent McIntosh, November 29, 1982).

18. See Mildred Fairchild Woodbury, "Susan Myra Kingsbury," in *Notable American Women*, 2: 235–36.

19. Interview with Hilda Worthington Smith, March, 1976.

20. Bryn Mawr College undergraduates actually had started the program but had operated it in a desultory fashion. It was Smith who made it viable. Smith credits Albert Mansbridge, pioneering leader of the British WEA, with providing inspiration. Mansbridge had been a guest lecturer at the college sometime during 1919 (see Hilda Worthington Smith, *Opening Vistas in Workers' Education: An Autobiography of Hilda Worthington Smith* (Washington, D.C.: By the Author, 1978), p. 106.

21. See Joyce L. Kornbluh and Lyn Goldfarb, "Labor Education and Women Workers: An Historical Perspective," in *Labor Education for Women Workers*, ed. Barbara M. Wertheimer (Philadelphia: Temple University Press, 1981), p. 19.

22. NWTUL women who endorsed the Bryn Mawr Summer School plan were Mable Gillespie, Frieda Miller, Agnes Nestor, Pauline Newman, Margaret Dreier Robins, and Rose Schneiderman.

23. Smith, "School Purpose," in *Women Workers at the Bryn Mawr Summer School*, Appendix H, p. 304.

24. Extant are application forms, alphabetically arranged and divided into categories of accepted and rejected students. A statistical analysis required selection of years for which both accepted and rejected sets were equally available. The choice of reasonable time spans was another consideration— 1924, 1929, and 1931 were selected. Every second accepted application was selected for the statistical analysis, giving an N of 155. For the rejected group, 14 were randomly chosen for each year, giving an N of 42. The fact that complete sets of data were missing for the years 1933 through 1938 precluded the possibility of analyzing the school's admissions policies for its entire duration ("Student Application Forms," ALES Papers–Wisconsin, Boxes 8–10, 27, and 55–57).

25. Since figures are unavailable, the degree of competitiveness in the admissions procedure is a matter of speculation. Based on my counts of the accepted and rejected forms, I estimate that in 1924, 105 of the 184 applicants were accepted (57 percent); in 1929, 98 of the 203 (48 percent); and in 1931, 91 of 116 (78 percent). These figures give an overall acceptance rate of 58 percent.

26. Leslie Woodcock Tentler, *Wage Earning Women: Industrial Work and Family Life in the United States, 1900–1930*. (New York: Oxford University Press, 1979), p. 59.

27. Ibid., p. 85.

28. Leo Wolman, *The Growth of American Trade Unions: 1880–1923* (New York: National Bureau of Economic Research, 1924), pp. 98, 106.

29. See U.S. Bureau of the Census, *Fifteenth Census of Population* (Washington, D.C.: U.S. Government Printing Office, 1930), pp. 6–11.

30. Ibid.

31. Smith, *Opening Vistas*, p. 160.

32. "1923 Publicity Brochure," HWS Papers, Box 12, Folder 221.

33. Bryn Mawr Summer School Curricula, ALES Papers–Wisconsin, Boxes 12–17.

34. Smith, *Women Workers*, pp. 62–65.

35. The School produced a voluminous archival record detailing its educational philosophy. Seemingly absent is an acknowledgment of John Dewey's influence. Two faculty members were highly conscious of the Deweyian impact and believe that the school deftly integrated theories of progressive, labor, and adult education (interview with Alice Hanson Cook, December 1980, and questionnaire response from Oliver S. Loud, 1982).

36. Amy Hewes, "Early Experiments in Workers' Education," *Adult Education* 6 (Summer 1956): 216.

37. "Unemployment Histories," ALES Papers–Cornell, Box 3.

38. "1924 Publicity Brochure," HWS Papers, Box 12, Folder 221.

39. Interview with Broadus Mitchell, January 1982.

40. Course Curricula of 1922, ALES Papers–Wisconsin, Box 2.

41. Course Curricula of 1934–1938, ALES Papers–Wisconsin, Box 22.

42. Smith, *Women Workers*, p. 7.

43. The intellectual freedom that students and faculty enjoyed was clear from questionnaires and interviews with former instructors: "In the general ferment of the 1930s . . . there was nothing unexpected or illegitimate about the interest and the engagement of teachers and students at Bryn Mawr with

the issues of the time—nothing alarming about representation of diverse radical 'sects' in the student group or faculty" (questionnaire response from Oliver Loud). This perception was substantiated in interviews with Esther Peterson, January 1977 and May 1981; Susan Shepherd Sweezy, July 1981; Colston Warne, September, 1976. The official archival record is less revealing. Euphemism and indirect wording are standard. Hilda W. Smith later described student activism of 1934: "[The unionized students] came into the School with very definite ideas of the kind of help they needed through an educational program. They were actually the younger leaders in the labor movement and had certain specific problems in mind on which they wished illumination.

Some of our critics at the College believe we should offer a cultural course, so called, making economics only incidental. The School believes that such a course would not attract the able, intellectual girls and that we should have only the more superficial students who would be interested in coming to the School. . . . We are not committed in our teaching to any one theory, social or political. We do attempt to give opportunity for a full discussion of all these theories, pointing out to the students the need for further study . . . to come to any understanding of these complicated questions" ("Statement by Miss Hilda Smith" [n.d.], Mary Van Kleeck Papers, Sophia Smith Collection).

44. Two-thirds (sixty-three) of the students at the summer school in 1934 were union members. More than half of these women were in three unions: the Amalgamated Clothing Workers, the Inter'l Ladies Garment Workers Union, and the American Federation of Full-fashioned Hosiery. Significantly, half of the women had joined their respective unions since June 1933—a response to Section 7A, National Recovery Administration (see "Meeting Minutes Bryn Mawr Board of Directors," October 21, 1934, HWS Papers, Box 12, File 223).

45. Interview with Colston Warne.

46. See *Philadelphia Record* (July 9, 1934), pp. 3–4; and *Philadelphia Inquirer* (July 10, 1934), pp. 1, 4.

47. Fifty-four, or 3 percent, of the Bryn Mawr Summer School's 1,610 students participated in the survey I conducted between 1977 and 1982. Statistical data and quotations are derived from the completed questionnaires.

48. Besides Carmen Lucia and Elizabeth Nord, other union activists are: Jane Ogden Arenz, Helen Carr Chamberlain, Carolyn Morreale Cancel-

mo, Janvier Gauthier, Freddy Drake Paine, Edith Berkowitz Parker, Bessie Weiss Rabinowitz, Ann Baden Sampler, Rose Marshall Sylvia, and Edith Kowski Wallstrom.

49. The former Bryn Mawr Summer School students in the oral history project are: Sara Barron, Amalgamated Clothing Workers of America (ACWA); Sara Fredgant, ACWA; Dolly Lowther Robinson, ACWA; Elizabeth Nord, Textile Workers Union of America; Carmen Lucia, United Cap, Hat and Millinery Workers Union; Bonnie Segal, International Ladies Garment Workers Union (ILGWU) *(The Twentieth Century Trade Union Woman Oral History Project,* Program on Women and Work, Institute of Labor and Industrial Relations, University of Michigan–Wayne State University, Ann Arbor, Michigan, 1978).

50. See Alice Kessler-Harris, "Rose Pesotta," in *Notable American Women: The Modern Period,* ed. Barbara Sicherman and Carol Hurd Green (Cambridge, Mass.: Harvard University Press, 1980), pp. 541–42.

51. These findings emerged from my questionnaire canvass. Additional information came from interviews: Marie Elliot Algor, August 1981; Alice Hanson Cook, December 1980; Katherine Pollak Ellickson, May 1977; Marguerite Gilmore, May 1977, and May 1981; Jean Flexner Lewinson, May 1977; Ida Craven Merriam, May 1977; Broadus Mitchell, January 1982; Esther Peterson, January 1977 and May 1981; Susan Shepherd Sweezy, July 1980; Caroline Ware, May 1977; Colston Warne, September 1976; and Constance Williams, November 1976.

52. See Thomas P. Roche, "Rosamund Tuve," in *Notable American Women: The Modern Period,* pp. 702–3.

53. See Alice Kessler-Harris, "Theresa Wolfson," ibid., pp. 742–44.

54. See Elizabeth Nelson, "Hazel Kyrk," ibid. 405–6.

55. See Ware, pp. 111–14.

56. Mary Kerewsky Friedman, class of 1923.

57. Mildred Olenio, class of 1930.

58. Ida Radosh, class of 1923.

59. Thelma Brown Haas, class of 1936.

60. Freddy Drake Paine, class of 1934.

61. Olive Heller, class of 1934.

62. Elizabeth Nord, classes 1923 and 1924.

63. Beatrice Owen, class of 1925.

64. Jean Flexner Lewinson, 1925 faculty.

65. C. A., 1928 faculty.

66. Susan Shepherd Sweezy, 1927 undergraduate assistant, 1933–1936 faculty.

67. Elizabeth Lyle Huberman, 1936 faculty.

68. See p. 112–13.

69. Mary Beard wrote to the Fact Finding Committee established to investigate the Seabrook Farms "eviction" that the situation confirmed her original opinion that the school was "an unnatural educational project—artificial from the women workers and artificial for the College sponsors" (Mary Beard to Fact Finding Committee, May 1935, Mary Van Kleeck Papers).

70. Bryn Mawr College alumnae numbered 2,500 in 1920.

71. Interview with Alice Hanson Cook.

72. The poems, essays and skit written by participants at the Bryn Mawr School for Women Workers are from the Hilda W. Smith Papers, Schlesinger Library, Cambridge, Mass., Box 13.

Chapter 5

Recognizing Regional Differences:
The Southern Summer School
for Women Workers

Mary Frederickson

Chapter 5

Although the 1880s have been designated as the "take-off" period for southern industry, the 1920s were the years when the region's cotton textile industry gained ascendency over its northern competitors and during which southern manufacturing continued a race for dominance in synthetic fibers, clothing, and shoes. The number of southerners in industrial work doubled between 1880 and 1890, and the movement of workers into manufacturing increased steadily for the next four decades. As in the Northeast fifty years earlier, no group felt the impact of industrialization more than the young women who left the region's farms to become operatives in southern mills and factories.

Despite the importance of working-class women in the development of industrial capitalism in the South, however, little attention has been paid to their history. This undocumented history includes the crucial role of women within the southern family economy and the determined and often militant efforts of southern women workers to improve their individual lives through collective action. Working women in the South sought support in these efforts from a variety of sources. At times they were sustained only by their own fortitude and the solidarity of their co-workers. In other cases, women workers joined trade unions, although organized labor often lacked the resources or motivation to assist them. As a result, numbers of working-class women fighting for autonomy and better working conditions joined forces with middle-class women's groups in order to change the character of the industrializing South.

The twin issues of industrial and racial reform had become central to southern middle-class reformers in the early years of the twentieth century. Efforts to mitigate the inequities in a racially segregated society paralleled work to channel the New South's industrial capacity toward creating a better society for all of the region's citizens. Southern women working in groups as divergent as the Methodist Women's Missionary Council and the Communist Party scrutinized southern society during the 1920s and 1930s and prescribed change. Within this broad spectrum of reform and revolution, the labor movement offered a consistent blend of activism and pragmatism. In the 1920s, however, the position of southern women within the labor movement was circumscribed. Middle-class women (with the exception of those in teachers' unions) had little or no contact with organized labor, while few southern working-class women were considered candidates for organization into craft-dominated unions. Therefore, working-class women looked outside the labor movement to find support for their efforts to organize, and middle-class women, concerned about industrial conditions, channeled their efforts into workers' education for women. Thus workers' education came to serve as a common ground for cross-class cooperation among southern women.

The single most important instrument for workers' education for women in the South was the Southern Summer School for Women Workers in Industry. Founded in 1927 by a group of women concerned about the human cost of industrialization, the school sought to build a network across the South which could both promote the organization of unions and fight for basic changes in the southern industrial system. For many years the Southern Summer School was directed by Louise Leonard McLaren, a native of Pennsylvania who came south in 1920 as YWCA National Industrial Secretary for the southern region. McLaren, together with Lois McDonald, the daughter of a South Carolina minister, provided the driving force behind the school.[1]

The origin of the Southern Summer School can be traced to the YWCA's work with women through its Industrial Department. In the nonunionized South the YWCA was an especially important organization for developing working-class leaders in dozens of southern communities. At the same time, through the YWCA middle-class women interacted with their working-class sisters in a way that both stimulated their reform impulse and provided practical experience on which to base an approach to solving the problems of southern industrial society.

The women working with the YWCA Industrial Department in the South, however, understood the limitations of an institution controlled and dominated by middle-class interests. Through their contact with the National Women's Trade Union League (NWTUL), the Bryn Mawr Summer School for Women Workers, and Brookwood Labor College, these women came to recognize the tactical importance of workers' education in a strategy of promoting union membership among southern workers. Taking these workers' education programs as their models, a coalition of working- and middle-class women created in the Southern Summer School an independent organization especially adapted to the needs of southern women workers.

In order to begin the process

of building such an institution, the school's founders reached out to individuals and organizations from across a broad political and economic spectrum that included women's groups, contingents of liberal southerners, and organized labor. This coalition secured funds, recruited a predominantly female faculty, and selected students through YWCA Industrial Departments and local trade unions. The school was an immediate success and generated a great deal of enthusiasm among organized women workers, unorganized workers in the YWCA, and southern middle-class reformers.

Students who came to the Southern Summer School were recruited by local "workers' education committees," which provided money for travel and tuition. All of the school's students were rank-and-file workers, and most were between eighteen and thirty-five years old. Between 1927 and 1934, the majority of the women who participated in the program were active in the YWCA Industrial Department; after 1934, most belonged to unions of textile, garment, or tobacco workers. Only white women attended the Southern Summer School. Although the school's leaders were concerned about the conditions of southern black workers and wanted to operate an integrated school, they bowed to the mores of a segregated society. The student body itself reflected the segregation within the southern industrial work force in the period prior to World War II, when few black women obtained manufacturing jobs.

At the Southern Summer School's six-week residence sessions (held at Sweet Briar College in Virginia in 1927 and afterward in schools and camps in western North Carolina) students received instruction in labor history, economics, and public speaking. As the school's faculty introduced southern women to the history of American workers, they sought both to increase the self-esteem of individual students and to encourage women to solve their problems collectively. The school was a place where southern women workers learned new ideas about the world and forged skills to use in the daily struggle of organizing and educating their fellow workers after returning home.

For the 300 women who attended the Southern Summer School's sessions between 1927 and the beginning of World War II, the opportunity to participate in an educational program designed specifically for them was a unique, exciting adventure. Motivations for attending were no doubt as numerous as the students, but thirst for education was a frequent theme. The organizers of the school realized the strength of this desire for learning and designed the school's program to channel this energy into the process of developing the leadership potential of the students. The curriculum in labor history and economics built on the experiences of the students, and the women were encouraged to express themselves and to develop communications skills by writing essays, poems, and plays. Above all, the school fostered among the workers a sense of self-worth as it prepared them for assuming leadership roles in the southern labor movement.

The women of the Southern Summer School created an atmosphere that encouraged students to expand their self-perceptions and to develop a sense of personal autonomy and group identity. In the first place, the school offered women a retreat from their social and familial obligations where they could talk to one another, reflect upon their lives, and obtain a fundamental sense of their own worth. Second, the school's faculty, young women who were themselves activists and dedicated to social change, became role models for their working-class students. Finally, the Southern Summer School offered women an ideological vision of a new social order in which a genuine democracy would be created. The social space to reflect and develop new ideas, nonpassive female mentors, and a new vision of the future provided students with the tools for forging the collective consciousness necessary for social change.[2]

The school's founders perceived the environment of the organization's summer sessions to be a key ingredient in creating the proper atmosphere for the education of women workers. The women who organized the Southern Summer School consciously sought to establish a cooperative community of middle-class and working-class women, teachers and students, in which all shared the work, studied together, and learned from one another. They wanted to create a true workers' school in which there would be no class lines and no formal academic hierarchy. To achieve this goal the faculty encouraged students to lead discussions, to ask questions, and to disagree openly with their teachers and with each other. When Louise Leonard McLaren wrote about the 1928 session, she emphasized faculty-student equality:

There was no line drawn between the faculty and the students such as is the rule in academic life; the simple fact that they all call each other by their first names is a kind of *symbol that the school is in a very real sense a cooperative undertaking in education in which the "faculty members" may learn as much as the "students."*³

Students were also cognizant of the special relationship between those who came to the school to learn and the faculty. As Polly Robkin, a student in 1934, recalled: "The school made a big impression on me. It was the first time I had ever been away from home, but that didn't bother me. The school was so informal—it was like everyone was on the same level—it seemed as if the teachers wanted to learn from us."⁴

In many ways, the school realized the goal of creating a community where women could come to share experiences and learn from each other. Most of the middle-class faculty members had several models to use as they worked to create a new organization that would bring middle-class and working-class women together. For example, Miriam Bonner, a faculty member who had taught at the North Carolina College for Women in Greensboro, described the atmosphere on that campus, saying, "There was a freedom about it . . . almost like a nunnery life in a way, and it was very comfortable and very pleasant." She depicted the Southern Summer School in a similar way, as a place where women could come together and talk with other women without pressure from bosses, husbands, or families. The Southern Summer School environment, to her, was "very friendly, very cooperative . . . just like one big happy family . . . a wonderful experience of freedom and security."⁵

In this supportive atmosphere, the Southern Summer School faculty encouraged students to speak about themselves, and teachers structured discussions that built on the individual experiences of working women. This was an important teaching method that prepared students to recognize their common history and to understand the need for communication and cooperation among women throughout the South. Furthermore, this teaching format helped southern working-class women realize the importance of organizing to protect their own interests. As an integral part of each teaching session, the faculty used the work histories of students as illustrations of specific historical developments within the southern region.⁶

While the Southern Summer School sought to foster the building of a collective identity among students, the faculty also wanted to give working-class students with limited formal education and few experiences beyond the restricted contexts of their home communities a larger, more universal orientation to history, economics, and the role of women in an industrializing society. To this end, background information was provided by courses in economics and labor history, and students developed communication skills in writing sessions and classes in public speaking. Thus, at the close of a summer term students who had initially concentrated on their own low wages, loss of a job, and individual employer were able to discuss across-the-board wage cuts and regional unemployment, as well as the implications of trade union organization and the advantages of industrial versus craft unions.[7]

Throughout its history, the Southern Summer School program was shaped by a board of advisers, faculty, and workers dedicated to expanding labor's political and economic role within southern society. As students from throughout the region came to the school they spoke about themselves, learned about each other, and reflected the influence of the five different instructors who, between 1927 and 1940, taught the core course in economics and coordinated the school's residence curriculum to give students a basic understanding of labor history and theory.[8]

In 1927, Broadus Mitchell of South Carolina, a young professor of economics at Johns Hopkins University, encouraged students, the overwhelming majority of whom were farmers' daughters, to discuss their individual role in southern industrial expansion. Lois MacDonald, a South Carolina native, former YWCA secretary, and member of the economics faculty at New York University, took over the economics course in 1928 and taught at the Southern Summer School for over a decade. MacDonald urged students to write about their role as women workers and to express their views on racial segregation within the southern region. In a labor economics course designed specifically for southern women workers, MacDonald focused attention on concerns of particular importance to southern workers and stressed the importance of improving conditions within southern industries. In 1937 the economics course was run by Caroline Ware, a Sarah Lawrence professor who had taught at the Bryn Mawr Summer School for Women Workers. Ware advised students to concentrate on learning union procedures and practices. In the late 1930s, under the direction of Leo

Huberman, author, organizer, and chairman of the Department of Social Science, New College, Columbia University, students wrote essays about the labor spy system, the Industrial Workers of the World (IWW), and the Gastonia strike of 1929. By 1940, the school came full circle in many ways when H. C. Nixon, a southern liberal scholar not unlike Broadus Mitchell, came to teach economics. Nixon, an academic political scientist and a Vanderbilt Agrarian, taught workers who had lived through the political and economic changes about which he had written.[9]

Parallel to the school's goal of educating workers in labor history and economics was its program to encourage self-expression and to foster self-esteem among the students. Communication skills were developed through basic writing and public speaking instruction. But beyond these practical lessons, the students were urged to express themselves in poetry, to write and produce plays, and to join in good-natured songfests. These activities opened new vistas to southern workers, whose educational backgrounds had been limited, and at the same time permitted an outlet never before available for long-dormant creative talents.

Learning traditional labor songs put students at the Southern Summer School in touch with a rich work culture from which southern workers often had been alienated. As they sang "Solidarity Forever," "The Internationale," and "I'm Labor," students at the school were stirred by words and music that had inspired generations of workers in other parts of the world. Students were also encouraged to incorporate the experiences of southern workers into new lyrics or traditional melodies. For example, to the tune of the gospel hymn "When First I Heard of Pentecost," workers wrote:

When first I heard of the CIO,
  I thought it must be right,
It seemed to suit the people,
  and be a great delight.[10]

Another original song written by a woman during the school's first session and adopted by classes that came later included these stanzas:

Southern girls awake, Southern
  girls arise
Better conditions make, get your
  share of the prize
Although there's work it's true,
  if we will dare and do
We'll get a decent living wage,
  and a little surplus too.

Chorus
Agitate, Educate, Organize
  today

*If we all together stay success
  will come our way
Agitate, Educate, Organize
  today
Oh, what fun when we get more
time to live and play.*[11]

The Southern Summer School's emphasis on student expression was part of a larger goal of illuminating and validating southern working-class culture. This ambition reflected, within the southern context, a national movement during the 1930s to define a "culture by and for the working class of America." Throughout the Depression era, reformers, intellectuals, and radicals alike sought, as Richard H. Pells has described, to "invest fiction and poetry with an almost missionary role in creating a new kind of society." Gradually concentration on novels and poems shifted to other art forms, one of the most important of which was drama.[12]

Over the years Southern Summer School students wrote and produced more than a dozen plays. Hollace Ransdell, who had worked at Brookwood Labor College, coordinated the majority of these productions. Ransdell asserted that the students had "a very dramatic sense" and on occasion even "ran away with the plot." Characterized by simple stories, colorful characters, and spontaneous dialogue, the plays focused on unemployment, the stretch-out, or bad working conditions and portrayed workers acting collectively to demand resolution of these problems.[13]

A pair of female characters generally had the leading roles in these plays. Traditionally one women portrayed a "good" person, while the other played a "bad" character. Moralistic plots, in which the good women always won, dominated scripts in which a union heroine played opposite a misguided nonunionist, a virtuous poor woman opposed a mean rich lady, or a well-educated but witless middle-class character lost out to an illiterate but clever working-class woman. Even the undesirable female characters, however, always demonstrated the potential to be enlightened and the capacity to understand a working-class woman's perspective.

Although female characters in Southern Summer School plays had the capacity for cooperating across class lines, male characters fell into three very separate categories. Working-class men, always good and kind, were sharp-tongued and headstrong. Capitalists were fat, well-dressed, cruel, calculating, intractable, and a bit ridiculous. Finally, the sheriff, a popular character to portray, represented capitalist law enforcers who were vile-talking and unsympathetic to the workers. Sheriffs were frequently the villains of these plays: workers who had turned against their own class. At times sheriffs could be subdued, either by force or by collective opposition to their reelection, but these men were always characterized as unscrupulous and potentially dangerous.[14]

Southern textile strikes provided students at the Southern Summer School with rich material to integrate into dramatic form, but one of the most powerful plays produced by the students focused on their everyday lives and working conditions. During the summer of 1928 students at the school performed a play entitled "Tobacco Shop," described by Louise Leonard McLaren as "an almost spontaneous production . . . [in which] what it meant to the girls to work in the hot, humid air of the tobacco factory was so well brought out by the characters that some of the spectators in the audience said later they almost began to feel the heat themselves."[15]

These plays were fun and exciting for the students, in part because they declared open season on bosses, law officers, scabs, and other banes of southern working-class existence. Yet there was more to the attractiveness of labor drama than mere entertainment to these young women. The plots distilled their work experience, the characters embodied their heroines, and the themes articulated their yearning for autonomy and control over their own lives. The plays cast women as strong, courageous individuals who were in the right and who had the ability to change people's minds and mobilize others for action. These qualities, aspired to by the students, were precisely those that the school's faculty sought to develop in order to provide the South with an indigenous labor leadership. Thus this women's theatre spoke effectively to both the needs of the students and the motives of the faculty of the school.

By the end of its first decade, the Southern Summer School had become well known within the southern labor movement, and 250 of the region's women workers had participated in the program. A thoughtfully designed curriculum, egalitarian relationships between the faculty and students, and a carefully selected student body all contributed to create a successful organization for southern women workers. As is true of any institution, however, the Southern Summer School had to adapt and, as McLaren wrote, "recognize the changing situation in the south." One of the most important turning points in the history of the school was opening the summer sessions to men. The transformation of what had been a tightly knit women's community into a coeducational workers' school involved substantial readjustments on the part of both women students and faculty.[16]

The first year men attended the school, the place where women students had openly voiced their opinions turned into a forum in which women had to defend their status as workers. In 1938, "a heated discussion" on the place of married women in industry "raged" for several days until, McLaren reported, "only statistics could convince differently those who argued that women's place is in the home." Moreover, while the CIO locals sending students to the Southern Summer School supported the theory of organizing workers regardless of skill, race, or sex, they selected more men than women as candidates for workers' education programs, and by 1940 over one-half of the school's students were male.[17]

Nevertheless, while admitting men meant the loss of the special camaraderie and supportive environment which Southern Summer School women had treasured, the move was a pragmatic one essential to perpetuate the school's influence in the southern labor movement and to ensure the continued advocacy within the movement of women and women's issues. Former students still looked to the school as both a vital part of their personal history and a conduit to increased participation in the labor movement. Female students coming to the school after 1938 also gained strength and inspiration from their contact with a workers' school dominated by women. For McLaren and the school's faculty and board members, the organization continued to be a place where they could come to renew their commitment to working for social change and to nurture the supportive relationships they had built over the years.

Throughout the Southern Summer School's history, the lives of the young women students graphically mirrored the basic social and economic changes occurring in the South in the 1920s and 1930s. The stories of Southern Summer School students recounted the hardships faced by those who worked the land, the movement of families into mill towns and urban centers, and the high price paid for economic survival. These women also told of ways in which they coped with their situations and "made do." Although each individual had a different history, the southern working-class women who came together at the Southern Summer School shared their experiences as workers, perceptions of their communities, and feelings about the hard times they had endured. Because of the Southern Summer School, these women left a written record. This written history, including student autobiographies and thematic essays, delineates the costs of industrialization as well as the benefits women workers gained in the changing social and economic structure of the South. The essays written by women at the school reveal the impact of these changes on personal lives and render understandable the political and social protests in which these women became involved.[18]

During the ten years from 1927 to 1937 when the Southern Summer School recruited only women workers, an average of twenty-five students attended the residence school each year. After 1937, when both women and men were admitted, approximately fifteen women attended each summer. All together, over 300 women came to the school. The women invited to participate in the six-week session were rank-and-file industrial workers recruited from a variety of industries across the South. The largest number of women were drawn from the North Carolina industrial piedmont, but women from Virginia, West Virginia, South Carolina, Georgia, Alabama, and Tennessee also attended. Occasionally a student from as far away as Texas would hear of the program through the YWCA or a local union, and in 1937 a group of women sharecroppers recruited by the Southern Tenant Farmer's Union (STFU) came to the school from Arkansas. The industries these women worked in varied as much as their native states. Workers came from textile mills, from tobacco industries, and from box factories and canneries. Some of the women had been domestic workers, and many, especially in the first few years, had done agricultural work. Although they were selected for their potential as rank-and-file leaders, the backgrounds and work histories of these women are representative of southern women workers generally; the industries and the working-class communities they represented were prototypes of the industrialized South.[19]

Because women came to the Southern Summer School from across the South and from a variety of communities and workplaces, the school's record allows a probing of work and family histories and the experiences of collective action among groups of women from agricultural and industrial backgrounds in rural areas, mill villages, and urban environments throughout the southern region. Moreover, comparisons can be made between two generations of southern women workers, for between 1927 and 1944 the school served two cohorts of women.[20]

The past, for most of the Southern Summer School women, revolved around the history of their family. Because they were young and only about 20 percent were married, they generally wrote and spoke of their family of origin. Almost one-half of the women who came to the school in the early years had been reared on farms. For their families, as for those of the rural women studied by Margaret Jarmon Hagood in the 1930s (*Mothers of the South* [1939]), while the concept of male dominance was accepted on one level, a rigid patriarchy did not exist. Young women had worked side by side with their mothers and fathers, performing numerous agricultural tasks, and their work experience reflected the diversity and flexibility required in agricultural labor. As one woman wrote:

The two oldest girls and I did the planting and plowing, pulling fodder and corn, picking cotton and chopping the winter's firewood from the woods. The smaller children did the hoeing and the weeding. With everyone in the field we often picked more than two bales of cotton a day

and hauled it to the store house.[21]

Because they had participated in all kinds of agricultural work, these women brought with them sex-role definitions which, when applied to a manufacturing setting, emerged as relatively egalitarian. Most of the young women at the school had not left the work force since they first entered it. They worked to support themselves and their families and viewed their domestic and public work as a dual responsibility. Because of low wages for men and the necessity of women's contribution to the family income, women in these families participated with their men in a joint economic partnership and continued an agricultural tradition of family work and shared wages far into the twentieth century.[22]

Many women who had grown up on farms had pleasant recollections about their agricultural backgrounds, which, although tempered with hard work, were relatively secure. A student in 1929 recalled that "we always had a place to sleep and at least one pair of shoes during the winter." One woman wrote that she was born in the Virginia countryside in "a little log cabin which is still a very dear spot to me." Another student remembered a home surrounded by oak trees and a happy childhood before she was old enough "to hoe corn and cotton, help tie and grade tobacco and after cotton opened, to pick cotton." This preadolescent child was hired out to work on other farms when there was not enough to do at home.[23]

Student writings chronicle the migration from farm to factory. In many cases this event was triggered by the death or ill health of a parent. From a young millworker in 1929 comes this testimony: "My father's health had been bad for several years. After he was not able to do farm work, we moved to the city. I was just 13. My sister who was two years older than I had to go to work in the mill to support the family."[24]

Moving into industrial communities, agricultural families readily translated a tradition of family participation for economic survival into the family wage economy:

Mother decided she would sell the farm for she was in debt and the farm was poor and small. She did not get much for it but did pay all she owed and had enough to go to the city where she could put my brother and me to work in factories. My brother got a job in a broom factory making $6.00 a week, I worked in a cotton mill and made between $4.50 and $7.00 a week. Mother washed, ironed and cleaned house for other people to keep the rest of the children in school.[25]

Even when each member had to go out to work, for many families a move into the industrial sector resulted in an improvement in living standards. Better housing and nearby schools were more frequently available than in the country, and while the paternalism of southern manufacturers varied from community to community, in many areas a company's philanthropy provided resources that had never been available to rural southerners.[26] A student from one mill community wrote: "We have a swimming pool, theatre, and two churches. We also have a grammar school. After a child has finished grammar school he can go to high school without paying tuition if he lives in the village. You can have insurance if you want it."[27]

Families working in manufacturing had more cash than had been available in the agricultural economy. As one woman put it, after going to work in the mill, she "got the taste of a dollar." Another student recalled being paid $1.01 on her first job: "I gave mother the dollar and kept the one cent. I was so glad to be able to give my mother money." A North Carolina woman remembered that soon after leaving her family's farm "marriage wasn't in my mind because I was having too good a time making money and being with people, and I was getting some things that I had never been used to having."[28]

But while industrial work provided some benefits, it also brought new problems. Many mill villages, especially in the 1920s and 1930s, were horrible places to live. Most reports of bad living conditions came from women living in cotton mill towns. One student described her community: "The houses we live in are not nice houses and they all need repairing. There is no water or bath in the houses. The mill village is very unsanitary as they have no sewer line for the waste water to pass out."[29]

However, unsanitary conditions and the difficulties poor housing presented for mill workers paled in significance compared to the loss of autonomy that characterized life in a mill village. For individuals who had been independent farmers, the fact that "employers seem to have sole authority over the people" made southern mill village existence a particularly demeaning lifestyle to accept. Students at the Southern Summer School described many different forms of employer control, but perhaps the most exceptional example came from a woman who lived in a mill village where "the lights are connected with the mill and are turned on at 5:00 in the evening and turned off at 10:30 at night. Again in the morning at 4:00 they are turned on and stay on until 7:00 in the morning."[30]

As these women and their families exchanged the hard life of southern agriculture for work in manufacturing, they became involved in an intricate set of trade-offs. The cost-benefit ratio varied greatly for different groups of workers, in specific places, and at particular times. On the one hand, agricultural families traded autonomy for cash wages, while on the other, they escaped rural poverty only to "eat up today what they work out tomorrow" at the company store. But if the resources promised to workers moving into southern industrial communities were often unavailable, nevertheless most manufacturing workers had a better chance than their rural relatives of obtaining housing with electricity and running water and at least a partial education for their children.[31]

Work dominated the lives of southerners hired as operatives in the region's factories and mills. For women entering industrial work in the 1920s and 1930s, the conditions under which they labored determined their tenure on the job and their response to speed-ups or stretch-outs. The working conditions in a particular factory or industry affected the short-term quality of women's daily lives (for up to twelve hours a day, six days a week) and their long-term health and well-being.[32]

Many women who took manufacturing jobs after growing up on farms considered industrial work less demanding than farm labor, although several years in a mill or factory usually altered that perspective. "At first I thought work in the mill a great experience," a student wrote in 1929, "but I soon grew tired of working in such a place and would often long to be out in the open again." After five years in the mill, one woman described "the dreadful monotony of reeling" as the worst part of the work. "The same old grind day in, day out. It does things to you," she wrote in her autobiography.[33]

The invariability of the work was one of many conditions women at the school considered when they described the factories where they held jobs. Industrial plants with hospitals and free medical services for employees were depicted, as were factories lacking ventilation, restroom facilities, or adequate seating. Conditions in garment factories were uniformly better than those in cotton mills. A Nashville garment worker described her unionized factory, complete with dressing room and a dining room that served hot meals, as "nice, clean and light." A fellow student employed in cotton textiles wrote that her work was "very tiresome" because she had to "stand up all the time." Furthermore, the cotton mill employee earned one-half the average wages a garment worker received.[34]

Heat, cold, poor lighting, and inadequate ventilation made tedious and boring factory jobs harder to bear. Yet other physical aspects of industrial work were even more noxious. One woman argued that in the rayon factory where she worked there was "something in the air that makes the girls faint." She had "known as many as twenty-seven to faint in one day." Women complained about dust so thick you "had to hold your breath" and dangerous chemicals in synthetic fiber plants where, one woman reported, "I have known several [employees] to lose their eyes . . . and two I know of lost their lives." While the immediate effects of dust and fumes were only too apparent, workers could only imagine the then-undiscovered threat of byssinosis or the still-unknown long-term damage done by chemicals.[35]

Early in 1929, conditions for southern textile workers worsened as employers began stretch-outs and speed-ups to increase production. While work in textiles had always been physically demanding and tedious, the pace in many mills had been tolerable. Many workers who lived near the mills went home for a midday lunch, and, as a North Carolina woman explained, "We didn't rush; we'd just stand around and talk. We just sort of kept our work going, you know, the machinery running." But with the stretch-out, she maintained, "they began wanting more work out of us. They'd put more work on you for the same pay. More work [and] they didn't know when to quit."[36]

When a South Carolina woman came to the school in 1929, she wrote an essay entitled "A Strike Against the Stretch-Out," which began:

For the benefit of those who may not know what the stretch-out is I will explain. In the weaving department of a cotton mill we had been running around the average of twenty-four looms. After the stretch-out system was introduced we were put on from eighty to one hundred looms and were given boys and girls to fill our batteries.[37]

After having worked six months under the new system, another North Carolina student wrote, "Everyone in the mill is completely worn out at stopping time. They go home unable to enjoy supper or anything else. . . . [S]ome of them '[are] just dragging along half dead and overworked until they don't know what it is to take a rest and feel good."[38]

With the stretch-out came new organizing efforts, as workers "rebelled against doing more work for lower wages." A Southern Summer School student who had gone out on strike in Danville, Virginia, in 1930 explained, "We started an organization because we made very low wages and worked long hours. We wanted to organize to try and get shorter hours and more money for our work."[39] Unions, primarily the United Textile Workers Union (AFL), gained some ground in the South in 1929–1930. Locals were established at Elizabethton, Tennessee and Marion, North Carolina after the workers walked out; and even in South Carolina, where the stretch-out system had resulted in so-called leaderless strikes, workers organized local unions. A South Carolina student at the school in 1929 wrote, "We had borne this abuse, for it was nothing short of that, for quite awhile. But please don't think we were 'contented cows' for we were far from being anything like contented."[40]

The willingness of these women to join unions in the late 1920s confirmed the school's prediction that southern workers, especially textile operatives, would form the next large group of American workers to organize. The women who came to the school in 1929, almost one-half of whom belonged to unions, held a basic commitment to collective action. For these women unions had made "life a little more worth living" and had brought "a happiness to people that they never had experienced before." The response of Southern Summer School students during the 1929 session provided an important impetus for expanding the program and enlarging the school's institutional base. The fact that so many southern women became involved in protests, walkouts, or clearly defined strikes during this period convinced the school's students that as a group they had an important role to play in ongoing effects to organize workers across the South.[41]

Throughout the school's history the percentage of students belonging to unions correlated directly with the rise and fall of union membership within the South. In 1927, when organized labor in southern states offered little to workers outside the crafts and building trades, only 25 percent of the workers who came to the school belonged to unions. During 1929 and 1930, as labor revolts in the South made national news, student membership in newly organized unions in hosiery, textiles, rayon, and other trades increased to 45 percent. By 1933, as gains made by the unions evaporated in the wake of severe economic depression, only 9 percent of the students at the school belonged to unions. Then, with the stimulus of New Deal legislation, labor organization increased throughout the South, and by 1934, 38 percent of the working-class women at the school were members of newly organized unions.[42]

The succeeding years, 1935 and 1936, brought new organizing activity, especially among the hosiery and garment trades, as northern unions continued to respond to the threat of competition from unorganized southern workers. Most important, the formation of the Congress of Industrial Organizations (CIO) in 1936, and especially the Textile Workers' Organizing Committee (TWOC) in 1937, increased organizing efforts among southern textile workers (in 1938 the TWOC claimed 25,000 southern members). At the same time, organization among southern garment workers escalated as the Amalgamated Clothing Workers of America (ACWA) launched drives to organize southern workers and stabilize the industry. During these years 80 percent of the school's students were union members. In the Southern Summer School's last years as a residence school, almost all of the women who attended came to the school as their unions' representatives.[43]

Because students came to the Southern Summer School throughout the transitional years of southern industrial development, preliminary contrasts can be made between two cohorts of southern women workers. The histories of these two groups of women reflect both changes and continuities in women's lives during a period of rapid social and economic accommodation.[44]

Among the first group of students, who came to the school between 1927 and 1934, about half had personally made the transition from farm to factory and had suffered through the worst years of the Depression as young adults. As we have seen, these women successfully adapted agricultural work patterns to an industrial setting. Moreover, in contradiction of the axiom of male superiority, the men and women in these families, subject to the demands of a family economy, practiced a relatively equal division of labor between the sexes. In the industrial family economy young women entered manufacturing and worked until they grew old; older women worked at home, often caring for their grandchildren. Husbands and wives frequently worked different shifts so that one parent could stay with the children. Nevertheless, women generally had primary responsibility for children and juggled schedules—their own, their husbands', and those of their female relatives—to provide continuous child care. As a North Carolina woman whose working life spanned the years between 1925 and 1950 explained:

I went back to work when my youngest girl was nine months old; my mother-in-law took care of her. But I worked on the third shift ten years; he worked on first shift. That way I could put the children to bed before I went to work at night; and then when I came home in the morning those that went to school, I stayed up and put them to school. And my sister stayed with me, and she worked on second shift. Managed that way, you know.[45]

These women, attuned from an early stage to working outside the home, organized their lives and their families around that necessity.

The second cohort of Southern Summer School students came after 1934. These women had come to maturity during the early years of the New Deal and had moved into industrial jobs at a time when a minimum wage, limited working hours, and the right to bargain collectively were becoming realities. After 1935 the majority of the women who came to the school had been reared in industrial communities rather than in agricultural areas. Like the women who came earlier, this second cohort viewed sexual divisions with a pragmatic eye. Men gardened and women canned, sharing tasks that in agricultural areas had been defined as women's work. Brothers worked in one factory for $6.00 a week, while sisters made from $4.50 to $7.00 a week on piecework in a mill on the other side of town. For both groups, the realities of women's lives belied the prevailing southern sex-role ideology that assumed that women did not work.[46]

Gradually, during the years between 1935 and 1940, with mandatory schooling and increased government regulation of hours and pay, family earnings gave way to higher wages for adult workers. Pay differentials by sex became more pronounced, and questions regarding women's place in the southern workforce became more common. During this period, some of the women who had attended the Southern Summer School before 1935, now older and married, but still in industrial jobs, came back to the school and found themselves warning younger students (after 1938, both male and female students) against the rhetorical argument that married women did not belong in industry. They maintained that few southern working-class women in the 1930s had stopped working outside the home when they married and contended that all women shared the responsibility for improving working conditions. Therefore, while changes were evident among the school's students in the transitional period between 1927 and World War II, women who had attended the Southern Summer School provided a sense of continuity for younger female students as they joined a growing network of southern women workers.[47]

The women who came to the school clearly viewed themselves as workers. Few of the students had ever voluntarily left the work force since they first entered it. They had left their jobs only when laid off or when fired for union participation or strike activity. This was true for the first cohort, women who entered industrial work between the ages of eight and seventeen, and for the second group of women, many of whom finished high school before beginning full-time work. Both groups of women worked to support themselves and to provide for their families. They referred to themselves as part of a "working class," to their neighbors and relatives as "working people." When asked to describe their communities, the women at the school demonstrated a keen class consciousness. A student in 1929 wrote that she did not like to live in a mill village because "the people are looked down upon as lower class." Class divisions, so obvious in isolated mill communities, were no less obtrusive in urban areas. A woman from Georgia wrote in 1932 that while Macon was a "good sized town and had people of all classes in it, the most exclusive section of the city is only a few blocks from the poorest section, which is the Atlantic Mill Village."[48]

Just as the women of the school had a well-developed sense of their class status, they also reflected a clear perception of their role as women workers. A young garment worker from Tennessee wrote in 1927:

Among the working class, women have always helped to make the living. Women at the present time are employed in almost all kinds of work. Women are gaining for themselves a place in the industrial world, but should be careful to keep a high standard and not remain content to be cheap labor.

This woman was active in the labor movement after she left the school, until her death in the late 1960s. In this early essay she established her recognition of class division in southern society, the prevalence of the family wage, and the importance of women's work in the expanding industrial sector. Her words reflect a consciousness of sex discrimination and an awareness of social and economic change.[49]

The Southern Summer School program encouraged students to recognize their importance both as women and as workers. Therefore, it is difficult to discern precisely how much student themes reflect the school's influence. Yet an overt working-class feminism emerges from the writings of the women who attended the Southern Summer School. Nascent in the minds of the students, this viewpoint was positively reinforced and further developed at the school. Thus, the feminism displayed in student essays represented an amalgam of old beliefs and new ideas, a synthesis of working-class pragmatism regarding sex roles and the intellectually rationalized belief in sex equality of the postsuffrage decades.[50]

For most working-class students, participation in the Southern Summer School marked a watershed in their experience, as it provided a first exposure to the world beyond the mill village or city factory. Forty years after her summer at the school, a Virginia woman claimed that the group was "responsible for whatever sense I have today." A North Carolina woman wrote in 1929 that the six weeks she spent at the Southern Summer School was "the first time ever in life that I could call my time my own." A striker from Marion, North Carolina, argued that the school "enlightened us . . . and put a fighting spirit in you," and a worker from Tennessee reflected that at the Southern Summer School she "caught on to a whole lot of things that I'd never dreamed about before."[51] The school encouraged students to discover their collective history as southern women workers and gave them the hope and inspiration to plan together for a shared future.

When students left the school, however, many returned to communities with few sources of support for their expanded social consciousness, augmented organizing skills, and goals for building a labor network among southern working-class women. The two groups that women most frequently represented at the school, the YWCA and local unions, did not always respond positively to the Southern Summer School program. The school's commitment to trade unions aggravated existing tensions within local YWCAs between the industrial women who were dedicated unionists and general board members with ties to manufacturers. For example, in Winston-Salem in 1929 the president of the YWCA ordered the industrial secretary not to meet with Louise Leonard McLaren because it had been decided that the "Southern Summer School had lined itself up with union workers and was therefore not to be trusted."[52]

Many of the students knew first hand the problems faced by women in trade unions before they came to the school, and they continued to argue for the full integration of women at all levels of union activity. A student from Birmingham stressed in 1935 that it was still necessary "to convince the men of women's ability and sincerity in unions." She argued that the survival of any union depended on the support of working women, who often dominated a factory work force and provided critical backing on picket lines and at relief stations during strikes. But she explained that women often could not play an active role in unions because of the double burden of working in the mill and at home. Nevertheless, locals across the region increasingly looked to the school as an institution equipped to train new union members. At least ten Southern Summer School students became CIO organizers after 1935 and further augmented the school's involvement in the southern labor movement.[53]

For some women, however, it proved difficult to sustain the reality of worker protests in local southern communities. To participate continuously in collective resistance, often without the support of a strong union, became an unattainable goal for many women who left the school with a deepened commitment to the southern labor movement. The tension that women workers felt between individual survival and collective gain is poignantly depicted in an exchange of letters between one of the Marion strikers and Louise Leonard during the fall of 1929. Leonard wrote to this former Southern Summer School student in October, after the second strike in Marion, in which six workers had been killed: "This morning I have a letter telling me that you have been scabbing in the mill since the murders and of course I am shocked to hear it. I hope there is some mistake about this and that you will write me and tell me how it happened." The student, a twenty-year-old cotton mill worker, replied:

Louise, I am sorry you heard that I was scabbing. I will tell you how it was and you be the judge. They had a strike on Tuesday and we didn't know anything about it until it was pulled and our boys got killed at the gate and then I quit work. . . . Our leaders never had any meetings to tell us what to do so nearly all the union people went back. I haven't worked but two days and they asked me not to go back and now I am back home and . . . have got no job no money no anything and my man is gone and I can't find out where he is whether dead or alive and I am in debt that it looks like I am going to have to do some scabbing so you can imagine what kind of shape I am in. I have got a little girl that has got to be clothed and fed . . . so now you have the truth from my heart what would you do if you was in my place.[54]

Despite the difficulties that many students faced once they returned home, the Southern Summer School provided the women who attended with a strong affirmation of their personal power and individual self-worth. Moreover, the school encouraged students to channel the strength that came from discovering their common history and culture as southern working-class women into new forms of political action. The school stimulated women to take public positions on collective bargaining, union power, women's rights, integration, and workers' education. For many women this type of encouragement was unique. As one North Carolina student recalled: "It was a great inspiration to me to feel like women were considered capable of participating."[55] At the Southern Summer School women could listen and learn, be exposed to new ideas and new world views. It was a place where southern working-class women, often for the first time, could speak their own minds.

In the spring and summer of 1929, workers in textile mills across the southern United States went out on strike to protest decreasing wages and increasing hours. These essays, written by students at the Southern Summer School for Women Workers in Industry during the summer of 1929, describe conditions in several southern mill communities and outline the factors which precipitated the walkouts.[56]

The Marion Manufacturing Company

The hours that the employees work at this mill are ten, eleven and twelve hours and twenty minutes. The day weavers and those that work in the cloth room get one hour off for lunch. The other departments get something less than an hour.

The condition in the mill is very bad. The floors are not kept as clean as they should be. Men and women use tobacco and spit on the floor. The toilets are not kept clean. They are not fit for a human to use. They sometimes overflow. These toilets are cleaned only in the day time. The weave room is very hot and has bad lights, has bad ventilation, and is very noisy. The other departments do not have good ventilation. There are but few seats provided for the workers and no washroom at all.

All these conditions could be made better if the company could be forced to look after this like it ought to be or if the owners of the mill thought enough of their help to have these conditions made better.

The company just recently built a YMCA. This is the only place in the Mill Village for amusement. In the YMCA is a swimming pool, ten pin alley, library, sewing and cooking department, shower bath department, and a basket-ball court. The people of the village pay ten cents for a shower bath, ten cents for bathing in the pool, and ten cents for a game of ten pins.

The employees of the mill walked out on a strike on the 11th of July, for shorter hours and for the same pay they were already getting for longer hours. This is the 9th day of August and we are still on strike. Do you blame us for striking?

—Unsigned, 1929

A Strike against the Stretch-Out

In the spring of 1929, the workers in the Monarch and Ottoray Mills of Union, South Carolina rebelled against the stretch-out system.

For the benefit of those who may not know what the stretch-out system is I will explain. In the weaving department of a cotton mill we had been running around the average of twenty-four looms. After the stretch-out system was introduced, we were put on from eighty to one hundred looms and were given boys and girls to fill our batteries.

We had borne this abuse for it was nothing short of that, for quite awhile. But please don't think we were "contented cows" for we were far from being anything like contented.

I will not take you back to the day of our rebellion. We came out of our mills on the day formerly mentioned and six weeks and two days hence found us back at work with a very small victory. Our work was only reduced to sixty-nine from seventy-two looms.

I will tell you a little of our hardships during our strike for we did not have a union at that time although we have one now that is growing in number and enthusiasm. We organized a relief committee which traveled over different parts of South Carolina and collected money and food for the most destitute of us that we might hold onto our cause. Wherever our committee went they always met people who knew about us and what a fight we were making and everyone was glad to help.

—Unsigned, 1929

The following essay comes from the collection of autobiographies written by Southern Summer School students in 1930.[57]

My Struggle to Escape the Cotton Mill

After mother and father were married, they lived on a homestead in Alabama. The house was built out of logs with one large room. The cooking was done in iron pots. Some little distance from the yard to the north was built the crib, in which to keep feed of different kinds. Here were horse and corn stalls, for then we kept a cow and father had to keep a horse to plow his little farm and to pull the buggy for it was miles to where anyone lived and too far to walk.

I've heard my father say after he had made a crop and there was no work to do on the farm he would walk two miles night and morning to work for as low as fifty cents per day to make enough to buy the things we had to have that he could not raise on the farm. In this way he worked some on the railroad and learned how to build railroad track and later became a section foreman. Father made good crops and I can remember the little barn filled to overflowing with corn, while the hayloft would be full of peanuts and hay and several nice hogs could be found in a pen nearby getting ready to be butchered for the winter's supply of meat and lard.

"Hard times" forced my father to rent this little house and move elsewhere to run a farm for someone who had capital to farm on a large scale. This was the beginning of the end, for we moved from place to place until the home was finally sold. Then I was old enough to start to school; but we lived too far from a school and I was too small to go alone, so all the schooling I had up until I was eight years old was a few months when my aunt taught me. All this time the family was growing larger, there being six children. The 1907 panic hit the country. We moved to a town in Alabama, to the cotton mills, and my father, my sister, and I went to work. I wasn't quite fifteen years old. In a short time another brother was born.

On going to work my sister and I were sent to the spinning room to learn to spin. My sister made better progress than I, but the bosses being harsh and I being timid I was half-scared to death all the time and could not learn the work. This kept up about three months. My father was making a dollar per day and my sister and I making fifty cents each per day. Then it was decided we had served our apprenticeship and should go on as "sides." I was given two sides of spinning and was paid eleven cents per side, making my daily pay twenty two cents, and was living in terror all the time in fear of the boss. When Father found I would no longer get fifty cents per day he told me to stay home. In the meantime my sister had been taken to the weave shop to fill "batteries," making seventy cents per day. After some red tape I was allowed to go to work in the weave shop and for nearly two years my sister and I worked for seventy cents per day. It took very little skill to keep this job going and there being no harsh bosses over me I was fairly happy here until Father began to insist that Sister and I become weavers. I hated the cotton mill and swore I would not stay in it all my life. My sister did not mind so much, tried, and became a good weaver.

After quite a struggle on my part to keep from learning to be a weaver, I gave it a thorough trial and found I could not learn weaving very easily, and being anxious to earn more money I began to think of how I could find better-paying work. Then I was allowed to go to the spooler and warper rooms where I worked at different times in both rooms making $1.25 per day and finally getting $9 per week.

The long hours and nervous state in which I worked had caused me to have much less strength than I would have had otherwise, and it was all I could do to keep the work up with the other worker who was required on the job and a boy to roll the bores for us. Then one day we were told that the boy could not help us anymore and I quit. My father had left the mill by this time because he had been too ready to talk to anyone he saw about conditions in the mill. With no one working in the mill but me, the company notified us to move and when I quit we were not living on company property.

The same day I quit the cotton mill I went to an overall factory to get work and succeeded. While talking with the owner of the business he told me that some of his employees made $10 per week and I thought if there was even a remote chance of me making that much money it was a wonderful opportunity for me so I went to work the next day. I worked four days that week and made $2.40 on piece work. I had worked eleven hours in the mill but here I worked nine hours and conditions were so different. A very nice, kind, patient young woman was my instructor and the superintendent was never harsh spoken. This was a union factory and I advanced so well that in a short time I was making as much as I had made after years of working in the cotton mill. However, the things that cotton mill life did to me have just now, after many years, begun to leave me.

—J. W., 1930

This excerpt from a Southern Summer School autobiography was written in 1938. The strike at the Loray Mill in Gastonia, North Carolina, was the largest and most famous of the series of walkouts in textile mills across the Carolinas and Tennessee in 1929.[58]

I Was in the Gastonia Strike

I had been working for the Manville-Jenkes mill in Loray, near Gastonia, for eight years—ever since I was fourteen. We worked thirteen hours a day, and we were so stretched out that lots of times we didn't stop for anything. Sometimes we took sandwiches to work, and ate them as we worked. Sometimes we didn't even get to eat them. If we didn't keep our work up like they wanted us to, they would curse us and threaten to fire us. Some of us made $12 a week, and some a little more.

One day some textile organizers came to Gastonia. They came to the mill gates at six o'clock, just when the daylight hands were coming out. They began to talk to the workers as they came out of the mill. Everybody stopped to listen. When the night-shift hands came up, they stopped to listen too. I was on the night shift. None of us even went into work that night, for the organizers were telling us that they would help us get more money and less hours if we would stick together in a union, and stay out.

This was the first time I'd ever thought that things could be better; I thought that I would just keep working all my life for thirteen hours a day, like we were. I felt that if we would stick together and strike we could win something for ourselves. But I guess we didn't have a chance—the way "the law" acted after we struck.

That night we had a meeting, and almost all the workers came. People got up and said that unless they got shorter hours and more money they would never go back to work. We all went home that night feeling that at last we were going to do something that would make things better for us workers. We were going to win an eight-hour day, and get more pay for ourselves.

The next morning, we were all at the mill at five o'clock to picket, but we couldn't get anywhere near the plant because the police and the National Guard were all around the mill and kept us a block away. We formed our picket line anyway, and walked up and down a street near the mill.

Every day for a week we picketed. One day, my husband, Red, went with me on the picket line. (He worked for another mill on the night shift.) Just as we started on the picket line two policemen came over and grabbed Red, put him in an automobile, and took him to jail. They beat him up with a blackjack, and broke his ring and tore his clothes. They thought he was one of the strikers, and they were arresting strikers right and left, hauling lots of them to jail every day.

In the second week of the strike, the bosses went to other towns and out in the country and brought in scabs. The police and the National Guard made us keep away from the mill, so all we could do was watch the scabs go in and take our jobs.

We kept on with our picket line, though we didn't have much of a chance to persuade the scabs not to go in, because of the police and the guards. We were treated like dogs by the law. Strikers were knocked down when they called to the scabs, or got too near the mill. Every day more and more strikers were arrested. They kept the jail-house full of workers. Strikers were put out of their houses. All over our village you could see whole families with their household belongings in the street—sometimes in the pouring down rain, and lots of them with their little children and babies.

We had a relief station where strikers could get food and groceries. Red, my husband, had been fired from his job in the other mill when his boss found out that he was trying to help us strikers, so he opened a drink stand near the relief station. One night about nine o'clock, the police came to the relief station as they usually went anywhere there were any strikers. I don't know what happened exactly, but there was a gun fight, and the chief of police was killed. Red, who was selling drinks there, was arrested along with a lot of others. Red and six others were accused of killing the policeman.

After Red was put in jail for the murder, my father and I moved to another town. I was expecting my baby soon, but I went to work in another textile mill. Except for what I read in the papers, I didn't know much about what was going on in Gastonia.

Seven months after the strike they tried Red and the six others accused of killing the chief of police. They had been kept in jail all this time. I couldn't attend much of the trial on account of the baby, but Red told me about it.

Almost everybody thinks that the workers were innocent, and many people believe that the chief was killed by one of his own policemen. However, Red and the others were convicted of murder, and given anywhere from five to twenty years in the penitentiary. Red and the others got out on bail, and all of them left the country and stayed away for two years. Then Red came back to get me and the baby and he was caught, and sent to prison. He served three years and four months of his prison term, and got out last year.

After the trial, I moved to High Point, and got a job in a textile mill to support the baby and me. We have had a hard time of it, but I think what we went through in Gastonia was worth it all because I think people all over the country learned about conditions of textile workers in the South, and it helped the labor movement in the South.

—Bertha Hendrix, 1938

Southern Summer School students based this play on an incident described in labor leader Mother Jones's autobiography. It was presented at the School in August 1933, and was recorded by faculty member Hollace Ransdell.[59]

Mother Jones' Tin Pan Army
The Women Mop Up Coal-Dale

Comic Sketch in One Act

Scene: The action takes place on a mountain road leading to the mines of the Valley Coal Company in West Virginia during the big coal strike of 1912.

Cast: Sheriff
      Deputy Sheriff
      Mother Jones
      Scab
      Mother of the Scab
      Union Official
      Women in Mother Jones' Army

When the curtain rises the sheriff is walking up and down with a gun over his shoulder looking anxiously down the road. The Deputy sits propped up against a tree, his gun beside him.

Deputy: Do you see 'em coming?

Sheriff: (Nervously) No. Oh Lord! I don't like this job!

Deputy: What's the matter? You ain't scared of a bunch of silly women are you?

Sheriff: You don't know what you're talkin' about. You ain't never faced Mother Jones and that army of wild cats of hers yet. She's a terrible woman. And that bunch of women obeys her like she had a magic spell over 'em!

Deputy: A withered up old woman like her! Why she is past eighty! What can she do? Them miners must be a weak lot to be led away by the dried up old prune.

Sheriff: You ain't never seen her or you wouldn't talk like that. There is something about that old woman. . . . I don't know what it is . . . but there is something about her that gets you. Didn't you hear about the rumpus she kicked up over the next valley last week?

Deputy: I heard she was raisin' hell over there with that army of wild women she's got, yellin' around like cats. Why didn't you smack 'em and send 'em home to their dishwashin' where they belong. That's what I would have done.

Sheriff: Yes you would! You'll have a chance pretty soon to try out some of your talk. I'll bet you shinny up a tree the first word she throws at you.

Deputy: Why don't you arrest her when she comes? Lock her up! That'll shut her mouth, I bet.

Sheriff: Arrest her! My gosh, man. I'd have that mob of women after me with their mops and brooms. The jail ain't big enough to hold 'em. They'd mop the life out of a feller before we got 'em there anyway.

Deputy: (Getting up) Listen! I believe the tin-pan army is approaching. Hear 'em?

Sheriff: Oh Lord! Yes, that's Mother Jones and her Mop Brigade all right. I wish I was out of here. I don't like this job. (Sounds of tin pan army are heard, gradually getting louder). (Sheriff edges away. Both look down the path, until Mother Jones appears leading a crowd of women with mops, brooms, etc. beating on pans with spoons. They shout to the tune of their beating:)

Women: Join the Union! Join the Union! Join the Union!

Sheriff: (Unconvincingly) Halt! Stop! Go back!

Mother Jones: Sheriff, the workers of America will not halt. And they will not go back. The workers are going forward!

Sheriff: (Weakly) I'll charge bayonets.

Mother J.: On whom?

Sheriff: On you fool women if you don't get back.

Mother: Bah, man! What nonsense are you talking? We're not enemies. We are just a band of working women whose husbands and sons and brothers are in a battle for bread. We want our brothers in Coaldale to join us in our fight. We are here on this road for the right to eat and work and live. And in the name of that right we demand that you let us pass. We're not going to hurt anybody now, if you'll behave yourselves.

Deputy: You're not going to hurt anybody. (Laughs) That's a good joke. (Shakes his bayoneted gun.) What do you think we're carrying these little things for? To pick our teeth with?

Mother: (Sternly) Put that little old thing away. (She shakes her mop at his nose.) Women, where is this man's wife? Go get her and tell her she'd better come and take this yelping yaller cur of hers home and clean him up, or we'll take a hand at it ourselves. (She advances on him threateningly.) Get back there. Get! Take that little old knife of yours home and use it to a better purpose than threatening hard-working women. Go mow down some of those whiskers on your face with it instead of threatnin' honest women who're fightin' for the right to get bread for their children. (She pulls his whiskers and pushes him back out of her way.)

Deputy: Hey, hold on there! That ain't no way to treat the law. I'll have you arrested for this. We got one of your fine union men in jail now. A common thief he is. Stole a pair of shoes.

Mother: If he'd only stolen a railroad you'd have elected him senator.

Sheriff: I ain't got nothing against you, Mother Jones, but I can't let you and them women of yours pass here, so you might as well turn around and go back. You ain't going a step further.

Mother: Who's going to stop us?

Sheriff: I and my deputy here . . . and this. (Thrusts out his gun.)

Mother: (Laughs scornfully) Do you think we're afraid of the likes of you? You'd better go ask that scabby old judge to give you another injunction to help—that old guy who plays golf while the miners starve, I mean. While we're serving humanity, he serves injunctions for the bosses. You'll find him in that swell country club where he plays around. Tell him the only club he allows the workers to have is the policeman's club—over the head. (A scab appears, stops when he sees the women, and takes refuge behind the sheriff.)

First Woman: Mother Jones, look! There's that Perkins scab slinkin' back there.

Second Woman: He thinks the law will protect him while he's sneakin' the bread out of our mouths.

Mother: Women, capture that man! Broom the life out of him, the sneakin' cur!

Third Woman: His mother's here. Let her tend to him! (Women grab scab, din in his ears with the pans, trip him up with their mops, push him with their brooms and haul him across the stage, stretching him out at his mother's feet as they shout, "Join the Union, Join the Union!" His mother bends over him and cries.)

Scab's Mother: Get me some water over there in the creek, one of you women. (Women talk together while one goes to creek and brings can of water. The sheriff takes advantage of the occasion to send his deputy off for help. He whispers loudly in the Deputy's ear.)

Sheriff: (Aside) Quick! Go call up the president of the Union and tell him to come up here as fast as he can and call off his wild cat women. Tell him they're clawing and scratching so I'll have to shoot 'em if he don't hurry. Scoot now!

Scab's Mother: (Sopping water on scab's forehead.) John, John, wake up! Come to, can't you? (Scab raises up slowly, cowering toward his mother as he sees women around him.) Come back to life there now, and join the Union!

Scab: (Looking fearfully at women.) Sure, I'll never scab again.

Sheriff: (Soothingly) Now Mother Jones, take these women away, won't you? I don't want to have to hurt 'em, but I can't stand for this . . . . (In answer to a signal from Mother Jones, the women charge the Sheriff with brooms, mopping at his feet and tripping him up. He stumbles, nearly falls and runs off pursued by the women. While this battle is going on, the Union president appears from the other direction and watches the proceedings in alarm.)

Union President: (Shouts up the path) Mother Jones! Watch out! The Sheriff has a gun. He'll shoot! (He wrings his hands and runs back and forth excitedly). Finally Mother Jones comes back followed by the women.)

Mother Jones: Fine work, women! You've done a good day's work, I'm telling you. Now I suppose you'll want to be getting back to your housework. Tomorrow morning we'll be meeting again at the same time, five o'clock, at Union headquarters. Goodbye to you. Take care of yourselves, and come ready for another scrap. We'll mop up the last scab tomorrow!

Women: (Leave, calling out greetings to Mother Jones.) Nothing like a good fight to scare sense into them scabs. Goodbye, Mother Jones. See you tomorrow, etc.

Union Pres.: (Anxiously) Didn't you get hurt, Mother Jones. Did any of the women get hurt?

Mother: Get hurt! Did we get hurt? (Dryly) No, *we* didn't get hurt.

President: But wasn't that the sheriff after you?

Mother: No, that was us after the sheriff. It was a grand fight!

Union Pres.: (Annoyed, says condescendingly) Well what do you think you got out of it?

Mother: Well while you and the other Union officials was taking your little beauty sleep in the hotel this morning, and the scabs was sneaking into the mines, we organized 500 men—took 'em right into the Union quick. We got 500 less scabs to fight now anyway.

Union Pres.: Took them into the Union? What do you mean? How could you do that? You didn't have the ritual!

Mother: Ritual be blowed! We made up one.

Union Pres.: Why you can't do that, Mother Jones! That's not according to the by-laws of the Union.

Mother: Say, what are we working for, to get men to join the Union and quit scabbing, or to teach 'em to say a little piece to rattle off just the way it reads in the book.

Union Pres.: Well, I think we ought to live up to what the rules say.

Mother: Yeh, if you had your way, you'd be so busy enforcing the rules that pretty soon you'd discover you didn't have no members to enforce 'em on.

Union Pres.: Say, how'd you get over here anyway. I heard them say over at the Hotel that one of the sheriff's men told the clerk at the desk to hold you and call him quick if you tried to go out. How did you get away?

Mother: Easy enough! That young clerk says to me when I came down: "Mother Jones, you mustn't go out. I've been given orders to watch this front door carefully and notify the deputy if I see you leave." "That's all right, sonny," says I, "Don't you worry about that. You just follow your orders and watch this front door carefully, and I'll go out the back door."

Union Pres.: Mother Jones, if you keep this up, somebody'll get hurt or killed, and then one of these days you'll land in jail and if they ever get anything like that on you, they'll hang you sure!

Mother Jones: That's all right, sonny. Let 'em do their worst. When I'm on the scaffold, I'll yell, "Long live the working class!" And the first thing I'm going to do when I see the Almighty is to tell Him how they're treatin' the miners on earth, living lean and lank and hungry as timber wolves! It's the producers, my son, not the meek that are going to inherit the earth. Not today perhaps nor tomorrow, but over the rim of the years my old eyes can see the coming of another day. But until that day comes, or until I leave this earth behind me, I'm going to fight like . . . well like my women fought today! And you men had better come and join us!

Curtain

Notes

1. See Mary Frederickson, "A Place to Speak Our Minds," in *Working Lives: The Southern Exposure History of Labor in the South*, ed. Marc S. Miller (New York: Pantheon Books, 1980), pp. 155–65; and forthcoming *A Place to Speak Our Minds: The Southern Summer School for Women Workers in Industry*, Indiana University Press.

2. See Sara Evans, *Personal Politics: The Roots of Women's Liberation in the Civil Rights Movement and the New Left* (New York: Vintage Books, 1979). The Southern Summer School provided the essential elements for the development among working-class women of what Evans has termed "an insurgent collective identity." In her work on the history of the women's liberation movement, Evans has defined three preconditions for this process: sufficient social space for a group to focus on itself as an entity, role models with whom members of a group can identify personally, and an intellectual framework for understanding society and directing efforts toward social change.

3. Louise Leonard, "The South Begins Workers' Education," *American Federationist* 35 (1928): 1381–89.

4. Interview with Polly Robkin, November 2, 1974.

5. Interview with Miriam Bonner Camp, April 15, 1976.

6. Student autobiographies, Southern Summer School Papers, American Labor Education Service Records, 1927–1962, Labor-Management Docu-

mentation Center, Martin P. Catherwood Library, New York State School of Industrial and Labor Relations, Cornell University, Ithaca, N.Y. (hereafter cited as SSS Papers, ILR).

7. See "Labor Economics, An Outline of the Economics Course at the Southern Summer School, Arden, N.C., 1930"; "Workers and the New Deal, a Discussion Course in Labor Economics Developed at the Southern Summer School for Women in Industry, 1934 Session"; and Caroline Ware, "Report on Economics Class, July 9–31, 1937," SSS Papers, ILR.

8. See "Reports of the Director, 1927–1940," SSS Papers, ILR.

9. See Daniel Joseph Singal, "Broadus Mitchell and the Persistence of New South Thought," *Journal of Southern History* 45 (1979): 353–402; Interview with Broadus Mitchell, August 14–15, 1977. Information about Lois MacDonald is from an interview with her, November 1974. Caroline Ware graduated from Vassar College in 1920 and received her Ph.D. from Radcliffe (Harvard) in 1925. She published *The Early New England Cotton Manufacture* in 1931, worked with the Columbia University Social Science Research Council during 1930–1932, and served as an assistant on the NRA Consumer Advisory Board and the National Emergency Council in 1934–1935. In 1935 she joined the faculty at Sarah Lawrence (interview with Caroline Ware, April 30, 1979). See memorial pamphlet, "Leo Huberman" (New York: Monthly Review Press, n.d.); Leo Huberman, "How to Spread the Work," in *Studies in Socialist Pedagogy*, ed. Theordore Mills Norton and Bertell Ollman (New York: Monthly Review Press, 1978).

10. "Southern Summer School Scrapbook, 1933," p. 47, SSS Papers, ILR; see also Philip S. Foner, *American Labor Songs of the Nineteenth Century* (Urbana: University of Illinois Press, 1975), p. 177.

11. "Songs of the Southern Summer School, 1938," p. 34, SSS Papers, ILR.

12. Student autobiographies and essays, SSS Papers, ILR. See also Richard H. Pells, *Radical Visions and American Dreams: Culture and Social Thought in the Depression Years* (New York: Harper & Row, 1973), p. 251.

13. Interview with Hollace Ransdell, November 1975.

14. Southern Summer School Playscripts, SSS Papers, ILR.

15. "Notes with playscript of 'Tobacco Shop,'" SSS Papers, ILR.

16. "Southern School Scrapbook, 1940," SSS Papers, ILR.

17. Ibid.; For women's participation in the CIO, see Ruth Milkman, "Organizing the Sexual Divison of Labor: Historical

Perspectives on 'Women's Work' and American Labor Movement," *Socialist Review* 10; no. 11 (1980): 125–32.

18. Student autobiographies and essays, SSS Papers, ILR. The life history material within this collection is weighted toward the years between 1927 and 1933. Most of the autobiographies were written anonymously; wherever possible students' home states or communities are identified.

19. "Student Statistics," SSS Papers, ILR; information obtained from each student usually included home community, age, marital status, educational background, age when started to work, years in work force, union affiliation, and religious background.

20. Students cannot be rigidly categorized into these cohort designations by age, life experience, or year of attendance at the school; however; the divisions provide a useful framework for interpreting the material in the life histories.

21. Margaret Jarmon Hagood, *Mothers of the South* (1939, reprint ed., New York: W. W. Norton & Co., 1977); quotation from student autobiography, SSS Papers, ILR.

22. Student autobiographies and essays, SSS Papers, ILR; interviews with former Southern Summer School students: Vesta Finley, July 22, 1975; Rosa Holland, July 22, 1975; Lillie Morris Price, July 22, 1975.

23. Student autobiographies, SSS Papers, ILR.

24. Ibid.

25. Ibid.

26. During this period manufacturers' reports, especially in the *Manufacturers' Record* (Baltimore and Atlanta, 1882–1958), the annual *Blue Book of Southern Progress (Baltimore and Atlanta, 1909–)*, and the *Southern Textile Bulletin* (Charlotte, N.C., 1911–; title varies), provide glowing accounts of conditions in southern industrial communities. On the other hand, reformers and political radicals painted a totally devastating picture of southern industrial life; see, e.g., Sinclair Lewis, *Cheap and Contented Labor: The Picture of a Southern Mill Town in 1929* (Philadelphia: Philadelphia Women's Trade Union League, 1929), and Myra Page, *Southern Cotton Mills and Labor* (New York: Workers Library Publishers, 1929). The Southern Summer School materials, written by southern women workers themselves, present a more balanced picture of life and work in southern industrial society.

27. Student autobiographies, SSS Papers, ILR.

28. Interview with Vesta Finley.

29. Student autobiographies, SSS Papers, ILR.

30. Ibid.
31. Ibid.; see also Lois MacDonald, *Southern Mill Hills* (New York: Alex L. Hillman, 1928), pp. 145–51; Ben F. Lemert, *The Cotton Textile Industry of the Southern Appalachian Piedmont* (Chapel Hill: University of North Carolina Press, 1933), pp. 63, 65; Herbert J. Lahne, *The Cotton Mill Worker* (New York: Farrar & Reinhart, 1944); George B. Tindall, *Emergence of the New South, 1913–1945* (Baton Rouge: Louisiana State University Press, 1967), pp. 325–27.
32. Lahne, pp. 102–28.
33. Student autobiographies, SSS Papers, ILR.
34. Ibid.
35. Citations regarding ill health were frequent in the student autobiographies; see also Lahne, pp. 160–61, 171–72; Mimi Conway, "Cotton Dust Kills, and It's Killing Me," and Chip Hughes and Len Stanley, "OSHA: Dynamite for Workers," in Miller, ed., *Working Lives*.
36. Interview with Vesta Finley.
37. Student autobiographies, SSS Papers, ILR.
38. Ibid.
39. Ibid.; evidence exists indicating that the strikes did have an effect on the stretch-out (see Tindall, p. 353).
40. F. Ray Marshall, *Labor in the South* (Cambridge, Mass.: Harvard University Press, n.d.), pp. 101–20; Lahne, pp. 216–31; citation from student autobiographies, SSS Papers, ILR.
41. Interview with Vesta Finley; interview with Bessie Edens, August 14, 1975; Liston Pope, *Millhands and Preachers: A Study of Gastonia* (New Haven, Conn.: Yale University Press, 1942), pp. 248, 258.
42. Figures tabulated from union affiliation records in SSS Papers, ILR; for national figures on female union membership, see Theresa Wolfson, "Trade Union Activities of Women," *Annals of the American Academy of Political and Social Science* 143 (May 1929): 120–31.
43. Union affiliation records in student biographical materials, SSS Papers, ILR; regional union membership figures from Marshall, p. 171.
44. Cohort group divisions based on material from student autobiographies and essays in SSS Papers, ILR, and on interviews with former Southern Summer School students, including Vesta Finley, Rosa Holland, Lillie Morris Price, Bessie Edens, and three former students from Macon, Georgia (August 1979).
45. Interview with Vesta Finley.
46. Anne F. Scott has persuasively argued that the prevailing image of the "southern

lady" did not correlate with the actual lives of southern white upper- and middle-class women in the first two decades of the twentieth century. For working-class white women, in both agricultural and industrial work, the ideology of southern womanhood appears to have had virtually no relevance, either as a prescription for behavior or as an image of women's role in the ideal society (see Anne F. Scott, *The Southern Lady: From Pedestal to Politics, 1830–1930* [Chicago: University of Chicago Press, 1970]).

47. "Report of the Director, 1936," SSS Papers, ILR; interview with Bessie Edens.

48. Student autobiographies, SSS Papers, ILR.

49. Ibid.

50. More research is needed on the beliefs of working-class southerners, both women and men, regarding women's role in southern culture. For an excellent discussion of the prevalence and importance of working-class feminism among late-nineteenth-century industrial workers in the Northeast, see Susan Levine, "Their Own Sphere: Women's Work, the Knights of Labor and the Transformation of the Carpet Trade, 1870–1890" (Ph.D. diss., City University of New York, 1980).

51. Student autobiographies, SSS Papers, ILR; interview with Vesta Finley.

52. Eleanor Copenhaver Report, Industrial Department, March 1929, p. 14, Archives of the National Board of the YWCA, New York, N.Y.

53. Student autobiographies, SSS Papers, ILR.

54. Louise McLaren to Minnie Fisher, October 16, 1929; Fisher to McLaren, October 23, 1929, SSS Papers, ILR.

55. Interview with Vesta Finley.

56. SSS Papers, ILR.

57. Student autobiographies, SSS Papers, ILR.

58. Ibid.

59. "Labor Drama," Box 111, SSS Papers, ILR.

Chapter 6

Partners in Progress:
The Affiliated Schools for Women Workers,
1928–1939

Marion W. Roydhouse

The Affiliated Schools for Women Workers was organized in 1928 as the coordinating body for workers' education programs for women. At that time, the progressive impulse for reform was still alive, and there were energetic groups of labor advocates struggling to found and fund workers' schools for women. Together they formed an innovative institution that established a network of women who shared ideas and hopes and gave each other much-needed emotional support.

The formal history of the organization shows a shift in focus through the 1920s and 1930s from an emphasis on individual and local solutions to an emphasis on national policies and more centralized responses to the needs of workers. This shift reflected reactions to an increasingly complex industrial society and the expanded purview of the federal government with the New Deal. The history of the Affiliated Schools also illustrates the nature of individual and collaborative efforts of middle- and working-class women to improve the work experience of women workers and to increase their participation in the public sphere.

The most important aspect of the Affiliated Schools was the informal exchange of information and the support provided for the task of building a workers' education movement focused on the needs of women workers. Such a focus was not found in the wider movement and was not provided to women by the American Federation of Labor's (AFL) official labor education organization, the Workers' Education Bureau. The Affiliated Schools, then, filled a vacuum in the 1920s and later provided needed resources for the rejuvenated labor movement in the 1930s.

Innovative in both form and goals, the Affiliated Schools served initially as a central coordinating body and a clearinghouse for information about faculty, students, and teaching methods, with the major goal of creating a long-lasting coalition for support among its members. The Affiliated Schools' main focus was to reduce overlapping fund-raising drives and recruitment efforts and to help schools exchange information, investigate joint problems, and evaluate experimental teaching methods. Between 1928 and 1938, the Affiliated Schools became an integral part of the movement serving women workers; after 1938, reorganized as the American Labor Education Service, (ALES), the organization sponsored annual conferences for teachers in workers' education and served both women and men in AFL and Congress of

Industrial Organization (CIO) unions across the country.[1]

The first suggestion for a central body to coordinate workers' schools for women came from the director of the Bryn Mawr Summer School for Women Workers, Hilda Smith, in 1926. The Bryn Mawr Summer School had been in existence since 1921; in 1925 the Wisconsin Summer School had begun, and the Barnard Summer School and the Southern Summer School were being organized. During 1926, Hilda Smith developed a proposal that addressed some of the problems she believed would arise as the number of residential schools for women workers continued to increase. The most pressing of these problems was the financial threat that overlapping fund-raising drives posed to those schools not yet on a steady financial footing and even to established programs like the one at Bryn Mawr, which faced new competition for limited monetary resources. The development of workers' schools for women was a "pioneer field," as Louise Leonard McLaren, director of the newly organized Southern Summer School, termed it, and there was a need to join forces in the face of financial difficulties and to create coalitions for support. There was sufficient interest in this idea for Hilda Smith to schedule a series of meetings during 1928 to discuss the development of such an organization.[2]

Out of these meetings came plans for the Resident Summer Schools for Women Workers in Industry, soon referred to as the Affiliated Summer Schools for Women Workers. After some discussion of an overarching central body, it was agreed that each school would remain autonomous and not delegate decisions on finances or policy. Member schools were reluctant to relinquish decisions on policymaking to a central body, especially when it became clear that Bryn Mawr would be the dominant partner in the coalition. Due in part to Hilda Smith's role in the formation of the first joint committee and her position as the first executive secretary of the Resident Schools for Women Workers, Bryn Mawr's predominance was also a result of the financial structure of the new organization. Funds raised by the Bryn Mawr Summer School were to be shared with the joint committee and used for both organizations.

By establishing a centralized committee, the founders of the Affiliated Schools created a new approach to solving their common problems. It took several years, however, for the organization to take shape. In its original form, the Affiliated Schools comprised two main committees, the education committee and the finance committee, and the organization was much less elaborate than Hilda Smith had envisioned. In the years between 1928 and 1932, the Affiliated Schools' patterns of fund raising and recruiting were set by the Bryn Mawr Summer School. In many ways, coordinating efforts prior to the organization's first reorganization in 1932 emphasized the winter fieldwork needs of the Bryn Mawr Summer School, and the work of the other member schools was given lower priority.

The first constitution of the Affiliated Schools, drawn up in December 1928, reflected the influence of Bryn Mawr and a focus on the fund-raising and recruiting role of college alumnae that differentiated Bryn Mawr from the independent schools, such as the Southern Summer School. The constitution defined the organization's purpose: "to extend educational opportunities to women workers in industry, by means of Summer Schools made possible through the use of college buildings and equipment and carried on through the cooperation of college alumnae and women workers in industry."[3]

The evolution of the Affiliated Schools can be traced through changes in its formal organization and also through the interplay of the different philosophical and organizational perspectives of the women who shaped the educational programs for women workers at that time. The Affiliated Schools reflected diverse constituencies, and member institutions had difficulty in agreeing on common policies and procedures. One of the essential debates was over the question of curricular focus for the schools for women workers. Bryn Mawr, because of its academic orientation, placed proportionately greater emphasis on science and cultural endeavors and favored an education that was broad in scope. Other schools, such as the Barnard Summer School and the Southern Summer School, served populations of students limited to a certain geographical area and often workers within specific industries. Rather than including courses in science and English literature, they emphasized economics and labor history and organizing techniques designed to meet the immediate needs of their students.

One of the primary contributions of the Affiliated Schools was to provide an effective educational support system for these individual schools. The first three schools for women workers to coordinate their activities were the Bryn Mawr Summer School, the Wisconsin Summer School, and the Barnard Summer School. After 1932, three other organizations became formally allied under the Affiliated Schools' banner: the Vineyard Shore Workers' School, the Southern Summer School, and the Summer School for Office Workers.

The Bryn Mawr Summer School for Women Workers was the first and most college-oriented of the workers' schools for women. Held for sixteen years on the campus of the prestigious women's school outside Philadelphia, the Bryn Mawr Summer School was founded by President M. Carey Thomas immediately before her retirement in 1922. With the assistance of the Dean of the college, Hilda Smith, and Professor Susan M. Kingsbury, director of the Bryn Mawr Carola Woerishoffer Graduate Department of Social Economy and Social Research, Thomas opened the doors of the college to women workers recruited from across the country. One hundred women came to the college each summer, supported by funds raised primarily by Bryn Mawr alumnae, after being selected from their local YWCA industrial club or trade union. At the summer school women industrial workers studied a variety of subjects from astronomy to English literature and from economics to public speaking.

As the Bryn Mawr Summer School developed closer ties to the labor movement, especially after the formation of the Congress of Industrial Organizations (CIO) in 1935, alumnae support began to wane, and the summer school's relationship to Bryn Mawr College grew strained. In 1935 and 1936, the summer school met in the Ramapo Mountains because of disagreements with college authorities over participation in local labor disputes. After 1939, and a permanent breach with Bryn Mawr College, the summer school moved to Hilda Smith's family home at West Park on the Hudson River, above New York City. Renamed the Hudson Shore Labor School, it operated as a coeducational resident school for workers until 1952.[4]

The Wisconsin School for Women Workers in Industry, the first residential program at a state-supported university, developed from the Industrial Department of the Madison YWCA. In 1924, the local YWCA organized discussions of labor problems attended by college students and working women. The following summer forty women workers from nine midwestern states were recruited through the YWCA Industrial Department to participate in the first eight-week residential program, planned by a committee of university faculty and students, women workers, and YWCA staff members. Alice Shoemaker, YWCA secretary in Madison, who had taught at the Bryn Mawr Summer School, became the first executive secretary. By 1928 the Wisconsin School had become the Wisconsin School for Workers, a coeducational school for workers at the University of Wisconsin.[5]

The Barnard Summer School, a nonresidential program, included women workers primarily from the garment industry in New York City. National Women's Trade Union League (NWTUL) activists, Hilda Smith and her assistant Ernestine Friedmann, a former YWCA Industrial Department secretary, persuaded Dean Gildersleeve of Barnard College to open the college facilities for an experimental school for women workers in 1927. This school geared its curriculum to the needs of young immigrant workers, many of whom had trouble using English as a second language. The Barnard Summer School functioned effectively until 1934, when lack of support from the Barnard alumnae and the impact of the Depression caused the organization to fold.[6]

The Vineyard Shore Workers' School, an eight-month residential program organized in 1929, joined the Affiliated Schools in 1933. Based on the conviction that workers' education should give women more than just training for work in the labor movement, Vineyard Shore offered a cultural focus as well as the "nuts and bolts" of economics and English that was the staple of other resident schools. It was Hilda Smith's demonstration project, designed as an answer to those within the movement for workers' education who called for a narrower, more pragmatic focus to curricula for women workers.[7]

The Southern Summer School, which held its first session in 1927, at Sweet Briar College in the hills of Virginia, aimed to reach women workers in the textile and tobacco industries of the South. But after the first summer, the Southern Summer School chose not to continue a close relationship with one college, on the Bryn Mawr model, and met in subsequent years in different camps and school facilities in the mountains of North Carolina, closer to the heart of the southern textile industry. Summer sessions concentrating on the needs of southern women workers were held every year until 1938, when, under pressure from the labor movement, men were admitted.[8]

By the early 1930s it had become apparent that not only women in industry needed workers' education programs—office workers did as well. The initial impetus for this idea came from the YWCA, which, through its Business Girls' Clubs, supported by the Federation of Business and Professional Women's Clubs, dealt directly with the growing number of women in the white-collar work force. In the summer of 1933, a workers' education session was held at Oberlin College, with Eleanor Coit of the Affiliated Schools' Joint Committee sent to help run the school. Proving successful, the Summer School for Office Workers was repeated, first at Oberlin and then, after 1936, at Northwestern University. The Summer School for Office Workers, like the Wisconsin Summer School, began as an experiment in workers' education for women, but by 1936 men were brought into the program. Initially men were in the minority, for in 1939 there were forty-four women and only sixteen men, but this balance shifted during the 1940s. In 1948, the summer school reoriented its program to accommodate the increasing number of white-collar workers, other than office workers, who were attending the sessions. After 1948, the summer sessions were called "White Collar Workshops."[9]

Serving a diverse constituency of member schools, the Affiliated Schools became a center for the examination of teaching methods and the evaluation of the impact of schools on the lives of student participants in workers' education programs. The Education Department was headed by Eleanor Coit, a former YWCA industrial secretary and proponent of pragmatic workers' education programs geared to the specific needs of the students. She argued that in workers' education the "'campus' is as broad as the area of interest of those who work. It is a campus without buildings, but with seats of learning where ever wage-earners are found." Coit's reports consistently echoed the need for curricula planned around "problems of concrete interest to the students." As head of the Education Department, Coit encouraged the development of courses on topics such as unemployment, industrial legislation, or the history of trade unions. Furthermore, Coit concluded that the educational process in the summer schools was far more successful when students were actively engaged in asking questions, participating in discussions, investigating a particular problem in small groups, and then leading discussions on the material for the rest of the school.[10]

Because the lack of written resources useful for the adult worker-student handicapped instructors at the residential schools, the Education Department worked to prepare new manuals and pamphlets written specifically for women workers. The Affiliated Schools' publications reflected the idea that workers needed easy-to-read texts that provided useful information in a clearly written format. Titles written under the auspices of the Affiliated Schools included: *The Scrapbook of the American Labor Movement*, by Gladys Palmer (Wharton School, University of Pennsylvania); *Your Job and Your Pay*, by Katherine Pollak; *This America*, by Jean Carter; and *Unemployment, a Problem of Insecurity*, by William Haber. These materials met a special need for students in workers' education programs and were widely used by those organizations belonging to the Affiliated Schools and numerous other worker groups both within and outside the labor movement.[11]

The Affiliated Schools conducted studies of student activities after they left the summer programs. Each school maintained its own network of former students, but the Affiliated Schools coordinated research on the impact of the schools on the lives of the students. In 1930, the Affiliated Schools facilitated a master's thesis by Mildred Price (University of Chicago) on the effects of adult education. The Affiliated Schools also sponsored a study prepared by Gladys Palmer entitled *The Industrial Experience of Women Workers at the Summer Schools, 1928–1930*, published by the Women's Bureau in 1931 (Bulletin 89); two economic surveys by Amy Hewes based on the industrial experiences of summer school students; and a cooperative study done in 1936 with Works Progress Administration (WPA) funds to examine the long-term effects of the residence programs. The last study concluded that the summer schools had a significant impact and that, although not all students became labor activists, a significant proportion did, and few students remained unchanged by their summer school experience. One of the last published studies sponsored by the Affiliated Schools was Eleanor Snyder's *Job Histories of Women Workers at the Summer Schools, 1931–34 and 1938*. Issued by the Women's Bureau in 1939, this work was hailed as one of the "increasingly useful studies of the experience of individual women workers" provided through "the initiative of the Affiliated Schools and the cooperation of the Women's Bureau."[12]

The staff of the Affiliated Schools maintained contact with former students, instructors, and supporters through correspondence, field visits, and regional conferences. Former summer school participants were encouraged to develop local workers' education activities, based whenever possible in unions, universities, YWCAs, and other community organizations. In some cases, former participants in the summer schools formed workers' education councils in their regions. By late 1931, many former summer school students were engaged in classes in over fifty cities. In some areas, former students were involved in promoting better working conditions for women, speaking on issues such as labor standards, unemployment insurance, and labor legislation.[13]

The activity of summer school alumnae furnishes the best evidence of the effectiveness both of the individual summer school programs and of the coordinating activities of the Affiliated Schools.[14] Many summer school students became active in unions. Elizabeth Nord, for example, chaired a new WTUL committee in Rhode Island, Theresa Gold did "special work" for the Boot and Shoe Workers in Massachusetts, and Louise Guigno organized for the Amalgamated Clothing Workers in Scranton.

Despite the financial impact of the Depression on the individual programs and on the Affiliated Schools (one-third of whose funds were lost in a bank closing early in 1932), the work of the organization flourished as it developed effective means of communication between the residence schools for women.[15] Board members and administrators from the schools shared ideas about fund raising, cooperated in finding capable teachers, and exchanged information about methods, materials, and curricula.

This cooperation, much of it carried out informally, was the core of the success of the Affiliated Schools. Louise Leonard McLaren and Hilda Smith shared a chocolate bar on the steps of a brownstone during a long day of knocking on doors; Lois MacDonald might meet either of them in Greenwich Village, where she had her apartment. Hilda heard of a vacant building for workers' classes while traveling on the subway one morning when she met Mary Van Kleeck from College Settlement as they were both strap-hanging. Eleanor Coit, the Education Department director, Hilda Smith, former head of the Bryn Mawr Summer School, Theresa Wolfson, professor at Brooklyn College, and Lois MacDonald, teacher at the Southern Summer School and professor of economics at New York University, together formed the backbone for the organization's daily work. Through a network in the New York City area, these women worked in coalition with working-class women like Josephine Kazcor, a graduate of Brookwood Labor College and an organizer for the United Textile Workers and the Amalgamated Clothing Workers, and Carmen Lucia, a graduate of the Bryn Mawr Summer School and an organizer for the Neckwear Workers' Union.[16]

The workers' education movement had no single coherent focus or unifying institution in the United States, and substantial theoretical and pragmatic differences existed between groups in the movement. Given this situation, and the need for support among the women in the male-dominated labor movement, the ability of the Affiliated Schools to bring together a variety of approaches and sometimes disparate groups was remarkable.

Given a constant shortage of funds, the Affiliated Schools' program of fieldwork, publications, coordination, and interpretation was a substantial achievement. But the issue of Bryn Mawr's domination continued to be discussed. By 1932, reorganization of the central body was suggested. It was generally felt that the Bryn Mawr Summer School should be separated administratively from the joint body. The need to incorporate legally, in order to relieve board members of individual financial responsibility, also became apparent. In addition, the board members recognized that the organization was changing direction, shifting its emphasis from an exclusive focus on the needs of member schools to a more generalized education service provided to any organizations and groups interested in workers' education for women.[17]

When the organization was incorporated officially in April 1932, the Affiliated Schools' Executive and Joint Committees prepared a constitution that outlined a new direction: service to a constituency wider than the providers of residential summer programs. This change necessitated strong labor representation on the board and sufficient funds to expand the winter classes, preparatory classes for the residence schools, and the publication series. By November 1932, a new set of by-laws had been drawn up, but by then the problem of funding for the separate organization made further work seem tenuous. As the Joint Committee prepared in 1933 for the final separation from the Bryn Mawr budget, it tried to decide which projects of the Affiliated Schools were most needed. By winter, it looked as though the Affiliated Schools would be able to continue only for a few months into the next year. It seemed that the experiment would fail as a result of the economic climate in which the organization was struggling to function.[18]

Recalling that "for six months we had been seeing newspaper reports of federal funds, allocated by the government to relieve unemployment," Hilda Smith went to Washington to attempt to raise money from both public and private sources. In the midst of the hectic activity of the first days of the New Deal no one could promise money for workers' education, and she left without securing any additional funds. Then, as soon as she returned to New York, a telegram arrived from Washington inviting Smith to work with Harry Hopkins's Federal Emergency Relief Administration (FERA) in the Emergency Education Division. This division was to provide work for unemployed teachers by establishing widespread programs in adult and workers' education. Hilda Smith hoped the Affiliated Schools would be called upon to provide the needed expertise and educational resources. With this in mind, she agreed to leave New York to join the New Deal, making what turned out to be a permanent move to Washington, D.C.[19]

Hilda Smith's move to Washington meant her resignation from the Affiliated Schools and the beginning of a long career in government. For the organization it was also a new beginning. Eleanor Coit filled Smith's place as director of the Affiliated Schools, and plans for cooperation with the FERA programs were anticipated. Support given to the Affiliated Schools in connection with FERA programs allowed for an expansion of the work of the organization, but led to a shift away from a primary commitment to the education of women workers.[20]

In 1933, the General Education Board of the Rockefeller Foundation gave the Affiliated Schools for Workers a grant of some $70,000, to be spread out over three years, which was intended to allow the organization to cooperate with the FERA programs. With the promise of additional funding, leaders and staff of the Affiliated Schools discussed ways in which the organization could cooperate with New Deal programs to develop workers' education. Coit voiced the fear that the basic principles of the Affiliated Schools might be lost at the local level because "many school authorities interpret workers' education programs somewhat differently from the Affiliated Schools, [and] there is a need of proceeding cautiously if the program is not to become one of general adult education." Therefore, it was decided that the Affiliated

Schools should support demonstration workers' education projects in communities where local organizations, including labor unions, would ensure the continuation of the programs after funding from the General Education Board grant had ended.[21]

The grant money brought with it the expansion and redistribution of staff. The organization added personnel in New York and field staff to be lent to FERA projects. Louise Leonard McLaren agreed to work as a liaison with Hilda Smith in Washington and to investigate possibilities for projects in the South. Others were appointed to evaluate requests from other regions—Alice Shoemaker in the Midwest, Ernestine Friedmann in New York. In addition, the organization expanded its publication series and established a traveling library.[22]

The next several years were busy ones for the Affiliated Schools, which provided services for the FERA and the WPA workers' education projects. The organization expanded its resources for specialists in workers' education by the mid-1930s. Requests for materials and advice about teaching methods came in from such diverse union groups as the Amalgamated Clothing Workers, the Federation of Federal Employees, the Railroad Equipment Painters, the Stationary Engineers, and the Boot and Shoe Workers. Teacher-training projects, college classes, the WTUL, and local adult education classes all asked the New York office on Second Avenue for assistance in program planning, curriculum development, and teaching resources. There was also a growing demand for resources from the traveling library.[23]

During these years, the Affiliated Schools' staff attended two New Deal–sponsored (FERA) conferences in Washington, D.C.: the 1934 Conference on Workers' Education, and, in the same year, the White House Conference on Unemployed Women.[24] In order to train new teachers in workers' education, the Affiliated Schools sponsored projects in Philadelphia and New York and supported teacher-training efforts undertaken in connection with workers' summer schools and classes. The organization also continued to sponsor innovative approaches to teaching. For example, the labor dramatics program that Affiliated Schools field representative Hollace Ransdell had developed at the Southern Summer School was continued in workers' education projects that she supervised in the textile centers of Rhode Island and the anthracite region of Pennsylvania. Jean Carter, who had taught at the Bryn Mawr Summer School, prepared a handbook in 1934 on methods of teaching for use with federal projects; Lois MacDonald wrote a pamphlet explaining the relationship between labor and the National Recovery Administration codes. Other publications discussing labor problems, teaching methods, and the work of the women's summer schools were produced by the organization during the 1930s.[25]

The expansion of activities in connection with the New Deal workers' education programs meant that the aim of the Affiliated Schools to promote new workers' programs could be realized. In the summer of 1933 Eleanor Coit directed a new experimental school for white-collar workers at Oberlin College. Known as the Summer School for Office Workers, and founded with support from the YWCA and the Federation of Business and Professional Women's Clubs, this new residential school initially enrolled only women; after 1936, it admitted men.

Working in collaboration with the New Deal workers' education programs changed the focus of the Affiliated Schools. The rapid organization of unions in the mass production industries created a demand for services in establishing workers' education programs for members of new local unions. In 1936, with funding from the Rockefeller Foundation coming to an end, the Affiliated Schools and each of the individual schools became more dependent on organized labor for financial support. Thus, from an organization focused solely on the needs of women workers and oriented to coordinating the work of independent residential workers' schools, the Affiliated Schools redirected its services to meet the needs of women and men in the organized trade union movement.

In 1935, John Edelman, research director for the Hosiery Workers, joined the board of the Affiliated Schools and became its labor liaison with the press. In the same year, Carter Goodrich, professor of political science at Columbia University, joined Edelman. Among the men elected to the Affiliated Schools board in the following years were Mark Starr, education director of the International Ladies' Garment Workers' Union (ILGWU); Max Lerner, editor of the *Nation* and professor at Williams College; Eduard Lindeman, from the New York School of Social Work and a long-time friend of the YWCA Industrial Department and workers' schools; Clinton Golden, of the Steel Workers Organizing Committee; and Henry Rutz, from the labor movement in Wisconsin and state director of workers' education.[26]

As the Affiliated Schools moved closer to the labor movement after 1935, the staff struggled to maintain academic freedom and open discussion in an atmosphere fraught with tension between the AFL and the newly organized CIO. Faced with the traditional AFL suspicion of intellectuals and middle-class allies and the intense factionalism that had developed in the labor movement, the Affiliated Schools worked hard to communicate that their aim was to support the labor movement, not to take sides in interunion politics.[27]

The Affiliated Schools trod a careful path in describing its purposes because of the diversity of the constituency it served. Writing in *Progressive Education*, Eleanor Coit stated that the programs of the Affiliated Schools were "consciously directed toward social change and the development of attitudes and abilities on the part of students which will make this change as intelligent as possible." Reform, it was clear from the Affiliated Schools' publications, was essential, but revolution was not the aim.[28]

In 1936, however, the board members of the Affiliated Schools faced the issue of whether they would become a CIO-affiliated Workers' Education Bureau. Board member Henry Rutz, with clear CIO sympathies, was convinced that the AFL workers' education program was defunct and that the Affiliated Schools should aim to "supplant or replace" the AFL-sponsored Workers Education Bureau.[29]

After great debate the board agreed that the Affiliated Schools should avoid becoming committed to one federation or group within the labor movement. The organization chose to remain independent, forgoing some financial support from organized labor but retaining a position which preserved its freedom in teaching and discussion.

By the late 1930s, reflecting the changed focus of the organization, the Affiliated Schools for Workers reorganized as the American Labor Education Service (ALES). Rather than an institution which fostered the special training of women through independent residential programs, the ALES aimed to provide service to the whole labor and workers' education movement. It continued to steer a middle course between the AFL and the CIO, but by adding new membership groups it sought wider financial support from labor, foundations, and individuals who could now join the organization.[30]

The ALES, with some funds from the Ford Foundation through the Fund for Adult

Education, carried on its educational service until the 1960s. Eleanor Coit, mainstay of the organization for three decades, retired in 1962 and the ALES disbanded. ALES historian Doris Brody believes that the tension between the commitment to freedom of discussion and the increasing political conservatism of organized labor created conflict and eroded the ability of the ALES to foster workers' education.[31]

The change in the organization to working with men and the organized labor movement during the 1930s leads us to question the roots of its original commitment to women and to women's issues. The question of the feminism of either the middle-class allies or the worker-students has no clear-cut answers. Certainly the origins of the schools lay in the work of the YWCA, and specifically its Industrial Department. A significant number of the original members of the boards of the member schools and the Affiliated Schools were women who had had some experience in the YWCA. Among them were Alice Shoemaker of Wisconsin, Ernestine Friedmann of Barnard and Vineyard Shore, Louise Leonard McLaren and Lois MacDonald of the Southern Summer School, Alice Hanson Cook, and Eleanor Coit. These women, and others like them, were trained in the YWCA tradition of commitment to the needs of women and belief that women could work together across class lines to improve the general quality of their lives and the position of women in society.

The women who formulated the workers' projects, however, almost consistently rejected any suggestion that what they were doing was primarily aimed at improving the status of women in society or that they were feminists. Instead, these women were committed to social reform, and specifically to the reform of working conditions within industrial society. Yet the same women also felt that they had a special commitment to women in the work force, as distinct from men. Therefore, the reforms they sought aimed to improve women's lives. At the same time, they felt that a more just society would not allow women to be exploited by poor working conditions, long hours, and low wage levels.

This was a position shared by others, one that historians have begun to analyze. Most recently, Susan Ware has concluded that prominent women of the New Deal—women like Eleanor Roosevelt, Katherine Lenroot, Molly Dewson, and Mary Anderson—were driven by a social feminism rather than by a feminism rooted in the push for equal rights for women. These women believed that women had specific social reform capabilities and that they had a special role to play in creating a more just society. An earlier generation of reformers, which influenced many of the women in the workers' schools—women like Florence Simms of the YWCA, Florence Kelley of the Consumers' League, and settlement house reformers Jane Addams and Ellen Gates Starr—rooted their position in similar concerns and motivations.[32]

Attaining women's rights was never a goal of the Affiliated Schools, and there seems to have been little discussion of women's issues at the workers' schools. And yet, the Affiliated Schools decided not to organize classes specifically for men when requested to do so by a group at Columbia University in the early years, though they did agree to provide advice and materials and to help find teachers.[33]

Thus, the decision to concentrate on women in the early years was not made by default. Hilda Smith recalled that at the Bryn Mawr Summer School they never talked directly of women's problems "because these were women, and we knew they were women, and we knew what they'd come for" and because there seemed little reason to discuss the political, social, or economic oppression of women in relation to the status of men.[34] This is not to say that the women did not discuss disparities in wage scales or the difficulties faced by married women in the work force, but they viewed these issues within the context of needed change in the industrial system, rather than as problems resulting from a male-dominated society. The summer schools were certainly feminist undertakings in the early years, and a network of women continued to be the main source of support. But it was feminism based on an idealistic belief in women's potential for fuller participation in society, rather than in the kind of commitment to change for women that led to the introduction of the Equal Rights Amendment in the same period.

The consequence of this vaguely formed social feminism was that the summer schools fostered a sense of camaraderie among the women and provided a place where they could develop their strengths and leadership talents away from the pressures of the outside world. This atmosphere was central to the impact of the schools on the worker-students; it made an increase in self-confidence one of the most long-lasting results of the summer sessions. When this atmosphere was diluted, it brought a crucial change in the effect the schools had on individual women.

A report written by Alice Shoemaker after the summer session at Wisconsin in 1932 reveals this ambivalence toward women and shows why the inclusion of men created an important change in atmosphere. In discussing the success of the session, Shoemaker pointed to the admission of men as a major achievement, concluding that "because of their superior experience, aggressiveness, and intellectual training, the men dominated both class discussions and student affairs, although many of the women did more thorough and intensive individual work."[35] Shoemaker did not perceive the impact of the "aggressiveness" of the men on the women students, nor was there any recognition that "more thorough and intensive individual work" by the women was the product of women's separate and different socialization. Women, long socialized to defer to men in the workplace and at home, could not find in this atmosphere the space to develop their own leadership abilities. Only those women with the strongest egos would emerge from such sessions willing to fight for and take the floor in union meetings. The rationale was that in the world of work men and women competed for leadership and that the workers' schools should reflect the world outside.

But the women's summer schools had been successful because they provided the opportunity for women to develop away from the overwhelming pressures of the male-dominated society. As the nineteenth century women's club movement and women's colleges had provided such a space for middle-class women, so the summer schools for women had given working-class women the opportunity to become active and effective leaders. In similar fashion, the Affiliated Schools for Women Workers provided support for women workers' education because it was an organization founded and run by women for women. The failure of the Affiliated Schools to come to terms with women's position in society or to perceive the ambiguities of their stance led the organization away from its concentration on women and toward a position more acceptable to the male-dominated organized labor movement.

The Affiliated Schools was an innovative organization, rooted in the work of both middle-class and working-class women. As a cooperative organization, it crossed class lines and, to a limited extent, racial lines as well. The very catholic nature of the political philosophy of the group, however, made the organization and the individual summer schools open to criticism from both ends of the political spectrum and all sides of the labor movement. The insistence of the Affiliated Schools on freedom of discussion caused major difficulties in securing funds and support from trade unions, despite the consistent aim of the programs to train active workers willing to undertake whatever reform efforts they themselves thought necessary.

The motivation behind the Affiliated Schools is reflected in the words of Helen Moscicki, a 1928 Bryn Mawr Summer School student who wrote:

"Education is the beacon light of every worker, the light which helps him carry on for a better and brighter future."[36] It is significant that Helen Moscicki chose to write "him," for it reflects the crucial ambivalence of the residential schools over the question of the role of women in American society and the need for a feminist commitment to women. But her comment also reveals the most significant tenet of the Affiliated Schools: that education for workers can play a vital role in social change and the reshaping of social conditions.

These poems were written at the Hudson Shore Labor School in 1940 and were printed originally in the booklet *"These Are the Words We Said,"* a collection of student writings distributed by the school.[37]

I

Your face, beautiful with belief,
You said,
No matter how bad things are, people will live
Who will be leaders, who will know and lead.
You said, They're not afraid.

Our country, North and South
West, East
Will grow alive and live with your belief,
With our belief, we people,
Our life and love of people, hope, and refusal of defeat

II

The living cells whose sum I am
Are warm,
Through the arterial rivers and veins
Blood runs, returns and runs,
And to each cell the blood,
According to its need,
Brings fuel, brings that cell bread
And each cell works, makes heat, makes me.
From work of all
I exist . . . Whole . . .

The sum of sums like me—the world.
Too bad the world has no impartial blood.

III

My parents kept me from children who were dark
So thoroughly that I was not aware
What they were doing
As they took me to school and left me at the door.

They hurried me through Harlem in the morning
To take the el. We lived above the hill.
They said, "After dark you must never take the el."
When I did I was frightened.

One does not speak to strangers in the city.
No need to be told you must not speak to negroes
For they were always strangers—in el-passed windows,
On ugly streets that were always far from home.

Forgive me please.
I will not say you are no different from me.
Strangers are different all; they make me shy.
But we are nearer, nearer body and mind
Than me and a debutante, or a Legion man.

—Ann McAvoy, 1940

Corky Row

Things have sure changed on Corky Row.
Things are just in the crack-up stage.
Gosh, it's fun to think back to the good old days:
How we saved for the pleasure of boat rides together;
How we loved the Sunday school picnics
because we got new dresses and ribbons;
How the boys teased and then treated us all to ice cream;
How the women loved to outdo each other
in the selection of clothes;
How the men were contented to play a game of cards
or an occasional game of checkers;
When everyone greeted one another
with a smile and a handshake.
Yes, sir, those were the good old days
before the mills closed down.
But things do change and it certainly has made
a lot of difference there.

Girls, forced to work in sweatshops,
to help support their families
Too tired at night to do anything
but nag and bemoan their past,
Not trying to help themselves.
Oh no! just nagging.

The boys have taken to drink
and never think of ice cream anymore.
Mothers get grayhaired worrying about their belongings
and how to keep them.
How they nag their families to a point of desperation.
No hate there really,
Just a lost feeling of days past.

Fathers are pathetic.
There is no work for them, but still they beg
for any kind of work
to help them keep their self-respect.
It is much harder for the men.
Instead of having their respect,
they are shunned and pushed around by all.

No more handshakes
when old friends meet,
Only a nod as they wearily pass by.
Love thy neighbor is very well to say
when you've got your belly full.
But try it on an empty stomach.

—Rita Gauthier, 1940

The following play was performed by students at the Hudson Shore Labor School, July 22, 1939. This production was billed as a "living newspaper" on the history of workers' education in the United States. The presentation was improvised by students and staff, largely from their own experience, with the exception of the first scene, which was taken from a written script. The play was performed on the front steps and porch of the Smith house, the family residence of Hilda W. Smith, which housed the Hudson Shore Labor School from 1939 to 1950.[38]

Workers' Education, 1939

At the beginning, the center lights go on. "Miss Smith" (played by a student) enters from the house and comes to the steps.

Miss Smith: Friends, neighbors and students . . . we welcome you here this evening and hope that you will share with us some of the fun we are having at Hudson Shore Labor School, and some of the ideas in which we believe. We are building a school here because we believe that the working people of this and other countries need and must have more education in order to help them understand and solve their problems, as workers and as citizens in a democracy. This need has existed for many years. When women were first beginning to go into the factories, early in the 19th century . . . .

(*Blackout.* Miss Smith down to position behind pillar. Characters in old fashioned dresses for Scene 1 enter, take their places. Lights up on porch area.)

SCENE 1: We First Go into Industry.
Lowell, Massachusetts—19th century
(Two girls are sitting on porch)

Helen: Did you see the new boarder at supper tonight?
Rose: Yes, wasn't she dowdy!
Helen: I suppose they'll put her up here with us. They always do.
Rose: I suppose they will. They're so crowded here, with all the new girls working at the mill. (There is a knock at the door.)
Helen: Shhh. Come in. (Pearl enters, in drab clothes, carrying suitcase. Helen and Rose rise, introduce themselves.)
Helen: You can put your bag over there.
Pearl: (putting it in corner) Thank you.
Rose: Won't you sit down?
Pearl: Thank you.
Rose: Have you come to work at the mill?
Pearl: Yes. A man at the farm where I live told me there were lots of jobs here at $5 a week, and that the work was easy, and the girls wear silk dresses. (Helen and Rose laugh.)
Rose: I hope you don't believe that!
Helen: Those agents will say anything to get the girls here.
Pearl: What! Do you mean it isn't true?
Rose: Of course it isn't. We work fourteen hours a day, from five in the morning until seven at night, with only a half hour at lunch. And when we get home at night we're so tired we can't eat our supper.
Helen: And we wear aprons—not silk dresses.
Rose: And do you know how much we make?
Helen: $1.50 a week, and we work *hard*.
Pearl: Oh! That's terrible! Oh, why did I ever leave the farm! Oh, don't you have any fun at all?
Helen: Now, now . . . certainly we have fun. We do a lot of reading, and we even have classes!
Rose: Yes, and we read novels too! Did you ever read a novel?
Pearl: Novels! Oh, no! Why, I've just read the scriptures and Pilgrim's Progress. . . . Do you mean you read *novels* here?
Rose: Yes, and other things too . . . poetry and . . .
Helen: And we have classes in philosophy and psychology and astronomy and we have a paper of our own, and Rose is the editor of it.
Pearl: Why! Why . . . a Lowell mill is just like a college!
(*Blackout.* Pearl and Helen exit. Rose goes to right pillar, where she remains for rest of play. Pillar lights up.)

Audience sings:
>Oh, you build and you turn,
>And you plow and you sow,
>And you hammer and you churn,
>Tell me, worker, what you earn?

Rose: (talking to Miss Smith) How long was it before women like yourself had a chance to study their problems?

Smith: It was many years. Organization had to come first, organization of the thousands of women who were going into industry. The first national organization was the Women's Trade Union League, founded in 1903. Along with this growth there were individuals in various communities doing what they could to further an interest in education. In 1915 . . .

(*Blackout.* Miss Smith goes onto porch and Mrs. Smith enters from inside. Porch lights up.)

SCENE 2: Others Realize our Problems.
West Park, 1915.

Mrs. Smith: Hello, Hilda, my dear. I'm so glad you're back.

Miss Smith: Hello, mother.

Mrs. Smith: You look tired, dear.

Miss Smith: I am—tired and discouraged.

Mrs. Smith: Why, isn't the community center at Bryn Mawr going well?

Miss Smith: Yes, as well as could be expected. People are having a good time and enjoying it, but so much more needs to be done.

Mrs. Smith: What do you mean?

Miss Smith: Since I've been living in Bryn Mawr I've seen people living and working in such terrible conditions—crowded rooms, no ventilation . . .

Mrs. Smith: But aren't there churches and organized charities to help the needy?

Miss Smith: Needy! They aren't people who need charity! They do useful work and all they ask is a decent wage for it. They're free citizens in a democracy and want to solve their problems.

Mrs. Smith: Well, why don't they protest to their employers?

Miss Smith: They don't dare. If they try, they're fired and blacklisted and can't get a job any place else.

Mrs. Smith: What can be done, then?

Miss Smith: They need organization. They've tried it in some places and had some success. Look at the employers . . . they're

organized and it's one of their chief sources of strength. But so many people can't see the strength they'd get from unions.
Mrs. Smith: Perhaps if they were educated to it . . .
Miss Smith: Yes, exactly. And that's what I want to do. I'm tired of charity work. Something much more important is needed.
(*Blackout.* Miss Smith back to position. Pillar lights up.)
Rose: What about the Women's Trade Union League? What did they do about education?
Miss Smith: Education was one of the main points of their program, and at a conference in 1916, they asked the women's colleges to help them. But the war interfered with the development of these plans. However, quite apart from a knowledge of these demands, one of the leaders in womens' education at the time, President M. Carey Thomas of Bryn Mawr College, was conscious of this need and anxious to help. We can see her speaking to Miss Smith, in 1920.
(*Blackout.* Miss Thomas enters from house. Miss Smith goes to porch. Porch lights up.)

SCENE 3: Others Suggest Ways and Means
Bryn Mawr College–1920.

Miss Thomas: Dean Smith, what would you think of a plan to open the doors of this college to women workers in industry?
Miss Smith: I think it's a splendid idea. There's a very great need for it, but how do you plan to do this?
Miss Thomas: There is nothing here at the college in the summer. There should be. If we are to build and keep our democracy, we must help every member of it to receive an education—women as well as men. Ten percent of the women in this country are in industry, and so far this college has never reached them. It can, and in the future we must see that it does.
(*Blackout.* Miss Thomas exits. Miss Smith goes back to position. Pillar lights up.)
Miss Smith: Plans were laid, and other people were brought in, people who believed in and had been trying to promote workers' education. The directors of Bryn Mawr unanimously voted the use of the college campus and equipment for this purpose. Committees for recruiting students were set up all over the country, and reports began coming in. Miss Ernestine Friedmann, one of the most active recruiters, reports . . . (Miss Friedmann comes onto steps in light.)

SCENE 4: We Gather from Various Industries.
America—1921

Miss Friedmann: New York—garment workers want to come to the Bryn Mawr Summer School. Boston—telegraph operators want to come. Minneapolis—soapmakers. Chicago—meat packers. Pittsburgh—steel workers. San Francisco—proof readers. . . (etc.)
(Miss Friedmann's back to audience. Audience sings.)
>We have gathered
>From the mills and factories,
>Wanting to understand
>The deep, wide world.

Rose: But how did it work? What were the classes like, and did the students have anything to say about what they were being taught?

Miss Smith: At first the instructors were almost as bewildered as the students.

(*Blackout.* Miss Hewes enters from inside. A few students gather from porch and audience. Porch lights up.)

SCENE 5: We Experiment in Cooperative Learning.
Bryn Mawr College—1921

>Myths of the Past
>Have lost their power,
>Time, time flying fast
>Brings a new hour.
>Nations despairing need a new creed,
>Seeking and sharing,
>Youth, youth must lead.

Miss Hewes: Let us consider first the HYPOTHESIS advanced for the explanation of this situation, giving due weight to both ideological and mechanical developments. Do not fail to give meticulous attention to the factors which must be correlated for the determination of unit cost.

Student: Excuse me, Miss Hewes, but I haven't understood a word you've said.

Miss Hewes: Well, just let me elaborate a little. FIRST: we must give due consideration to the requirements of successive technological changes. SECOND . . .

Student: But Miss Hewes . . .

Miss Hewes: Just a moment. SECOND: We must describe and evaluate the newer forms of corporate organization. THIRD: we must consider mass production as limited by and consistent with a developing or declining market. FOURTH:

Student: Miss Hewes, we can't understand any of what you're saying. There's just no . . .
Miss Hewes: (ever gentle) But I'm sure that if you'll just let me finish . . . FOURTH: We must calculate the revaluation of man hour compensation . . .
Student: But, Miss Hewes, there's no point in your finishing. We don't know what any of those words MEAN. We don't know what you're TALKING about, and we didn't come here for all that.
Miss Hewes: (sitting down) Oh, dear. Perhaps I haven't made enough effort to understand what your problems really are. Now tell me, what is it you want to learn about?
Student: Well, now in my shop there's been twenty people thrown out of work because of some new inventions. . . .
Second Student: And in my shop we've been trying to get a union organized but the conditions aren't so bad, so nobody's interested.
Miss Hewes: I am sorry. I didn't understand what you needed to know. I see now . . . these are the problems we must start with.
(*Blackout.* Pillar lights up.)
Rose: If these students were chosen from all over the country, in order to get most of the industries and sections represented, why weren't there any Negroes? Aren't they important too?
Miss Smith: The students themselves asked this question in 1926.
(*Blackout.* Students enter from audience and porch. Sit on steps. Porch lights up.)

SCENE 6: We Extend Our Experiment.
School meeting—1926.

(The students reenact an actual occurrence in 1926. The chairman opens meeting and asks for further recommendations to the Board of Directors. One student moves that four scholarships be set aside for Negro workers. Another student rises to say that she thinks that is all very well, but if they let Negroes in, the day will come when they will let Japanese and Chinese too, and then what will the world come to? Other students challenge her. She is from the West Coast, and knows how they work for nothing there and depress wages in general.)
Student: But that would be the point in letting them come. They'd learn what it means.
(There is further argument. Student moves that along with the four Negro scholarships, four be set aside for workers from foreign countries. Motion is seconded, voted on, passed. Foreign student from Sweden comes up from audience, students reach out their hands to

her. She stands at bottom of steps and speaks to audience, thanking them for admitting foreign girls.)

Swedish Student: On behalf of the Swedish labor movement and myself, I want to thank you all for admitting foreign students to this school. The workers everywhere must get together in order to learn and understand each others' needs and problems. I hope my being here will help bring closer to you the problems, struggles, and hopes of the Swedish workers. And from you I will be able to take back to my people the story of your problems and struggles. Then we will have more understanding of the problems that concern us all and we can work together toward a better world.

(She sits with the other students.)

(Negro girl enters from porch, stands in back of group of students and sings: "I'm gonna lay down my sword and shield." Students and audience join in chorus: "Ain't gonna study war no more."

(*Blackout.* Exit. Pillar lights up.)

Rose: But with only a hundred students how can you hope to reach very far, and how are all the others going to get a chance?

Miss Smith: Other schools are growing up. In 1927, the University of Wisconsin opened its doors in the summer to industrial workers; in 1928, the Southern Summer School opened in Sweet Briar College, Virginia; in 1929, a winter residence school called Vineyard Shore was held here at West Park; in 1930, two former students started the workers' school of the Pacific Coast at Occidental College; in 1933, an office workers' school was started at Oberlin College; and now Hudson Shore Labor School, with nineteen years of continuous existence behind it on the Bryn Mawr campus.

Rose: How do the workers from so far and wide find out about the school?

Miss Smith: We have recruiting committees from all over the country.

(*Blackout.* Porch lights up on students.)

SCENE 7: We Come to the School.

(Scene shows a student who has been to the school telling other students about it, encouraging them to apply. Questions and answers about the school, how much it costs, what they teach, who's there, etc. At end of scene there is a blackout, audience sings "We have gathered," while people for next scene are taking their places. At end of song, lights up and student goes to steps from audience.)

SCENE 8: We Want to Know Other Workers.

(Student says: "I want to go to that school because these are my problems—trying to interest different workers in doing something about their problems." She then goes from one to the other of three workers, who are pantomiming their work in three different spots—a domestic worker, a beauty operator, and a textile worker. She suggests that each come with her to a discussion of the Wagner Act. Domestic worker is only mildly interested but says she can't come until late, if at all, etc. The textile worker is not interested. Says: "I've got a good job, good conditions, a good boss, why should I worry about that stuff?" The beauty operator is anxious to come but can't get off. At the end, student turns to audience and says: "This is my problem. How am I going to interest these workers in these matters which are so important for them?")
(*Blackout.* Students for next scene take their places. Lights.)

SCENE 9: We Want to Learn from Other Workers.

(Two girls in bathing suits lie on porch pantomiming swimming. Instructor teaching them. Third student enters. General repartee. Instructor finally calls REST. They sit around, talking. Instructor tries to interest them in a current events forum to be held that night. All they want to do is swim. Almost no response, except one student who is promptly booed down by the rest. Instructor turns to audience in gesture of despair: "I'm STUCK.")
(*Blackout.* Pillar lights up.)
Rose: She must be glad to know that there is a school where she can learn from other workers how to handle similar problems.
Miss Smith: Yes, and a school where she can exchange ideas with other girls in different situations.
(*Blackout.* Porch lights up.)

SCENE 10: We Want to Study with Other Workers.

(Two men, members of a grievance committee, are sitting on the porch. Girl enters, submits a complaint from the other women workers in the factory. Men try to boo her down on grounds that women are always complaining, but they don't do anything about it and they are lousy union members anyway . . . etc. Girl tries to convince them of their stupidity and selfishness, and ends up with fact that she's going to Hudson Shore Labor School and they will see some action when she gets back with a new sense of confidence in herself as a union leader

and an educator of the other women who need to learn to speak courageously for their own rights.)
(*Blackout*. Pillar lights up.)
Rose: But in lots of American communities there are women whose voices are being heard, aren't there?
Miss Smith: Yes, and you'll find some of them at the school too.
(*Blackout*. Porch lights up.)

SCENE 11: We Want to Cooperate with Other Workers.

(Three girls on steps, beefing on the conditions in their shop. "Let's go on strike. That last one was fun." "Yes, let's. There's no excuse for the toilets being in such shape," etc. Several minor complaints come forth. Another girl enters, tries to calm them down: "Just because they've got a union they can't go mad with power; strikes aren't the only way of getting things", etc. Suggests they form a grievance committee and learn together what good grievance procedures and techniques can be. This they decide to do by contacts with other workers who are studying similar problems at Hudson Shore.)
(*Blackout*. Pillar lights up.)
Rose: There must be a great demand for a place where such things can be freely and fearlessly discussed. (In quick succession, the following people speak from the audience.)
First: There is. The United Radio, Electrical and Machine Workers would like to have a conference at the Hudson Shore in September.
Second: The Amalgamated Clothing Workers would like to come in October.
Third: The Industrial Division of the YWCA would like to have its leaders' conference here early in October.
Fourth: A local of the ILGWU has already had a conference here, and now I should like to make a request for Local 32 for a conference here late in the fall.
(Miss Carter rises from audience and goes to steps.)
Miss Carter: One of the main reasons that the Bryn Mawr Summer School has moved into a permanent home at West Park is in order to meet just such needs as these. Now, as the Hudson Shore Labor School, it extends its hospitality to these and many other workers' education groups. May you all come for study and discussion of your problems—and may you all carry back to your organizations the same spirit of service that our students are taking back to their own communities from this summer's school.
(During this speech five girls come out of the house and stand behind her. After she has finished the audience begins to hum the verse to Hans Eisler's "United Front." The five girls speak.)

First: Back to Pittsburgh, to help develop the educational facilities there.
Second: Back to Boston, to help work for better social legislation.
Third: Back to Chicago, to make my fellow workers feel they must become conscious members of our American communities.
Fourth: Back to Bridgeport, knowing now that my job is not an isolated thing, concerning myself alone, but that it is an important part of society.
Fifth: Back to Wheeling, West Virginia, with a new feeling of what the words "tolerance" and "internationalism" can mean.
(Audience sings "United Front" chorus slightly changed and follow students from porch to barn, for "Folk Festival.")

> *Chorus: So—march, two, three,*
> *So—march, two, three,*
> *To the work that we must do.*
> *March back to the mills and the factories,*
> *For the world is in need of you.*

Notes

1. Doris Cohen Brody, "American Labor Education Service, 1927–1962: An Organization in Workers' Education" (Ph.D. diss., Cornell University, 1973).

2. Louise Leonard McLaren to Lucile Kohn, November 15, 1933, American Labor Education Service Papers (hereafter cited as ALES Papers), Labor Documentation Center, Martin P. Catherwood Library, New York State School of Industrial and Labor Relations, Cornell University, Ithaca, N.Y., Box 1. Hilda Worthington Smith, *Opening Vistas in Workers' Education: An Autobiography of Hilda Worthington Smith* (Washington, D.C.: By the author, 1978), pp. 193–94.

3. "Constitution of the Joint Committee of Affiliated Summer Schools for Women Workers in Industry," adopted December 8, 1928; Executive Committee Minutes, April 1928, ALES Papers, Box 1.

4. Smith, *Opening Vistas*, pp. 113ff.; Hilda Worthington Smith, *Women Workers at the Bryn Mawr Summer School* (New York: Affiliated Summer Schools for Women Workers in Industry and the Association

for Adult Education, 1929). The papers of the Bryn Mawr Summer School were deposited in several repositories: see the Hilda Worthington Smith Papers, Schlesinger Library, Radcliffe College, Cambridge, Mass.; Hilda Worthington Smith Papers, Franklin D. Roosevelt Library, Hyde Park, N.Y.; Bryn Mawr Summer School Papers, State Historical Society of Wisconsin, Madison, Wisconsin; Marion Park Files, Bryn Mawr College Archives, Bryn Mawr, Pennsylvania.

5. Alice Shoemaker, "The Wisconsin School," in Affiliated Schools' Scrapbook, ALES Papers, Box 38; Report of the Educational Department, October, 1933, ALES Papers, Box 1.

6. Smith, *Opening Vistas*, pp. 171–73; Executive Committee Minutes, April 28, 1933, Box 13; Joint Administrative Committee Minutes, November 12, 1932, Box 13; Education Department Report, October 1933, Box 1 (all in ALES Papers).

7. Smith, *Opening Vistas*, pp. 183–90, 202 ff.; interview with Hilda Worthington Smith, March 11, 1975, deposited with the Southern Oral History Program, University of North Carolina, Chapel Hill, North Carolina. In New York City in the 1930s Hilda Smith helped organize classes in pottery and art for an art workshop that was run with much success by Mabel Leslie, a former electrical worker and officer of the WTUL who had studied in Europe.

8. See Mary Frederickson, "A Place to Speak Our Minds: The Southern Summer School for Women Workers" (Ph.D. diss., University of North Carolina at Chapel Hill, 1981).

9. See Chapter 7.

10. Eleanor G. Coit, "Progressive Education at Work," in *Workers' Education in the United States*, ed. Theodore Brameld (New York: Harper & Bros., 1941), p. 165; Education Department Reports, November 1931 and October 1933, ALES Papers, Box 1.

11. ALES-sponsored printed works and mimeographed pamphlets included Jean Carter, *Mastering the Tools of the Trade* (English grammar); Olga Law Plunder, *Methods of Teaching English to Workers' Classes*; Jean Carter, *This America: A Study of Literature Interpreting the Development of American Civilization*; Colston Warne, *Money and Banking*; Caroline Ware, *The Worker Goes to Market*; Hilda Worthington Smith and Jean Carter, *Education and the Worker-Student*; Lois MacDonald and Emmanuel Stein, *The Worker and the Government*; Lincoln Fairley, *Company Unions*; Esther Porter, *Dramatizing Industrial Scenes*; George S. Mitchell, *Some Problems of the Textile Industry*; Elsie Gluck,

An Introduction to American Trade Unions; John C. Kennedy, *Unemployment and Its Problems*; and Helen D. Hill, *The Effect of the Bryn Mawr Summer School as Measured in the Activities of its Students*. The Affiliated Schools also produced a series of "scrapbooks" which contained collections of articles and student-produced collections such as "Women's Experience in American Industry" and "The Labor Drama." In addition to these, publications produced jointly with other organizations appeared, such as the *Annotated List of Material for Workers' Classes*, produced with the American Federation of Teachers.

12. Mildred Price, "The Effects of an Adult Education Project Upon a Group of Industrial Women" (M.A. thesis, University of Chicago, 1930); Eleanor M. Snyder, *Job Histories of Women Workers at the Summer Schools, 1931–34 and 1938* (Washington, D.C.: U.S. Women's Bureau, 1939, Bulletin no. 174); quotation from "Foreword" of Snyder, *Job Histories*, written by Carter Goodrich, p. vii; Amy Hewes, *Women Workers and Family Support: A Study Made by Students in the Economics Course at the Bryn Mawr Summer School* (Washington, D.C.: U.S. Women's Bureau, 1925, Bulletin no. 49); Amy Hewes, *Women Workers in the Third Year of the Depression* (Washington, D.C.: U.S. Women's Bureau, 1933, Bulletin 103); and George F. McCray, *An Evaluation of Workers' Education*, published by the WPA Workers' Education Program and the Chicago Committee of the Affiliated Schools, 1936, ALES Papers, Box 13.

13. Education Department Report, November 1931, ALES Papers, Box 1.

14. Ibid. See also Florence Hemley Schneider, *Patterns of Workers' Education: The Story of the Bryn Mawr Summer School* (Washington, D.C.: American Council on Public Affairs, 1941).

15. Joint Administrative Committee minutes, January 1932, ALES Papers, Box 1.

16. Files of the Executive Committee and Joint Administrative Committee, ALES Papers.

17. Ibid.

18. Shoemaker to Kohn, November 15, 1933; McLaren to Kohn, November 15, 1933; Meeting of the Board, Minutes, November 18, 1933, ALES Papers, Box 1.

19. Hilda Smith stayed with the FERA after its reorganization under the WPA until 1943; she then moved into war work for the Public Housing Administration. In 1945 she became a lobbyist for the National Committee for the Extension of

Labor Education, working unsuccessfully for a bill to fund labor education. After 1950 she held a variety of positions as consultant and staff member to various foundations, ending her working career at the Office of Economic Opportunity in 1965. Her papers are deposited in several places, but the Hilda Worthington Smith Papers, Schlesinger Library, Radcliffe College, Cambridge, Mass., contains the full manuscript of her autobiography.

20. Smith, *Opening Vistas*, p. 234; Interview with Hilda W. Smith; Eleanor Coit File, ALES Papers, Box 13.

21. Executive Committee Minutes, January 1934, ALES Papers, Box 13; Supplement to Director's Report, January 1935, ALES Papers, Box 13.

22. Director's Report, January 1935, ALES Papers, Box 13.

23. Executive Committee Minutes, Education Department Report, November 1932, Box 1; Report to Directors, March 1, 1934, Box 13 (both from ALES Papers).

24. Eleanor Roosevelt had supported the Affiliated Schools' fund-raising appeals in the past. Executive Committee Minutes, December 10, 1933, Box 13; Smith to Coit (1933?), ALES Papers, Box 5.

25. The Affiliated Schools published an annotated bibliography on workers' education, as well as a series of "Scrapbooks" that were collections of articles. Two examples were "Snapshots of Workers' Education Here and Abroad," and "Teaching Economics in Workers' Education."

26. Information on these men was drawn from Executive Committee Minutes and the general correspondence. It is clear from these sources that they could devote less time to the organization than did the original female board membership.

27. For a discussion of the workers' education movement and organized labor in the 1930s see Mark Starr, "The Current Panorama," in *Workers' Education in the United States*, ed. Theodore Brameld (New York: Harpers & Bros., 1941), pp. 89–113.

28. Eleanor Coit, "The Affiliated Schools for Workers," *Progressive Education* (April–May 1934) in ALES Papers, Box 36.

29. Special Board Meeting Minutes, March 28, 1936, ALES Papers, Box 13.

30. Executive Committee Minutes, June 6, 1936; Report of the Director, February 18, 1938, ALES Papers, Box 13.

31. For an examination of the ALES after 1939, see Brody, "The American Labor Education Service," Constitu-

tion and By-Laws, 1939, ALES Papers, Box 1.

32. There is a growing body of literature on "social feminism" and the roots of women's involvement in reform movements in the late nineteenth and early twentieth centuries. see Ellen Condliffe Langemann, *A Generation of Women: Education in the Lives of Progressive Reformers* (Cambridge, Mass.: Harvard University Press, 1979); Nancy Schrom Dye, *As Equals and As Sisters: Feminism, Unionism, and the Women's Trade Union League of New York* (Columbia: University of Missouri Press, 1980); Susan Ware, *Beyond Suffrage: Women in the New Deal* (Cambridge, Mass.: Harvard University Press, 1981); Stanley Lemons, *The Woman Citizen: Social Feminism in the 1920's* (Urbana: University of Illinois Press, 1973). Or see the autobiographical writings of the women themselves: Jane Addams, *Twenty Years at Hull House* (New York: Macmillan Co., 1961), Mary K. Simkhovitch, *Neighborhood: My Story of Greenwich House* (New York: W. W. Norton & Co., 1938).

33. Joint Administrative Committee, Minutes, April 1932; Executive Committee Minutes, April 14, 1928, ALES Papers, Box 1.

34. Interview with Hilda W. Smith conducted by the author.

35. Education Department Report, 1932, ALES Papers, Box 1.

36. "Bryn Mawr and the Industrial Girl," by Helen Moscicki, Bryn Mawr, 1928, in Mildred Price, "The Effects of an Adult Education Project," p. 131.

37. From "These Are the Words We Said," ALES Papers.

38. From the Hilda W. Smith Papers, Schlessinger Library, Cambridge, Mass., Box 15, folder 260.

Chapter 7

Education in Working-Class Solidarity: The Summer School for Office Workers

Alice Kessler-Harris

On first acquaintance, the Summer School for Office Workers (SSOW) appears to have been much like the other summer schools for women workers that originated in the 1920s. It was designed, said the organizers, "to bring together women office workers from different sections of the country in order to study the present economic system and the part which they as workers play in our industrial and social life."[1] The school was residential, was located on a college campus, attracted a committed group of students, and drew an impressive faculty from the best eastern and midwestern schools and colleges. Like other labor schools, the SSOW hoped, in the words of one of its founders, to encourage students to engage in "effective group action, growing out of a greater understanding of the forces affecting the students' economic and social lives."[2] Beyond these broadly stated purposes, however, there were enormous differences.

In contrast to other residential workers' education programs, the SSOW had a special mission: to break down the barriers between clerical and manual workers. The rationale for this new avenue into workers' education emerged out of changes in the nature of office work in the early part of the twentieth century, changes that sparked a debate about the relationship of office workers to manual workers and cohered around definitions of class. By the 1920s, the typical office had grown from a small, personal workplace to a large, impersonal center, the people who worked in these centers were increasingly female, and their work was becoming increasingly subdivided as the principles of scientific management took hold. The resulting reduction of most office jobs to routine, noncreative, and repetitive tasks accompanied an enormous growth in the work force.[3] Once a relatively select and largely male group, the clerical sector altered to become the most rapidly expanding segment of the work force.

As the character of office jobs changed, some noted the disappearance of the appurtenances that had made office work the province of the middle class. No longer could most office workers expect to exercise judgment and initiative, nor could they expect promotion. Rather, office jobs took on the form of blue-collar labor, with its demands for rote work and its insistence that workers give up any notion of careers in management. And increasingly office workers lacked the assurances of job security that had previously compensated for low pay. Social scientists in Europe and in the United States began to wonder how office workers fit into the lexicon of class. From the perspective of their tasks at work and in their relationships to supervisory staff, office workers seemed more akin to manual laborers than to the professionals and managers who had traditionally constituted the middle class. In terms of income, social relations, and relative leisure, office work increasingly failed to provide a life-style significantly different from that to which manual laborers aspired.

As the real lives of these two groups of workers grew closer, those in the office sectors feared, and therefore rejected, association with manual laborers. Most refused to join unions, for example, yet their real wages and their working conditions declined in the very decades that saw visible improvement in the lives of production workers. Some social scientists feared the likelihood of bitterness and frustration, with inevitable political consequences, as the benefits of a middle-class life-style became unattainable. Others, however, expected a future rapprochement between manual and nonmanual workers. When the new class of workers grew to maturity, it was thought, they would recognize their affinity with blue-collar workers and begin to identify with them instead of hoping to be like their bosses.[4]

The Summer School for Office Workers emerged out of this climate of debate about the class position of people who worked in offices. The idea came originally from Grace Coyle, a long-time social worker in the Industrial Department of the YWCA who was later to become a professor at Western Reserve University. In 1929, Coyle had just completed a lengthy study of the 4 million people employed in offices that effectively demonstrated the place of women at the bottom of the scale. These women not only suffered the disadvantages of declining wages and job satisfaction, but they were also likely to be the daughters and wives of men who were manual laborers. Convinced that the failure of members of this growing sector of the work force to understand their affinity to other workers deprived them of the capacity to act in political concert, Coyle persuaded Eleanor Coit, director of the Affiliated Summer Schools for Women Workers, to develop a program for office workers. Coit set to work to assemble a board of consultants. To economist Paul Douglas, she explained: "This group of workers are not admitted to either Bryn Mawr or Wisconsin Summer schools, and only a few clerical workers [are admitted to] the Barnard School. Because of the distinct economical problems of this group and the increasing need for a realization of their group problems on the part of clerical workers we have felt that a new school organized to meet the needs of this group would be valuable."[5]

Others in the early years of the school stated the case even more strongly. White-collar workers, argued economist Elinor Pancoast, were less "economically mature" than industrial workers. They had a different psychology, rooted in an older belief in a continuing opportunity to "rise to positions of business power and security which formerly set office workers apart from industrial workers."[6] To avoid feelings of isolation, an enhanced sense of individual responsibility, self-blame, and perhaps ultimately fascism, it was, noted one influential SSOW faculty member in 1936, "high time that these girls working in offices identify their economic interests with those of the girls working at the machines of industry."[7] The average industrial worker had long ago learned that her security lay in collective struggle; the SSOW meant to teach office workers not only the lessons of collective action but those of class consciousness as well. "The integration of the individual office worker with his group by the development of a sympathetic understanding of the labor movement" was its primary purpose.[8] Office workers had to learn something about working-class solidarity.

If the idea of the school was to enlighten office workers about their real places in the work force, its form derived from the decade-long experience of residential summer schools for women begun at Bryn Mawr in 1921. Bryn Mawr and its successors at Barnard, Wisconsin, and in the South had successfully demonstrated the advantage of residential experiences for women as a way of maximizing the strengths of a shared female experience in the process of organization. To the women who organized the SSOW the model must have seemed ideally suited to office workers. Here was a rapidly growing group of female workers, seduced by the possibility of white-collar work into jobs that seemed to offer upward mobility but that in fact increasingly held only limited possibilities. SSOW founders firmly believed that even a brief education, sensitive to the particular roles of office workers, could encourage them to see the work force and their places in it more realistically.

What had worked in the 1920s ran into difficulties in the 1930s, however, for both the form of education for women and its content faced the challenges posed by a newly aggressive labor movement. In the 1920s, workers' education for women had relied heavily on women's organizations. Recruitment, funds, and personnel had come from women's networks. But the Depression and the New Deal created a political climate more conducive to trade union organization than ever before. The still craft-centered American Federation of Labor (AFL) and the more spirited Congress of Industrial Organization (CIO) remained, however, primarily committed to old definitions of class, relegating white-collar workers to secondary places in a struggle that centered on control over heavy industry. In an effort to accommodate itself to the vision of a militant unionism, the SSOW shifted course. Instead of encouraging office workers to see themselves as a new proletariat, the school emphasized the need to bring a broader range of white-collar workers into trade unions. It stretched its concept of office workers so far that the focus on the special problems posed by socioeconomic change for a particular group virtually disappeared. In a period of heightened class awareness, the school abandoned its concern for the sensibilities of female office workers in the interests of a larger class that it could neither define nor fully understand.

The SSOW's increasing identification of broader categories of workers as candidates for unionization led it to an ever-closer alliance with, and finally dependence upon, the labor movement. But the 1930s no more solved the problem of how to place this new class than had the earlier decades, and when union militancy settled into day-to-day existence, the school found itself the servant of a labor movement whose main interests still lay in the old blue-collar sectors. This was not necessarily failure, for the SSOW served the labor movement effectively until its demise in 1962. But the cost of such service was abandoning notions of developing class consciousness among a new group of workers.

Confusion, however, emerged only later. In the beginning, Coit pursued the notion of an office workers' school energetically. To refine the new vision, she consulted leaders of the old progressive coalition that had spearheaded reform for women workers in the early years of the century and representatives of self-defined feminist groups. These included Elisabeth Christman of the National Women's Trade Union League (NWTUL), traditional arbiter between working women and trade unions; Margaret Williamson of the YWCA; Frances Cummings of the National Federation of Business and Professional Women's Clubs, then among the most militant of feminist organizations; as well as representatives of the National Jewish Welfare Board, the League of Girls Clubs, and the Women's Bureau of the Department of Labor. Although she hoped eventually for trade union involvement, Coit did not, in the initial phases, work closely with any union leaders. The start-up committee consulted only with the Brotherhood of Railway Clerks, and with the Stenographers, Bookkeepers, and Assistants Union. Several factors probably explain Coit's failure to reach out for trade union support. The craft-centered and production-oriented AFL had never encouraged unionization among office workers. Organized office workers were few and far between. In 1930 fewer than 2.5 percent of all women clericals belonged to trade unions, most of them to the Stenographers, Bookkeepers, and Assistants—a left-wing union which aroused Coit's fears that the school "should not be flooded by the communists." Much as Coit claimed to regret the absence of "adequate representation" from the organized clerical workers, she never filled the gap in the planning stage, and she waited until 1931 to add a member of the Bookkeepers, Stenographers, and Accountants Union to the committee.[9]

Together the planning group developed a concrete notion of what the school might be. Discussion focused on two issues: the mechanisms by which clerical workers could be encouraged to develop a group identity, and the potential for divisiveness inherent in separating clerical workers and industrial workers from each other in an educational institution. Underlying both was the implicit acknowledgment that women who were clerical workers shied away from either using trade union tactics or allying with those who did. As one student put it somewhat later, "Office workers don't consider themselves as really part of the 'working class.'"[10] But since, in the eyes of the SSOW organizers, this was a misperception that inhibited office workers from adequately understanding the world around them, undermining it became the school's first task.

Planning discussions expressed some of these concerns concretely. Trade unionist Philip Ziegler, president of the Brotherhood of Railway Clerks, preferred, as he wrote to Alice Shoemaker of the Wisconsin Summer School, "to have our women members associated with workers in other trades rather than segregated. For the purpose of developing labor solidarity and giving workers some understanding of each other's problems I felt that there should be no separation as between trades and classes." Like other members of the committee and the clerical workers they surveyed, however, he soon agreed that the differences between women factory and office workers warranted separate instruction. His members, for example, reported that "they didn't think" they "would fit in with the factory girls" and they "were so far ahead of the factory workers in education that they would be under a handicap if they were placed in classes with the factory workers."[11] Others thought that the clerical workers would have difficulty getting "acclimated" to the greater militancy of the factory workers and feared that they would be overwhelmed by them.[12]

The upshot of the debate was an agreement to reach unity through separation. Committee members, as Coit put it, agreed "that every effort must be made to have this educational project developed in such a way as to make the clerical group feel increasingly a part of the larger group . . . to emphasize the common interests of the clerical workers with other workers."[13] Unwilling to challenge the clerical workers' strong sense of identity, the committee urged separate standing within the Affiliated Schools for Workers network. The SSOW was to have its own board of directors, with which the head of the Affiliated Schools would deal. The board would work closely with the schools for industrial workers, yet be free to develop its own direction. This, it was felt, would create a consciousness "on the part of clerical workers that they had distinct problems" while opening the door to trade union activity.[14]

The planning committee's first official statement of purpose trod the narrow line between class consciousness and the individuality and upward mobility widely attributed to clerical workers. Faced with surveys that revealed office workers to be interested in job achievement, Coit wrote to Frances Cummings that the school would "offer to office workers an opportunity for study and for development in the understanding of life. The school," she went on, "is planned as a workers' education project. It is especially concerned in the group interests of office workers and in a deeper understanding by those workers of their economic life."[15] All mention of trade unionism, collective action, and social awareness were carefully excluded.

These relatively innocuous goals proved to be far too cautious in the context of the changing times. Between 1929 and July 1933, when the first group of thirty-three female clerical and office workers actually met, the stock market crashed, Herbert Hoover was driven from the White House, and a New Deal was proclaimed. Stimulated by these amazing economic circumstances, the labor movement stirred, providing a focal point for working-class efforts to organize. Simultaneously, Communist Party activity increased, raising economic issues to the forefront of consciousness. All these things led to more immediate involvement with economic issues. So, when the first call for applicants went out, potential students were told that the program was "planned to give the office worker a better understanding of the social and economic forces which are controlling her working life, and to form a basis for further study and for intelligent action in her community."[16] Applicants between twenty and thirty-five years old were asked to pay $12 a week for all expenses. They were not told that the committee hoped for fifty students.

Recruiting proved more difficult than the staff anticipated. Relying on networks of volunteer organizations such as the YWCA, the staff had already been forced to push back a projected 1932 start-up by a year. Even so, two requirements hindered the effort. Because they wanted young women to return to their communities with the ideas and inspiration gathered from their experience, the committee agreed to admit only "girls who have had some preparatory work in local classes." And even these "girls" had to provide part of their own expenses if their local committee or organization could not or would not subsidize them. On June 26, 1933, Coit complained that they still had only fourteen definite students. And on July 25, ten days before the summer school was to open, they were still recruiting. The thirty-three students who finally met at Oberlin College for the two-week opening session represented a range of experience. They came from fifteen cities and eleven organizations. Most were sent by community organizations and business girls' clubs. Three were members of office workers' unions. Among them were stenographers, bookkeepers, file clerks, secretaries, and office machine operators.

From the beginning the SSOW adopted the content and pedagogical style that had become the hallmark of the industrial schools. Classes focused on issues of economics, social ethics, and community life. They utilized materials drawn from popular literature, but attempted to expose students to a broad spectrum of opinion and encouraged the use of the college library. In 1933 the reading list included Charles and Mary Beard's *Rise of American Civilization* and Harold Faulkner's *American Economic History*, as well as an array of fiction and biography. But most important, an extraordinary group of teachers (Theresa Wolfson, Orlie Pell, and Clara Kaiser among them) managed to turn the classroom into a vital forum for discussion, debate and critical thinking.

Teachers began with the students' concrete experience and moved from there to generalization and abstraction, and finally to the formation of informed opinion. They were concerned not with memorization so much as with the ability to think, argue, and influence. Because so much depended on teaching skills, instructors were carefully selected for their flexibility and adaptability. All instructors were expected to aid individual students in resolving the problems that emerged out of their own work experiences and at the same time to guide discussions to fruitful conclusions for the group as a whole. Since the entire group in the first two years was female, issues such as the passing over of women for promotion, unequal pay, and sexual harassment were important parts of the discussion.[17]

These methods proved enormously successful. Before they left, participants in the first summer institute formed a continuation committee to help recruit for next year. They prepared to work in small groups in their own communities, urged the school to extend the program to four weeks in 1934, and debated the feasibility of a six-week session. And they raised, but did not resolve, two issues of continuing importance. How, they asked, should occupational lines be drawn? And should men be admitted to the SSOW? For the moment, they recommended that the school be restricted to female office workers—or those temporarily unemployed who were usually office workers. And they urged every student to return to her community and conduct local classes in the winter. To maintain contact, they undertook to put out a newsletter, called "The Office Worker."[18]

Students seem to have been more amenable to notions of unity and more class conscious than organizers believed. At any rate, SSOW founders were delighted at the awareness of group interests that emerged from this two-week session. At its culmination, students wrote and presented a play that stressed the capacity of office workers to learn that they too were workers. It included a rousing rendition of the following song to the tune of "Polly Wolly Doodle."

The Union is the place for me,
The place for working girls
Who want some time to sing and play
And money we can spend.

Chorus
On the line, on the line, on the picket, picket line
We'll win our fight, our fight for the right
On the picket, picket line.

The girl who scabs is the girl who's yellow
And is a sight to see
We'll kick her out, We'll keep her out
With the picket, picket line.

As plans proceeded for the second, and then the third and fourth sessions, questions implicit in the early discussions began to emerge as problems. Only three of the first-year students were trade union members. But, according to one participant, "We all came to the decision that the office worker needed unionization, and left with the resolution to help strengthen the office unions in those cities where there are none."[19] The desire to incorporate more trade union members into the program meshed with faculty and student beliefs that unionization was the only answer to unpredictable working conditions. Wolfson put it this way in 1934: "Organization is a very important method for dealing with the economic problems that office workers are facing and for that reason we are anxious to have that point of view represented at the school."[20] To seal the bond between the school and the trade union movement, the school abandoned its earlier policy of recruiting through local women's organizations like the YWCA and sought out active trade unionists instead. The continuation committee urged that the second-year group "should give more consideration this year to the question of workers' organization."[21] Graduates of that group wrote to William Green, then president of the AFL, urging him to add a national organizer for office workers to his staff. "We feel," wrote Henrietta Klebe, chair of the 1934 continuation committee, "that it will be to the benefit of office workers if they enter the labor movement and it will be a particular benefit to the American Federation of Labor to have them in their ranks."[22]

Individuals followed through on these group initiatives. Doris Pieper of Chicago, for example, attended the 1935 session of the school at Bucknell

College. Within a week after she returned home, she had contacted John Fitzpatrick of Chicago Federation of Labor about a charter for office workers. And two weeks later, she proudly announced the receipt of a charter for Stenographers, Typists, Bookkeepers and Assistants Union number 20074.[23] To her first organizing meeting she invited another SSOW graduate who had been influential in setting up a national committee to do research on clerical workers.

As the CIO began an aggressive campaign to organize office and white-collar workers in the late 1930s, the importance of trade unions in the SSOW increased. By 1935 a third of the students belonged to trade unions.[24] In 1936 the first convention of the United Office and Professional Workers of America (UOPWA) included ten SSOW graduates, and in 1937 nearly half of the SSOW's residential students belonged to trade unions. The shifting composition, in the context of economic depression and organizational struggle, led to questions about curriculum and about the degree to which the summer school should serve unions.

Attracting trade union members in the new climate of trade union militancy required compromises in both residential conception and program format. Active unionists could rarely spare four weeks for study and contemplation. Ambitious plans to expand to seventy-five students had already created difficulty in recruiting students, leading school administrators to settle for a split program.[25] Beginning in 1935, some students would come for four weeks, others for two. The disruption of the residential community this heralded foreshadowed even greater difficulties to come when organizers decided to add weekend seminars to the residential programs. Weekend seminars addressed concrete issues of union organization and activity, of arbitration and grievance procedures, and of particular industrial problems, rather than the general socioeconomic questions that were at the heart of the residential school program. They succeeded in appealing to a broader constituency and they provided needed services, but at the cost of the sense of community and purpose so crucial to the summer school idea.

These internal changes had a broader political context. After 1936, efforts to organize office workers centered largely in the CIO, and for nongovernment workers, in the newly formed UOPWA. But not even the CIO was wholly committed to office workers, and these unions relied heavily on money and advice from left-wing groups, including the Communists.²⁶ But the Left had no more adequate an analysis of the proletarianization of office workers than had the old AFL. Nor did they consider the extent to which women's issues needed a specific focus. For their purposes, office workers were simply part of a larger middle class whose organization and support were necessary for victory in the crucial industrial sectors. If the school were to participate effectively in the trade union movement, then it had to play a role in developing a sense of unity among all white-collar workers. Its mission would have to change to address these issues. Feminist support and, specifically, women's issues such as had emerged during the first year were less important in this context than broader working-class alliances.

Not all students were prepared to make such connections. One second-year student, after reading a newspaper report describing the 1934 investigation for Communist activities of a FERA school directed by Orlie Pell at Oberlin, wrote to a fellow student, "You remember my surprise one night at school while you were there at the singing of socialist songs? Why did they have printed copies of these songs and encourage singing of them?"²⁷ She was not sure, she continued, that she believed in "organizing groups along certain lines, such as unions."

But many of the school's most active graduates accepted and encouraged the kind of reaching out implied by Socialist politics. "I am now YCL [Young Communist League], too," wrote a former Newport, Kentucky, student who was then editing the *Office Worker* to Orlie Pell. "Thought you might like to know that. We are working hard now in the AYC (American Youth Congress). We have rather a good unit." And she went on to describe some of the activities of other students. She had, she said, visited with one in Indianapolis. "She is working in the union there, also in the YCL, very active in the YW (Young Women's Christian Association). Myrtle Powell is also in all three of these besides taking an active part in the American Youth Congress." Then she continued, "I don't know whether either of the girls care if Marion Barbour knows they are in the YCL but I wouldn't mention it, but I thought you particularly would like their political backgrounds."²⁸

Pell understood the risks of diversity and willingly accepted them. She supported the notion of admitting men to the summer school, shepherding it through the committee in the winter of 1935, and writing enthusiastically in the summer, "We *are* going to have men! We have accepted several already and a few more may come in."[29] Among others, Pell believed that the school should be open to political discussion, urging that the "divergence of political opinion" be handled by selecting "representatives of various political opinions among each radical group." Admitting retail clerks and bringing office workers into closer contact with industrial workers might contribute to easing tensions. Students in the 1936 session supported this notion, and the committee in consequence cautiously agreed to take "a few well qualified" retail clerks for the 1937 school.[30]

These decisions influenced the school's curriculum and direction. For in order to attract a broader array of students, the committee began to experiment with different formats and new content. As Clara Kaiser, teacher and supporter, wrote in 1938, "Perhaps what is needed is the widening of its constituency by the inclusion of teachers, social workers and other professionals.... The focus in the curriculum under these conditions ought to include the wider problems of all white-collar and professional workers."[31] And indeed, in 1936 the school began to appeal to other white-collar workers through a series of conferences called White-Collar Workshops. The first of these occurred in the summer of 1936, in conjunction with the regular session of the school. Speakers on the general theme of "The Place of the White-Collar Worker in the Labor Movement" included representatives from unions of teachers, post-office clerks, state and federal employees, and the newspaper guild, as well as stenographers, typists, and bookkeepers. They raised questions about the efficacy of industrial or craft union methods for white-collar workers and about whether white-collar workers would take unified political action with industrial workers. Eleanor Coit recorded immense satisfaction with the conference, which, she wrote, "afforded to a group of white-collar workers" the opportunity "to think constructively about their place in the labor movement."[32] A successor conference held in 1937 raised the issue of organization explicitly. Participants were asked to address the question, "Should there be a different approach for middle-class and professional workers toward the labor movement than that of the industrial workers?"[33]

Students responded to the issue of white-collar identification with sufficient enthusiasm to encourage the SSOW national committee to raise the issue of expanding the school's constituency yet again. "One of the important questions now under discussion," reported Eleanor Coit in October 1937, "is the possible extension of the admission policy of the school to include white-collar workers other than office workers, such as teachers and social service employees."[34] These students, she suggested, might be financed by scholarships from the national offices of white-collar unions. To serve these new groups, the SSOW added a new training seminar to its summer sessions beginning in 1937. Primarily designed to teach the principles of workers' education to teachers, the seminar served union education programs.

The issue that had haunted the school's founders in 1933 had by now been resolved. In 1933, students had been asked to identify with workers. Ironically, as opportunities to organize broadened, the school's sense of itself narrowed. In 1937 students were asked to understand that "all of our girls are not individual workers but are part of a great many white-collar workers who needed to be made aware of their part in the entire social scene."[35] Thus students were no longer workers, but white-collar workers. They could, however, organize. As one faculty member put it, the psychology of the students had changed. "In the early days of the school," she said, "most of the students had a more academic interest in the labor movement, assuming that it did not concern them personally. Now their place in the labor movement is accepted."[36]

This shift to a labor movement orientation created inevitable pressures. In December 1937, the SSOW committee debated "whether the emphasis which certain unions feel it is necessary to put on immediate needs in contrast to long-range objectives would cause the school to modify its curriculum in any way."[37] Although then, and in the future, the committee affirmed the school's humanistic orientation, classroom problems became more specifically defined and the curriculum inevitably more problem oriented. Workshops included instruction on preparing graphs, charts, and other visual materials. Techniques of trade union organization were specifically discussed.[38] True to their original pedagogy, teachers continued to use students' own experiences as launching pads. In 1939, for example, the school stressed the theme of community organization, and a course in community relationships discussed three problems: securing facilities in a disadvantaged community, racial discrimination, and education for trade unionism in a community club.[39]

By the end of the 1930s the shape of the school had emerged. From a school for office workers, it had broadened gradually first to include retail clerks and then to serve other white-collar workers. Originally an institution supportive of union organizing, it had taken organization as a major goal, adding a full-time trade union person to its faculty in 1939. And from seeking out a wholly female student body it had moved eagerly to recruit men, who constituted nearly a third of the students in 1939 and whose members would increase steadily thereafter until, in some years in the 1950s, they made up a majority.

None of these changes smoothed the path of the executive committee. In the first seven years, the school moved from campus to campus. Oberlin twice, Bucknell, then Northwestern hosted the summer session until the school finally settled in the Chicago area, first at the Chicago Theological Seminary and the University of Chicago and then at Lake Forest College. Annually, the board debated the length of its session—four weeks or three—discussed how two- and four-week students were to be integrated, wondered whether trade union members and nonmembers could or should learn together, and attempted to find new ways to integrate residential students into the increasingly important workshops and seminars. The board experienced constant difficulty in recruiting. "At last I have some applicants for the summer school!"[40] wrote a local committee member to Orlie Pell in 1939. Each year the number of students able to stay for a four-week residential period dwindled: twenty-three in 1936, sixteen in 1938, twelve in 1939.[41] After the discouraging 1939 figures were in, the board voted reluctantly to shorten the session to three weeks. And each year, the service component of the curriculum grew to encompass the most significant portion of the school's activities, at least numerically. Contacts with women's groups that had provided initial funding and guidance, as well as students, now became minimal. The YWCA, WTUL, and Business and Professional Women's Association retreated in importance as trade unions filled the gap. A 1943 fund-raising letter described the school as "a labor school supported by unions and individuals interested in workers' education for white-collar workers."[42]

The executive committee had come to this description after a long and agonizing discussion spearheaded by the special report it commissioned in 1941 to explore options and goals. Elinor Pancoast, professor of economics at Goucher College and a long-time teacher in the school, took on the task of gathering data and surveying former students. Inconclusive as the final report is, it provides graphic evidence of the school's record. Only eighty-one of 285 students bothered to return their questionnaires. Of these, fifty-three were union members, and one-third (seventeen) of these had joined unions after their summer school experience. While many students continued to be active in community groups, more than half (forty-six) of those who returned questionnaires had never participated in local classes. As one former student put it, "I didn't answer the questionnaire which was sent to me because I didn't think I had anything new to tell you."[43]

Among the suggestions adopted by the faculty, several encouraged ways of creating closer friendships with white-collar unions. These included inviting their education directors to a special institute during the school's summer session, exploring the possibilities of classes in union organizing techniques, and including in the literature statements about what the school could do for the labor movement. While the final report insisted that the school could continue to serve union as well as nonunion groups, the faculty wondered whether "some adjustment of the curriculum is necessary in order to speed up the adaption of non-union students to the objectives of the school."[44]

The war years provided the circumstances that led the SSOW to move increasingly toward short-term institutes, workshops, and weekend conferences for trade union leaders and for particular unions. Time pressures pushed sessions down to two weeks and then to one, and into instrumental topics. Sessions focused on such topics as safeguarding labor standards and labor's demands in the postwar world. And the faculty suggested programs that would teach negotiation, grievance, and arbitration skills—all topics geared to the needs of paid union officials and activists.[45] Workshops were organized for telephone workers, and the training programs for teachers in workers' education took on larger dimensions. As the war ended, the structure of the summer schools involved a grab bag of activities. The two-week session held at Lake Forest in 1946 included, in addition to the two-week residential school, a one-day institute on the international labor movement, a course in community relations, a seminar in the techniques of worker education, and a special course in economics that stressed such topics as price control, full employment, social security, and trade unionism.[46] Residential students could participate in one or more of these programs. But they were designed to meet the needs of transient participants. The 1947 session stressed the "arts of communication" in the two-week residential school, and special projects included a leadership seminar for professional workers and a "week-end" school for Chicago postal and telephone unions. "Current economic and social issues constituted the core of the study program," wrote one commentator, "with special interest shown in living costs, housing discrimination and labor legislation."[47]

The school never entirely abandoned its attempts to recruit young women who "are interested in exploring further the problems and the role of the white-collar workers in the world today," but this goal was undermined by the continuing pattern of union services and by the all-inclusive definition that the term "white-collar" assumed. In 1948, the SSOW changed its name to "White-Collar Workshops" in recognition of the fact that postal employees and telephone workers as well as teachers and social workers had replaced the original secretaries and bookkeepers. Much of the early enthusiasm remained intact. "It was a wonderful revelation to me," wrote a 1946 student, "to find out that a mixed group can live together in peace and harmony regardless of race, color or creed."[48]

But the residential school that struggled to survive in the late 1940s and early 1950s resembled the earlier incarnation very little. In 1951, two-thirds of those resident students who came from the United States were paid union staff from AFL, CIO, and independent locals.[49] The 1952 session continued the trend, and in 1953 the board of directors met to decide how to handle the situation. In an acrimonious meeting on February 11, 1953, the board debated the school's direction. Eleanor Coit made the initial presentation. In the context of "the present day scene," she suggested, and in view of the comparatively small number of cities and unions that had "sent students to the school in recent years," she wanted to consider some changes. She was, she said, cognizant of new white-collar organizing efforts in both the AFL and CIO. But she wondered whether "the school's special function is to meet the needs of rank and file white-collar workers and local union officers, or to answer the more specialized needs of selected union leaders."[50] The board members argued at length and then concluded that they did not want to restrict the school to "the specific training of union leaders." And it agreed that it "should not give up the resident work" if it was at all possible to continue it.

For the following nine years, the school continued its resident work somewhat haphazardly but focused its major energies on a series of workshops designed to explore the impact of automation on white-collar workers. In 1962 the parent body, the American Labor Education Service, decided to dissolve. With scarcely a whimper, the board of directors of the White-Collar Workshops, among whom sat some of those who had founded the Summer School for Office Workers thirty years before, concurred. Twenty-nine years after the school's first classes, the board left its tasks to be "picked up by other groups in the economy."

If it did not meet its original expectations, the SSOW nevertheless served a useful purpose in educating several hundred women in community activism and trade union leadership. It was not entirely the fault of either the school or its organizers that notions of working-class solidarity that had formed the initial conceptual foundation for the school later foundered. External events of the SSOW's first decade simply captured the school, undermining its theoretical anchors. Caught up in the prevailing trade union militancy, the school abandoned the female support system that had earlier given it stability and a relatively independent financial base. The heady unionization campaigns in which office and other white-collar workers participated left little room for understanding the organizational consequences of dependence on a movement in which both women and white-collar workers were on the periphery. In an attempt to encourage unionization, the SSOW increasingly urged office workers to identify not with blue-collar but with white-collar workers, undermining an initial sense of broader unity among the "working class." And even when white-collar workers organized, the labor movement's own conviction that its base lay among manual workers provided no new impetus for the school to continue to participate in programs of economic awareness. Office workers were again left uncomfortably situated, somewhere between the labor movement and white-collar professionals. By the end of the 1930s, the white-collar workshops, having all but abandoned their earlier initiatives toward a broader education, had no choice but to pursue an alliance with an ambivalent trade union movement. This new group of workers remained isolated from the mainstream of labor, possessing, still, aspirations to upward mobility that had relatively little hope for success. In the 1960s—ironically, shortly after the White-Collar Workshops dissolved itself—debates about the nature of a "new working class" opened once again. Sparked by a vital women's movement and by rapid changes in office technology, the discussion once again poses the issue of how these new workers function in the class structure.

We Went to the Summer School

The following are excerpts from letters of former students of the Summer Schools for Office Workers, written in the 1930s and 1940s, and a skit, "We Take Our Stand," written and performed by the school's participants in August 1936. The skit points to the need for solidarity between office and factory workers.[51]

I have heard so much talk about "widening our horizons." The Summer School for Office Workers did that for me. I feel that if my experience in Summer School did nothing more than give me a personal view of business girls' working conditions in the various cities in the United States, it was worth the price. But the Summer School for Office Workers did more than that; it taught me definitely that I must have something to say about the way our affairs are run, and that I can do something about it; that I must be concerned about other business girls' problems as well as other workers' problems. We were not told what to do (each student determines the channels through which he can work most effectively), but our course of study gave us intelligent insight into economic and industrial problems.

—Leona B. Hendrix, n.d.

There were two main reasons why I went to the Summer Institute for Office Workers in 1933. The first one was that I was very much interested in studying and discussing unemployment, low wages, and depressions. I had been out of a job for a year and had had lots of time to ponder about the whys and wherefores of these things.

The second reason was curiosity. I had become very curious about the kind of school that would attract office workers to the extent that they would "sacrifice" their precious two weeks' vacation in order to attend.

The Institute proved to be a fascinating exchange of experiences and ideas. There were no dull, cut-and-dried recitations from memory; instead there were intensely interesting, full-of-life discussions of things which were real and important, of problems which challenged my thinking. I felt as though a door had opened in my brain and rooms which hadn't been used for years were swept and dusted, and after two exciting weeks of School there was no lack of occupants for the new space. Summer School inspired and challenged me and made me want to think. I saw opportunities for work that I hadn't been conscious of before and now I actually wanted to take advantage of them.

Did it last? Well, in 1934, I had a job and I managed after much difficulty to get two weeks' leave so that I could go back to attend the last two weeks of the now-full-fledged Summer School for Office Workers.

So, from my own experience, I say, for a mental stimulus with a powerful drive, try the Summer School for Office Workers.

Frances E. Scott, n.d.
Philadelphia, Pennsylvania

It is almost five years since I first attended the Summer Institute for Office Workers and its influence is still a major factor in my life. . . . It was something that happened inside me as the result of the stimulating experiences of learning and thinking with the group of office workers at the Summer School.

In the first place it gave me an abiding interest in life outside myself—an interest that seems to grow more interesting and more challenging each year—an interest in trying to help to get a more abundant life for a larger number of people. By "more abundant" I do not mean merely material abundance, such as better living conditions and more security (although that's part of it) but also more opportunity for education and chances to know the cultural and beautiful sides of life. It is hard to think of justice on an empty stomach, and hard for the victim of injustices to think of peace and love and beauty. So it's an ever-engrossing problem to try to make the cycle of life read more food, more justice, more peace, more love, and more beauty, instead of no food, no justice, no peace, no love, and no beauty. It is this interest that has lifted me out of myself and has shown me opportunities of doing things that I never saw before attending the Summer School.

Another important outcome of attending the school is the ever-growing circle of interesting people whom I could not have met were it not for contacts made at the Summer School—vital and interesting people doing exciting things in the labor movement and in the fields of education and social work. Some of these persons are acquaintances, and it is a privilege to meet them and hear their views; and others are friends, people who are interesting to know. These friendships are sincere and lasting because of the bond of a common interest in a common cause. And it is all possible because I was lucky enough to get to go to the Summer School for Office Workers.

—Marian V. Carrol, n.d.

We Take Our Stand

SCENE 1: The office of the Gormon Corporation. There are four girls at desks—two typists and two bookkeepers. Clara gets up and goes to Rose's desk. She whispers to her and then turns to the other girls:

Clara: Did you notice that the machinery isn't running?
Jane: Yes. It's awfully quiet in there. Has something gone wrong?
Clara: No. Not with the machinery.
Ruth: Something is wrong with the pay everyone here gets and the hours we all work.
Clara: That's why the place is so still. The shop workers are having a meeting.
Ruth: I think we ought to be in on it.
Mary: What for? They'll get into trouble for stopping in the middle of the day.
Ruth: Well, we ought to stop too.
Mary: And lose our jobs?
Clara: Mary, you don't understand. The factory workers are talking about a strike for better wages and shorter hours.
Mary: I wouldn't mind a raise. But I need my job.

Education in Working-Class Solidarity · 245

Ruth: So do we all.

Clara: Let's face the facts. When and if the shop workers go on strike, what are we going to do?

Ruth: We've got the same reasons for striking that they have. $15 a week for a bookkeeper is no pay. It's a bribe.

Clara: And $12 a week for a typist isn't enough for room and board.

Jane: Don't forget that Mary and I are only getting $11 a week.

Clara: And I haven't forgotten all the overtime we've worked without even a word of thanks, not to speak of getting paid for it. We're certainly no better off than the factory workers.

Ruth: And they don't have to come to work dressed to look like twice their pay like we do.

Mary: But half a loaf is better than none.

Ruth: Let's not talk so much. What are we going to do?

Mary: I say mind our own business.

Jane: Eleven dollars worth? I'm for striking if the factory workers do.

Ruth: I agree with Jane.

Mary: I'll stick with you. But I still don't see why we should support the factory workers. We want better pay, but they couldn't help us. Why should we help them?

Clara: If we help them win their demands, they'll help us win ours.

Jane: You think you're different, Mary, because you've got a desk of your own to work on. But you and I get a dollar less than the factory girls. (As she talks, Hannah, Grace and Mac enter, wearing aprons/smocks.)

Clara: What's up, Hannah?

Hannah: We've decided to go on strike unless Mr. Williams signs the agreement right now.

Grace: And we want you to come out with us.

Hannah: In fact, if you girls say you're ready to strike, the boss may give in without a strike.

Clara: We're all with you.

(The boss enters as she finishes.)

Williams: Why aren't you working? You've still got an hour before lunch. (To Hannah:) What are you doing here in the office?

Hannah: Mr. Williams, unless you sign the agreement today and grant us union wages, an eight hour day, and union recognition, we're all going on strike.

Williams: Who's we?

Hannah: All the factory and all your office workers.

Williams: What have the office workers got to do with it?

Clara: We all know the factory workers deserve better conditions.
Williams: (to factory workers) Bring the agreement into my office. We'll talk it over. (He exits.)
Ruth: I think he gave in.
Clara: I think so too.
Mary: He was pretty angry at us. I wonder what he'll do?
Clara: Here they come. (Hannah, Grace and Mac rush in, waving agreement.)
Hannah: Thanks to you girls, we've won. Wait til the shop hears this. (They exit.)
Williams: I'm surprised at you girls.
Clara: Why Mr. Williams?
Williams: I thought at least my office staff was loyal to the firm.
Clara: But we didn't do anything against the firm. Those factory workers deserve decent wages and they'll do better work if they get them.
Williams: I don't care what they do. Most of them can be replaced in five minutes if I wanted. But you girls. You've worked here a long time. I feel almost like a father to you. And then, whose side do you take? Aren't you satisfied here?
Jane: We certainly could stand a raise in pay.
Williams: I'll consider it. But you'll have to prove that you're loyal to the firm. All right, Jane, type this up. "We the undersigned hereby agree never to join a union or participate in any strike against the Gormon Corporation." Now I want everyone to sign that.
Jane: That's not fair.
Clara: It's not legal to make us sign that.
Williams: Then you're not loyal to the firm. I'll fire all of you if you don't sign that pledge.
Clara: We won't sign.
Williams: (shouting) Your signatures or your jobs.
Mary: But, Mr. Williams . . .
Clara: Come on, girls. . . . We'll be back when you're ready to sign a union agreement. (They exit as Williams crumples up typed pledge. Blackout.)

SCENE 2: A picket line. The four office workers are picketing up and down and humming "On the Line." Suddenly, Hannah, Grace, Mac and a group of factory workers rush out. The office girls greet them and there is general excitement.

Clara: What happened?
Grace: We couldn't stand it any longer.

Education in Working-Class Solidarity

Clara: But what about your agreement?

Hannah: He was breaking it right and left. Anyhow, what did you expect us to do? Scab? (They all hug and shake hands. One of the girls starts the rest in singing—to the tune of "The Old Gray Mare.")

> Mr. Williams ain't what he used to be
> ain't what he used to be
> ain't what he used to be
> Since the union came.

Hannah: (picketing with Clara) You know, Clara, this is the first time the factory workers have supported the office workers on strike.

Clara: And I think it's only the beginning. (Blackout)

SCENE 3: The entire group of strikers is sitting and talking among themselves.

Hannah: Are we ready to start the meeting? All right, Mac, what did you want to say?

Mac: If it weren't for the office workers, we wouldn't be out on strike now. The boss told us tool and die makers today that he's willing to take us back right now but we've got to forget about the office workers.

Grace: Is that so? Don't forget that this is a joint strike. You had no right to see the boss without the rest of us. But we're not going back until all of us are ready.

Ruth: And we won't be ready until we win.

Mac: Well, then you're going to keep it up without us. Why should we suffer because the office workers are on strike?

Mary: And on whose account were the office workers locked out?

Mac: Well, are you going back or do we go alone?

Hannah: The office workers have been out for sixteen weeks; we've been out for twelve. We've stuck together because we know this strike belongs to all of us. We're not going to give in now.

Mac: Then you refuse to go back?

Hannah: It's up to the strikers. All those in favor of going back without the office workers. (Mac says "aye") Mac, do you know what this means?

Mac: It means we go back without you.

Clara: We'll win our strike without them.

Hannah: Those tool and die workers would be all right. But they've got the same idea you office workers used you have. They think they're better than the rest of us.

Clara: If we were all in one union, they would have to stick with us.
Grace: It won't be long before they understand. Now they don't consider us because we are unskilled workers. But if the office workers learned better, they will too. (laughter) How about a song before we go back to the picket line. (Strikers sing "Solidarity" starting to leave as they finish the song. Blackout.)

SCENE 4: The picket line. Strikers are picketing and singing "Please, Mr. Boss." They sing the song twice and then start to hum as Clara steps off the picket line and says to the audience:

Clara: When workers, whether they are office or factory workers, go out on strike, they need not only their own solidarity but that of the labor movement, and the aid of all those who think they have a right to decent conditions. Come on up and join our line. Help us sing; help us picket; and help us win.

Audience follows directions and join the picket line on the stage, until the entire group—actors and audience—move on out of the theater/hall together.

Notes

1. "The Summer Institute for Office Workers, Oberlin College. July 15–29, 1933," American Labor Education Service Collection, Industrial and Labor Relations Archives, Cornell University (hereafter cited as ALES), SSOW Miscellaneous 1933, Box 91.

2. Orlie Pell, "Summer School for Office Workers," *School and Society* 65 (June 28, 1947): 477.

3. For this development, see Harry Braverman, *Labor and Monopoly Capital: The Degradation of Work in the Twentieth Century* (New York: Monthly Review Press, 1974), and Michael Crozier, *The World of the Office Worker* (New York: Schocken, 1973), p. 1. For statistical data, see Alba Edwards, *Comparative Occupational Statistics for the United States: 1870–1940*, (Washington, D.C.: U.S. Government Printing Office, 1943) and Janet Hooks, *Women's Occupations through Seven Decades*, Women's Bureau Bulletin no. 218 (Washington, D.C.: U.S.

Government Printing Office, 1947), pp. 74–77.

4. The outlines of this debate are sketched in C. Wright Mills, *White-Collar: The American Middle Classes* (New York: Oxford University Press, 1951), esp. chaps. 9 and 14; Emil Lederer, *The Problem of the Modern Salaried Employee* (New York: N.Y. State Department of Social Welfare, 1937); and Lewis Corey, *The Crisis of the Middle Class* (New York: Covici, Friede, 1935), chaps 6 and 11.

5. Coit to Douglas, January 3, 1930; SSOW Correspondence 1929–30, ALES, Box 91.

6. Elinor Pancoast, "Summer School for Office Workers," *American Federationist* 43 (October 1936): 1052.

7. Theresa Wolfson, "Should White-Collar Workers Organize?" *Independent Women* 15 (November 1936): 356.

8. Pancoast, p. 1053.

9. Coit to Douglas, April 16, 1930, SSOW Correspondence 1929–30; and Coit to Doris Madow, January 24, 1931, Office Workers Summer School, Correspondence 1931 (both in ALES, Box 91). Also see Minutes of the Committee, November 4, 1929, SSOW Minute Book, ALES, Box 91.

10. Miss Pell's Class, 1939, p. 2, SSOW Class Notes 1939, ALES, Box 95. The writer went on to say, "In a company where I worked once, the stenographers and clerks would not have anything to do with the factory girls, because they considered themselves much better in spite of the fact that they were making $14.00 a week to the factory girls' $28.00."

11. Ziegler to Shoemaker, April 1, 1930, SSOW Correspondence 1929–30, ALES, Box 91.

12. Typescript, November 12, 1930, Memos on Meeting of Committee to form SSOW 1930–31, ALES, Box 91.

13. Coit to Ziegler, July 16, 1930, SSOW Correspondence 1929–30, ALES, Box 91.

14. Quoting Grace Coyle in typescript, November 12, 1930.

15. Coit to Cummings, July 15, 1930, Office Workers Correspondence 1931, ALES, Box 91.

16. "The Summer Institute for Office Workers, Oberlin College," and "Memorandum on the SSOW: a New Experiment in Adult Education," SSOW Plans etc. to 1933, ALES, Box 91.

17. See the Director's *Reports of the Summer School for Office Workers* (1934, 1935, and 1936), passim. See also the various articles published about the school by its faculty, including Pancoast (n. 6 above); Clara Kaiser, "The Office Worker," *Social Work Today* 5 (May 1938): 20–21; and Orlie Pell, "A Workers School for the Office Worker," *American Federationist* 42 (June 1935): 622–24.

18. Minutes of the First

Meeting of the Continuation Committee, Continuation Committee file, ALES, Box 91.

19. Marion V. Carroll to Frank Morrison, November 17, 1933, Continuation Committee file, ALES, Box 91.

20. Minutes of the Third Meeting of the Admissions Committee of the SSOW, June 5, 1934, p. 3, ALES, Box 91.

21. Minutes of a Meeting of the Office Workers Summer School Committee, May 11, 1934, SSOW Correspondence NYC, ALES, Box 91.

22. Klebe to Green, October 30, 1934, Henrietta Klebe file, ALES, Box 92.

23. Questionnaire of Doris Pieper, August 15, 1935; Pieper to Jean Carter, August 7, 1935 (both from Doris Pieper file, ALES, Box 92).

24. Minutes of the Meeting of the SSOW Committee, December 31, 1935. Also see Kaiser, p. 21.

25. Coit to Cummings, June 26, 1933, and July 5, 1933; Minutes, June 5, 1934 (both in SSOW Correspondence NYC to July 31, 1933, ALES, Box 91).

26. For a discussion of this point see Sharon Hartman Strom, "Challenging 'Woman's Place': Feminism, the Left, and Industrial Unionism in the 1930's," *Feminist Studies* 9 (Summer, 1983), pp. 359–86; and Robert Shaffer, "Woman and the Communist Party, USA, 1930–1940," *Socialist Review* 45 (May–June 1979), pp. 73–118.

27. Ethel Gordon to Klebe, August, 1934, Henrietta Klebe file, ALES, Box 92.

28. Velma Noyes to Pell, October 15, 1936, Noyes file, ALES, Box 92.

29. Pell to Noyes, July 1, 1936, Noyes file, ALES, Box 92. Also see Minutes of the Meeting of the SSOW Committee, December 31, 1935, ALES, Box 91.

30. Minutes of the Meeting of the SSOW Committee, December 31, 1935, and December 31, 1936 (both from ALES), Box 91.

31. Kaiser, p. 21.

32. Eleanor Coit, "Office Workers' School," *Journal of Adult Education* 7 (October 1936): 504; and Conference on Chicago White-Collar at SSOW, August 1936, ALES, Box 95.

33. Summaries of Discussion at SS for Workers Conference, Evanston, August 14, 1937, p. 1, Conference, Chicago White-Collar at SSOW file, 1937, ALES, Box 95.

34. SSOW, Report of Director, 1937, p. 5; see also Report, 1939, p. 7, for increasing dependence on trade union support.

35. Theresa Wolfson, "March of Time," p. 5, Conference, Chicago White-Collar at SSOW file, 1937, ALES, Box 95.

36. SSOW, Report of the Director, 1937, p. 1, ALES.

37. 1937 Minutes, December 31, 1937, p. 6, SSOW Minute Book, ALES, Box 91.
38. Wolfson, "March of Time," p. 4, ALES.
39. Lucy Carner, "Memo on Community Relationships Course," SSOW Classnotes, 1939, ALES, Box 95.
40. Elizabeth Wright to Pell, June 14, 1939, File K, ALES, Box 92.
41. Coit, "Office Workers School," p. 503; SSOW Report of Director, 1939, p. 7, ALES.
42. Marie Algor to Samuel Collins, September 8, 1943, Philadelphia Weekend School file, 1943, ALES, Box 94.
43. "Representative Character of the Returns," Elinor Pancoast Report, ALES, Box 96; and Florence Cobb to Coit, December 18, 1941. Correspondence, NYC. to 1944, ALES, Box 91.
44. Appraisal of the SSOW, January 1, 1942, pp. 3–4, Elinor Pancoast Report, ALES, Box 96.
45. Report of Director, January 24, 1942, p. 4, ALES.
46. "Office Workers' Summer School," *Adult Education Journal* 5 (October 1946): 178. See also "Office Workers' Summer School," *Adult Education Journal* 6 (October 1947): 189.
47. "Office Workers Summer School," *Adult Education Journal* 6 (October 1947): 189.
48. Lydia B. Toedtli, September 25, 1946, Student Reports 1946–52, Box ALES, 98.
49. Annual Report of the American Labor Education Service, Inc., 1951, p. 5, and 1952, passim.
50. Annual Meeting, Board of Directors, White-Collar Workshops, Feb. 11, 1953, p. 1, ALES, Box 97.
51. The letters and the skit, "We Take Our Stand," are from the ALES Collection.

Chapter 8

The She-She-She Camps: An Experiment in Living and Learning, 1934–1937

Joyce L. Kornbluh

Soon after she arrived in Washington in September 1933, to start her job as Specialist in Workers Education in the Federal Emergency Relief Administration (FERA), Hilda Smith was asked by FERA director Harry Hopkins and his assistant, Clarence Bookman, to "do something" to meet the needs of jobless women.[1] The program that she initiated and developed promoted educational camps in a nationwide New Deal experiment for women on relief. Nicknamed the "she-she-she camps" by their detractors, these projects were frequently compared to the successful Civilian Conservation Corps (CCC) camps in which unemployed men were put to work on highly visible public service projects in order to develop practical skills. The she-she-she camps were considerably less successful, however, and much less extensive than their counterparts for men.[2]

The camps and schools program for women was short lived. From 1934 to 1937, 8,000 to 10,000 women enrolled in over a hundred centers, generally for six to eight week periods. In late 1935, the program was transferred to the National Youth Administration (NYA); it lasted only until the fall of 1937, when federal funding to the project was cut and most of the camps were closed.[3]

Smith's project highlighted the limited place of women workers in the New Deal. Hopkins hired her as a workers' education specialist, but her position was vague and controversial and her efforts to promote and fuse education and relief programs for women were treated for the most part with benign neglect. Although women's organizations around the country, aware of the plight of jobless women, pressured New Deal administrators to handle the problems of female unemployment, the inequities in women's receipt of public relief increased and their list of economic grievances grew longer throughout the Depression decade.

By 1932, 2 million women in all occupations felt the financial, physical, and mental efforts of being without paid work. A new and alarming phenomenon developed in the country—bands of young, homeless women roaming the streets, reluctant to seek aid, frequently sleeping in train stations or behind heating ducts in subway bathrooms. "It's one of the great mysteries of the city where women go when they are out of work and hungry," Meridel Le Sueur wrote in 1932. "A woman will shut herself up in a room until it is taken away from her and eat a cracker a day and be quiet as a mouse so there are no social statistics concerning her." At the height of the Depression, National Women's Party activist Helena Weed observed, "Men thronged the breadlines; women hid their plight."[4]

Private charities exhausted their resources for those women who did seek help, and New Deal agencies concentrated on ameliorating the lot of male heads of households, still regarding women as peripheral workers. They remained antagonistic toward hiring women while men were out of work. Many of the New Deal projects discriminated against women in their hiring practices, regulations, and wage scales. Women were denied access to higher paying public service jobs, were paid lower wages, and, if married, were subject to layoffs from their public and private sector employment. Women made up only a small percentage of the recipients of federal work relief jobs. By the end of 1934, only 142,000 women had received emergency work relief, in contrast to approximately nine times that number of men.[5]

In March 1932, during his frantic first hundred days, FDR had developed the idea of a national work conservation program for young, jobless males, and he announced the program in his acceptance speech at the Democratic National Convention in July of that year. The concept of work camps for unemployed youth, foreshadowed in the writings of social philosophers Thomas Carlyle, John Ruskin, and William James, had been tested in a number of European countries in the 1920s, where young people were conscripted or volunteered for public service for periods of six to eighteen months. It is probable, although Franklin Roosevelt denied it, that he was influenced in his thinking by William James, his Harvard professor in 1912, who had called for "youth armies" working on national service projects in a "moral equivalent of war."[6]

The Civilian Conservation Corps bill (S.B. 598), signed by Roosevelt on April 1, 1933, was the first New Deal measure designed to deal directly with the unemployment problems of young men. It enrolled 2.5 million males during its ten-year period, paid them $1.00 a day, and maintained them for an average of a year. The CCC was one of the most publicized and successful of the New Deal experiments, reflecting the president's lifelong commitment to forest conservation, his romance with rural life, and his assessment that the "tree armies" of jobless males that he had started as a relief measure while governor of New York State were a sound investment of public funds since they utilized a hard-hit age group in work not ordinarily performed by private industry.[7]

Meeting in March 1933, a month before the CCC bill was passed by Congress, the National Women's Trade Union League (NWTUL) called for a parallel network of schools and camps for jobless women to be financed by the Costigan-LaFollette-Wagner relief bill, housed on public property, and modelled on the YWCA residential camps for young women in industry. Hilda Smith incorporated this recommendation in a memo that she circulated to New Deal administrators in August 1933 to solicit their aid for workers' education schools and activities, and she expanded it two months later in her response to Hopkins's and Bookman's request that she do something for unemployed women.[8]

The network of schools and camps for jobless women would not have developed, however, without the leadership and active intervention of Eleanor Roosevelt. The first lady, in the center of the New Deal's political sisterhood, used her contacts, influence, and prestigious White House facilities to advocate aid for the forgotten women of the Depression and New Deal years. Aware of the NWTUL proposal through her close connections with leaders of that organization, Eleanor Roosevelt had also been influenced by the concept of a young workers' corps of eighteen- to twenty-five-year-olds, an idea advanced in a slim 1932 volume, *Prohibiting Poverty*, by Prestonia Mann Martin, the granddaughter of educational philosopher Horace Mann. The book, which went through eight editions between 1932 and 1934, drew heavily on Edward Bellamy's *Looking Backward* for its vision of a utopia in which youth would be organized industrially to produce needed goods and services for the whole society. "It may be possible to try out some of these ideas under emergency relief," Eleanor Roosevelt replied to a correspondent who had written enthusiastically to her about Martin's book.[9]

Prodded by the continuing destitution of jobless women and inspired by this "Utopia drafted by a woman," Eleanor Roosevelt did initiate such a project in spring 1933. She asked FDR for funds to "provide healthful employment and useful instruction amid wholesome surroundings for needy young women." The president sent her proposal on to Hopkins, who agreed to the plan, allocated monies from the national relief appropriations, and instructed the New York director of emergency relief to comply with Mrs. Roosevelt's requests for a model camp for unemployed women to be started in her home state.[10]

Camp TERA (Temporary Emergency Relief Administration) opened June 10, 1933, in a Depression-closed employee vacation facility owned by the New York Life Insurance Company in Bear Mountain State Park, about an hour's drive north of New York City and not far from the Roosevelt homestead in Hyde Park. For the next four years it was identified by the press, the public, and its personnel as Mrs. Roosevelt's special project, since she and her daughter served on the advisory board, sent holiday presents, corresponded with staff and participants, and made occasional visits.[11]

At the start, Camp TERA benefited from the sponsorship of two powerful and highly visible public figures, Mrs. Roosevelt and her ally, Secretary of Labor Frances Perkins, who helped preside at the camp's opening. But TERA soon generated public confusion as to how this experiment compared with the CCC program and whether females would be paid to perform public service. From 1933 to 1937, when the camp program folded, the purpose of TERA and the camp projects for women that followed continued to be misunderstood. Camp administrators were confused about how to synthesize educational goals and relief objectives, and relief agency personnel were never clear about how the program's administration should be divided among the national, state, and county levels.

The needs of jobless women, however, were so acute, and the response of the recovery program was so inadequate, that Camp TERA stirred the public imagination and sparked headlines across the country in the days immediately following its opening. Letters and telegrams received at the White House pledged facilities owned by individuals and organizations for similar projects. Young women wrote to "Mrs. President" and "Madam Secretary" to apply. The YWCA director in Macon, Georgia, offered the Y's fully equipped 87-acre camp; the president of Temple University's Women's Club volunteered her family estate in Maine; the welfare director in Cincinnati, Ohio, promised that if Camp TERA was successful, his city would initiate a camp for needy girls.[12]

Twenty-year-old Marie Ether, the oldest of an Idaho farm family of thirteen children, was one of the many who wrote her congressman asking to attend such a program. "We haven't had no crop for three years and the prospects look bad for this year. As their is no job in sight around here and as I do not have a high school education, I thought it would be educational to go."[13]

Hilda Smith also thought that it would be educational if numbers of young women like Marie Ether could attend federally funded residential programs where they could take classes, develop group skills, exercise critical thinking, and experience personal growth. She visualized these schools as modelled on the Bryn Mawr Summer School for Women Workers and anticipated a program where unemployed women would be educated to understand the economic conditions that affected their lives and so could translate that knowledge into community action.

Her proposal to Hopkins and Bookman called for New Deal–financed experimental residential schools, to be run for two-month terms, to help jobless females develop a sense of "social responsibility." Hopkins's immediate response to Smith's proposal was favorable. But, in contrast to the speed with which other New Deal projects were being launched, he did nothing to expedite implementation of her recommended program for a number of months.[14]

Social workers, the network of women in national government positions, and women's organizations stepped up their campaign to lobby New Deal administrators to develop more adequate work relief policies and programs for women. At a White House conference on women's needs engineered by Eleanor Roosevelt and FERA women's director Ellen Woodward in November 1933, Harry Hopkins admitted that "the government has not done what it should [about jobless women] and feels pretty humble about it." He pledged government monies and determination to "care for unemployed women" and asked the hundred or so conferees for advice on how to extend that relief. Conference participants suggested establishing special public works jobs for women, earmarking 20 percent of federal funds for state-initiated women's work relief, and developing a network of schools and camps for jobless girls and women, a project that was being discussed by Smith, Mrs. Roosevelt, and members of the NWTUL.[15]

As time passed with no further action on her plan or on any other women's work relief projects, Smith requested to speak at a conference of FERA field representatives held in Washington in February 1934. A number of the FERA staff opposed her proposal, anticipating "serious discipline problems if women were brought together to live." Undaunted by these reactions, Smith launched a publicity campaign through the publication of a widely distributed pamphlet, "The Woman with the Worn Out Shoes," which outlined the plight of jobless females and the problems of destitute transients and summarized the recommendations for a network of schools and camps that might help keep these women constructively occupied and off the streets.[16]

Together with Eleanor Roosevelt and Ellen Woodward, two of her most vocal and influential advocates in the support system of social feminists in the national government, Smith orchestrated a White House conference in April 1934 that convened eighty women from national community and social welfare organizations, public agencies, and New Deal offices. The participants expressed a range of suggestions for a schools and camps program, including the need for health- and morale-building activities and a curriculum that would educate jobless women for more intelligent participation in a democratic society.[17]

One government staff member cautioned that, in a recent national survey of FERA administrators, over half had indicated that they had no interest in such a proposal and that there was no need in their states for such a program.

Assistant FERA administrator Aubrey Williams, who was pinch-hitting for Harry Hopkins at the conference, pledged "limited funds" to carry out the plan, while making clear his displeasure with the term "workers' education," a component of the recommended curriculum that he felt "smacked of class distinctions."[18]

Despite precarious support, Smith moved quickly after the conference to set up a national advisory committee to consult with her office and to advise the states in curriculum development, the selection of teachers and students, and budgetary allocations. The national advisory committee included many national and New Deal leaders during the next few years.[19]

A comprehensive *Memorandum on Standards and Procedures in Establishing Resident Schools and Educational Camps for Unemployed Women*, which Smith sent to Hopkins in May, reflected her vision of a well-rounded educational program that integrated workers' education, social sciences, and English. The *Memorandum* also recommended vocational guidance, health education, and opportunities for cultural and recreational activities. It advocated the discussion method of teaching to help students analyze their economic and social worlds and a system of self-government to enhance their skills for problem solving and community participation.[20]

Hopkins approved the proposal as a relief measure and wrote to state relief administrators in May 1934 that limited funds were available for resident programs for jobless women. He asked states to telegraph detailed plans and budgets within the week for proposed projects to open in summer 1934. His memo stipulated that states would be responsible for obtaining rent-free facilities, appointing local advisory committees, and supervising each program. He gave no role to Smith's national office in the hiring of personnel and ignored the national advisory committee's proposal that it supervise budgets and consult on program development. Twenty state relief administrators wired within a few days that they were ready to apply.

The program would be confined to on-site education and group activities. CCC administrators had vetoed the national advisory committee's recommendation that young women in the resident programs be used, as men were, in reforestation and community service projects since, they claimed, "work outside the camps [for women] was not practicable and the supervision and transportation costs would be greatly increased." Thus, significant work and training opportunities for women in the program were curtailed from the start.[21]

Less than a month after Hopkins's approval, Smith and Mrs. Roosevelt used a White House press conference to publicize the start of a national program "intended to serve as social and educational laboratories [from which] women will go forth to cope more intelligently and with renewed strength and courage for their special problems." They estimated that each school would cost $6000 for approximately sixty students drawn from relief rolls for an eight-week term.[22]

Within a few weeks, twenty-eight schools and camps were operating within twenty-six states and the District of Columbia. Smith drafted and distributed "Suggestions for Organization of Curriculum and Teaching in the Residential Schools and Camps for Unemployed Women" to all project personnel and to state relief administrators. The manual succinctly summarized much of progressive education philosophy regarding education for democratic living. It recommended a system of participant self-management and group decision making about the administration and content of each project. It included a statement of Smith's long-time desire to help workers help themselves through workers' education.

She defined workers' education in all of her publications as: a curriculum that "offers men and women workers . . . an opportunity to train themselves in clear thinking through the study of those questions closely related to their daily lives as workers and as citizens."[23]

Noble though Smith's ideals were, they contributed greatly to the confusion of purpose that quickly swamped the program. They implied a long-range, far-reaching approach to problems that, in the press of the New Deal's focus on economic recovery, appeared to require short-term, stop-gap solutions.

The schools and camps for women were organized by state relief agencies in cooperation with local YWCAs, some ongoing workers' education programs, women's clubs, churches, and settlement houses. Federal funds covered food and maintenance, which averaged $8.00 a week per enrollee, staff salaries, and the upkeep of buildings used in the programs. In addition, in 1935, the women participants received spending money of fifty cents a week. State or private funds were solicited for equipment and to meet other organizational costs.

Smith's role was to administer the program as part of her job in the FERA Emergency Education Program. She was aided by a small Washington staff that included Ernestine Friedmann, who was also spending time on the WPA teacher training projects. In 1935, Smith received permission and funds to hire eight field staff for three months; they also split their time between helping organize the WPA summer teaching training centers and the women's schools and camps. The state supervisors of workers' education, hired by the emergency relief program in twenty-four states by 1934, also aided the organization of the programs. The mix of state, local, and national direction, however, subjected the program in many areas to cross-purposes and confusion.[24]

Hasty and haphazard recruiting, pressures to fill quotas, lack of advance publicity, and poorly informed county relief and welfare workers meant that most of the women participants arrived at the residential programs ill informed about what to expect. Although local advisory committees and camp directors in some states had time to interview some applicants, for the most part enrollees were sent to the projects from the relief offices. Most of the women were under twenty-five and single; a third had never worked or had held only relief project jobs. Approximately 90 percent were Caucasian, and many came from small towns and rural areas, a pattern that continued through 1937. "I was told to be ready to leave in three days. I didn't know what the course of study would be or in what line of work," one woman later wrote Smith.[25]

Many had anticipated vocational training and thought they would be assured of jobs following the program. "I attended with the idea that the school, being a government school, would mean a lot in securing a job. The school was a good idea but if you can't get a job after you return home, the government school can't mean very much." A group of young women who had been to TERA wrote to Mrs. Roosevelt that they had gained health and an interest in life during their stay, but could not find paid work on their return to the city. "Now, after four weeks of tramping through the streets, more than one girl says there is nothing left except suicide or tramping on the roads." Smith estimated later that only one-fifth of the enrollees in 1934 and 1935 found paid work on their return home, many in New Deal–sponsored relief projects.[26]

Despite Smith's emphasis on educational activities, it was the harsh realities of the times that determined the real focus of the camps. Most county agents sent women who needed food and shelter first and foremost. A Washington staff person from Smith's office reported, after visiting a number of sites: "To see a group of girls assemble on the first night was to receive an immediate and tragic impression of the results of unemployment, Thin, emaciated girls . . . they were overcome by the sight of a simple supper. Many showed symptoms of long fatigue, exhausted nerves and mental strain. Many expressed anxiety in leaving husband, father or brothers unemployed, thankful, however, to relieve them of the burden of another person to feed for the summer. All were bewildered in trying to understand what was happening in their own lives."[27]

There was frequently a discrepancy between the expectations of what "should" happen and the actual camp experience. A camp director reported, "The first week the girls would not sing in the dining room as I, who had been brought up on private camp traditions expected them to do. . . . I realized that they were there to eat. Singing marred the flavor of corn bread dripping in butter . . . and made questionable the assurance of a second helping." Staff, too, did not always match Smith's vision. Many of them, also hired from relief rolls, looked on their subsidized stay in the residential programs as a chance to escape their own desperate family and community conditions and to live and eat well for a few months in a supportive and healthy environment.[28]

The seventy-five camps and schools operating in 1934 and 1935 reflected regional and cultural differences. In Arkansas, black sharecroppers' daughters lived on the campus of a Negro agricultural college. In New Jersey, a project was run for jobless professional women, the only one of its kind in the country. In Philadelphia, forty women lived and studied in a midtown YWCA. In Ohio, unemployed clericals spent six weeks in a small frame house on the Oberlin College campus in connection with the Summer School for Office Workers run by the Affiliated Schools for Workers. In the Ozarks, women from mountain families took part in a project run collaboratively with the Opportunity School, an ongoing program for illiterates. In New York City, trade union women, now jobless, lived in a Barnard dormitory. Out in North Dakota, young women left Indian reservations for the first time to go to a resident project in a nearby town.

Nine of the projects in 1934 were connected with ongoing workers' education programs on the campuses of universities in Wisconsin, California, and Ohio. Despite Smith's recommendation that workers' education be included in each curriculum, these were the only centers to include those kinds of materials and discussions. In most of the schools and camps, participants did not have the maturity or the experience in the work force or in workplace organizations to discuss labor history and labor problems. In addition, the open antagonism to unionism felt by some participants in a number of the camps and schools and by their neighbors in the surrounding communities prompted Smith to recommend in late 1935 that the term "social civics" replace the term "workers' education" and that discussions focus on current events and community problems instead of workplace issues.[29]

In all of the projects, participants divided their time between site maintenance, study, and recreation. Food preparation, house cleaning, and curtain sewing were considered laboratory work in some places since the staff assumed that the participants would be homemakers. A number of the projects ran beauty shops; some trained the young women to sew simple dresses. Some held sessions on table setting, home cleanliness, and personal hygiene. Commenting on the "she-she-she" focus of her experience, one young woman wrote Smith, "Most of us got the impression that they wanted to teach us something useful if we got married immediately and that that was the only proper thing to do."[30]

The scope and quality of the education classes varied among the projects. The teaching methods recommended by the national office were based on progressive education ideals. Many of the schools and camps scheduled three or four morning classes daily. Reports from the individual projects indicate that there was an attempt to discuss different social systems, the new social security legislation, the cooperative movement, war and peace, and simple economic trends. Participants supplemented classwork with trips to local businesses, public housing projects, cooperative stores, union meetings, museums, and education centers.

Two-thirds of the camps and schools scheduled classes in English grammar, composition, reading, and public speaking. Poor library facilities hindered reading programs in a number of the sites, but staff encouraged the women to read daily newspapers and current magazines, and a number of the projects dramatized current events through student-developed skits based on the WPA "living newspaper" model. Almost every camp published a newspaper, many with superficial social notes and gossip but some with book reports, poems, and short essays on personal experiences. In one project, enrollees sent weekly reports to their home-town newspapers; in a number of centers, the women took part in mock forums and debates. Some of the centers ran small co-op stores for refreshments and toilet articles; a few set up a simple "credit union" that made modest loans. In an attempt to broaden the social vision of the participants, guest speakers from Washington, nearby community groups, and local educational institutions spoke on topics such as good business practices, the League of Nations, the cooperative movement, and the artist in a democracy.[31]

Smith's 1935 report pointed out that an attempt was made "to develop a professional interest in some type of work for which the student was fitted and in which she might have a genuine professional pride. Very few of the girls had thought of work from the point of view of a life interest and quite naturally, their immediate concern was to earn a few dollars." Many of the projects included sessions on personal and job counseling and group discussions on practical employment problems. In some camps the women practiced filling out job applications, studied community job-referral facilities, and role-played job interviews.

Although vocational training was not an original purpose of the program, several of the camps did train the young women for office or domestic work. Some of the projects attempted to organize follow-up programs to help the women find jobs and to continue to develop the interests and skills developed in the summer programs.[32]

Recreational activities, nature study, organized sports, and student government formed a part of the daily schedule. However, in a number of the projects, social life became an issue. Harry Gersh, a teacher at Camp Jane Addams in the mid-1930s, recalls that for many of the girls from New York City evenings were a problem:

These campers were neither Girl Scouts nor YW girls. . . .
They were, for the most part, slum-raised, street-wise women transferred from teeming neighborhoods and crowded city apartments into the clean, brisk and totally foreign air of a state park. . . . Camp Jane Addams was fenced and campers were not permitted outside the fence. Inside, there were 153 female campers, 18 female staff, one old man hidden in the kitchen, one married man with wife present and two young male teachers. . . . It was a most unnatural environment for these young women. . . . The above is reported only because it illustrates a basic flaw; the planners and directors of the camps didn't really understand with whom they were dealing and, therefore, how to deal with them. No one had thought that sexual isolation would be a problem."[33]

Eventually, at Camp Jane Addams and at many of the other projects, there were weekly dances to which young men from nearby CCC camps were invited. In addition, through the student government process, some of the young women negotiated a periodic weekend back at their homes.

Community reactions varied in response to the programs. In some areas, residents pitched in to donate furniture for the facilities and volunteer their labor to clean the site, fix appliances, and help with daily chores. In other areas, projects were viewed suspiciously. In July 1936, for example, the Rockland County (N.Y.) American Legion accused Camp Jane Addams of using public funds to promote communism, citing as evidence that the camp was gated and restricted to outsiders, that the enrollees sang the "Internationale" and other labor songs, and that the staff provided a forum for anti-American speakers. It was one of a number of similar attacks mounted by the American Legion and the Hearst newspapers against the WPA emergency education program and the camps project through the period, adding to the accumulation of negative reactions that eventually led to their demise.[34]

Despite many problems and shortcomings, the program's paramount contribution was to help restore health and self-confidence to the thousands of young women who had come to the resident projects emaciated and exhausted by their long struggles with Depression problems. Eye glasses, dental work, and in some cases minor operations were negotiated for the women in a number of communities. Seventy-five percent of the women reported weight gains, and many attested to "a new outlook on life."[35]

On their evaluation surveys, which were part of a follow-up research project recommended by the national advisory board for the 1934 and 1935 sessions, participants testified to their positive experiences:

It seemed like someone did have an interest in whether we lived or starved and was trying to help.

It was a blessing for me to have the opportunity of spending eight weeks in a school building up my physical and mental strength, being sure of food, shelter and above all companionship. Since returning home, things have been much brighter even tho I am still unemployed.

After going to the FERA school, I felt that while conditions might be bad, they are not hopeless.

I came filled with thoughts of myself and my family. I'm going with interest in each and every one of you. I didn't know I could do what I've done here. I'm taking home more than I brought. I'm taking thoughts of beauty and kindness which will help me when the clothes that I made here have been used up.

It's not only that I am getting enough to eat for the first time in three years, but I am beginning to think of myself as a real person again.[36]

Late in 1935, after the FERA was transformed into the Works Progress Administration, the program for jobless women was transferred for administrative convenience to the National Youth Administration (NYA), which had been established to provide work opportunities for eighteen- to twenty-five-year-olds to produce goods and services for pay instead of receiving relief. This shift brought about changes in the program. These, however, were not significant enough to revitalize the project, since there was still a lack of serious commitment on the part of the New Deal administrators to provide enough funds and support staff to help put the project on a firmer foundation.[37]

Hilda Smith remained chair of the national advisory committee and was a major influence in the program's continuation. Administration of the camps program was assigned to NYA staff person Dorothea de Schweinitz, a national advisory committee member who had previously worked for the U.S. Department of Labor, and a five-person group at the NYA. Smith and de Schweinitz hoped that the NYA would create 150 camps and schools to serve 15,000 young women, but funds were never made available for more than a third of that number.[38]

Under the NYA, the project shifted its focus to give young women under age twenty-five who had never held a job some rudimentary vocational skills, in addition to group living, education, and physical rehabilitation. Seventy-five percent of the enrollees in 1936 and 1937 were under age twenty; most of them were Caucasian and came from rural areas or small towns where there were no jobs, no job training, and no other NYA project.

As in former years, the camps and schools were housed in donated or low-rent college or school buildings, YWCA camps, or on private estates. From January 1936 through the fall of 1937, when the program was eliminated, approximately 6,000 young women were enrolled in about fifty projects; exact figures are hard to obtain, since some of the women enrolled in several sessions and some of the camps were open year-round and included several terms. Most of the projects, however, folded after a single three- or four-month session because of administrative problems and difficulties in recruiting participants and obtaining necessary federal and state financial and political support.

Under NYA regulations, the women worked an average of three hours a day for maximum wages of $25 a month, from which they paid approximately $15 for room and board. The NYA required that each girl have $5.00 in cash each month after her expenses were paid. Work projects for the women's camps aimed to be socially useful and to prepare the enrollees for their future in their homes, workplaces, and communities. Most of the work, however, was sex stereotyped, emphasizing manual skills and good work habits and providing training in homemaking and child care. Girls prepared hospital dressings, sewed for institutions and for families on relief, painted signs, repaired books and toys, produced Braille materials, and did simple clerical tasks and mimeographing for other WPA projects. In some camps, they worked in nearby communities as playground and nursery school aides.

Many of the camps lacked equipment and supplies for serious work. Production of even the simple objects was hindered by poor administration, cumbersome procedures for ordering and obtaining materials, and an uneven flow of supplies to the camps. Despite the limitations of the work projects, a number of camps and schools undertook imaginative learning projects and incorporated some self-government into their programs.[39]

In 1936, Smith still discussed the program as "a social laboratory in which it is hoped that the girls will acquire the skills, poise, a knowledge of resources and experience in self-government and democratic procedures." A staff report highlighted the programs' objectives in 1936, which included: "to develop an understanding of the obligations of citizenship . . . to develop qualities of initiative and cooperation for solving social problems . . . to develop attitudes and abilities for community service."[40]

Opposition to the work camp programs for women, however, continued to be a problem. Although there is no documentation, the national advisory committee reports imply that many NYA administrators attempted to scuttle the projects, claiming that they did not understand their purpose and objectives and questioning their necessity. Although NYA deputy director Richard Brown admitted that the national staff and national advisory committee had done a good job of interpreting the program, he told national advisory committee members in September 1936 that other New Deal agencies needed to see "eye-to-eye" with them about the program and that other government agencies needed a better understanding of its concept and objectives.[41]

In alerting the national advisory committee to the continued confusion about the program's objectives, Brown was communicating an administrative message that the program was in trouble. Some government officials complained that the costs of the program for women were higher than the costs of nonresidential NYA programs, that it was difficult to plan useful public work for inexperienced young women, and that the quality of the articles made in the women's camps was spotty. They cited problems in filling the camp quotas of approximately eighty enrollees because, they claimed, parents were reluctant to let young women live away from home even during the Depression. They cited cases where schools and camps were attacked by local community members or by the American Legion as sponsoring leftist discussions and programs.

Some of the issues raised pointed to real problems. Recruitment for the women's schools and camps had grown more difficult under the NYA because wages for the young women were so low after room and board were paid that the girls could not send money home to their families and could scarcely buy toilet articles or pay for other personal needs. Complaints had been lodged by some communities fearful of the forums and free discussions and suspicious that radical, anti-American ideas were being taught by federally paid staff who were outsiders to the community. Some of the camp staff were left-wingers, reflecting the variety of political affiliations current in the 1930s.[42]

Transportation to and from the residential projects remained a major problem throughout the four years, since the federal government never appropriated travel funds for enrollees, who had to depend on the National Guard, public school buses, camp staff, or private individuals to drive them to the projects. Finding qualified staff was also a continuing difficulty. During the FERA years, regulations required that teachers be hired from relief rolls. Teaching staff during the WPA period was borrowed, for the most part, from other WPA divisions. Many interested persons were discouraged from accepting jobs with the program because of changing government regulations and procedures, the hasty organization of many of the camps, low wage scales, uncertain job tenure, limited free time, and no vacation pay. Although a 1937 study of close to 500 staff members of the women's camps program indicates that about 60 percent had attended some college and 30 percent had a college degree, it was hard to find teachers competent in their fields who could also function effectively with young adults in an intense residential experience.[43]

Early in 1937, government appropriations for emergency education were reduced, and, alarmed at the implications of this move for the women's camps project, Hilda Smith again called on Eleanor

Roosevelt's help through a memo to the White House. She suggested that $500,000 be allocated for twelve to fifteen demonstration projects in 1937–1938, which would serve 3,500 to 4,500 young women in a work and study program to include vocational counseling, follow-up job training, and placement when the women returned to their homes. The national advisory committee met on August 3 and endorsed this proposal. It recommended that the NYA concentrate on spring and summer residential programs to reduce the costs of heating the facilities. It suggested more on-the-job training opportunities, where enrollees could earn higher wages and obtain valuable vocational experience. It also underscored the need for residential projects for older women under the auspices of the WPA Adult Education Division.[44]

The August 1937 meeting was the last for the national advisory committee. On August 16, Mrs. Roosevelt paid a surprise visit to the 130 campers and staff at Camp Jane Addams (the renamed Camp TERA) and, meeting with them on the dock overlooking Lake Totorati, shared her "unofficial opinion" that the camp would be closed the following month for lack of funds. The following day, the *New York Times* announced that the girls' camps would close as of October 1, 1937. The reason given was the "relatively high cost of the camps as compared with other NYA residential work projects which will be continued and expanded." The article stated that costs of $45 per enrollee per month had been planned for the women's work camp projects, while the actual costs ranged from $38 to $58 per month (an average of $48— three dollars more than the budgeted amount). The article also assured the public that this move would have no effect on the boys in NYA work camps or in the CCC.[45]

The *Final Report of the National Youth Administration, 1936–1943* claimed that the work camps for women were the forerunners of a highly successful NYA network of residential programs developed from 1937 until the war years and that they helped prepare NYA administrators for problems in coordinating and organizing work and living situations involving large numbers of people. What the official report failed to point out was that abandonment of the program meant abandonment of significant efforts to help unemployed women. The report concluded: "Consequently, the final abandonment of the old program did not constitute a complete loss, although some of the best characteristics of that program, namely self-government, cooperative management, personal guidance, and workers' education were now relegated to a less important role."[46]

Smith persisted in her advocacy of the schools and camps program for women and attempted to revive the concept in 1940 in connection with war defense. Writing to Mrs. Roosevelt about the need for programs for jobless women aged twenty-five to forty who were too old to be eligible for NYA projects, she stated: "The CCC camps with their millions of dollars for wages, education work, travel and supervision constantly remind me of what we might do for women from the same families. As so often is the case, the boys get the breaks; the girls are neglected."[47]

Her friendship with Mrs. Roosevelt had given her carte blanche in bringing her visions and problems to the White House and, through the first lady's intervention, had secured the attention of FDR and the limited support at the program's start of a few New Deal administrators. Smith and Mrs. Roosevelt shared a warm belief in the equal rights of women who, if given the proper intellectual "tools," could "work out their salvations wisely and well." But neither Smith nor Mrs. Roosevelt, nor their cohort of liberal women in New Deal government, had the power to mount a long-term, comprehensive, federally supported national educational program for jobless women.

Smith was primarily an educator and a reformer. Her adherence to the goal of a well-educated citizenry at all economic levels was grounded in her commitment to preserve democracy and the existing economic system through the educational process. Her view of education was comprehensive and ambitious, addressing the mind, body, and spirit of adult learners. The schools and camps program for women, which she pursued with evangelical zeal, reflected these philosophical and moral commitments. However, the program was too broad in its concept and too diffuse in its impact to take root in the crisis-oriented emergency relief programming of the New Deal period.

The camps and schools for women floundered owing to external pressures and internal contradictions. Externally, the she-she-she camps were seen as a social aberration by a country that had never used public resources to meet the nonvocational work needs of women or, for that matter, of men. The camps challenged the status quo by suggesting that women might go beyond their roles in the home to play extended, or different, roles in the workplace, in the labor force, and in public life.

The internal contradictions sprang from a mixing of goals. Early in the planning of the program, women in the schools and camps were barred from the kind of direct public service experience that men received in the CCC. Although the camps for women were an emergency relief effort, they were overseen by individuals who held long-term educational goals that fit awkwardly with the short-term emergency relief nature of New Deal programming.

There were no institutional models for preparing women to succeed in the workplace other than those developed by the higher education network of women's private schools and by the cross-class experiments for women workers in the residential programs coordinated by the Affiliated Schools for Workers in the 1920s and 1930s. These schools, such as the Bryn Mawr Summer School for Women Workers, were based on the concept that society must provide and pay for broad-based education for working-class women so that they can participate more actively in solving social problems. This model was too ambitious in the context of a temporary relief program because of the short duration of the camps, the lack of total focus on education, and the expectations of the enrollees, who needed job training and paid work.

Other issues also led to the program's demise: developing a federally funded and supervised education program in a country committed to local control of the content and format of public education; finding staff qualified to work with young female adults in residential settings; working within the New Deal emergency program, with its quixotically shifting personnel, variable congressional appropriations, and changing budgets and regulations; and mediating tensions—still not resolved—between federal and state responsibility for local programming.

What had the young women gained in these residential projects? Some of the objectives of the camps and schools had been attained in some degree. Certainly, mental and physical health improved; self-confidence quickened; group skills improved. Young women broadened their life experience, confronted new social and intellectual stimuli, and tasted the first freedoms of moving away from family households and home-town communities.

The program attempted to give young women some control over their lives at a time when the United States had lost control over its economy. On balance, although the program might have gone further, it was bound by ideological and financial limitations rooted in the New Deal's preoccupation with economic collapse and recovery, shaped by gender stereotypes, and influenced by an emphasis on educating individual women rather than on shifting their relationships to their families, workplaces, and society.

The she-she-she camps left neither long-term policies allocating public resources for the education or job training of women nor reforestation projects that would make a nation proud. They were a small but significant experiment directed to establishing a principle—that government has a responsibility in meeting women's education and job-related needs. They linked the programming of some of the New Deal education projects to the philosophical and moral concepts of earlier progressive philosophers and educators. In so doing, they underscored the need for women to be an educated and active citizenry and promoted the use of public resources for those who had been America's forgotten people.

The monologue "For Sale" was written in a creative writing workshop at the School for Unemployed Workers in Madison, Wisconsin, that was held from August 10 to September 18, 1935. The WPA instructor of the workshop considered it the best piece of work in his class and staged it for participants and community members in a theater on the University of Wisconsin campus.[48]

For Sale

SCENE: A dirty clothes-strewn hovel. Upturned ash trays; piles of dirty clothes; broken shabby furniture litter the room which serves as home to the room's single occupant. She is a haggard and hard looking women with bright spots of rouge smeared on her drawn face. As the curtain rises, she squats on a chair, displaying a pair of bare, muscular legs. Her arms are drawn up under her chin. She smokes continuously during the entire scene, sometimes slinging the cigarette away before finished and starting another. A bottle of hard liquor stands on the floor.

Sally: (Spoken in spurts, as if thinking aloud.) "Yeah, just good old Sally—that's me. I ain't so hot to look at, but damn it, I never thought I'd come to this. Two bucks between me and starvation. (A long pause; her eyes become glassy and a cynical smile pulls her mouth tight.) Hell, eight months ago, Ida bought a pair of flimsy socks with two bucks. (Loud mirthless laughter) Said I'd be back to work in a day or so. Said I should just sit tight til the storm blows over. Those pie-eyed saps don't know what a storm is. They're still eating their cake. Then the relief department—"Go to your family. You can't get relief here." Hell, I don't have a family. Why should anyone worry about a dame like me?—Huh, once I went to church—kinda got a kick out of it—so nice and peaceful—like you used to think you'd like to be. All the pretty statues with the little do-funnies draped around 'em—and the pretty lights that came through the window. (Uproarious laughter. Slowly she pours out a generous shot. Picking it up, she assumes an air of affected gaity and parades around.) Oh yes, Mr. Zilch, I work in the perfume department. That's what makes me smell so good. (Takes a small drink). Well, I just can't recall but I believe I get about twelve dollars a week. Oh yes, I work ten hours a day. They say it's eight only but you know what little mistakes people make.—I figure I can pay up my room this week if I take the guy from Dallas. Oh, he's a nice guy. I imagine he's a very nice man. (Gulps down the rest of the drink.) Damn it, his wife should see him. Then she'd know how NICE he is.—Now, I ain't got a job at all. Now I can sell my whole damn body for anything I can get. Now I can go to hell. (Strides aimless around room.) Might as well get good and drunk. What've I got to lose? Good thing the sap left his alky here this morning—Hm, must be nearly 9:30—I hear him coming now—I think I'll spring the news on him. Will he give me hell! (Laughs and laughs as if hysterical. Falls into chair. Steps are heard coming up several flights of stairs. Her body seems to weaken; her face become more haggard.) God, me and a baby. Starving on a liquor diet as it is. I can't stand it any longer. I tell you I'm losing my mind. Those steps—those steps—why doesn't he come—get it over with—me and a baby—she won't get relief either. The hell with the department of outdoor relief. I can still make a living—selling my body. (Laughs more deliriously.)
Man: How's about it, Sally?
Sally: Yeah—yeah, come and get me. Just good old Sally.

—Helen Olson, 1935

In spring, 1936, young, unemployed women in the WPA-sponsored residential school in Philadelphia wrote papers in their English class from which the following excerpts are taken. They are typical of the kinds of essays written by the participants in the New Deal schools and camps for unemployed women.[49]

When I was fourteen years of age, I had to quit school and go to work. My first job was not very pleasant as there were long hours and very small pay. The work was in a shirt mill. In applying for the job I went to the employer's house and asked him for a job. He told me to come in the next morning, so I had to go before school. I worked that way for about a month, and then was old enough to quit school.

We worked nine hours a day. Sometimes if we did not get enough work out in the day time we had to go back at night and work until nine o'clock. For this work, I received on an average of seven dollars a week, for fifty-two hours and more.

After working there about three and a half years, I got very disgusted with the conditions so I looked for another job which I got. As soon as possible, I quit the old job. For a while I thought I was in heaven but it soon wore off, and was just as bad as ever. About a year later, the NRA came along and made things very nice for the workers. Soon after, the mill got organized and conditions got better so fast that the workers did not realize what was happening. I think it happened too quick for them for when the time came to fight to keep these conditions, the workers did not know enough about fighting for better things in life to respond the way they should have.

Everybody thought the NRA was in to stay but it quickly fooled the people. If the NRA had not gone out just as quickly as it had come in, the different employers had not moved South and all the girls that were put idle would still be working, and there would not be so much of the cheap labor going on, as the people in the South always work cheaper.

My experience in getting jobs was never very hard but the conditions were so bad that it was very hard to keep a girl. I worked until this past January when the firm I worked for moved part of their mill South. This, of course, put some of the people idle for some time. The things I work on will not start until next summer as I work on woolen coats for men and these orders only come through in the spring.

My next job was doing housework and I got that through the welfare. I was given the address and the same day I went over to see the woman and she wasn't sure until she saw her husband and told me to come over Sunday. So I called her up Saturday afternoon and her husband answered the phone and told me to start Monday morning. Sunday came and I went over to see her and went into a conversation. She asked me different things and I asked her what the wages were and she asked me what I got in the private tea room and I told her. I thought I would take it because I did not have another job on hand.

So I worked one year. There was more work to do and I did not get a raise so I quit. I told her I needed more money. She said she couldn't afford it. I said she then does not need me. I stayed home and she came after me. I still did not go to work and stayed home a week. On Sunday her husband came over and said he would give me a raise—it wasn't much. So I went to work and kept on working and worked another year and I did not get the raise I was promised and I did all the work there ever done so I quit.

I thought two years for small wages was plenty for a girl who has to give help at home.

The following excerpts are from papers written by the young women at Camp Arcola in Pennsylvania, during the summer of 1936. They give insight into the process through which individuals became engaged in group activities and collective learning.[50]

My first knowledge about Camp Arcola was when our [relief] visitor came to our house and asked me if I'd like to go to a resident school. He gave me a few days to think about it. In those days I thought a lot. I couldn't make up my mind to what good it would be for me until I went to the meeting at Pottsville and met Miss Segelbaum. She told us a lot of things we would learn such as swimming, dramatics, sewing and working in the kitchen. I went home after the meeting and told my mother that I'd made up my mind to go for maybe learning to live in a group and associating with different people would help me get work.

When we had our meeting before we came to this camp we talked about what we would like to do when we got here, if we would like to cook, or sew, or clean or do other things. Miss Segelbaum told us a lot more about the camp and we were all anxious to come. I knew before I came up here that they were all going to try to fit us in for a good job and I was pretty sure we could learn a lot up here. When I got here and had the different meetings and the committees and all the interest groups, I knew we would learn more than I had expected. I do think it is a very good idea in having this camp because when anyone hires you to work for them, they can expect more from you than just anyone that never came to this school. We are learning much more than girls who just sit around the house and are out of work. I know I learn a lot about waitress work and other things, too. In the time that we have left, I would like to know more about English and politics and how to make different things such as belts and covers, and do a lot of things in our social science work shop. I do think we are all going to have a good time and learn plenty more before we go home.

When I first heard of my opportunity to come to Camp Arcola, I sort of hesitated. I thought I would get homesick and not like the camp. After I thought it over, I finally decided to come because I realized that it would be quite an experience. Now that I have been here four weeks, I am certainly glad that I accepted the opportunity, I have gained more confidence in myself by being able to get up and speak in front of a group and have also learned how to adjust myself to a new environment. . . . I find that I have learned quite a few things. For instance, I was never interested in politics before coming here and now I find it is a really interesting subject. I made a chart on a political party from which I learned a lot about everyday life that I didn't know before.

It took several days for the girls to get acquainted. Then slowly and surely they began going around in groups. In the meantime, the cooperative store was organized and I was elected manager. The store surpassed all my wildest fancies of what it would be like. The girls are one great bunch.

I like very much the idea of cooperative living. The committees are very well organized and the council selected by the girls are doing a very good job. On the whole the camp is much more than I expected and the girls much nicer.

Although we were told that it was a camp where we make our own rules and regulations, I myself believed that the director would make rules which we would have to abide by. It was pleasing to find that we could set up our own government and also to really have a chance at cooperative living.

Camp Arcola is doing a great deal for me in more ways than one. First of all, I have learned to get along with strange girls. Never before had I the opportunity to get in and live with a group and get along as well as I have been doing. It is doing every one of us more good than we realize. Secondly, the camp is teaching me how to handle all kinds of situations. We are learning to express our own ideas and see them carried out. Third, there are so many subjects and interests to get into and learn things. The counselors are enthusiastic to show what the girls really can do. I hope to accomplish more speed on the typewriter and broaden my knowledge in English. I am getting first aid instructions and am very grateful for this.

All in all, I really think the camp is worthwhile if the girls take advantage of the groups offered in camp. Also a chance to indulge in sports and running a store.

I have been able to gain some more experience in office work and typing, taking dictation and answering the phone. I have enjoyed being on the library committee as it gave me the opportunity to be chairman and also work in the library. In the politics group I have really gotten a better idea of the different parties which will enable me to vote more intelligently in the Fall. Up to this time my coming here was worthwhile.

Notes

1. Federal Emergency Relief Administration (hereafter FERA), *Concerning Workers' Education* (Washington, D.C.: FERA, December–January 1934–35), 1: 44.

2. Oral history of Hilda W. Smith conducted by Ashley

Doherty, May 30, 1969 (in Smith Collection, Franklin D. Roosevelt Library, Hyde Park, N.Y., container 1, folder "Interviews," p. 11).

3. FERA, *Report on Educational Camps for Unemployed Women, 1934 and 1935* (Washington, D.C.: FERA, May 1936), appendix 2; Susan Ware, *Beyond Suffrage: Women in the New Deal* (Cambridge, Mass.: Harvard University Press, 1981), p. 113.

4. Lois Scharf, *To Work and To Wed* (Westport, Conn.: Greenwood Press, 1980), chap. 6, and Alice Kessler-Harris, *Out to Work: A History of Wage-Earning Women in the U.S.* (New York: Oxford University Press, 1982), chap. 9, are excellent summaries of conditions for women during the Depression and New Deal years. "Employment Conditions and Unemployment Relief: Unemployment Among Women in the Early Years of the Depression," *Monthly Labor Review* 38 (April 1934): 792, n. 7; Meridel Le Sueur, *Ripening* (New York: Feminist Press, 1982), p. 141; Helena Hill Weed, "The New Deal That Women Want," *Current History* 41 (November 1934): 181–82.

5. Weed, p. 183.

6. Chicago Council of Social Agencies, *Work Camps* (Chicago: Chicago Council of Social Agencies, December 1941), pp. 1–2.

7. William E. Leuchtenburg, *Franklin D. Roosevelt and the New Deal, 1932–1940* (New York: Harper & Row, 1963), p. 52.

8. Women's Trade Union League, "Memorandum of Suggestions to Labor Conference, March 1933," Smith Collection, Franklin D. Roosevelt Library, Hyde Park, N.Y., Box 10, file "Public Relations–Labor, 1933–1938"; Hilda W. Smith, "Plan for Resident Schools for Unemployed Women in Need of Relief," Hilda Worthington Smith Papers, Schlesinger Library, Radcliffe College, Cambridge, Mass. (hereafter Smith Papers), Record Group A-76, file 290.

9. Joseph P. Lash, *Eleanor and Franklin* (New York: W. W. Norton & Co., 1971), pp. 510–11, 699.

10. Ibid.

11. *New York Times*, June 2, 1933 (10:6); "Memorandum, May 31, 1933," FERA, Women's Camps Section, Old Subject File, FERA, (hereafter cited as FERA Collection). National Archives, Washington, D.C.

12. Letters and telegrams from individuals and organizations offering facilities for the women's camps program can be found in FERA Collection, Record Group 69, file 984.

13. Ether to Congressman Lemke, July 12, 1933, FERA Collection, Record Group 69, file 284.

14. Hilda W. Smith, "Plan for Resident Schools for Unemployed Women in Need of Relief," Smith Papers, Record Group A-76, file 290. Schlesinger Library.

15. Ware, pp. 106–7; Weed, p. 183.

16. Hilda W. Smith, *People Come First* (New York: Adult Education Fund, Ford Foundation, September 1952), p. 78; FERA, *Report on Educational Camps for Unemployed Women*, p. 8.

17. 1934 FERA *Report*, p. 10; *New York Times*, April 29, 1934 (20:7).

18. "Summary of White House Conference on Problems of Jobless Women, April 30, 1934," FERA Collection, Record Group 69, file 360.

19. Members of the national advisory committee included Dr. Louis Alderman, director, WPA Emergency Education; Josephine Brown, intake and certification, WPA; Richard Brown, National Youth Administration; Mary Bethune, National Youth Administration; Mary Anderson, Women's Bureau, Department of Labor; Helen Gifford, National Board, YWCA; Eleanor Coit, Affiliated Schools for Workers; Dorothea de Schweinitz, National Youth Administration; Ellen Woodward, director of Women's Work, WPA; and Elizabeth Wickenden, WPA.

20. Smith, *People Come First*, pp. 75–76 and appendix G.

21. Ibid., p. 78.

22. *New York Times* June 16, 1934 (17:8).

23. Hilda W. Smith, *Suggestions for Organization, Curriculum, and Teaching in Residential Schools and Educational Camps* (Washington, D.C.: FERA, July 1934); American Labor Education Service Collection, New York State School of Industrial and Labor Relations, Cornell University, Ithaca, N.Y. (hereafter ALES Collection), Record Group 5225, Box 15, file "Schools and Camps for Unemployed Women."

24. 1934 and 1935 FERA *Report*.

25. Ibid., pp. 21–22.

26. As quoted by Lash, p. 205; 1934 and 1935 FERA *Report*, p. 4; *Monthly Labor Review* 39 (November 1934): 1110.

27. 1934 and 1935 FERA *Report*, p. 5.

28. Ibid.

29. Ibid.

30. Ibid., p. 17.

31. 1934 and 1935 FERA *Report*; in addition, I examined reports from about fifteen of the projects, which I found in the National Archives, the Smith Papers at the Schlesinger Library, Radcliffe College, and in the ALES Papers in the archives at Cornell University.

32. 1934 and 1935 FERA *Report*, pp. 34–36.

33. Harry Gersh, "The She-She-She Camps: An Episode in New Deal History," unpublished paper in the Smith Papers.

34. *New York Times* July 3, 1936 (3:4); also see articles in Smith Papers, Record Group A-76, file 297.

35. 1934 and 1935 FERA *Report*, p. 6.

36. Ibid.

37. Funds for the women's camps program under the National Youth Administration were provided through a separate allocation from the NYA budget. Presidential letter no. 5064, July 13, 1936, established a limit of $1,111,000, of which only $700,000 was actually allocated for the women's project. The camps program operated as an official work project and closed October 1, 1937 (Palmer O. Johnson and Oswald L. Harvey, *The National Youth Administration*, Staff Study no. 13 (Washington, D.C.: Advisory Committee on Education, 1938), p. 17.

38. Ella Ketchin, *Report on the National Youth Administration Camps for Unemployed Women* (Washington, D.C.: National Youth Administration, 1937), p. 48.

39. Ibid. p. 62.

40. Smith to Eleanor Roosevelt, November 18, 1936, in Smith Collection, Franklin D. Roosevelt Library, Hyde Park, N.Y., Box 21, file "Correspondence." also see Adeline Taylor, *NYA Camps for Jobless Women* (Washington, D.C.: National Youth Administration, 1936), p. 18.

41. "Minutes of the Advisory Committee, Monday, September 21, 1936," ALES Collection, Record Group 5225, Box 15, file "Schools and Camps."

42. Statement of Charles Taussig to the National Youth Administration Advisory Committee, February 8, 1938, National Youth Administration Collection, National Archives, Washington, D.C., Box 608, file "NYA Papers."

43. Ketchin, p. 42.

44. "Memorandum to Mrs. Roosevelt, June 1, 1937," notes made by Hilda W. Smith, and "Minutes of the National Advisory Committee Meeting, August 3, 1937" (both from Smith Papers, Record Group A-76, file 290).

45. *New York Times* (August 17, 1937) (24:4).

46. Federal Security Agency, *Final Report of the National Youth Administration, 1936–1943* (Washington, D.C.: U.S. Government Printing Office, 1944), pp. 84–85.

47. Smith to Eleanor Roosevelt, May 15, 1940, Smith Papers, Record Group A-76, file 290, "Correspondence."

48. From ALES Collection,

Box 15, file "Wisconsin School for the Unemployed."

49. From *Report of the Resident School Camp for Unemployed Girls*, March 23-May 17, 1936, Philadelphia, Pa., in ALES Collection, Box 15, file "Educational Camps for Unemployed Women—Philadelphia."

50. From Pennsylvania's Girls' Camps, National Youth Administration Collection, National Archives, Washington, D.C., file "Arcola Resident School Camp, Summer 1936."

Chapter 9

To Rekindle the Spirit: Current Education Programs for Women Workers

Barbara Mayer Wertheimer

"What do I want from workers' education?" a trade union woman asked in 1928. She answered her own question in an article in the American Federation of Labor (AFL) newspaper, the *American Federationist*: "I want workers' education to teach me the truth about our economic system, our government, laws, customs and traditions. I want workers' education to give me that which no other educational institution has given me since I first entered the public schools, and which I cannot obtain anywhere else.[1]

Although much has changed in the fifty-four years since Nettie Silverbrook wrote these words, her goals sound familiar. There are many similarities between her experiences at the Bryn Mawr Summer School for Women Workers, Brookwood Labor College, and the Boston Trade Union College that she attended in the 1920s and the experiences and goals of women in contemporary labor education programs. Common themes run through labor education in her day and in ours.

Women played a key role in the development of labor education in the early twentieth century, and, following a hiatus in the post–World War II period, programs run by and for trade union women have become increasingly important. As in Nettie Silverbrook's day, the profession is still a small one, even with the expansion in union and university workers' education services. The field has depended on the personal influence and persuasiveness of individuals. Labor education activities have been deemed expendable when funds run short in unions and universities, and labor educators periodically must fight to maintain the existence of classes and other education services for women and for men.

Action-oriented education for change has been the hallmark of labor education. It is a field that has continuously sought to meet new needs and new demands while retaining a basic philosophy and a set of methods that we owe to the pioneers of our field. Meeting the needs and demands of women workers in the contemporary period has been one of the new developments in labor education. This chapter focuses on that process, the changes that World War II brought to labor education, and the renascence in programming for women workers in the late 1960s and 1970s. It indicates the ways in which the women's movement has reached union women and discusses the burgeoning number of projects and programs that offer a special outreach to work force women and, increasingly, to men as well. It details the major components of some of these programs and reviews several of the most innovative projects that have contributed new and different directions to the field.

World War II, a watershed for labor unions and for women workers, brought full employment and the end of many Depression-initiated emergency recovery programs developed under the government's Works Progress Administration. Wartime industries hired millions of women who entered the paid work force for the first time. Offering good pay and on-the-job training, blue-collar jobs opened to women and minorities as never before in our country's history. Many of the new jobs in heavy industry were unionized, and large numbers of women became part of an organized work force that was racially integrated, at least in a number of locations. Major issues for working women became the fight for equal pay, community services, and child care.

Researchers have now documented what happened to women's employment when the war ended and numbers were laid off to open jobs for returning servicemen. Women, however, did not retreat to their kitchens, but took lower paying service and clerical employment, the kinds of jobs that many of them had held prior to the war. As the postwar economy boomed, expanded services opened millions of new jobs in offices, hospitals, and education systems to women throughout the United States. Not until the 1960s, however, did union organizing successes among teachers, health-care workers, and government employees match the union membership gains that women had experienced during the war in the mass production industries.

The postwar years brought an increasing emphasis on higher education. The GI Bill of Rights helped many older male students attend college for the first time. Community colleges developed and expanded, their goal being that no American should be more than 100 miles from access to higher education. Increasing labor unrest and impatience with stringent governmental wage controls in the postwar period led state legislatures to fund labor education centers at state universities in an effort to promote industrial peace. These labor education centers, often staffed by people with trade union background and experience, began to reach workers through education programs held on the campus, on the job, and in the union hall.

Unions began to lobby for passage of a Labor Extension Service bill modeled on early Civil War legislation that had given farmers the benefits of government-funded agricultural extension services. Although the nation had become increasingly industrialized, Congress never recognized this basic inequity in publicly supported education services, nor passed appropriate legislation. Nevertheless, postwar university-based labor education services began to become available to workers on a state-by-state basis. Offered to groups of workers, predominantly to male union leaders and activists, these classes and programs were administered and taught by male educators who used classroom materials and case studies reflecting men's experiences in the labor force and in their unions.

By 1950, the labor force participation of women had soared beyond wartime peaks, a trend that has continued through the present period. Today, 44 million women workers represent over 43 percent of the work force. These women now have the same educational levels as men, and they need and expect to have the same permanent commitment to holding paid jobs. As a result, they have demanded more status as workers, improvement of the jobs they hold, and more opportunities to obtain those higher paying and more challenging jobs from which they have traditionally been barred. They seek equal pay for equal work, paid maternity leave, access to on-the-job training, and an end to sexual harassment. They also seek increased responsibilities in their unions and workplace organizations.

The Civil Rights movement, passage of the Equal Pay Act (1963) and of Title VII of the Civil Rights Act (1964), and Executive Order 11246 (1964), in addition to the implications of their continuous work force participation, led women workers to reassess their roles in the workplace and in their unions. Many started taking advantage of expanded educational opportunities at community colleges and universities to enhance their skills and broaden their understanding of social issues in our rapidly changing nation. Many responded favorably to the new courses and conferences offered by a few unions and university labor education programs that focused on the participation of union women in determining conditions in their workplaces and union policies in their workplace organizations.

These developments depended on the foresight and efforts of union and university leaders and labor educators, the financial support of several foundations, and the push from union women who had the motivation and energy to undertake the challenge of adding these education programs to their full-time jobs and their union and homemaking activities.

From small, tentative, and experimental beginnings, labor education programs for women workers have come to play a key role in encouraging women to develop self-confidence, learn new personal and organizational skills, and become part of a sisterhood of women with shared purposes and common goals. Today, labor education for women workers is a recognized and respected component of the labor education movement, drawing inspiration and strength from earlier periods of workers' education activities and responding to the current needs and interests of union women and their organizations.

The renascence of labor education programs for women workers actually began in the 1940s and 1950s with the early work of the United Auto Workers (UAW) and the International Union of Electrical Workers (IUE), two unions with concrete positions on women's issues and a firm commitment to labor education for women.[2] University labor education programs for female union staff, leaders, and rank-and-file members developed in the early 1970s and augmented the pioneer work of these unions. Model university programs for women were established at Cornell University and at the University of Michigan. Through the 1970s, new programs for women workers developed in organizations such as the Coalition of Labor Union Women (CLUW) and Nine to Five: the National Association of Working Women.

The UAW Women's Department, established in the 1940s, began advocating convention resolutions on issues important to women workers during World War II. In 1970, the union's convention resolutions included UAW support for the elimination of discriminatory state laws, job protection during maternity leaves, and the establishment of expanded child-care facilities. The women's rights' resolution, adopted at the 1974 UAW convention, staked out a clear women's position that indicated the direction UAW women members want to go.[3]

The IUE carried out an equal pay for equal work and an antidiscrimination policy as early as 1952 through the programs of its Education and Social Action Department.[4] To carry out convention resolutions on equal pay, the union joined in forming the National Committee for Equal Pay, which was active in getting the 1963 Equal Pay Act passed by Congress. The union's interest in working to end discrimination predates Title VII of the 1964 Civil Rights Act and has led to programming, starting at the national level, that has moved into the district and local structure of the union. The union sees its education program as the vehicle for achieving its wider union goals; conferences and other education programs aimed at increasing women's involvement in every aspect of union life are a regular part of the union's ongoing program.

It is the policy of the International Executive Board that a national women's conference take place every second year. The first such conference, held in 1967, was built on the theme: "The Status of the IUE Woman: Her Responsibilities, Contributions, and Goals." This conference laid the groundwork for the union's first self-survey to determine where IUE women were in the union, what offices they held, and the extent to which they were underrepresented as local union officers. Succeeding surveys have shown that programs focused on increasing the participation of IUE women have helped women to move into union positions they had never held before and to run for office and for committee posts in increasing numbers.

The IUE's Women's Council, established in 1972, advises the International Executive Board and works to gain union support for women's issues. The chair of this council sits on the board, but has no vote. To further the Women's Council mandate, a special women's program is held at each union convention, not only to educate those who choose to attend but also to increase the visibility of women, close to 38 percent of the union's membership, at its national conventions.

Five years after the formation of the Women's Council, the IUE revamped its structure to increase the decision-making role of women in the union. It did this by providing a model constitution for all new IUE locals, mandating that the local union executive board consist of five people, two of whom were to be secretary and the social action chairperson, posts traditionally held by women.

University programs that have pioneered in developing labor education services for women workers and women union members have benefited from the early efforts of union leaders and workers' education practitioners. Both the program at Cornell University and that at the University of Michigan were led by women experienced in labor education who used approaches and methods firmly rooted in the successful labor education programming of the past. A labor advisory committee worked with each program. Teaching methods involved students in the learning process through class discussions, simulation exercises, panel discussions, role play, the use of films, and other participatory education methods. Both of these programs have flourished and have been central to the development of labor education for women workers, not only in New York and Michigan, but throughout the country by way of the assistance they have provided other university and union labor education programs.

In 1970, what is now Cornell University's Institute for Women and Work did not exist. But the New York City Extension Division of Cornell's New York State School of Industrial and Labor Relations (NYSSILR) began to offer seminars and courses for union women staff, leaders, and active rank and file. Part of the purpose of these programs was to bring women leaders together to get to know each other, since there were relatively few at that time, and to develop an initial support network. Out of a series of monthly brown bag lunch meetings that provided information on topics such as working women and the law came rap sessions on the problems of women in unions.

As a result, the group constituted itself a planning committee for a major conference held in January 1974, attended by some 600 New York City union women. This conference, which predated by several months the initial organizational meeting for CLUW, indicated that the time was at hand to mobilize women in unions and associations across all jurisdictional lines to communicate with each other and to act on their common concerns and needs.

Parallel to this development, I received a one-year grant in 1972 from the Ford Foundation to study the barriers to the participation of women in unions. With Anne Nelson as collaborator, we proceeded to survey some 115 local unions in the New York City area to learn what positions women held. The study focused closely on seven unions, eager to cooperate with the research, that represented a cross-section of occupations and had a female membership of more than 25 percent.[5]

Out of this study came the design for Trade Union Women's Studies, a two-pronged labor education program for union women that started in September 1974 with assistance from the Ford Foundation. One aspect of this program included short courses and conferences that provided specific information in a number of areas, such as grievance handling, public speaking, and sexual harassment. The second component of the program included a year-long evening college credit program in labor studies and leadership skill development that provided thirty-six weeks of intensive training. In addition, union women also could earn nine credits toward a college degree.

The courses, specifically designed for union women, were developed to put working women back into the pages of labor history, into case studies, collective bargaining games, and all of the written resources used in these programs. These materials built a sense of self and sisterhood for women workers and union members, in addition to providing a knowledge of how unions work. The course work and the supporting materials encouraged women to examine ways of working within union structures to attain leadership positions and to effect change.

The Program on Women and Work (POWW) at the Labor Studies Center of the University of Michigan's Institute of Labor and Industrial Relations (ILIR) also started in the 1970s, following an initial series of meetings in southeast Michigan that brought together women from unions and university labor programs in that area. Because union members in Michigan are spread over a wide geographic area, the ILIR's Program on Women and Work on the Ann Arbor campus of the University of Michigan concentrated on Saturday workshops and a residential Michigan Summer School for Women Workers, held annually on campus each August since 1974.[6]

The one-day conferences, initiated in the fall of 1973, focused on one main subject or theme for a six- to eight-hour session: women and the law, collective bargaining issues, child care, union administration, women in politics, working with committees, effective speaking, or assertion training. In 1974, POWW experimented with bilingual programs on issues for Hispanic women workers and union members. The popularity and importance of the annual Summer School for Women Workers led to the start of an annual winter residential program, cosponsored by Michigan State University and the University of Michigan and held in late winter on the East Lansing campus. In 1979, under a grant from the Michigan state legislature, the Union Women/Minorities Leadership Training Project started providing programs for union women and minority members at six of the state's university labor extension service centers.

During the 1970s, several new organizations of women workers emerged, offering labor education for women as part of their ongoing programs. Although they differ in membership and methods of operation, their goals are similar: to improve job conditions for women workers, to help them gain equal opportunity under the law, to gain increased respect for women workers, and to help women participate more fully in their labor organizations. Only two of these pioneering organizations will be discussed here—Nine to Five: the National Association of Working Women, and the Coalition of Labor Union Women (CLUW). Established within six months of each other—Nine to Five in October 1973, and CLUW in March 1974—both organizations were initiated by women who were workers and feminists, often with considerable political expertise gained through participation in the Civil Rights movement of the 1960s. Nine to Five reaches out to organize clerical workers, and CLUW enrolls union women. Both organizations have a chapter structure, growing memberships, and huge potentials for helping working women improve their workplace conditions.

Now a national organization with 12,000 members, fifteen chapters, and the goal of doubling this participation by 1983, Nine to Five had its official beginnings in Boston in 1973. The ten founding members believed that clerical workers needed a collective voice in order to improve their salaries and workplace conditions. They took their first action by passing out Nine to Five job surveys to clerical workers in downtown Boston. Similar groups began to organize in other major cities, supporting themselves through local fund-raising campaigns, membership dues, foundation grants, newsletter subscriptions, literature sales, and speakers' fees as the seriousness of the office workers' movement became recognized. The city groups formed a loose affiliation in 1976.

Beginning in the early 1970s, Nine to Five chapters chalked up an impressive list of workplace gains in banks, insurance companies, and offices. Chapters won salary increases, job posting requirements, safer working conditions, and procedures for dealing with sexual harassment for their members. Through member education and direct action, the Nine to Five chapters filed suits under Title VII of the Civil Rights Act, lobbied, organized letter writing campaigns, and designed public information techniques to challenge offending employers and to educate the public about issues affecting office workers.

The education program of the national organization and its chapters has raised the consciousness of office workers across the country. Member education is a central activity in each chapter, with classes and workshops, public forums, community publicity, and national and chapter newsletters that share program ideas, publicize worker complaints, and announce settlements won on equal employment and other workplace cases.

CLUW began with a series of regional meetings in 1973 to assess whether women were ready to assert their needs for more representation at every level of union leadership. A national founding meeting for a new organization, called for March 1974, brought 3,500 union women to Chicago, several thousand more than anticipated. They came by every means of transportation from all sections of the country to launch this new organization.

Four guiding principles were set at that meeting: to increase the number of women in trade union leadership positions through affirmative action on the job and in the unions; to support legislation on women's concerns; to move women into political office; and to organize the millions of unorganized women workers. An elected national executive board was established to govern CLUW, with a team of officers who ran the organization between board meetings. Paralleling the structure of most unions and associations in the U.S. labor movement, the organization established a convention procedure to pass resolutions and set policies to guide the officers and the chapters.

From these beginnings, CLUW has grown to include sixty-five chapters and 15,000 members. Education is essential to its leadership development function. Each CLUW Chapter has an education committee; the national organization has established the CLUW Center for Education and Research, which has received several foundation grants to conduct research and assist chapter development of education programs. Through the national organization, chapters obtain educational materials on collective bargaining of working women's issues, organizing CLUW chapters, and the need of union and other working women for an Equal Rights Amendment. The annual regional summer schools for union women,[7] in which CLUW cooperates, provide another valuable way to reach potential members. CLUW also works in coalition with other women's groups on issues such as pregnancy disability and equal pay for work of comparable worth.

By 1975, with the sustained growth of programs for women within key unions, the development of university-based education programs for union and nonunionized women workers, and the creation of new organizations like Nine to Five and CLUW, the concerns of working women had become central issues for many union and university labor education programs. Moreover, the specific programs designed for union women by CLUW and for office workers by Nine to Five offered new models of labor education for women.

It is important to examine the current education programs in major unions and to trace the university-based programs beyond the pioneering efforts of the Cornell and the University of Michigan programs in the early 1970s. We need to look at the increasing cooperation between union and university programs and to analyze the contribution of those organizations, created in the last decade, to meeting the needs of working women in this period.

While only a few of the many programs for union and working women can be described or even mentioned in this chapter, the projects that are discussed illustrate the range and the direction of contemporary labor education programming for women. As they have developed and expanded, these programs have had an important impact on the field of labor education. Today, as in the period before World War II, increasing numbers of women unionists and feminists with the training and credentials for the field are choosing labor education as their life work. As veteran labor educator Larry Rogin has written:

Everyone interested in labor education is again in the debt of women labor educators. They have demonstrated an ability to reach a neglected audience in imaginative and creative ways. They and several men in the field as well, have thought deeply about their work. . . . Perhaps they will inspire other groups who have special needs to experiment with special programs. It is in this fashion that labor education will expand and will attract new participants, first to classes and programs, then into further union activity and leadership.[8]

Among the heartening trends of the past decade's activities in developing labor education programs for women workers is the growing cooperation between unions and universities in planning and conducting these programs. This unified approach reflects the increasing number of women and men at university labor education centers who are concerned with working women's issues. It is also an indication of the growing number of women union members who have attended union and university programs for women workers, including the regional summer schools, and who now constitute a new pressure group for the expansion of such programs.

Increasingly, during the 1970s, labor unions set up women's divisions or departments and encouraged their education divisions to hold classes and workshops to meet the growing needs and concerns of women members. In several instances, international union leaders have found the resources of university labor education centers useful in carrying out their policies to plan regular conferences and education programs for women members.

Recently, the AFL-CIO Executive Council, which now includes two women members, took an official stand on working women's rights. In May 1982, Lane Kirkland, the AFL-CIO president, stated that "the primary concern of the AFL-CIO is that working women continue to suffer from widespread wage discrimination in the workplace." Kirkland affirmed that "the Federation has redoubled its efforts to see that all workers are paid equally for work of comparable value and to remove all barriers to equal opportunity for women."[9]

Kirkland recognized the issue of comparable worth as one important concern that has mobilized union women. Other issues that stimulate working women to action include health and safety on the job, child care, bargaining for maternity-paternity leave, sexual harassment, job training, and, more recently, the impact of the recession and the federal budget cuts on working women. These issues have become the basis for workshops and courses offered by labor education programs in unions and universities and at the residential summer schools for union women. In addition, throughout the 1970s, working women increasingly supported the Equal Rights Amendment, which served as a means of educating and unifying trade union women with other women's groups and organizations.

At the same time that programs for and about women workers have gained acceptance, there has been a growing recognition that the concerns of working women—health and safety on the job, vacations, seniority, decent wages and working conditions, viable grievance procedures, education leave, and flextime, to name a few—are issues that affect men as well as women workers. Long before Betty Friedan discovered that women need men to make their workplace gains permanent, union women were making continuous efforts to obtain the support of their male union leaders and to involve male rank-and-file members in education programs about working women's—and men's—issues.

The Communication Workers of America (CWA) is one of the unions with a national women's program that receives support from the union president for the work of its Women's Division. In 1978, the CWA invited the Institute for Women and Work at Cornell to help plan and conduct a national women's conference. The union's president, Glen Watts, asked all CWA regional directors to attend the conference, participate in workshops, and learn more about the concerns of women members. Taking the interests of its women members seriously, this union has continued to work on the problems emphasized at the 1978 conference: job stress, impact of high technology in the workplace, safety and health, and pay equity.

Moreover, the staff of the CWA Women's Division has worked with all CWA districts to conduct regional conferences on the national conference model. Each district has completed its second or, in some cases, its third such conference. Seven were held in 1982, each lasting several days and involving several hundred members. These conferences included discussions of the impact of technological change on women workers, plenary sessions on political issues, and workshops to develop basic skills for increased participation in the union. Sexual harassment, a subject that has come into the open in the past few years, is discussed at almost every CWA women's conference, where the film *Workplace Hustle* is often part of the program.[10]

The formation of local women's committees is encouraged as a way of organizing women's programs in each state. For example, CWA district 4 held a regional women's conference in June 1981 in connection with Women's Awareness Month and with the cooperation of Ohio State University's Labor Education and Research Service. Programs in CWA locals throughout the state focused on women's roles in the labor movement, while the district women's conference highlighted organizing.

Finally, the CWA is seeking to increase the participation of women in discussions on the quality of work life. To this end, a national labor-management committee brings representatives of the union and the American Telephone and Telegraph Company together. Vice-presidents of the national union staff and local officers sit on these committees locally, and the training programs for union representatives are becoming an important source of skills development for CWA women as well as men.

A second union that serves as an example here is the Service Employees International Union (SEIU), whose membership of 650,000 is 40 percent female. In 1980, SEIU's national convention passed a resolution calling for a national women's conference and for a women's committee for the union. Planned by this women's committee, the first SEIU National Women's Conference took place at the University of Connecticut in June 1981. More than 400 women from across the country attended this meeting, the purpose of which was to establish a regional structure for women's committees and programs.[11]

A model SEIU regional women's program has been developed by the women's committee of the Public Employee Federation (PEF) in New York State. Union members attend Saturday seminars and discuss concerns such as child care and pay equity. Through grass roots committees, this group was instrumental in persuading the state to adopt an Albany childcare center as a pilot project and pushed for the state to fund additional on-site childcare centers. Most recently, the PEF in New York State has received funding from New York State's Professional Development and Quality of Worklife Committee to hold a two-day, state-wide women's conference (August 1982) focusing on developing leadership skills.

One of the more unusual ways of developing union-university cooperation was initiated by SEIU through its film festivals. In 1981, in conjunction with the Smithsonian Institution in Washington, D.C., SEIU's education department sponsored a successful, well-attended summer film festival to bring labor films, many about women workers and women in unions, to a wider audience. The success of the program led SEIU to enlist the cooperation of university labor education centers in cosponsoring similar film festivals. By fall 1982, these had been held in five states in an attempt to inform the public about the labor movement, including the issues of women workers.

In unique cooperation, SEIU and the National Association of Working Women, Nine to Five, have joined many of their efforts and programs. SEIU has established a separate district 925 within its structure to concentrate on the organization of white-collar and clerical workers. SEIU provides support funding to Nine to Five and staff to spearhead organizing drives, and Nine to Five is included in all SEIU's women's programs.[12]

The support of SEIU's president, which is wholehearted and is essential to this effort, includes the view that the union is committed to a twenty- or thirty-year campaign to organize clerical workers under the SEIU banner. This is another instance where the top leadership of the union supports efforts to enlist active participation of women and sees the organization of clerical workers as a key mission. The composition of the union staff, which is close to 50 percent female, also reflects this focus.

The women's program of another major union, the American Federation of State, County, and Municipal Employees (AFSCME) developed from a women's caucus that became active at the union's 1978 convention. The union response was to appoint a woman coordinator with the responsibility for organizing four regional women's conferences that were held the following year. More than 1,200 women attended these programs, which focused on issues such as collective bargaining, pay equity, and sexual harassment.

One of the purposes of the regional meetings was to determine what AFSCME women wanted in the further development of women's programs. In 1980, regional conferences for clerical workers focused on the special concerns of this group, which is predominantly female. At the 1980 AFSCME national convention, major responsibilities for women's programs were shifted to the district council level, although the national Education Department continues to publish pamphlets on women's issues and to send representatives to meet with organizations, such as the National Pay Equity Committee, that are concerned with working women's issues.

On the district council level, women's conferences are sponsored by district women's committees. In Pennsylvania, for example, AFSCME works with Pennsylvania State University's labor education center to plan and conduct its women's conferences. In New York, District Council 37 has an education fund under its collective bargaining agreement with the city that supports a wide range of labor education and job training programs for its 110,000 members. The women's committee of D.C. 37 sponsors an annual conference and other education programs for women, while Cornell's Institute for Women and Work conducts a branch of its year-long Trade Union Women's Studies program for D.C. 37 members; this program is aimed at increasing participation in the union at the same time that college credits are earned.[13]

The George Meany Center for Labor Studies is a continuing education arm of the AFL-CIO. Located on a campus in Silver Spring, Maryland, close to Washington, D.C., it offers a residential training program for union staff. Throughout the year, five-day sessions are conducted on special subjects, including an annual leadership training session on women's issues that helps meet the need for skill development and technical competence that union staff women seek. This institute provides sound background on labor laws important to women, the current economics of women in the work force, and information on pay equity, health and safety problems, and other issues. The program offers an opportunity for women staff from a cross-section of labor organizations to share experiences and learn practical leadership skills in a supportive environment.

During the decade of the 1970s and on into the 1980s, university labor education centers have initiated a variety of new programs, many of them innovative in design and targeted to meet the changing needs and concerns of the growing number of women in the labor movement. A number of university labor education centers have come a long way in developing programs for union women, supporting them through staff assistance, and hosting the annual regional summer schools for union women. Equally important, women are more in evidence as staff members on labor extension faculties; by 1982, almost every university labor education program had at least one woman staff member.

A university base has provided some labor education programs with a research component. POWW at the Labor Studies Center of the University of Michigan developed a national oral history project, "The Twentieth-Century Trade Union Woman: Vehicle for Social Change," with a grant from the Rockefeller Foundation, that has collected and transcribed, interviews with seventy-five union women who were active in the union movement in the past six decades.[14] From the outset, applied research has been one of the key activities of the Institute for Women and Work at Cornell. The study that explored the barriers to the participation of women in unions resulted in the book, *Trade Union Women: A Study of Their Participation in New York City Locals*.[15] Another year-long study looked at the use women made of union-negotiated, company-financed tuition refund monies and reported these findings in a book, *Where Are the Women?* by institute staff member Mimi Abramowitz.[16] Other research of the Institute on Women and Work has followed graduates of its year-long Trade Union Women's Studies leadership training program in a longitudinal survey of their progress in obtaining positions of responsibility in their unions, in CLUW, and in their communities.

Among recent Institute for Women and Work programs was a national conference for union leaders involved in the issue of pay equity, planned with the cooperation of the AFL-CIO Department of Education and the national CLUW. The institute is now deeply involved in a pilot two-year program to train ten minority group women as labor educators. Funded by the Muskiwinni Foundation, this project provides intensive training in labor education methods and field experience for ten minority group women, each sponsored by her union or association, which agreed to share some financial costs of the program and to utilize the women in labor education following the two-year period.

In a variation of the year-long, college-credit program for union women, the Institute for Women and Work has developed a parallel project, Public Service Women's Studies (PSWS), designed to help women employed by New York State to move up the job ladder. PSWS focuses on human relations and organizational skills, written and oral communications, and workplace-related mathematics to help women advance through the state's civil service system and to encourage them to work for a college degree. The program, planned in cooperation with the Civil Service Employees Association, receives partial tuition reimbursement from New York State.

Throughout the country, university labor education programs have started including programming for union women. At the University of Alabama in Birmingham, a series of workshops for women leaders has been planned on health and safety, political action, women in labor history, communications skills, and basic unionism. Health and safety programs also are a special focus of the Labor Occupational Health Program of the University of California at Berkeley. At Ohio State University, the Labor Education and Research Service worked with the Women's Film Program of Cincinnati on an award-winning documentary, *Pregnancy and the Working Woman.*

Other programs for women workers have been conducted through labor education centers at the University of California at Los Angeles, the University of Connecticut, Rutgers, the State University of New Jersey, the University of Kentucky, the University of Maine, the University of Oregon, and Indiana University—a major change in labor education programming that has taken place in the 1970s and 1980s. These and other university labor education centers have cooperated in the most outstanding example of collaboration between university and union labor educators, the highly successful regional summer schools for union women. Over the past seven years, close to 2,000 union women have attended these schools, held in the Northeast, Midwest, South, and Far West regions.

Begun through the efforts of the Committee on Programs for Union Women of the University and College Labor Education Association (UCLEA), with the cooperation of the AFL-CIO Department of Education and CLUW, these regional schools bring together women from a cross-section of unions and experienced women labor educators. The regional schools, run on a shoestring budget, have served as a training ground for union activists as well as for women new to the field of labor education.

The regional summer schools seem to inspire as well as inform trade union women, who return to their unions and communities with increased motivation and skills to participate in workplace organizations, local union women's committees, and CLUW chapters. Although a number of women still use their vacation time and pay their own way to these week-long activities, growing union support for sending more women members to these regional programs is evident. The high spirit and dedication to the labor movement exhibited at these programs led one male labor educator who attended a regional summer school for women workers graduation to comment, "It's like the Thirties all over again!"

Perhaps as a testimony to the reality that women are in the work force to stay, new organizations of women workers have emerged in the contemporary period that share similar goals. Some of these groups are small and work effectively in one city or region: for example, Chicago's Women Employed, Union Women's Alliance to Gain Equality (Union WAGE) in California, and the National Congress of Neighborhood

Women in New York City. The Nine to Five organization and the national CLUW, whose beginnings have already been reviewed, have made major gains in the past decade on the national as well as the local level and have incorporated education activities into all of their projects.

By 1982, the informal affiliation of city groups that Nine to Five formed in 1976 had become a permanent nationwide organization, Nine to Five: National Association of Working Women. Its steady growth is due to its chapter and national leaders, who have a keen sense of public relations. Over the years, "Nine to Five" has become a byword for women workers, as has the organization's slogan: "Raises, Rights, and Respect." In the last decade Nine to Five chapters have expanded their programs to include an annual three-day summer school. At the 1982 school, the organization's fourth, 300 women workers gathered at Bryn Mawr College to discuss such issues as closing the gap between men's and women's earnings, mobilizing women for more impact on the political process, maintaining and enforcing equal employment laws, and devising methods for women to have a role in restructuring offices that have installed new technology. The 1982 school initiated a national membership drive to double the number of Nine to Five chapters in the coming year.

The education programs of Nine to Five prepare workers for the opposition they meet during organizing drives and help them to succeed in building effective chapters. Its extensive materials include a four-session course on labor history, developed and tested with a grant from the National Endowment for the Humanities.

As a model of union and association cooperation, the SEIU–Nine to Five linkup bears close watching. This development, which has accelerated the awareness of many labor unions of the need to organize women office workers, has led to a women's organizing campaign in the Washington, D.C.–Baltimore area, launched with support from the AFL-CIO Industrial Union Department and CLUW. SEIU and six other major labor organizations are targeting banks, insurance companies, hospitals, universities, industrial operations, and food services to educate unorganized women about their need for workplace unions. Public education takes place through a media campaign, telephone polls and interviews, a women's resource center, and other community outreach programs.

Over the past decade, CLUW has emerged as an organization that seeks increased power for women in the labor movement. In addition to its success in raising funds from unions and foundations, organizing unorganized women, supporting legislation, and developing coalitions with like-minded groups, CLUW's education and leadership development programs have successfully expanded. One major CLUW research and education project, "Empowerment of Union Women," examined the positions women hold in labor organizations and developed a manual that provides information and "how to do it" material for CLUW chapters to use in developing women union leaders.

Recently, CLUW received additional funding from the Carnegie Corporation of New York for a two-year leadership training program for CLUW members and chapters that would extend its Empowerment of Union Women project. Union and university labor educators serve on the project's advisory board, another example of important cooperative links that help realize one of the project's goals—to encourage CLUW chapters to utilize university labor education resources in their own areas. Other recent CLUW research and education projects include Project Opportunity, a demonstration program in ten selected CLUW chapters designed to develop a network of "opportunity advisors" to link CLUW members with family and individual needs to community and educational resources; and the research and writing of a book on women in health-care settings where unionized hospital workers fight for better wages and working conditions.

These programs bring visibility to the national CLUW, its leaders, and its chapters and result in increased financial support from unions and foundations and a growing membership; in fact, they have necessitated the assignment of a CLUW staff member as organizing director to work full time on establishing new chapters.

Today, labor education for women workers is recognized by many unions and universities as both a legitimate and an important component of workers' education. Since the 1970s, the growing cooperation in programming between union and university labor educators has been of benefit to union women and to working women's groups that have a commitment to unionizing unorganized women. A range of new programs and a wealth of new resources—study guides, films, filmstrips, monographs, and books—have been produced for and about women workers. Even *Nine to Five*, a highly successful Hollywood film starring Jane Fonda, Lily Tomlin, and Dolly Parton, served to call attention to many issues of women workers.

Foundations and government grants and contracts have been important in providing support for new and innovative programs that have demonstrated the range and possibilities of labor education focused on meeting the needs of a particular group. This funding supported pilot projects when many unions and universities were not prepared to do so. Foundation funding has helped labor educators to demonstrate ways that ideas useful in one context are adaptable to others and, similarly, to show that traditional methods can be used in contemporary settings to meet new needs.

During the past decade there has been a growing awareness by the labor movement of the importance of organizing women workers. To do this, unions had to realize how central the public image of the labor movement is and that education is a critical process in arousing the consciousness of women workers as well as public awareness of their issues.

Unions have realized that they must demonstrate a concern for women members if they want additional working women to join their ranks. Increasingly, unions have sought publicity in the media for their women's conferences and activities. More union resources have been made available in support of education programs for women union members and other women workers. The Industrial Union Department of the AFL-CIO has cosponsored training conferences with CLUW for women union members and has promised to increase the number of women organizers employed on its national staff. More local unions sponsor women members to attend summer schools for women workers and other classes and workshops organized by university labor education centers. In New York City, many unions provide scholarships for women to attend the Institute for Women and Work's college credit program, Trade Union Women's Studies. There is more financial support for CLUW.

Women are still a long way from equality. The current economic recession and political backlash against working women will affect many union leaders. Union struggles to retain the gains of recent years are taking priority, and education, especially for women members, is considered expendable. Furthermore, the pressure to implement affirmative action through unions diminishes when these laws are not enforced by the federal government. In addition, recession layoffs involve conflicts between traditional seniority rankings and hiring patterns that have resulted from affirmative action.

These problems put new demands on labor educators and increase the need for workers' education that will help unions change to meet new times. Unions need to develop increased membership participation, especially among the growing numbers of women in their ranks. They need active member support for organizing drives. Unions seek ways of initiating effective new coalitions to press for the social policies and legislation that are so badly needed by working people.

Despite the gains in the past decade, there is a distance to go before obtaining support for education programs for women workers, although we now number over 30 percent of the labor movement's membership. In this process, it is still crucial to gain support of union and university program leaders. As Patsy Fryman, an assistant to the president of the Communication Workers of America, said in a 1979 conference on developing education programs for union women: "Unless you gain the support of the principal officer within a union, your project ideas may go nowhere."[17] At the same conference, university labor educators indicated that many of their directors expected them to do programs for union women "on our own time" and did not consider these activities a legitimate use of staff time or budget monies which would count in favor of the educators when they came up for performance review or promotions.

As recently as 1981, it was necessary to devote a session at the Southern-Midwestern regional meeting of UCLEA to "Special Issues Faced by Women Labor Educators on the Job." Speakers addressed the fact that some labor education centers have not fully integrated programs for women workers into their budgets or their planning. Other issues addressed by speakers included developing essential materials for courses for women unionists; getting more working women, especially Latino and black women, to become labor educators; eliminating sexism from existing labor education materials; and integrating issues of sexism into all labor education courses. More work needs to be done in reaching other groups of women workers: older women, especially retirees; Hispanic women; and part-time workers, who make up one-third of all women workers.

Although this chapter has focused on programs for union women and other working women, labor education has a special role in reaching out to male union leaders and rank-and-file members. Especially in a period of shrinking jobs, men and women must understand how sexism and racism affect workers and how these problems can be eliminated. Men who have attended women's conferences and workshops often have learned a new respect for the articulation of women members, how it feels to be in a minority, and the concerns that most affect union women. Labor educators and union leaders need to develop new ways to reach male members and increase their understanding of the continuing role of women in the labor force and the implication this has for unions and for families.

The labor movement must organize women workers in order to grow. As the labor movement expands, there will be room for new leaders, women as well as men, who should not constitute any threat to incumbent union activists. The process of changing attitudes has begun and must continue, with information on subjects relating to women in the labor movement incorporated into programs, classes, and materials for all workers.

We do not know how much will change if a shift in the center of power occurs and women participate in proportion to their numbers in the work force and in unions. We must continue to seek the day when changes come because women are in a position to make things happen rather than merely to obtain changes through pressure on union leaders. We may yet arrive at a point when we can stop counting the number of women and men in leadership positions. Then, human concerns will take precedence over issues raised because racial, gender, or ethnic groups feel that they have not been heard. Not only is there a key role for labor education in this process; there is also enough challenge and excitement in developing and facilitating the necessary programs to last most labor educators twice a lifetime.

Barbara Kohn is a forty-three-year-old worker and mother of four children from a small town in southeastern Michigan, who has taken a number of classes offered by the University of Michigan's Institute of Labor and Industrial Relations and has attended several of the Michigan Summer Schools for Women Workers. She was interviewed by Joyce L. Kornbluh in October 1982.[18]

Interview with Barbara Kohn, United Auto Workers

Barb, tell me a little about yourself. Where do you work?

I've always worked, all my life since I was twelve. I put myself through high school by working. Then I married and worked in an office while my husband went to college. But I couldn't stand office work. It was too confining, too few people around. And I love people. So I quit and went to work in a TV factory where they make coils.... And after being there for seven years, I had to make a big decision to quit and go to work for General Motors. It was a big decision. I went to work at the auto plant fifteen years ago.

What do you do?

I'm a stripper (laughs). It doesn't mean taking off your clothes. A stripper is a person who stands on the other side of a pattern press and when six layers of material for the car upholstery come down, we tie it up and put it into a gondola and it's taken to the department that makes seats for the Oldsmobile.

How did you hear about the first workers' education class you attended?

I think there was a brochure. I had always been involved with the union as a silent majority. My husband was president of his local union.... So I lived union, but I lived it through him. Because of *his* involvement. His idea was for me not to get involved. My first venture in my local union was to edit the local union newspaper. I came down to Ann Arbor to a writing workshop for newspaper editors. It was $5.00 for a Saturday workshop. Since I was going to do the union newspaper, I thought why not? Our local union had never sent a woman to *anything*. And we are a woman-oriented shop. Run by men! So I came to the ILIR workshop that Saturday and that's how I got on the ILIR mailing list.

What were some of the other classes you took?

Basic Unionism, to learn about my local union. Assertive Training. I think I take an assertive training course every year. It's helped me come out of a shell. I've learned more through those assertive training classes. Collective Bargaining. I think I've taken pretty much all the classes. But Assertive Training is always on my list.

What was the reason you came to the classes?

To broaden my horizons, to learn more about my workplace, and to be able to speak out for people. The role of a woman in the generation I was brought up in was to be a housewife first, subservient to her husband. To be seen but not to speak. Or if you did speak, to speak softly. Decision-making was the male's job. You just didn't make decisions. You didn't do anything to push yourself ahead, to broaden yourself. You were locked into your own little world. You were dominated by others. I didn't want to be part of those "yes" people. I wanted to be part of the people in the decision-making, but I didn't know how to do it effectively.

Is that why you took the classes?

Yes, if I was going to write the union newspaper, I wanted to *know* what I was writing and *understand* what I was writing about in an intelligent way. So that's why and how I started with the writing class and I must say it was the best local union newspaper our local has ever had.

Did you have any trouble getting to the classes?

At first the officials in my local union were very reluctant to send me. Then I went to the executive board of my local to ask if three or four women could go with me to the classes. And it was met by an immediate "No." "If you want to go, Barb, we'll send you, but we're not going to waste union dollars on a bunch of women going off. What are they going to do? What are they going to do for the union when they get back?"

Well, the male union executive board members weren't going to give us a chance. But I went. And my enthusiasm for what I had learned in those labor classes—I *used* it. When I got back, I *used* the learning. I was able to *speak up*. And that was the result of the classes in effective speaking and the classes in assertive training. I didn't hold back. I let them know I could speak up. And what I had learned about the union contract. I was able to speak up and I wasn't afraid of my male counterparts.

So they decided that I should become chair of the local union women's committee. Give me something to do. And it's been very effective. I've gotten more women involved.

I'm interested in what the Summer Schools for Women Workers were like for you.

Very frightening at first. I was *alone* the first year when I went. I didn't realize that all the other women felt alone too. We had no idea of what the summer school was going to be like. We had no idea of what would be taught and what we were going to learn that would be beneficial to ourselves and other people.

What had you expected?

I really didn't know. I came into it blind. I thought I was going to learn basic unionism. I had watched [the union officers] hold a union meeting and I felt I could probably do as well. But I had no idea how the parliamentary procedure rules should be followed. But I did have to learn to conduct a meeting. Being chair of the women's committee, I really needed that.

I also needed the strength to stand up there and carry it off. I had no idea of how to do it. *Now*, I can be very authoritative. *Before*, I knew I was going to learn something but I didn't know what.

Now I go back to the local union after these classes and I am bubbling over with enthusiasm about what I've learned. I tell and I tell and I tell until people get sick of hearing me and they say, "When are *we* going to get to go?"

What did you like the most in the summer school program?

I formed some close friendships with women who have been in like situations that we've been in in our plant. It was a cross-section of women in unions from all walks of life and all modes of work. Not just from the Big Three auto companies, but from little workplaces, food places and telephone companies. And the problems *they* face. It's a problem-solving school. It doesn't solve the problems for us but it gives us the insight so that we can go back and tackle the problems and solve them.

How did it do that for you? Help you solve the problems?

I think through the summer school classes, I have a different outlook. Before, I used to punch the clock, and if I had a problem, I complained to the union. The people in the union couldn't care less. They would go by the contract. Go by the union books. Now I'm finding that even though I'm just chair of the women's committee, which has no real voice, I *do* have a voice. People come to me and say, "Gee, Barb, this is what is happening." Nobody else seems to care.

Why do they come to you, Barb?

I guess I've made it known that's what I am here for. Women have to look out for women. And now, through the assertive training, I'm not afraid to speak up to mingle in groups. I used to stand on the outside. I'm not afraid now to walk into any break area [in the plant] and sit down with someone and say "How do you like your job." And they'll tell me, "Well, the foreman's been riding me" or "I'm not getting any satisfaction with my grievance," and I can ask why.

Now, I can honestly be really concerned. Before, I cared only about me and my job. I care now about a lot more people and I think *they* care about a lot more people as a result.

What else was important to you at the Michigan Summer School for Women Workers?

I value the friendships I've gleaned from the schools. I've met people from all over Michigan and formed some close friendships. We keep in touch. That was an important part of the schools, living together. I came from a basically white area and I have really found that I don't have any prejudices. Now, I've met Blacks and Hispanics and I find that we're all the *same*. Now we have a few Blacks and Mexicans in our plant and some of them are my closest friends. The summer school was my first experience of living in a dorm and living with all these different ethnic and racial groups. And I learned a lot from that. I've always called myself a Christian but I didn't know what Christianity really meant until I was able to live with other people. I am very happy with that. We are very isolated in a small village away from the big cities.

What was the group experience like for you at the summer school?

I think last year really stands out in my mind. We had a play-acting thing, a role play, about sexual harassment. Now I see that every day in my plant on my job—favors being dispensed to women if they go along with the boss's wishes. And that really doesn't need to be. At one time, I would never have been able to explain this to women, to tell them that this doesn't need to be.

The group experience at the summer school made me more aware of it [sexual harassment]. Before the school, I had figured that the woman was loose, or that the boss was showing favoritism to women who were being nice to him. But the role play thing we actually did showed me that these things happen when the women DON'T want it to. And so, I was able to go back to the plant and say to some women, "Look, you don't have to let the foreman tell you dirty jokes. You don't *have* to let the foreman pat you on the bottom if you want three minutes personal time to go to the bathroom and take a smoke." The role play really helped me convey to them that we're all equal. It was something I had overlooked before.

How did you feel in the group?

Uncomfortable at first because I was new. I had never, *never* done anything like this before and I was older in my forties. It's easier when you are a child. I was afraid to make a mistake. But we all make mistakes.

When did you begin to feel differently in the group?

When I could look out and see the other women begin to identify with *me*, and I could identify with *other* people. Because we are all so isolated. When I could look around and see people with the same identical problems.

How did you relate to the teachers?

Feedback was encouraged by the instructors. It was not a teacher-student thing. We were all together. Someone would mention an issue and you looked around in the group and saw women nodding, identifying with the problem. "Yes, we have that situation too where I work." It was *all* group. Everyone had something to add.

It was not a teacher standing three feet above us talking down while we listened. It was all group—a feedback thing.

The teachers weren't doing the teaching. We were teaching ourselves. The teachers brought that out in us. I had expected to come to these classes and sit behind desks like a college student because I didn't know what it was going to be like. It was informal. More relaxing.

Can you give an example of how the teachers brought out the learning in you?

If we were in the speaking class, right away, I would not get up and say anything. On a one-to-one basis, I can probably talk more than you can. But don't get me up in a group to speak. I turn to jelly. I have to go to the bathroom. I get all nervous and sweaty.

So it was in such a *relaxed* way that you didn't even know you were *participating*. You were asked to tell something about yourself in the group. At least to give your name, tell what you do, what you are affiliated with. Well, everyone likes to talk about themselves. As the time advanced in the class, we were able to get into little clusters, maybe solve a problem or debate.... These things were done in such a way that we were really teaching ourselves.

What else in that situation helped you to learn?

The fact that I wasn't alone. That everybody was basically there for the same learning process that I was going through and I wasn't as afraid as I thought I was.

What about learning is important to you, Barb?

It's broadened my understanding. I was very closed in. Now, I'm hungry for more learning constantly. The classes have helped me to go beyond my own little circle. If I'm in a store, or traveling, or at work, I feel assertive enough to go up to a person and ask questions and get involved. I'm trying to get involved now with the substance abuse issue in our plant. We have a bad problem, a bad situation with alcoholism and drugs. You really have to gain the confidence of people to help, to get behind the problem, to find the causes that are making their lives to be messed up. And you've got to be truly genuine to gain their confidence. With all the substance abuse problems that we have now in the plant, if I can help *one person*, I can truly say that it was worth *all* the classes that I've taken.

Learning in these classes has given me the confidence to think of someone other than myself. And it has helped. All the classes have helped me to think to do this. They have made me aware of my own potential. The classes put me back into the mainstream. I was so *narrow*. Walking down a *narrow* road. Now, I am branching out. Coming to classes and learning. I'm spreading myself among my fellow people at work. I have to be busy now. I don't want to stagnate.

What way do you learn best, Barb?

Informal. Oh, yes, definitely. We've had some tremendous speakers and they have motivated me to get off my duff and do something. Because you can't do anything unless you get off your duff and do it yourself. You've got to want to do something. *Then*, if you meet someone who impresses you, you feel you want to strive.

If you learn in an informal way with people you admire ... here you are, sitting around a table, rubbing elbows, drinking coffee, all *equals*. And you really see that these people have gone someplace and you want to do the same. Do like they have done and accomplish what they have accomplished. It's the real motivation, the real motivation.

How do you define learning, Barb?

Not keeping something to yourself. You can learn and absorb vast amounts of knowledge but then it can collect *dust*, like an unopened book. But unless that book is opened and fed back out through your mouth, no one is going to know what is in that book. It's up to you to put that knowledge back out, to use it. To me, learning is not just keeping knowledge to yourself, but giving it back. That's the learning process. *Using* the knowledge.

Do you see any changes in yourself, Barb? How have you used your learning?

One of the classes was about women's rights. And I first thought, what are they talking about? And then I came to see that I don't have any rights unless I stick up for myself. But then, I found that I was able to get a loan. In *my* name. I was somebody then. I could get a loan. I could get credit. I could open a savings account. I could buy a car. I could do this as a woman. I was not aware of that *before*. Because I was a woman, I was silent. I didn't *know*.

This learning process *opened* me to be able to ask questions without being fearful. To be able to take no for an answer but to ask "Why?" or "Why not?" It helped me to have a *voice*, to speak up for my own rights.

Have there been any other changes, Barb?

I never had to make decisions for myself. At first it was my father and mother. Then my husband. Then the minister. Then the employer. I felt like a puppet on a string and someone else was pulling the strings. You perform. Now, I don't feel I have that many strings attached anymore. Because, when I lift my hand, *I'm* doing it.

Women have been pushed into a role. Be a good girl. Be a good girl. Be a good wife. Get out there and make some bucks, but be quiet. No voices, no voices. Just be the silent person. But I don't think this country can run without us. We're intelligent beings. We have a lot to feed back, not only into our homes, but into our workplaces, our communities, our politics.

I've been finding my voice. I've even surprised myself. I never thought I had something worthy to be said. And now, in the last couple of years, people are asking me my opinions. Now, I'm being looked to for advice. And if I can do it, I'm sure that other women can do this if they have the opportunities.

"We Came Here Stripped," and "Better Than B-12" appeared in *The Voice*, the student-written newspaper at the 1982 Southern School for Women Workers, Austin, Texas, sponsored by the University and College Labor Education Association (UCLEA). They were written by members of the American Postal Workers Union, AFL-CIO in Texas and Florida.[19]

We Came Here Stripped

In our observations of the UCLEA summer school, we did not observe one single person who was not profoundly interested in bettering her local union and in equal rights for women.

The classes we attended were both motivating and informative. It was plain to see that the instructors were dedicated to the labor movement. They encouraged and stimulated us to overcome our inhibitions. Women's abilities were revealed in films of the early labor movement, where women have always been involved. We especially liked a quote from the film *Talkin' Union*: "My husband was Secretary Treasurer and every pay-day I would go down and collect the dues."

The instructors also motivated us in our ambitions and taught us how to use our abilities and skills in order to help our local unions.

One thing that was very evident was the fact that all the union representatives had the same goal—to achieve quality in their unions, and equality for women. There is no doubt in our minds that the women who attended this school will go back home to their own locals and create a lot of commotion.

We came here stripped and went home fully equipped.

—Debra Butcher,
Ruby Dixon, and
Melba Gallant, 1982

Better Than B-12

Since my arrival at the Austin airport to attend the 1982 Southern School for Union Women, one very noticeable characteristic about many of the women who attended (staff and students) was just how nice they are. As my stay lengthened, this characteristic niceness became more and more evident. But these ladies are anything but pushovers as they are dedicated and committed to a cause. In fact, I have not met such a conglomeration of committed people since my flower child days. If I learn nothing this week except that I'm not alone, that there is a bunch out there making waves, causing changes, being heard and yet at the same time being themselves, sincere, people-oriented, and union-minded women, I'd still be proud.

I've asked myself what makes me want to be so involved, to jump in, totally submerging myself when I've got a man at home protesting (mildly, as he too is involved in our Union) my involvement and children demanding my time. An honest look at my feelings reveals that I can't help myself, that it's biological forces making me do this. It is because I'm devoted to my family that I so fiercely want to strike out at anything encroaching upon my personal rights, beliefs and territory. It is because I want my children to grow up strong, honest, and free that I must stand up and protest each manipulation, each lie, each imprisoning element. Just as it is invariably the females in the animal kingdom that rush out and protect their family in danger and risk their lives so their young ones might go free, it is precisely the woman in me that pushes me forward.

Getting together this week has strengthened me, redefined my purposes, and refocused my goals. I've learned that at the same time we are sensitive to the needs of others, we must be aware of our rights and willing to stand up for them, but not too proud to say we need each other to make things work. Yes, I honestly believe together we can make anything work as we have the knowledge, tools, and resources. At the end, the world will know that nice guys (gals) do indeed finish first.

—Betty Tsang, 1982

The following valedictory speech, was given by a member of the United Steelworkers of America, AFL-CIO, who participated in the Trade Union Women's Studies Program of Cornell University's New York State School of Industrial and Labor Relations in New York City. The one-year program, which includes courses in labor studies and training in leadership skills, offers college credits that can be applied to a college degree.[20]

Valedictory Speech

Friends, classmates, teachers, Cornell and Empire State faculty, officers of DC 37, union officials and guests. It is with a great feeling of pride that I speak this evening as Valedictorian of the Trade Union Women's Studies Class of 1981. In the past year, we have shared an invaluable experience. As a group, we have increased our knowledge and awareness. Our consciousness has been raised as women, union members and workers. We have shared our problems, dreams and lifestyles. We have met new friends and come to know a feeling of closeness and sisterhood. I know I echo the feeling of the entire class when I say that we will go forward from this time and place with an added dimension and a personal enrichment, not only from academic absorption but from our own co-mingling. There were days when each of us thought that the struggle was too difficult, but here and now we know the struggle was worth it.

First I must speak of my classmates, many of whom have goals . . . dedicated and aspiring. . . . I speak of you ladies, who in addition to taking care of families, holding down necessary jobs, have been actively involved in union affairs. You ladies have added on yet another time-consuming role, that of educating yourself on the union front. . . . In addition to hours spent in class, there were many, many hours spent reading, researching and writing assignments, precious hours that made us realize that although some of us had been away from the school scene for a long time, our brain cells only needed a little motivation. Being "women on the move."

We ourselves got it together. Now that is over. In addition to the knowledge we gained from our studies, there emerges a totally overwhelming satisfaction. We made it.

I want to thank all of you for these months of friendship and intellectual exchange. I also want to thank all my classmates for their wonderful support and confidence in me as a person. I know that I do your bidding when I also express our gratitude and thanks to everyone who has made this experience come true. . . . For the 1981 Trade Union Women's Studies class, I say to you, we don't always pass through the doors that education opens for us, but we can always be warmed by the vast amount of sunlight that comes through them.

There are some gifts that are priceless beyond measure. This is one of them. We are "Women on the Move." Thank you most sincerely.

—Susan Tindall, 1981

Lynnette Rich, a cashier in Battle Creek, Michigan, is vice-president of Local 951 of the United Food and Commercial Workers' Union. Dottie Jones, former autoworker and chief steward for UAW Local 630 at the Chrysler plant in Ypsilanti, Michigan, is currently working as assistant director of the Walter P. Reuther Senior Centers in Detroit. Lynnette and Dottie, both poets in their spare time, have attended and co-taught many classes and workshops sponsored by the Program on Women and Work of the Institute for Labor and Industrial Relations at the University of Michigan.[21]

Factory Worker

Been working on this line ten years and some.
I work hard just to get the job done.
I go home and try to get some rest,
Knowing full well I've done my best.
I can see those parts in my sleep,
After all, I've done the same thing
Week after week.
Why don't the boss believe me when I say,
"These parts ain't worth a damn."
He says, "Run them anyway."
People say I don't care,
I have no pride in my work.
But what do they know.
Let them work a few days in my place
And see how it feels to be part of
The factory rat race.

—Dottie Jones, 1980

On the Wings of a Dove

On the wings of a dove we go forward,
Spreading peace, hope and love.

As watchful eyes gaze towards the clock,
We eagerly prepare for a better day.

For Mother Time is on our side.

We are the women of the nation,
A rainbow of colors, beautiful for any eyes to behold.

No longer silent, but free for all to hear
Our cry for dignity and equality.

For we are the gentle people,
The bearers of God's fruit.

On the wings of a dove, we join hands and go forward.

—Dottie Jones, 1980

Sisterhood

She came from the ghetto
And I from the suburb.
She came, a woman of colour
And I, a "number one" (government classified)
She struggled with discrimination daily
And I thought I was free of all that . . .
Allowed by some great proclamation to do
Whatever I wished.
She and I dreamed (and do dream)
The same dreams. . . .
Quality lives and jobs,
Equality in our endeavors,
The right, unabridged by any government or state, to stand
Female and Free.
She and I, heritages intact, dreams identified, have met . . .
Have joined hands . . .
Realize the power within us. . . .
She and I
    Have become
        WE.

—Lynnette Rich, 1980

Hope

I don't believe
  one person can do it; no,
    not even two.

I believe the job too large,
  the struggle all-encompassing
    the time too short
  for our success, for *just* us two.

Hello in there!
  Do you hear me?
    Is anyone home?

I need you
  and you need me. . . . .
    we all so very much need each other
      if any of us
        are ever
          to be
            free.

—Lynnette Rich, 1981

Conviction

I believe in women

The women in aprons, the women carrying briefcases, holding textbooks
and/or babies, stringing telephone wire, repairing automobiles, playing
guitars and pianos,
using artist brush and easel, writing furiously into the night. . . .

I believe in the women
marching, singing, chanting
or quietly standing and watching
banners held high
words illuminating our paths, our lives, dreams and soon-to-be realities.

I believe in the women of all ages, from every walk of life, rich and poor
forming a never-ending circle,
building bridges of caring and strength
gathering all people together
        to make this world an infinitely better place in which to live.

—Lynnette Rich, 1982

Notes

1. Nettie Silverbrook in *American Federationist* 35 (January 1928): 100.

2. Gloria Johnson and Odessa Komer, "Education for Affirmative Action: Two Union Approaches," in *Labor Education for Women Workers*, ed. Barbara M. Wertheimer (Philadelphia: Temple University Press, 1981), pp. 204–17.

3. Ibid.

4. Ibid.

5. Barbara M. Wertheimer and Anne H. Nelson, *Trade Union Women: A Study of Their Participation in New York City Locals* (New York: Praeger Publishers, 1975).

6. For a detailed description of this program, see Joyce L. Kornbluh and Hy Kornbluh, "Conferences: The One-Day Model," in *Labor Education for Women Workers*, ed. Barbara M. Wertheimer (Philadelpia: Temple University Press, 1981), pp. 54–61.

7. The schools are sponsored by the Committee on Programs for Union Women of the University and College Labor Force Education Association, in which the AFL-CIO Department of Education also cooperates.

8. Lawrence Rogin, "A Summary Discussion," in *Labor Education for Women Workers*, p. 267.

9. *AFL-CIO News* (May 22, 1982), p. 7.

10. Interview with Lela Foreman, director of Women's Activities, Communications Workers of America, July 1982.

11. Interview with Pat Thomas, education director, Service Employees International Union, July 1982.

12. Ibid.

13. Interview with Andrea DiLorenzo, former AFSCME staff member, July 1982.

14. *Working Womenroots: An Oral History Primer* (Ann

Arbor: Institute of Labor and Industrial Relations, University of Michigan, 1979), pp. 4–6.

15. Werthheimer and Nelson, Trade Union Women.

16. Mimi Abramowitz, *Where Are the Women? A Study of Worker Underutilization of Tuition Refund Plans* (Ithaca, N.Y.: Institute for Women and Work, New York State School of Industrial and Labor Relations, Cornell University, December 1977).

17. Summary Report, "Developing University and Union Workers' Education Programs for Women," Conference Proceedings, Institute for Women and Work, New York State School of Industrial and Labor Relations, June 15, 1979, n.p.

18. Interview with Barbara Kohn from Jean M. Golaszewski and Joyce L. Kornbluh (eds.), *Women Workers View Their Learning* (Ann Arbor: Institute of Labor and Industrial Relations, University of Michigan, 1983), pp. 59–67.

19. From *The Voice*, 1982 Southern School for Women Workers, St. Edwards University, Austin, TX, sponsored by the University and College Labor Education Association in cooperation with the AFL-CIO.

20. From the archives of the Institute for Women and Work, Cornell University, New York State School of Industrial and Labor Relations, Metropolitan Division.

21. "Factory Worker," "On the Wings of a Dove," "Sisterhood," "Hope," and "Conviction" are from the archives of the Program on Women and Work (POWW), Labor Studies Center, Institute of Labor and Industrial Relations, University of Michigan.

Chapter 10

Memories of a Movement:
A Conversation

Lyn Goldfarb

Cook

Gilmore

Rogin

Peterson

In its sixty-year history, the movement for workers' education for women workers has become a tradition, carried on from generation to generation. The residential schools for women workers, remarkable in their clarity of vision and purpose, ideological framework, and understanding of material and social conditions, have become the foundation and force behind many developments in labor education today. The early residential schools became models for the schools for women workers that emerged forty years later, when it became clear that women workers still desired programs and schools designed for their particular concerns.

Despite their short history, in the Twenties and Thirties, the residential schools for women workers lived on in the spirit and activities of the students and staff who attended and taught at these programs. As activists in the labor movement, in labor education, and in government and community organizations and agencies, they continued their work in ways that kept the spirit and philosophy of their labor education experience alive.

As a labor educator coming of age in the 1970s, I was profoundly influenced by the women and men who shaped a movement that gave working women the tools to break through many barriers and gain power and justice in their own right. Labor education is not just a concept on paper, but is a reality kept alive by their stories and the vibrancy of their commitment and accomplishments.

Through oral histories and the continued visibility of those former participants in the early programs for women workers, I have learned from their voices, their experiences, and their memories. In many ways, the schools and their teachings, as well as the ideology and methodologies on which they were based, seem as real to me fifty years later.

As a graduate student with a commitment to feminism and the labor movement, I met Marguerite Gilmore, then working at the U.S. Department of Labor's Women's Bureau, who introduced me to Hilda Smith. Meeting Hilda—Jane, as she is often called—was a turning point in my life. During the hours of oral history interviews I conducted with her, she shared her life with me—her visions, her ideas, and her belief in the profound effect that education could have on women workers. It was a transforming experience for me. Labor education became the vehicle for my own work.

These next few pages are interviews with four pioneers in

the early workers' education movement: Alice Cook, Esther Peterson, Marguerite Gilmore, and Larry Rogin. Their work spanned the breadth of labor education programs and projects, and their interviews reflect a cumulative experience. They were not interviewed in one setting, yet their four interviews are interwoven to form a complete story.

Alice Hanson Cook, a graduate of Northwestern University, did graduate work at the University of Frankfurt-am-Main in Germany. She started teaching at the Bryn Mawr Summer School for Women Workers in 1928 and continued to teach there and at other residential programs for women and men workers for the next thirty years. Serving on the executive board of the YWCA, and as staff for the Industrial Department of the YWCA in Chicago and Philadelphia, she planned classes and programs for working women. She is currently Professor Emeritus at the New York State School of Industrial and Labor Relations, Cornell University.

Esther Peterson, the recreation director at the Bryn Mawr Summer School for Women Workers in the early 1930's, has taught courses and organized for several unions: the International Ladies Garment Workers' Union, the American Federation of Teachers, and the Amalgamated Clothing Workers of America. She served as a labor lobbyist in Washington, D.C. for several international unions and for the AFL-CIO. In 1960, she became director of the Women's Bureau of the U.S. Department of Labor and became the executive director for President Kennedy's Commission on the Status of Women, which Eleanor Roosevelt chaired. She served as Consumer Affairs Advisor in presidential administrations from Johnson to Carter and had a seven-year tenure as Consumer Affairs Director for the Giant Food Corporation. She continues to work in related fields.

Marguerite Gilmore began her work in labor education in 1929 at the Vineyard Shores School for Women Workers as secretary, tutor, and teacher of recreation and music. She directed the Chicago workers' education activities under the Federal Emergency Relief Administration and the Works Progress Administration, trained unemployed teachers as part of these New Deal programs, and, during the past thirty years, worked for the War Labor Board, the Wage Stabilization Board and the Women's Bureau of the U.S. Department of Labor.

Although Larry Rogin did not teach at any of the residential programs for women workers, he remained close to those activities through his long-term involvement with workers' education. An instructor at the Brookwood Labor College from 1935 to 1937, he has been active in labor education for almost half a century. He directed education programs for the American Federation of Hosiery Workers and for the Textile Workers' Union of America. Rogin headed the AFL-CIO national Education Department from 1960 to 1967 and is currently a program coordinator at the George Meany Center for Labor Studies.

What did the experience mean to the women who attended the residential schools for women workers? What was its impact?

LARRY:
The early years were years in which the labor movement was weak and declining. The women's schools were schools both for the development of the individual and for the broadening and interpreting of her experience. Most women workers, except in the few industries where unions existed (most obviously, the garment industry), were unorganized. So the women's schools had a mix of organized and unorganized women workers, some women who had no experience or knowledge about unions at all, and a good many who had been through pretty harrowing experiences and efforts to organize. The women, naturally, came away [from the residential schools] more union-minded. The ones that weren't union-minded were influenced very much by the activists who came from unionized industries.

MARGUERITE:
It enlarged their horizons to know what was going on, to understand why there was this great Depression and what they could do about it when they got back [from the schools]. And I think that was what was important. When they found out what needed to be done, they prepared themselves to do something about it when they went back. They just didn't sit back; they wanted to do something about it.

ALICE:
For many of the women, it was the high point of their whole lives. It put them in touch with ideas, books, and people whom they otherwise would never have met, not only the teachers but other working women from all over the country.

ESTHER:
In the first place, it gave the women techniques, which was important, techniques of speaking and organizing. It gave them an understanding of the

labor movement. We had to be so careful in recruiting students. They would think, "Oh, it will help me get a better job." No, but it will help you to understand your job. And that was the rough part because many of them just wanted to improve their lot. But, you see, this was a training ground for these women to develop leadership. I think they needed that opportunity. We had mock meetings, for example. They said that they would never dare to stand up in union meetings ... in front of all the men. But we developed them. We'd put on plays. They'd take parts; they played that they were men. They experienced the kind of heckling they would get. They took the parts of the boss, the citizens. We call it roleplay. The whole point was to be practical . . . . where you are today, not some theoretical something down the pike. This brings it all back to me. It was such a wonderful experience. Terrific. When I think of the women who developed out of those schools, they became terrific trade union leaders, it's fantastic. It's something that we have lacked until CLUW came along. Those programs developed a real source of leadership.

ALICE:
And usually, during the last week of the school, we really tried to link these women back into their communities by getting them to think about where they could work. If there was not a union, what kinds of organizations existed where they could be active. Was there a Consumers' League, a YWCA? What was going on in the churches, and so on. Many of these women did become active. And when unions became more widespread, many of these women went into positions as activists, and as officials.

Looking back at these programs, were these schools feminist? Were they thought of as feminist at the time? In retrospect, what do you think?

LARRY:
These early workers' education activities were very close in time to the climax of the feminist movement, which was the campaign for the women's suffrage amendment. The schools for women workers started with that as a background. There was this success story. The programs for women workers were also related to the Women's Trade Union League, which was feminist, and to the Industrial Department of the YWCA. And so, yes, I'd say they were [feminist-oriented]. I don't know if we ever thought about it that way at the time. It's hard to go back and try to

recreate what a feeling was. If what you mean by feminist is getting an understanding of the problems of women and giving them a decent place in society, [the programs] were feminist.

ESTHER:
I didn't think of it as feminist. We didn't think in those terms in those days. I didn't, anyway. Maybe others did, but I didn't. But I remember the women's focus. I know you've heard this song; I think it's the first working girls' liberation song. I helped write the music, and Fannia Cohn wrote the words. I worked so hard on it. (singing)

In the black of the winter in 1909,
When we fought and bled on the picket line;
We showed the world that women could fight,
And we rose and won with women's might.
Hail the waistmakers of 1909,
Taking a stand on the picket line,
Breaking the power of those who reign,
Pointing the way, smashing the chain,
And we gave new courage to the men
Who carried on in 1910.
  (I love that)
And shoulder to shoulder,
We will win through the ILGWU

I think it's terrific. It's 1910, and the women did it. I will never forget the story of the strike of 1909–1910 as long as I live. Great strong feminists were they. But I didn't think of them as feminists. I just thought of them as strong women.

MARGUERITE:
With my interpretation of feminist, I wouldn't think so. They were concerned about things that women were concerned about but it was not a separatist school. Their husbands came up sometimes from New York City, came for weekends to Vineyard Shores. There was certainly not anything in the teaching that was just feminism . . . that came along later. The programs were about their status and stature as women workers.

ALICE:
I think they saw the possibility of what their rights could be. And, in this whole atmosphere, feminist issues, and feminist assertiveness had its effect. And the effect on trade union women was to make them respond to what really, in my view, was a new kind of institution. And it focused not simply on remedial education . . . but training women to play a really influential role in an important social institution— the labor union.

LARRY:
The schools for women workers were special because of one very important reason: they were women's schools and the staffs were women. Not entirely, but the majority of teachers were women. So there was a concern for women as part of society, women as people. They were free to express themselves in every way; they didn't have to be afraid if they talked about certain things that some man would come in and tell them what to do, or would be critical. The programs were unusual in this regard.

Why do you feel the schools were successful?

ALICE:
In eight weeks, one can do a great deal. It is possible to raise difficult and controversial problems and have time to work them through. We tried not to shy away from difficult problems. One issue was the race question, which at that time had not been faced up to in this country. Later, when I was working at the Southern Summer School for Women Workers, we were not allowed to have black women because the laws of the state forbade the integration in any way in the same institution of white and black persons.

By the end of the third week of the school, even if the issue had not come up, we felt that we as the faculty must raise the question of race relations in the South. We needed at least three weeks to work this issue through so that we could arrive at some understanding of what the problems are, and how white women could deal with these issues with their fellow workers. That length of time was very important to us. And I think it became an intense experience for the women who were involved in the schools, certainly for us as teachers. It did really have the effect of changing lives, changing the directions of life for those who participated in the programs.

LARRY:
The longer-term school was a much more effective device but I don't know how you could accomplish it now because of cost. In the old days, if you had a job, you never had seniority. There were no union contracts, so if you went away for six or eight weeks, either you got a leave, or you got another job in the same industry, or you went back to your old job. Nowadays, going away for six or more weeks can cause all kinds of problems unless your union sponsors you.

ESTHER:
It was interesting to me, this tremendously strong, democratic process that Hilda Smith

insisted on: the faculty having a say and the students having a say. Having grown up in a more authoritarian background, I couldn't see how you could suddenly give power to people like that. And we did have problems with it. It was during the roughness of working through the democratic process that we decided to proceed with supporting the Seabrook strike, and events like that. I think that probably I, for one, didn't have the judgment and the maturity at that time to make some of those decisions. But, majority ruled out—in one way it was good and another way it was bad, but on the whole I think it was good.

You really have to begin to have faith and trust in people. It was a great experience for the young women to think that they had a say in shaping the schools' policies. I think it was rough, but it worked.

MARGUERITE:
The teachers were excellent. They didn't come to the schools to teach, or they weren't accepted unless they were very interested in helping people grow. We had good faculty at the summer schools. They were real people in themselves, not just teachers, but people who had a feeling of really being part of the world as they helped the students feel part of the world. They were not pessimists. They were helping to enlarge the vision of the women to see what kind of a world it was and what they could do to even make it better.

It was informal. The classes were not so large, and they were able to communicate individually, particularly in the residential schools like Bryn Mawr or Vineyard Shores. You'd have more time; you'd see more people. Everybody was working towards a common goal, and the faculty met almost daily. If there was a problem with one person or another, they could deal with that problem and help them get over it. It was an extraordinary educational experience.

LARRY:
The programs then were not institutionalized; people were not being trained to fit into something. If you take our union education now, we train people to fit into unions, and, to some extent, that is true in the women's schools and programs today. But the schools and programs we are talking about in the early period, existed when unions didn't amount to much in the society and the people who wanted to build unions were exploring changes in the structure, changes in the philosophy of the labor movement. I think this meant that they were much more open.

If you think of the experience

of six weeks of very close association with other concerned women and faculty, I think it must have been a remarkable experience for all of them. It was the living together, the working together on projects, and the evenings together—the whole thing had a tremendous impact.

Was there a special need for women's schools in the Twenties and Thirties? Do the same needs exist today?

ALICE:
I think it is a different need. Back in the Twenties, the need was, to a great extent, that of immigrant women who never had education in this country and were doubly or triply handicapped for that reason. Many of the men in the labor movement were also immigrants. However, I think with the rise of the women's movement in this country, it became apparent that this important social institution, the unions, were not responding with equality to the special needs of women.

MARGUERITE:
Today life has changed again. Women have more freedom but they need a lot more too. Unions are important, but they're more a part of the country. I think that women's rights, equal rights, are not yet a part of the country. This is the emphasis that must be taken. I think some of the methods that were used then, when the faculty really tried to understand the problems of the workers, was the key.

ALICE:
Thanks to the recent equality legislation, to the existence of the Status of Women Commission, the work of the Women's Bureau, union women see the possibility of what their rights can be. And in a sense, this whole feminist atmosphere . . . has had its effect. The effect on trade union women is to make them respond to what, in my view, is a new kind of institution. Labor education for women workers today is training women to play a really influential role in an important social institution.

LARRY:
I think I'm probably in a minority among men in the labor movement in this. I think that the society, the situations, and the unions haven't changed enough as yet. . . . I see a role for women's schools concentrating on training for skills and building support systems. . . . I don't think that it's the only education that is needed but I think it is still very useful. The role models are needed. There aren't enough role models as yet of women in unions, in administrative, key positions. I

really feel that the need isn't over.

What contributions did the women's schools make to the field of adult education?

LARRY:
The schools for women workers, even more than union education in general, approached people through their jobs and through their institutions. While the problems that women face in society were part of the focus, what stands out was the development of educational methods that came out of the women's schools. There was a heavy focus on teaching methods that would be effective. I think that was because of a different view of how people developed. A lot of that came from the YWCA where the industrial secretaries were basically group workers, not teachers.

I think that there's still more attention in the women's schools and programs today on teaching methods than there is in the general labor education field. It is very interesting that the early schools for women workers were the sources of most of our literature on teaching methods. You don't see anything coming out now that deals with the kinds of teaching problems that the articles and pamphlets addressed at that earlier time.

ESTHER:
I think that it had a very great impact because we were really experimental in method. And that's where Hilda Smith was absolutely magnificent. I don't think that anyone has really analyzed the contributions that we made in the methods of teaching. I'll never forget sitting down with Jane [Hilda Smith] and having her explain that what we had to do was to have the students see the whole world and where they fit into it. This was important. These were all new concepts to me; an old gym teacher was what I was. She had the vision and I don't think there's been anything else like it.

We started the use of "role play." We started that back in the Twenties and Thirties long before there was anything else like it. I'd go to conferences later and say, "My word, that was figured out at the Bryn Mawr Summer School." I had to laugh at role playing. We never had a title for it. We'd just ask, "What was it like when the cop did this?" "What was it like when the boss said these things?" We acted out the whole thing .... a living newspaper.

We didn't have textbooks. It was the experiences that were our textbooks. In recruiting students, the only things that they needed to be able to do was read and write. The program was all built out of their lives and it began with who they are and where they are. I think that is a lesson I learned there that helped me all through my life. If I am studying unemployment, I go to the unemployment office and talk to the people. You have a user concept. You don't start way up there and come down. I learned that at the Bryn Mawr Summer School for Women Workers.

ALICE:
I think that what we used to call a discussion method, which Eleanor Coit so strongly advocated, has become more an accepted means of teaching in the universities than it was at the time the women's schools for women workers were pioneering in that field. Certainly in the WPA days, the attempt to train teachers . . . unemployed public school teachers, to teach labor education, was an effort to bring them from the textbooks and lectures into dealing with real problems, and drawing materials for the future.

What was the impact of the early schools for women workers on the field of labor education?

ALICE:
Hilda Smith went from Bryn Mawr and work with the summer schools to Washington, D.C., very early in the Roosevelt administration, after the WPA was established by the government as a means of providing employment. She went to work in that program and visualized that workers' education could be nationwide, and could reach unemployed workers through training unemployed teachers.

An astonishing number of states had these programs. It was the result of these programs, I think, that state universities were ready to pick up workers' education programs when that time came. All of these things, I think, grew directly out of the WPA and constituted a kind of transition from the summer schools for women workers to the university labor education programs.

LARRY:
I think there is a similarity in giving confidence to people. There is a concern for their problems, an awareness of the difficulties. And there's some training to help them solve these problems.

What are some of the differences between that early period in workers' education and the activities in the field today?

ALICE:
A difference is the very high use today of university-trained people as teachers, and the

movement into the universities as the major educational resource for these schools. The early schools were conducted under independent auspices but they were also often held at college locations and brought in university teachers.

A much more vocationally-oriented training goes on in most of the schools for women today. The "how to" courses, the bread and butter courses, compare with the attempts of the schools in the early years to provide a background with considerably more depth on the general subjects: economics, history, literature, even psychology. Now that kind of teaching does not often exist today and it couldn't work very well because the courses today are so much shorter.

Did the women's schools of those years have any impact on the labor movement?

MARGUERITE:
Yes, I think the schools had an impact on the labor movement. In the first few years, there weren't many union people involved. There were women from the ILGWU and from some of the other unions. In 1929, when I was just coming into the field, that's when unions were just coming in, and the schools had a great deal of influence on them. The labor movement wasn't that aware of women coming into the work force, so the schools took the lead in helping unions recognize women. The unions were invited in and a comraderie began to exist between them and it gave the young women new ideas and I think it gave the unions an idea of how women could help.

LARRY:
Did it impact on the labor movement? No, because during this period and also during the beginnings of the big growth of the labor movement in the Thirties, the role of women was submerged rather than expanded. If you take the unions in the period in which I first got involved with unions, you saw the unions struggling. There was still some role for women, but they were gradually forced out of it . . . when the unions grew, with a few exceptions.

But if you look at the unions in the textile industry, there were more women. When the Textile Workers Organizing Committee was set up, we had, I guess, two women on the executive board. It soon became one, and then none. And the same thing was true in the garment unions. There were many more women in the garment unions in the Twenties but they tended to be pushed aside. Before institutions became established and viable, there was much more room for women in them than afterwards.

ESTHER:
I don't think the labor movement thought of these programs as a way of women gaining movement. I don't think they cared about it at that time. I think they saw these activities as an educational force. At the same time that Hilda Smith was working to expand labor education services, the trade unionists began to do far more in education. We all began to work on a national labor extension services bill, that Hilda worked on so hard, to try to get support for labor education.

There were a lot of things going on and I think the labor movement awakened to the fact that they had to have schools for their members and perform other educational activities. The summer schools began to admit men and the schools became not just for women. I think it affected the way the labor movement looked at these programs.

What were the contributions of middle-class women?

LARRY:
The people who started the women's schools did not come out of a trade union background. While some of the staff in the women's schools had some background in labor problems or in organizing and working with unions, a large number did not have that experience and tended to get involved with the unions as through their experiences in the summer schools. It required a real concern for many of these middle-class women. Many stayed in and around the labor movement and made their careers that way; others stayed in labor education.

You need to look at the decline of the women's schools coming in a period when they couldn't raise the money to keep them going. It needed little money to keep the institutions going in the early days but then it began to take more money. I look at the Brookwood [Labor School] experience. I don't know if it was the same experience for the women's schools but I think it reflects part of it. Money was contributed to Brookwood, much of it coming from outside the labor movement. As long as there was no strong union movement challenging the society, when workers were downtrodden and didn't have much hope, you could raise money from outside sources.

ESTHER:
You see, we raised the money for all these scholarships at meetings and teas. I went to so many teas raising money to get

scholarships. The money that was raised there came mostly from the upper class. I think that it was a little bit of the "lady bountiful" image, helping the poor working girl who is at the factory. I can remember going to those [fund-raising] meetings and talking about these bright young women who were just hungry to learn. But then, of course, the husbands of some of these [wealthy] women got angry because we were teaching the young women workers about trade unions.

MARGUERITE:
A number of these wealthy women, a lot of whom had been active with the Women's Trade Union League, and carried on in that tradition, they might not have known the deep principles of the schools but they thought it was a wonderful idea and they supported it. Middle- and upper-class women would have meetings and make contributions to the schools. Bryn Mawr alumni in many cities set up committees to raise funds and select women to attend the school. A lot of people were supporting the schools and that's why in 1933, during the Great Depression, the schools went under because they couldn't afford to contribute any more. They'd give teas and bridge parties to raise funds. In many cases, they didn't understand the principles of unions but they thought these are poor girls, working hard, who need to have a break and get to know more about the world. It was a desire to help other women look at the world and give more to the world.

How did the change to including men in the programs affect the women's schools?

ALICE:
The change came with the massive organizing of tens of thousands of people who had never been organized before. I think there was a real pressure then to bring men into the schools because they actually needed this education. But I think that the real pressure came from the needs of the unions and the fact that the schools themselves were changing.

I was at the Southern Summer School for Women Workers when it changed over to include men and we had only three or four men there the first summer. It was still predominantly a women's school; there were women faculty and most of the students were women. I don't think we felt any change in emphasis or curriculum at that point. When the Bryn Mawr school changed, it was after it had moved to Hudson Shore. I went back in 1942 and by that time, it was accepted that we have coeducational schools. I don't remember thinking that it was continuous with the old Bryn Mawr Summer School [for Women Workers]. It became a different school, and not just because men were there. There were shorter sessions. There was a closer link to reality in teaching about organizational problems, collective bargaining problems, and labor law. I think there was a conscious decision to change from a more humanities-based program to "how to" classes.

By then, evening classes in the localities were much more available, thanks to the WPA programs and the labor colleges in the big cities. When I look back and when I did some research on what was actually taught at those schools, I found that they were very practically oriented. They taught parliamentary procedure, public speaking. The effort was to offer trade unionists the chance to express themselves with some coherence on their feet and to be able to think through problems and present them with some logic.

How did the experience of teaching at the schools for women workers affect you personally and professionally?

ESTHER:
Personally, along with other experiences of the period, it changed my life completely. It gave me a whole new direction. I left my old profession completely and wanted to throw my lot with the labor movement. Here I was out of college, graduated with honors, and I didn't know a thing about the labor movement. I just didn't understand the world. I became converted to the trade union movement at that time as the avenue for accomplishing the things that I believed in. I became converted.

Politically, it did mean a lot to me. I was the recreation director at the Bryn Mawr school and of course I went to all the classes. The thing that I did that was creative was to translate their economics classes into rhythm and to dance and to drama. I am told it was a terrific original method which added to the teaching of economics and labor history.

ALICE:
Beginning with my teaching at Commonwealth College, these programs gave me an exposure to the ways of thinking of working-class men and women and it certainly shaped my professional interests. When I had the opportunity to go abroad to do my graduate work, I chose to do my dissertation on labor education. And while I never got my graduate degree because Hitler interfered with that, I went through the process and thought of myself from

that point onward as a professional labor educator. I began then to have the interest that has been consistent ever since of comparing this country with Europe, my interest in comparative labor movements, particularly in labor education.

My experience with the labor movement and then in Germany—all that experience became part of a single role that made it possible for me to move right into an academic setting [at Cornell] and I was also active in the extension work at Cornell, teaching classes to trade unionists and doing research on labor unions.

MARGUERITE:
I had gone to the YWCA camps for a number of years where I was a counselor. And the YWCA told me about the Carhart Overall girls' strike, what troubles they were having and that it would be interesting if some of us just went over to chat with the strikers. That was kind of a start for me. My family was startled at the time. I took economics and labor problems at Wheaton College and got more and more interested. Ernestine Friedmann was teaching there and she took me once a week to the Boston Labor College where she was teaching economics and current events in the evenings to working people and she used me to help tutor them. At Wheaton, we also set up an arrangement with the young women at the Bedford Textile Mills there and we'd have regular meetings.

Ernestine asked if I wanted to be on the staff of the Vineyard Shores School which I certainly did. After being there several years, when that school closed down, I got a fellowship from the University of Chicago to study labor problems. And that really affected my career. The more I read and the more I heard about labor problems, the difficulties workers had getting decent wages and working conditions and how much they were being cheated out of the good things in life, it just sent my life in those directions.

These women and men—the pioneers of labor education—have had a profound effect on the development of contemporary labor education programs. Today, as in the past, schools for women workers address concerns and build skills, confidence and leadership unparalleled in any other kind of program. In these programs, women of different unions, generations, racial and ethnic backgrounds understand common experiences and shared differences.

Meeting and working with

these pioneers has been a rare opportunity to learn history from the people who lived it. In sharing their experiences with us, they provide a new generation of worker-educators the opportunity to carry this proud tradition forward. And thus we keep the spirit and soul of the movement alive.

Photographs

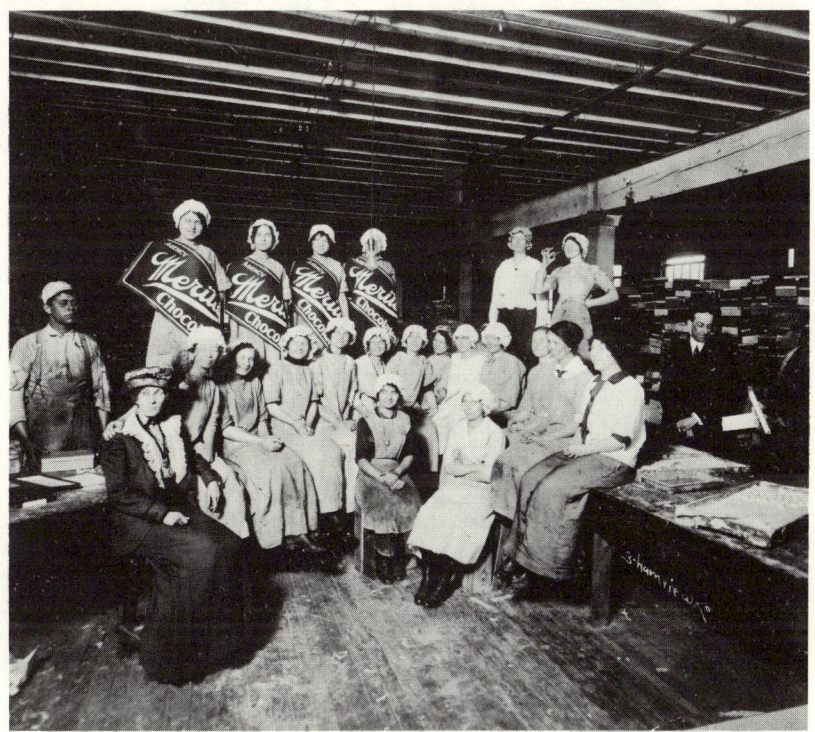

Noontime factory Bible class at a Birmingham, Alabama, YWCA (ca. 1915).
Source: National Board, YWCA Archives.

YWCA Industrial Girls' Club, Kalamazoo, Michigan "Rosenbaum's Add-a-Link-52 Hustlers" (no date).
Source: National Board, YWCA Archives.

Industrial girl delegates at the Blue Ridge YWCA Conference (no date, probably 1920s).
Source: National Board, YWCA Archives.

*Folk dancing at the ILGWU Unity Center (ca. 1919).
Source: ILGWU Research Department.*

*An English class at the New York Women's Trade Union League
Headquarters (early 1920s).
Source: New York State Department of Labor Archives.*

Directing Board of the Bryn Mawr Summer School for Women Workers (June 1921). Left to right: Dr. Susan Kingsburry, Miss Ernestine Friedman, Mr. Henry Clay, Dean Hilda Smith, Miss Leila Houghteling.
Source: The Schlesinger Library, Radcliffe College.

The Machine Dance. Bryn Mawr Summer School for Women Workers (1932).
Source: The Schlesinger Library, Radcliffe College.

The Robots. Bryn Mawr Summer School for Women Workers (1932).
Source: The Schlesinger Library, Radcliffe College.

An ILGWU symposium on women in the labor movement (July 1925) at Unity House, Forest Park, Pennsylvania. Fannia Cohn is at the far right, seated on the platform steps. Source: New York Public Library, Fannia Cohn Papers, Rare Books and Manuscripts Division, Astor, Lenox and Tildeu Foundations.

Play entitled "Work and Wealth" produced by Hollace Ransdell. Southern Summer School (1929). Source: Michael Studio, Asheville, N.C.

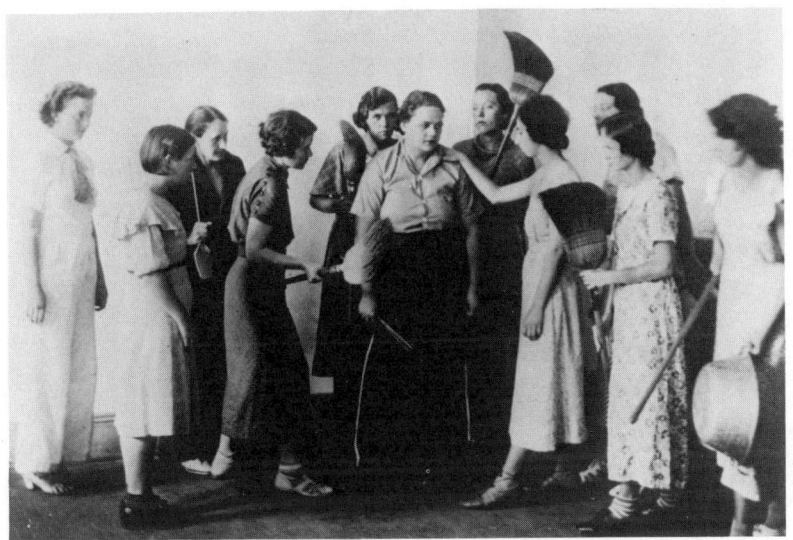

Students at the Southern Summer School for Women Workers perform "Mother Jones' Tin-Pan Army" (1933).
Source: National Archives and Records Collection.

Summer School for Office Workers, Chicago (1940).
Source: The Schlesinger Library, Radcliffe College.

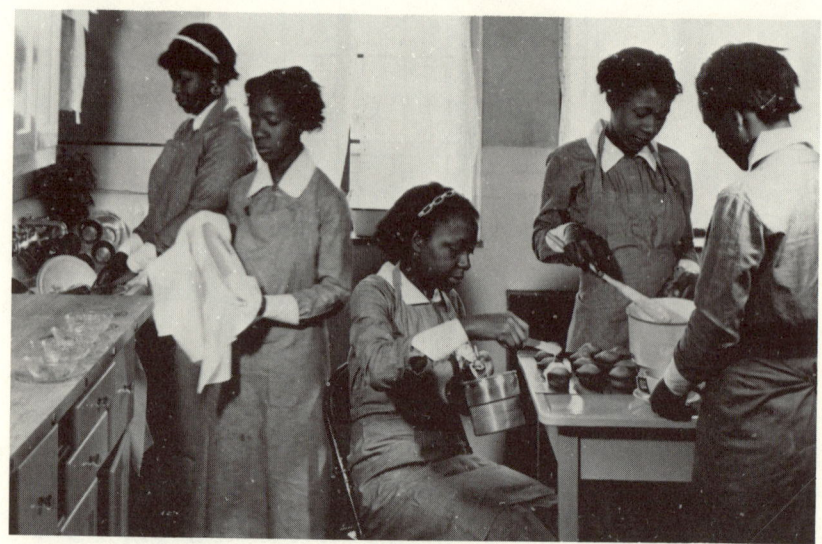

Unemployed young women get training in domestic arts in a WPA educational camp for household employees in Michigan (ca. 1934).
Source: Archives of Labor and Urban Affairs, Wayne State University.

FERA Educational Camps for Women, 1934 and 1935.
Source: The Schlesinger Library, Radcliffe College.

A performance about domestic workers at a WPA program in Illinois (mid 1930s).
Source: National Archives and Records Collection.

Hudson Shore study class, 1939.
Source: The Schlesinger Library, Radcliffe College.

Unemployed women at WPA Camp Eleanor Roosevelt perform a puppet show (1935).
Source: National Archives and Records Collection.

Palmers' Lodge, South Carolina, a WPA educational camp for unemployed women (ca. 1935).
Source: The Schlesinger Library, Radcliffe College.

An educational trip to Washington, D.C. (1930s).
Source: Archives of New York State Department of Labor.

Eleanor Roosevelt, Bessie Hillman, and Hilda Smith at a
graduation banquet of the Hudson Shore Labor School for
Women Workers (early 1948).
Source: The Schlesinger Library, Radcliffe College.

A workshop at the 1975 Michigan Summer School for Women Workers, Ann Arbor, Michigan
Source: Labor Studies Center, Institute of Labor and Industrial Relations,
University of Michigan.

A trade union women's studies class at Cornell University's New York State School of Industrial and Labor Relations, New York City (late 1970s).
Source: Institute for Education and Research on Women and Work,
New York State School of Industrial and Labor Relations, Cornell University.

UCLEA Southern Summer School for Women Workers, Austin, Texas (June 1982).
Source: Texas AFL-CIO.

Public Employee Federation Summer Women's Conference in Lake Placid, New York, 1982.
Source: Service Employees International Union.

Selected Bibliography

Abramovitz, Mimi. *Where Are the Women? A Study of Worker Underutilization of Tuition Refund Plans*. Ithaca, N.Y.: Institute for Women and Work, New York State School of Industrial and Labor Relations, Cornell University, 1977.

Adams, Frank. *Unearthing Seeds of Fire: The Idea of Highlander*. Winston-Salem, North Carolina: John F. Blair, 1975.

Anderson, Mary. *Women at Work*. Minneapolis: University of Minnesota Press, 1951.

Barbash, Jack. *Universities and Unions in Workers' Education*. New York: Harper and Brothers, 1955.

Bloom, Jonathan D. "Brookwood Labor College, 1921–1933." Master's thesis, Rutgers University, 1978.

Boone, Gladys. *Women's Trade Union Leagues*. New York: Columbia University Press, 1942.

Brameld, Theodore, ed. *Workers' Education in the United States*. New York: Harper and Brothers, 1941.

Brody, Doris Cohen. "American Labor Education Service, 1927–1962: An Organization in Workers' Education." Ph.D. dissertation, Cornell University, 1973.

Carter, Jean, and Smith, Hilda W. *Education and the Worker-Student*. New York: Affiliated Schools for Workers, Inc., 1934.

Chafe, William H. *The American Woman: Her Changing Social, Economic, and Political Roles, 1920–1970*. New York: Oxford University Press, 1972.

Chambers, Clarke A. *Seedtime of Reform*. Minneapolis: University of Minnesota Press, 1963.

Cohen, Ricki Carol Myers. "Fannia Cohn and the International Ladies' Garment Workers Union." Ph.D. dissertation, University of Southern California, 1976.

Cook, Alice H., and Douty, Agnes M. *Labor Education Outside the Union: A Review of Postwar Programs in Western Europe and the United States*. Ithaca: New York State School of Industrial and Labor Relations, 1958.

Curti, Merle. *The Social Ideas of American Educators*. New York: Charles Scribner's Sons, 1935; Rev. ed. Pageant Books, Inc., 1959.

Davis, Allen F. *Spearheads of Reform: The Social Settlements and the Progressive Movement, 1890–1914*. New York: Oxford University Press, 1967.

Dwyer, Richard E. *Labor Education in the United States: An Annotated Bibliography*. Metuchen, N.J.: Scarecrow Press, 1977.

Dye, Nancy Schrom. *As Equals and as Sisters: Feminism, Unionism, and the Women's Trade*

Union League of New York. Columbia: University of Missouri Press, 1980.

Edwards, Alba. *Comparative Occupational Statistics for the United States: 1870–1940*. Washington, D.C.: U.S. Government Printing Office, 1943.

Evans, Sara. *Personal Politics: The Roots of Women's Liberation in the Civil Rights Movement and the New Left*. New York: Knopf, 1979 Vintage Books, 1980.

Frederickson, Mary. "A Place to Speak Our Minds." Ph.D. dissertation, University of North Carolina at Chapel Hill, 1981.

Freire, Paulo. *Pedagogy of the Oppressed*. New York: Herder and Herder, 1972.

Hansome, Marius. *World Workers' Educational Movements*. New York: Columbia University Press, 1931.

Harrison, J. F. C. *Learning and Living, 1870–1960: A Study in the History of the English Adult Education Movement*. London: Routledge and Kegan Paul, 1961.

Hill, Helen D. *The Effect of the Bryn Mawr Summer School as Measured in the Activities of Its Students*. New York: American Association of Adult Education, 1930.

Hodgen, Margaret T. *Workers' Education in England and the United States*. London: Kegan Paul, Trench, Trubner, & Co., 1925.

Hourwich, Andrea T., and Palmer, Gladys L. *I Am A Woman Worker: A Scrapbook of Autobiographies*. New York: Affiliated Schools for Workers, 1936.

Hooks, Janet. *Women's Occupations through Seven Decades*. Women's Bureau Bulletin No. 218. Washington, D.C.: U.S. Government Printing Office, 1947.

Jacoby, Robin Miller. "The British and American Women's Trade Union Leagues, 1890–1925: A Case Study of Feminism and Class." Ph.D. dissertation, Harvard University, 1977.

James, Edward T., and James, Janet W., eds. *Notable American Women, 1607–1950: A Biographical Dictionary*. 3 Vols. Cambridge: Harvard University Press, 1971.

Kennedy, Susan E. *America's White Working Class Women: A Historical Bibliography*. New York: Garland Publishers, 1981.

Kessler-Harris, Alice. *Out to Work: A History of Wage Earning Women in the United States*. New York: Oxford University Press, 1982.

Koch, Raymond, and Koch, Charlotte. *Educational Commune: The Story of Commonwealth College*. New York: Schocken Books, 1972.

Kornbluh, Joyce L. "A New Deal for Workers' Education: The Workers' Service Program Under the Federal Emergency Relief Administration and the Works Progress Administration, 1933–1942." Ph.D. dissertation, The University of Michigan, 1983.

Lagemann, Ellen Condliffe. *A Generation of Women: Education in the Lives of Progressive Reformers*. Cambridge: Harvard University Press, 1979.

Lash, Joseph P. *Eleanor and Franklin.* New York: W. W. Norton, 1971.

Lederer, Emil. *The Problem of the Modern Salaried Employee.* New York: N.Y. State Department of Social Welfare, 1937.

Lemons, J. Stanley. *The Woman Citizen: Social Feminism in the 1920s.* Urbana: University of Illinois Press, 1973.

Leuchtenburg, William E. *Franklin D. Roosevelt and the New Deal, 1932–1940.* New York: Harper & Row, 1963.

Levine, Louis. *The Women's Garment Workers.* New York: B. W. Huebsch, 1924.

MacDonald, Lois. *Labor Problems and the American Scene.* New York: Harper and Brothers, 1938.

MacLeech, Bert. "Workers' Education in the United States." Ph.D. dissertation, Harvard University, 1951.

Mills, C. Wright. *White-Collar: The American Middle Classes.* New York: Oxford University Press, 1951.

Mire, Joseph. *Labor Education.* Madison, Wisconsin: Inter-University Labor Education Committee, 1956.

Noggle, Burl. *Into the Twenties: The United States from Armistice to Normalcy.* Urbana: University of Illinois Press, 1974.

Norton, Theodore Mills, and Ollman, Bertell, eds. *Studies in Socialist Pedagogy.* New York: Monthly Review Press, 1978.

O'Neill, William L. *Everyone was Brave: A History of Feminism in America.* New York: Quadrangle, 1971.

Palmer, Gladys L. *The Industrial Experience of Women Workers at the Summer Schools, 1928–1930.* Women's Bureau Bulletin No. 89. Washington, D.C.: U.S. Government Printing Office, 1931.

Pells, Richard H. *Radical Visions and American Dreams: Culture and Social Thought in the Depression Years.* New York: Harper & Row, 1973.

Pesotta, Rose. *Bread Upon the Waters.* New York: Dodd, Mead and Company, 1944.

Roberts, Richard. *Florence Simms: A Biography.* New York: Women's Press, 1926.

Robins, Margaret Dreier. *Educational Plans of the National Women's Trade Union League.* Chicago: National Women's Trade Union League, 1914.

Robinson, Marion O. *Eight Women of the YWCA.* New York: National Board of the YWCA, 1936.

Rogin, Lawrence, and Rachlin, Marjorie. *Labor Education in the United States.* Washington, D.C.: National Institute of Labor Education, 1968.

Schaefer, Robert J. "Educational Activities of the Garment Unions, 1890–1948." Ph.D. dissertation, Teachers College, 1951.

Scharf, Lois. *To Work and to Wed.* Westport, Conn.: Greenwood Press, 1980.

Schneider, Florence H. *Patterns of Workers' Education: The Story of the Bryn Mawr Summer School.* Washington, D.C.: American Council on Public Affairs, 1941.

Schwartztrauber, Ernest E. *Workers' Education: A Wisconsin*

Experiment. Madison: University of Wisconsin Press, 1942.

Sicherman, Barbara, and Green, Carol Hurd, eds. *Notable American Women: The Modern Period.* Cambridge: Harvard University Press, 1980.

Simon, Rita James, ed. *As We Saw the Thirties: Essays on Social and Political Movements of a Decade.* Urbana: University of Illinois Press, 1967.

Sims, Mary S. *The YWCA: An Unfolding Purpose.* New York: Women's Press, 1950.

Smith, Hilda Worthington. *Women Workers at the Bryn Mawr Summer School.* New York: Affiliated Schools for Women Workers in Industry, 1927.

———. *People Come First.* New York: Adult Education Fund, Ford Foundation, September 1952.

———. *Opening Vistas in Workers' Education: An Autobiography of Hilda Worthington Smith.* Washington, D.C.: By the author, 1978.

Snyder, Eleanor M. *Job Histories of Women Workers at the Summer Schools, 1931–1934 and 1938.* Women's Bureau Bulletin No. 174. Washington, D.C.: U.S. Government Printing Office, 1939.

Soltow, Martha Jane and Wery, Mary K. *American Women and the Labor Movement, 1825–1974: An Annotated Bibliography.* Metuchen, N.J.: Scarecrow Press, 1976.

Starr, Mark. *Workers' Education Today.* League for Industrial Democracy, 1941.

Stensland, Per Gustaf, "Education and Action in an American Union." Ph.D. dissertation, Teachers College, 1950.

Stewart, Annabel M. *The Industrial Work of the YWCA.* New York: Women's Press, 1937.

Tentler, Leslie Woodcock. *Wage-Earning Women: Industrial Work and Family Life in the United States, 1900–1930.* New York: Oxford University Press, 1979.

Van Kleeck, Mary. *Working Girls in Evening Schools.* New York: Survey Associates, 1914.

Wandersee, Winifred D. *Women's Work and Family Values, 1920–1940.* Cambridge, Mass.: Harvard University Press, 1981.

Ware, Caroline F. *Labor Education in Universities.* New York: American Labor Education Service, Inc., 1946.

Ware, Susan. *Beyond Suffrage: Women in the New Deal.* Cambridge, Mass.: Harvard University Press, 1981.

———. *Holding Their Own: American Women in the 1930s.* Boston, Mass.: Twayne, 1982.

Wertheimer, Barbara M. *We Were There: The Story of Working Women in America.* New York: Pantheon, 1977.

———. ed. *Labor Education for Women Workers.* Philadelphia: Temple University Press, 1981.

Wertheimer, Barbara M., and Nelson, Anne H. *Trade Union Women: A Study of Their Participation in New York City Locals.* New York: Praeger, 1975.

Wilson, Elizabeth. *Fifty Years of Association Work Among Young Women.* New York: National Board of the Young Women's Christian Association, 1916.

Wolfson, Theresa. *The Woman*

Worker and the Trade Unions. New York: International Publishers, 1926.

Manuscript Collections

Bryn Mawr, Pennsylvania. Bryn Mawr College. M. Carey Thomas Papers.

Cambridge, Massachusetts. The Schlesinger Library. National Women's Trade Union League Papers; Hilda Worthington Smith Papers.

Detroit, Michigan. Archives of Labor History and Urban Affairs. Wayne State University, Selma Borchardt Collection; John Edelman Collection; Mark and Helen Starr Collection.

Gainesville, Florida. University of Florida. Margaret Dreier Robins Papers.

Hyde Park, New York. Franklin D. Roosevelt Library. Hilda Worthington Smith Papers.

Ithaca, New York. New York State School of Industrial and Labor Relations. Cornell University, American Labor Education Service Papers; Workers' Education Bureau Collection.

Madison, Wisconsin. Wisconsin State Historical Society. American Labor Education Service Papers; David Saposs Collection; Textile Workers Union of America Collection; Wisconsin School for Workers Papers.

New Brunswick, New Jersey. Institute of Management and Labor Relations. Rutgers University. Bryn Mawr School for Women Workers Papers.

New York, New York. New York Public Library. Fannia Cohn Collection.

New York, New York. Tamiment Library. New York University. Rose Schneiderman Papers.

New York, New York. The Archives of the National Board of the YWCA. Industrial Department Records.

Northampton, Massachusetts. Smith College. Sophia Smith Collection. Eleanor Coit Papers; YWCA National Board Papers.

Washington, D.C. Library of Congress. National Women's Trade Union League Papers.

Washington, D.C. National Archives. Federal Emergency Relief Administration Collection; National Youth Administration Collection; Works Progress Administration Collection.

Index

Abramowitz, Mimi: *Where Are the Women?*, 302
Academic freedom, 120–21, 142 n43, 201, 205
Active Worker's Schools (New York), 52
Adesska, Florence, 33 n41
Affiliated Schools for Women Workers, The, 189–221, 230, 273; admission of men to, 200–204, 220 n26; and Bryn Mawr Summer School, 190–92, 197, 203; curriculum of, 191, 193, 194; educational philosophy of, 191, 194, 198–203; and feminism, 202–5; funding of, 190–91, 197–98, 200, 205; organization of, 190–91, 197–99, 200; programs and functions of, 189–90, 191–92, 194, 196–97, 199–200; publications of, 194–95, 200, 218 n11, 220 n25; and unions, 192, 200–202, 205
AFL-CIO, xvii, 297, 301, 302, 303, 304, 306
Algor, Marie, 124
Amalgamated Clothing Workers of America (ACWA), 52–53, 56, 166
America, Helen, 116
America Federation of Labor (AFL), 8, 201; and white-collar workers, 228, 229, 233–34, 240; and women, 49, 89, 93, 189; and WTUL Training School, 16, 33 n31
American Federation of Labor-Congress of Industrial Organizations (AFL-CIO), xvii, 297, 301, 302, 303, 304, 306

American Federation of State, County, and Municipal Employees (AFSCME), 300–301
American Labor Education Service (ALES), 189, 201–2, 241. *See also* Affiliated Schools for Workers
American Legion, 267
Anderson, Mary, 7, 12, 18, 34 n47 and n49, 49, 114

Barbour, Marion, 235
Barnard Summer School, 190, 191–92, 193
Barron, Sara, 124, 144 n49
Beard, Mary, 128, 145 n69
Berkowitz, Edith: "We Shall Be Free," 62
Berry, Margaret, 124
Black women, 12, 16, 264; at Bryn Mawr Summer School, 116, 125–26; in YWCA, 79–80, 88, 102–3, 105 n28. *See also* Race issue
Blanshard, Paul, 52
"Blue Triangle Houses" (YWCA), 78, 80
Blum, Emanuel, 120
Bonner, Miriam, 153
Bookman, Clarence, 255
Brandeis, Louis D., 40
Bread and roses, 6, 136. *See also* Social, cultural, and recreational activities
Brody, Doris, 202
Brookwood Labor College, 47, 48, 51, 53, 56, 87, 150, 338–39
Brotherhood of Railway Clerks, 229
Brown, Richard, 269

Brown, Thelma, 102
Bryn Mawr College, 304
Bryn Mawr Community Center, 114, 141 n20
Bryn Mawr Daisy: poems and essays from, 129–37
Bryn Mawr Summer School for Women Workers, 109–45; admission of men to, 192, 339–40; and Affiliated Schools for Women Workers, 190–92, 197, 203; and black students, 116, 125–26; and communism and socialism, 120–22; curriculum of, 118–21; during Depression, 119–22; educational philosophy of, 109, 110–12, 115, 118–19, 128, 142 n35; faculty of, 109, 118, 120–21, 124–25, 126, 127; finances of, 112, 128, 139 n13; founding of, 110–14; impact of, 122–29; as model, 150, 227, 259, 273; and Seabrook farms strike, 122, 145 n69, 333; and social activism, 120–21, 122–24, 142 n43, 143 n48; students at, 87, 115–18, 121–24, 125–26, 141–44 n24–25, n43–44 and n48–49; and unions, 118, 120, 143 n44 and n48; and WTUL Training School, 35 n54, 109–45; and YWCA, 90–91, 118. *See also* Hudson Shore Labor School
Bucknell College, 233–34, 238
Burgess, Sarah, 131–32
Burns, Agnes, 26–29
Butcher, Debra, 316

Camp TERA (Camp Jane Addams), 258, 263, 266, 271
Career patterns of students, 195–96, 330; at Bryn Mawr Summer School, 122–25, 128–29, 143–44 n48–49; at Summer School for Office Workers, 233–34, 239; at WTUL Training School, 11, 20–21, 34 n53

Carnegie Corporation, 139 n13, 305
Carner, Lucy, 84–85, 86
Carrol, Marian V., 243–44
Carter, Jean, 199–200; *This America*, 195
Caspar, Bella, 13
Chicago Theological Seminary, 238
Christensen, Ethlyn, 96
Christian Socialism, 111
Christman, Elisabeth, 17, 228
CIO. *See* Congress of Industrial Organizations
Civilian Conservation Corps (CCC), 255, 256–57
Class consciousness, 44; and office workers, 225–30, 236–37, 241, 249 n10; and Southern Summer School, 152–57, 167–68, 182 n2. *See also* Cross-class coalitions
Clay, Henry, 109
Coalition of Labor Union Women (CLUW), 290, 294, 295, 302, 303, 304–5, 306
Coeducationalization, 92, 157–58, 193–94, 200–204, 232, 235–36, 238, 339–40
Cohn, Fannia Mary, 9–10, 11, 31 n14, 114, 331; and ILGWU, 41–43, 44–47 passim, 48–51, 53–54
Coit, Eleanor, 94, 96, 336; and Affiliated Schools for Women Workers, 194, 196, 198, 200, 201, 202; and Summer School for Office Workers, 226, 228–29, 230, 231, 236–37, 240–41
Collins, Ruth, 129–30
Columbia University, 203
Communication Workers of America (CWA), 298–99
Communism, 42, 50–51, 120–22, 149; and office workers, 229, 231, 235
Congress of Industrial Organizations (CIO), 89, 93–94, 189–90, 192, 201; in the South, 155, 158, 165, 170; and white-collar workers, 228, 234, 240

Cook, Alice Hanson, 96, 124, 202; interview with, 328–41
Cornell University, 290, 291–92, 298, 301–2, 317–18
Coyle, Grace, 96, 226
Cross-class coalitions, xi–xvii, 39, 48, 56, 149–50, 338–39; at Bryn Mawr Summer School, 112, 115–16, 118, 125–27; and class tension, 9, 12, 19–20, 34 n52, 48–49, 81–83, 140 n17, 169; at WTUL Training School, 5, 8, 15, 31 n9, 339; at YWCA, 77, 79, 81–83, 94–95, 97, 99–102, 150
Crouch, Diamond, 102–3
Cummings, Frances, 229, 230
Curriculum, 340; of Affiliated Schools for Women Workers, 191, 193, 194; of Bryn Mawr Summer School, 118–21; of current labor education programs, 292–93, 310, 336–37; of ILGWU, 44, 46, 55–56, 59–60; at she-she-she camps, 260–61, 264–66, 268–69, 278–79; of Southern Summer School, 151–52, 154; of Summer School for Office Workers, 231–32, 236, 237–38, 239–40; of WTUL Training School, 5–6, 8, 10, 11–14; of YWCA, 84–85, 94–95

Dana, Henry Wadsworth Longfellow, 109
Derry, Kathleen, 13, 14
de Schweinitz, Dorothea, 268
Dewey, John, 119, 142 n35
Douglas, Paul, 13, 14, 109, 226
Dressner, Sadie, 118
Dubinsky, David, 53–54, 57
Dyche, John, 40

Edelman, John, 200
Educational philosophy, xv–xvi, 39, 54, 329–30, 332–34, 335–37, 340; of Affiliated Schools for Women Workers, 191, 194, 198–203; of Bryn Mawr Summer School, 109, 110–12, 115, 118–19, 128, 142 n35; of current labor education programs, 291–92, 293, 294, 336–37; of ILGWU, 39, 41, 43–47, 54–57; of she-she-she camps, 257, 259, 260–62, 264, 269, 271–74, 278–79; of Southern Summer School, 152–57, 182 n2; of Summer School for Office Workers, 231–32, 234–36, 237–38, 239–42; of WTUL Training School, 5–6, 7, 17–21, 30 n4; of YWCA, 77–78, 83–84, 86, 336
Eliot, Laura, 31 n9
Ellickson, Katherine Pollak, 125. *See also* Pollak, Katherine
England, 111–12
Ether, Marie, 258–59
Europe, 58, 80–81, 111–12
Evans, Sara, 182 n2

Faculty, 333, 336–7, 340–41; at Bryn Mawr Summer School, 109, 118, 120–21, 124–25, 126, 127; at current labor education programs, 313–14; at ILGWU, 44; at she-she-she camps, 263–64, 270; at Southern Summer School, 152–53, 154–55; at Summer School for Office Workers, 232; at WTUL Training School, 10, 13
Fairchild, Mildred, 122
Fancy Leather Goods Workers, 39, 52
Faxon, Mrs. Henry D., 31 n9
Federal Emergency Relief Administration (FERA), 198–99; and she-she-she camps, 255, 259–67, 270
Feminism, 49, 54, 202–5, 235, 272, 330–32, 334; social, 109–10, 138 n5, 139 n7, 202–3, 260; working-class, 168–69

Finances: of Affiliated Schools for Women Workers, 190–91, 197–98, 200, 205; of Brookwood Labor School, 338–39; of Bryn Mawr Summer School, 112, 128, 139 n13; of current labor education programs, 292, 293, 299, 302, 303, 305, 306; of ILGWU, 41; for she-she-she camps, 255, 257, 259, 261, 262, 268, 269–71, 282 n37; of WTUL Training School, 6–7, 8, 11–12, 14–16, 20, 33 n31
Fitzpatrick, John, 234
Ford Foundation, 201, 292
Frankfurter, Estelle, 109
Franklin, Stella, 31 n9
Fredgant, Sara, 124, 144 n49
Friedman, Mollie, 56
Friedmann, Ernestine, 84, 95–96, 193, 199, 202, 262, 341
Fryman, Patsy, 307
Fulton, Margaret, 116
Funding. See Finances
Furriers' Union, 39, 52

Gastonia strike, 175–77
Gauthier, Rita, 207–8
Gersh, Harry, 266
Gildersleeve, Dean Virginia C., 193
Gilmore, Marguerite, 125; interview with, 327–41
Goins, Irene, 12
Gold, Theresa, 196
Golden, Clinton, 200
Gompers, Samuel, 43
Goodman, Sadie, 99–101
Goodrich, Carter, 200
Graduate Department of Social Economy and Social Research (Bryn Mawr), 113, 140 n17
Green, William, 49, 89, 233
Guigno, Louise, 196

Haber, William: *Unemployment, a Problem of Insecurity*, 195

Hagood, Margaret Jarmon: *Mothers of the South*, 160
Haigwood, Ruby, 116
Hand, Frances Fincke (Mrs. Learned), 122
Haray, Margaret, 16–17, 34 n43
Hardie, Kier, 53
Hardman, J. B. S., 52, 72 n32
Harrison, J. F. C., 111–12
Health care, 15, 33 n34, 59, 263, 267
Hearst newpapers, 267
Heath, Venus M., 67–69
Hendrix, Bertha, 175–77
Hendrix, Leona B, 242
Henry, Alice 10
Herbst, Alma 96
Herstein, Lillian, 124, 126
Hewes, Amy, 109, 119, 120, 124, 195
Hill, Helen, 18
Hochman, Julius, 53
Honour, Margaret, 124
Hopkins, Harry, 198, 255, 257, 259, 260–61
Huberman, Elizabeth Lyle, 124, 127–28, 129
Huberman, Leo, 154–55
Hudson Shore Labor School, 192, 208, 339–40; publications from 205–17; "*These Are The Words We Said*", 205–8. See also Bryn Mawr Summer School for Women Workers
Huntzinger, Leona, 63–64

ILGWU. See International Ladies' Garment Workers' Union
Indiana University, 303
Industrial War Service Centers (YWCA), 78–79
Institute for Women and Work (Cornell), 298, 301–2, 306; publications of, 301–2
Institute of Labor and Industrial Relations (ILIR). See University of Michigan

Index · 367

International Congress of Working Women, 81
International Ladies' Garment Workers' Union (ILGWU) Education Department, 39–74; curriculum at, 44, 46, 55–56, 59–60; education philosophy of, 39–41, 43–47, 54–57; founding of, 39, 40–42; after 1935 reorganization, 53–56; and social activism, 39, 45–47, 51, 54–55; and socialism, 42, 46, 50–51; and spiritual needs, 43–46, 55; during twenties, 49–52
International Union of Electrical Workers (IUE), 290–91

James, Williams 256
Jones, Brownie Lee, 96
Jones, Dottie, 319–20
Jones, Mary Harris (Mother), 177–82

Kaiser, Clara, 232, 236
Kazcor, Josephine, 197
Kemp, Marjorie, 16
Kennan, Ellen, 120
Kingsbury, Susan M., 91, 113, 114, 192
Kirkland, Lane, 297
Klebe, Henrietta, 233
Kohn, Barbara: interview with, 309–15
Kornbluh, Joyce L.: interview by, 309–15
Kosovicz, Mary, 130–31
Kyrk, Hazel, 124

Labor drama, 156–57, 199, 232–33, 265, 330, 335; examples of, 177–82, 208–17, 244–48, 274–75
Labor education, current, 56, 287–323, 336–37; curriculum of, 292–93, 310, 336–37; educational philosophy of, 291–92, 293, 294, 336–37; funding for, 292, 293, 299, 302, 303, 305, 306; and labor union programs, 290–91, 297–301, 306–8; and union-university cooperation, 296–97, 298, 299, 303, 305; and university programs, 290, 291–93, 301–3
Labor education, history of, 31 n5, 39, 47–50, 56, 110, 288–90, 296, 327
Labor unions: and current education programs, 290–91, 296–301, 303, 306–8; and efforts to organize women, xvii–xviii, 5, 49, 93–94, 288; in garment industry 39–40, 52, 58; in the South, 149–50, 164–66; and white-collar workers, 228–30, 233–34, 237–42, 300; and women activists, xvii–xviii, 89–90, 149–50, 164–66, 169–70, 303, 309–10, 337–38; and women's education, 39, 54, 87; and women's issues, 290–91, 297, 306–8, 334; and workers' education, 8, 87, 139 n13, 150, 333. *See also* individual unions
Lake Forest College, 238
La Zar, Jennie, 65–67
Legislative efforts, xvii, 5, 77–78, 81–83, 87
Leonard, Louise, 92, 170. *See also* McLaren, Louise Leonard
Lerner, Anita Marburg, 124
Lerner, Max, 200
Le Sueur, Meridel, 255–56
Lewinson, Jean Flexner 125, 127
Life and Labor, 10; articles from, 21–29, 57–69
Lindeman, Eduard, 200
Lipschitz, Dora, 13
Lockwood, Helen Drusilla, 124
Loud, Oliver, 124
Lucia, Carmen, 123–24, 128–29, 144 n49, 197

McAvoy, Ann, 205–6
McDonald, Lois, 85, 86, 96; and Southern Summer School, 150, 154, 196, 200, 202

McDonald, Marie, 59
McIntosh, Millicent Carey, 124, 140 n17
McLaren, Louise Leonard, 95, 96; and Affiliated Schools for Women Workers, 190, 196, 199, 202; and Southern Summer School, 150, 152–53, 157–58, 169. *See also* Leonard, Louise
Maniloff, Sylvia, xviii
Mansbridge, Albert, 111, 141 n20
Marriage: and careers, 11, 16–17, 34 n43, 167
Martin, Prestonia Mann: *Prohibiting Poverty*, 257
Mayer, Helen, 116
Men: admitted to womens' education programs, 92, 157–58, 193–94, 200–204, 232, 235–36, 238, 339–40
Merriam, Ida Craven, 125
Michigan State University, 293
Michigan Summer School for Women Workers, 311–14
Mitchell, Broadus, 120, 124, 154
Mittelstadt, Louisa, 8–9, 11, 31 n10
Monroe, Edna, 98–99
Moscicki, Helen, 205
Muskiwinni Foundation, 302
Muste, A. J., 51, 109

National Conference of Industrial Women (YWCA), 81–82, 83, 104 n21
National Congress of Neighborhood Women (New York), 303–4
National Consumers League (NCL), 109
National Recovery Act (NRA), 53, 120–21, 200
National Women's Trade Union League (NWTUL or WTUL) Training School for Women Organizers, 5–35, 48–49; accomplishments of, 20–21; curriculum of, 5–6, 8, 10, 11–14; educational philosophy of, 5–6, 7, 17–21, 30 n4; faculty at, 10, 13; fieldwork at, 6, 10–12, 14, 17–19; finances of, 6–7, 8, 11–12, 14–16, 20, 33 n31; founding of, 6–8, 30 n1, 31 n9; and health care, 15, 33 n34; as model, 7, 109, 150; and other women's organizations, 114–15, 141 n22, 193, 228, 257; scholarships to, 7–8, 15–17, 33 n31; social, cultural, and recreational activities of, 6, 15; and social activism, 7, 14, 17–19; and socialism, 9–10; students at, 8–10, 11, 16, 20–21, 26–29, 33 n41, 34 n53, 86–87
National Youth Administration (NYA), 255, 267–72
Nelson, Anne, 292
New Deal: and Bryn Mawr Summer School, 120–22; and unionism, 53, 165; and women, 202, 255–56, 259–61, 267–68, 271–72; and workers' education, 195, 198. *See also* She-she-she camps
Nine to Five, 306
Nine to Five: The National Association of Working Women, 290, 294–95, 299–300, 304
Nixon, H. C., 155
Nord Elizabeth, 123–24, 126, 128–29, 144 n49
Northwestern University, 194, 238

Oberlin College, 194, 200, 238, 264
O'Connor, Julia, 12, 13
Ohio State University, 302–3
Olson, Helen, 274–75
O'Neill, William L., 138 n5
Opportunity School, 264
O'Reilly, Leonora, 31 n9

Palmer, Gladys, 124; *The Industrial Experience of Women Work-*

ers at the Summer Schools, 1928–1930, 195; *The Scrapbook of the American Labor Movement*, 195
Pancoast, Elinor, 227, 239
Pell, Orlie, 232, 235–36, 238
Pells, Richard H., 156
Perkins, Frances 258
Pesotta, Rose, 124
Peterson, Esther, 125, 129; interview with, 328–40
Phoebe Anna Thorne School (Bryn Mawr), 113, 140 n17
Pieper, Doris, 233–34
Pollak, Katherine: *Your Job and Your Pay*, 195. *See also* Ellickson, Katherine Pollak
Powell, Myrtle, 235
Poyntz, Juliet Stuart, 41–42, 43–47 passim, 57–61, 70 n8
Price, Mildred, 195
Program on Women and Work (POWW, University of Michigan), 293, 301, 319
"Proctocol of Peace," 40

Race issue, 16, 149, 151, 206, 288, 312, 320, 332
Rand School, 40–41
Ransdell, Hollace, 156, 177
Rich, Lynnette, 319, 320–22
Richman, Lena, 109
Robins, Margaret Dreier, 7, 9, 10, 12, 15, 33 n34
Robinson, Dolly Lowther, 124, 144 n49
Robkin, Polly, 153
Rockefeller Foundation, 198, 200, 301
Rodolfo, Sophie Schmidt, 129
Rogin, Larry, 296; interview with, 328–38
Roosevelt, Eleanor, 257–58, 260, 261, 270–71, 272
Roosevelt, Franklin Delano, 256
Russell, Alys, 111

Rutgers, the State University of New Jersey, 303
Rutz, Henry, 200–201

Sapos, David, 51, 52, 114
Saunders, Laurance, 109
Schlesinger, Benjamin, 40
Scholarships, 7–8, 15–17, 33 n31, 49, 91–92, 151
Scott, Anne F., 185 n46
Scott, Frances E., 242–43
Scott, Melinda, 11, 31 n9
Seabrook Farms strike, 122, 145 n69
Segal, Bonnie, 124, 144 n49
Selden, Helen Schuldenfreid, 129
Service Employees International Union (SEIU), 299–300, 304
Sex-role definitions: and educational training, 17–19, 84, 264–65; and marriage and career, 11, 16–17, 34 n43, 167; Southern, 158, 160–61, 166, 167–69, 185 n46
Sexual harassment, 21, 312–13
She-she-she camps, 255–83; accomplishments of 267, 273–74; closing of, 271–73; community reaction to, 266–67, 270, 272; curriculum of, 260–61, 264–66, 268–69, 278–79; educational philosophy of, 257, 259, 260–62, 264, 269, 271–74, 278–79; essays from, 274–79; establishment of, 259–61, 281 n19; under FERA, 255, 259–67, 270; funding for, 255, 257, 259, 261, 262, 268, 269–71, 282 n37; government resistance to, 259–61, 267–68, 269–72; under NYA, 255, 267–72; recruitment for, 268, 270; social life at, 266; staff of, 263–64, 270; students at, 262–63, 264, 266, 268; vocational training at, 263, 266, 268–69
Shoemaker, Alice, 96, 193, 199, 202, 204, 229
Silverbrook, Nettie, 287

Simms, Florence, 77, 78–83 passim, 95
Smith, Alexia, 17
Smith, Hannah Whitall Pearsall, 111
Smith, Hilda ("Jane") Worthington, 124–25, 219 n19, 327, 332–33, 335, 336, 338; and Affiliated Schools for Women Workers, 190, 192, 193, 196, 198–99, 203; and Bryn Mawr Summer School, 110, 113–14, 118, 124–25, 128, 142 n43; and she-she-she camps, 255, 257, 259–63, 268–72
Smithsonian Institute, 299
Snyder, Eleanor: *Job Histories of Women Workers at the Summer Schools, 1931–34 and 1938*, 195
Social, cultural, and recreational activities: at Bryn Mawr Summer School, 120; at ILGWU, 43–46, 55; at WTUL Training School, 6, 15; at YWCA, 78, 90, 97
Social activism, xvi, 39, 52–57; and Affiliated Schools for Women Workers, 201; and Bryn Mawr Summer School, 120–21, 122–24, 142 n43, 143 n48; and ILGWU, 39, 45–47, 51, 54–55; and Southern Summer School, 154; and WTUL Training School, 7, 14, 17–19; and YWCA, 77, 85, 95, 150
Social feminism, 109–10, 138 n5, 139 n7, 202–3, 260
Socialism, 235; and Bryn Mawr Summer School, 120–22; and ILGWU, 42, 46, 50–51; and WTUL Training School, 9–10; and YWCA, 82–83, 95
Social unionism, 43
Southern Summer School for Women Workers in Industry, 92, 149–86, 190, 192, 193, 332; accomplishments of, 169–71; admission of men to, 157–58, 193, 339; curriculum of, 151–52,

154; educational philosophy of, 152–57, 182 n2; essays from, 171–82; faculty at, 152–53, 154–55; founding of, 150–51; and labor drama, 156–57, 177–82; and race, 151, 332; and student expression, 155–57; students at, 87, 151, 158–59, 165–71; and transition from agriculture to industry, 160–62, 166–67, 173–74, 184 n26; and unions 150, 164–66, 169–70
Southern Tenant Farmer's Union (STFU), 159
Southern United States, 79, 92–93, 149–51, 164–66
Speer, Mrs. Robert, 114
Spencer, Jennie, 87–90; "My Transition," 90
Starr, Helen Norton, 51
Starr, Mark, 53–54, 55–56, 57, 124, 200
Stenographers, Typists, Bookkeepers and Assistants Union, 229, 234
Stolberg, Benjamin, 54
Strikes, 7, 10–11, 40, 49, 89, 133–35; coal, 177–82; Gastonia, 175–77; Seabrook Farms, 122, 145 n69, 333; Southern textile, 164–65, 179, 172–73, 185 n39
Student-industrial movement (YWCA), 83, 97, 99–102
Students, 86–87, 329–30; at Bryn Mawr Summer School, 87, 115–18, 121–24, 125–26, 141–44 n24–25, n43–44 and n48–49; at she-she-she camps, 262–63, 264, 266, 268; at Southern Summer School, 87, 151, 158–59, 165–71; at Summer School for Office Workers, 233–34, 239; at WTUL Training School, 8–10, 11, 16, 20, 26–29, 33 n41, 86–87; at YWCA, 86–87
Suffrage (vote), 26, 104 n14, 110, 112
Sullivan, Rose, 12

Summer School for Office Workers, 192, 193–94, 200, 225–51, 264; accomplishments of, 241–42; admission of men to, 194, 200, 232, 235–36, 238; and class consciousness, 225–30, 236–37, 241, 249 n10; compared to other schools, 225, 227–28, 231; curriculum of, 231–32, 236, 237–38, 239–40; educational philosophy of, 231–32, 234–36, 237–38, 239–42; fees for, 231; letters from, 242–44; and other women's organizations, 288–29, 238; recruitment for, 231, 233, 238; students at, 233–34, 239; and unions, 228–30, 233–34, 237–42
Sweet Briar College 93, 151, 193
Sweezy, Susan Shepherd, 124, 127

Tentler, Leslie, 117
Textile Workers' Organizing Committee (TWOC), 165, 337
Thomas, Martha Carey, 110–14, 118, 140 n14–17, 192
Thompson, W. O., 120–21
Tindall, Susan, 318
Tippett, Tom, 87–88
Trade Union Women's Studies, 292–93
Training School for Women Organizers. *See* National Women's Trade Union League
Tsang, Betty, xviii, 316–17
Tuve, Rosamund, 124

Unions. *See* Labor unions
Union Women's Alliance to Gain Equality (Union WAGE, California), 303
United Auto Workers (UAW), 290–91
United Cloth Hat and Cap Makers, 39, 52
United Labor Education Committee (New York), 39
United Office and Professional Workers of America (UOPWA), 234
Unity Centers, 41, 45, 59–60
Unity House, 44–45, 56–57, 58–61
University and College Labor Education Association (UCLEA), 303, 316
University of Alabama, in Birmingham 302
University of California, 302–3
University of Chicago, 10, 12–14, 238
University of Connecticut, 303
University of Kentucky, 303
University of Maine, 303
University of Michigan, 290, 291, 293, 301, 309–15, 319
University of Oregon, 303
University of Wisconsin, 92, 190, 191, 192–93

Van Kleeck, Mary, 196
Vineyard Shore Workers' School, 87, 192, 193
Vocational training, 263, 266, 268–69, 337
Voice, The (Southern School for Women Workers, Austin, Texas), 316–17

Walker, Amy, 31 n9
Ware, Caroline, 124, 125, 154, 183 n9
Ware, Susan, 138 n5, 202
Warne, Colston, 122, 124, 125
Watts Glen, 298
Weed, Helena 256
White-Collar Workshops, 236, 240–41
Whitehead, Myrtle, 8–9, 11, 32 n20
Williams, Aubrey, 260
Williams, Constance, 125
Williamson, Margaret, 228–29
Wisconsin Summer School for Woman Workers, 92, 190, 191, 192–93
Wolfson, Theresa, 51, 124, 196, 232, 233

Women: in the home, 29, 136; in the labor force, 5, 288–89; and New Deal, 202, 255–56, 259–61, 267–68, 271–72; unemployed, 255–56, 259–60, 263, 274–75. *See also* Labor unions

Women Employed (Chicago), 303

Women's Bureau (Department of Labor), 7, 195, 229

Women's Trade Union League. *See* National Women's Trade Union League

Woodward, Ellen, 259, 260

Worker's education. *See* Labor education

Worker's Education Association (England), 111

Worker's Education Bureau, 39–40, 48, 56

Worker's University at Washington Irving High School (New York), 41, 46

Working conditions, 22–26, 63–69, 129–35, 162–64, 171–75, 276–77, 319; stretch-outs and speed-ups, 164, 172–73, 185 n39

Workplace Hustle, 298

Works Progress Administration (WPA), 195, 336, 340. *See also* New Deal

WTUL. *See* National Women's Trade Union League

Wylie, Laura, 126–27

Young Woman's Christian Association (YWCA) Industrial Programs, 77–106, 257; accomplishments of, 86–87, 88, 90, 96; and black women, 79–80, 88, 102–3, 105 n28; curriculum of, 84–85, 94–95; educational philosophy of, 77–78, 83–84, 86, 335; Industrial Clubs of, 77–78, 80, 84, 85, 86, 87–88, 92, 96; and labor unions, 81–83, 93–94, 169; and other women's organizations, 80, 84, 90–93, 95–96, 150–51, 192–94, 202; publications of, 97–103; and recruitment for summer schools, 90–93, 115, 231, 233; and religion, 78, 82–83, 84, 94; secretaries and staff of, 77, 84, 94–96, 118, 124, 150, 193–94, 226, 335; and social activism, 77, 85, 95, 150; social and recreational activities of, 78, 90, 97, 120; summer conferences of, 85–86, 87–88

Ziegler, Philip, 229–30.